THE PEOPLE(S) CALLED METHODIST

VOLUME 2

UNITED
METHODISM
AND
AMERICAN
CULTURE

THE PEOPLE(S) CALLED
METHODIST

FORMS AND
REFORMS OF
THEIR LIFE

William B.
Lawrence

Dennis M.
Campbell

Russell E.
Richey

Editors

Abingdon Press
Nashville

UNITED METHODISM AND AMERICAN CULTURE, VOLUME 2
THE PEOPLE(S) CALLED METHODIST:
FORMS AND REFORMS OF THEIR LIFE

Copyright © 1998 by Abingdon Press

This book is printed on acid-free recycled paper.

Library of Congress Cataloging-in-Publication Data

The people(s) called Methodist : forms and reforms of their life /
edited by William B. Lawrence, Dennis M. Campbell, Russell E. Richey.
   p.   cm.— (United Methodism and American culture: vol. 2)
   Includes bibliographical references.
   ISBN 0-687-02199-5 (alk. paper)
   1. United Methodist Church (U.S.).   2. Methodists—United States.
I. Lawrence, William Benjamin.   II. Campbell, Dennis M., 1945– .   III.
Richey, Russell E.   IV. Series.
BX8233.P46   1998
287'.6—dc21   98-42781
                                                       CIP

---

99 00 01 02 03 04 05 06 07—10 9 8 7 6 5 4 3

MANUFACTURED IN THE UNITED STATES OF AMERICA

Contents

Editors' Preface vii

Introduction 1
　　William B. Lawrence

PART ONE: A Portrait of American Methodists and Their Leaders

United Methodists and American Culture: A Statistical Portrait 27
　　John C. Green and James L. Guth

United Methodist Congregations in North Carolina and California:
　　Regional and Generational Trends 55
　　Jackson W. Carroll and Wade Clark Roof

Patterns of Giving Among United Methodists:
　　Member Contributions to the Local Church......................87
　　Charles E. Zech

United Methodist Leaders: Diversity and Moral Authority 109
　　Daniel V. A. Olson and William McKinney

United Methodist Ordained Ministry in Transition (Trends in
　　Ordination and Careers) 129
　　Rolf Memming

Paying the Preacher Her Due: Wages and Compensation Among
　　United Methodist Clergy..151
　　Patricia M. Y. Chang

PART TWO: Methodist Peoples and the Shaping of American Culture

"Playing in the Dark"—Methodist Style: The Fate of the Early African
      American Presence in Denominational Memory, 1807–1974 175
            Will Gravely

Black People in the Methodist Protestant Church (1830–1939)............ 193
            James M. Shopshire Sr.

Methodist Missions to Korea: A Case Study in Methodist Theology
      of Mission and Culture..219
            Stephen S. Kim

Hispanic United Methodists and American Culture.............................241
            Justo L. González

One Eye on the Past, One Eye on the Future: Women's Contributions
      to the Renewal of the United Methodist Church 257
            Barbara Troxell and Patricia Farris

CONCLUSION

United Methodism and American Culture: Testimony, Voice,
      and the Public Sphere...279
            Donald G. Mathews

Contributors 305

Editors 308

Endnotes..309

Preface
United Methodism & American Culture

This volume is one of a series of publications deriving from research, consultations, and conferences undertaken with the assistance of a major grant from the Lilly Endowment, Inc. This five-year study has been based at the Divinity School of Duke University and directed by Dennis M. Campbell and Russell E. Richey. William B. Lawrence served as Project Associate, and counsel was provided by an Advisory Board composed of Jackson W. Carroll, Director of the Ormond Center, Duke University; Rosemary Skinner Keller, Dean of Union Theological Seminary, New York; Donald G. Mathews, Professor of History, University of North Carolina, Chapel Hill; Cornish R. Rogers, Professor of Pastoral Theology, Claremont School of Theology; and Judith Smith, Associate General Secretary, Office of Interpretation, General Board of Higher Education and Ministry.

The project began under a planning grant that made it possible for the principals to engage in exploratory conversations with a wide array of church members, including board and agency leaders, bishops and district superintendents, clergy and laity, United Methodist faculty, and researchers in other Lilly-sponsored studies. From the counsel received through such exploratory discussions, the project came to pursue three primary objectives:

1. to provide a careful fresh estimate of the history of Methodism in America, with particular attention to its twentieth-century experience;
2. to attempt a portrait of United Methodism at the dawning of a new century;
3. to explore policy issues, with a view to the church's effective participation in American society and the world in the future.

We pursued those objectives through sponsored research; through dialogue with the several commissions, committees, and projects that were launched during the 1992–96 quadrennium to study United Methodism; and through a series of conferences and consultations. Approximately seventy-five church leaders, scholars, and researchers participated in the final conferences, each working on a specific aspect, theme, or issue from the comprehensive task. From their efforts, we are pleased now to share some of the results in the second of what will be three volumes of essays.

These three volumes, organized thematically, will touch on all three of our objectives for the "United Methodism and American Culture" project but focus on the first two. The third objective will be addressed in a policy-oriented volume, also to appear from Abingdon Press, on questions facing the church at the dawn of the new century. Much of the research undertaken as part of this project could not be accommodated in these few volumes and will appear in the future in *Quarterly Review, Circuit Rider, Methodist History,* and other media.

From the start of this project, Abingdon committed itself to be the "publisher of record" and to make the results appropriately accessible to United Methodism. As part of that commitment and this project, Abingdon has already published *The Methodist Conference in America* (Richey) and will publish a two-volume collaborative effort (also involving Richey), *The Methodist Experience in America,* one volume of which will be narrative, the other a historical source book. These two volumes and perhaps others are currently slated to appear also in CD-ROM form.

The project will culminate in three synthetic "statements." One of these, like this volume, will address the church's leadership and be most appropriate for clergy and clergy-to-be. A second will be aimed at the adult laity of the denomination. A third will be in video form and be usable in an even wider set of contexts.

Through these "publishing" efforts we seek to open conversations about the future of our church and its role locally and globally in the decades and century ahead.

Introduction

William B. Lawrence

The Forms of a People

Who are the people called "Methodists" in the United States of America?

Their presence cannot be ignored. The United Methodists, for example, are more widely distributed across the country than any other Protestant denomination. Like Roman Catholics, they can be found in almost every county (or countylike unit) in the country.[1] Approximately 15 million Americans, nearly 8% of the adult population, claim a United Methodist affiliation.[2] On an average Sunday in the autumn, five times as many persons sit in the pews of United Methodist church buildings as sit in the bleachers at professional football games in the nation. So American United Methodism has significant human resources.

United Methodists' economic impact cannot be ignored, either. During the most recent year for which statistics are available (1995), United Methodists contributed nearly $3.5 billion to their local churches. The churches, in turn, disbursed most of those billions in their local communities through support for their staffs, management of their facilities, and operation of their programs. Further, they have more financial resources than simply their current income. Counting real estate and other investments, United Methodist congregations have more than $30 billion in assets.[3] Besides the wealth of local churches, approximately 40,000 active and retired clergy are vested in the denomination's pension program, which includes one of the largest portfolios of benefit funds in the country.

Nor can their institutional vitality be ignored. United Methodists have some level of affiliation with more than a hundred colleges and universities, several schools, and thirteen theological seminaries. Cities across the country, such as Indianapolis, Houston, and New York, have a "Methodist" hospital in their health care system. While many of these health care and educational institutions only consider themselves to have been historically affiliated with the people(s) called Methodists, the retention of the name or the acknowledgment of the historic tie is itself significant. Apparently the "Methodist" connection has some importance for the organization—whether it be local identity, public

1

relations with potential donors, or a legal requirement for maintaining access to some endowment.

Beyond these "affiliations," United Methodists own or control a wide array of institutions through their annual conferences, through other levels of conferencing, or through corporations that these conferences have created. They operate scores of facilities that offer outdoor recreation, camping, hostelry, health care, residential retirement, child care, and countless other social services.[4]

Yet their human, economic, and institutional vitality may be something less than could be inferred from these bits of evidence. Of the fifteen million or so Americans who claim to be United Methodists, only about eight and one-half million can actually be documented by the denomination's statisticians. Of the millions seated in the pews, it must at least be said that they represent a decreasing share of the American population. Though the church still receives offerings in the billions of dollars each year, income growth is scarcely keeping pace with rises in the cost of living. Though the gross revenues are increasing each year, larger portions are being used by local churches simply to maintain aging buildings, provide compensation (including benefits) for clergy, and otherwise sustain the organization's internal functioning. Moreover, the institutions that have traditional ties to the United Methodism are finding various ways to loosen those ties, to distance themselves from the church, to identify their church affiliation as historic rather than present, and to establish their self-image by intellectual achievement, research success, or quality of service rather than by denominational affinity.

So Methodism is sizable, yet shrinking; influential, yet diminishing; substantial, yet diaphanous. That is the aggregate picture of the people(s) called Methodists in the United States near the close of the twentieth century.

But who are the people in the aggregation, the people(s) called "Methodists"? What, if anything, makes them different from any other describable and definable entity? Are they the embodiment of particular social and cultural characteristics? Are they the bearers of unique theological, spiritual, or liturgical traditions? Are they an identifiable body at all, or merely a connected association of groups and individuals, held together by pension and polity? Are they "united" Methodists? Or are they simply sharers of a label "Methodist"? Have they some distinctive marks? Are they distinguished by their devotion to a certain body of doctrine? Are they committed to specific moral disciplines? Are they the product of a certain institutional history? Are they a "people" called Methodist? Or are they more accurately "peoples" called Methodist?

And what is their place in the social, political, and cultural milieu of the United States? How have they helped form American culture? How have they been formed by American culture? With what aspects of American culture are they specifically linked? What features of the culture have been altered because of the presence of people(s) called Methodist?

A clarifying word, by way of ecclesiastical genealogy, may be in order. There are many peoples who constitute the Methodist family and who trace their lineage to John Wesley. Within the United States, some of their institutional forms are easy to identify and are historically well-known: United Methodist, African Methodist Episcopal, African Methodist Episcopal Zion, Free Methodist, and Wesleyan churches, for example. Others have abandoned eponymous markers like "Wesleyan" or "Methodist," perhaps in favor of celebrating certain doctrinal emphases, such as the Pentecostal Holiness churches.

Not all of the people called Methodists actually call themselves Methodist.

Further, not all of the people who are called United Methodists have a common spiritual genealogy. This is a denomination with a durable tradition of hymnody, but an ephemeral interest in catechism. Hence, United Methodists may be able to sing the songs of grace with greater joy than many other Christians, but there is no assurance that any teaching about grace inscribed in the song will actually be imbedded in the souls of the singers. United Methodists are governed by a *Discipline*, but they do not necessarily adhere to a discipline. Steeped in an early opposition to slavery, Methodists found ways to be flexible about it. Reluctant to be doctrinaire about abortion, United Methodists have an official position[5] which seems both to please and to dissatisfy so-called pro-life and so-called pro-choice contenders. Content to be dualistic about homosexuality, United Methodists have declared that homosexuals are "persons of sacred worth" who are welcome in the church; but they have said that homosexuality is contrary to Christian teaching, so homosexual persons are not welcome in the ordained ministry.[6]

A Denomination of Peoples

The examination of "United Methodism and American Culture," of which this volume is one part, has not attempted to study the entire

Methodist family. It has focused only on the largest institutional and spiritual household of the bodies within that broader lineage.

But despite that limiting definition, a variety of people(s) can be called Methodist and still be lodged within the United Methodist Church. The task herein is to describe this variety of people(s) near the close of the twentieth century. One portion of the descriptive task is contemporary; hence, the essays gathered in the first part of this book are the work of social scientists whose presentations and analyses of data create a profile of the denomination at present. Another portion of the descriptive task is historical; thus, the essays in the second part of this book cast a critical eye on the way that stories of some of the people(s) called Methodist have been told, on portions of the history that have not been fully disclosed, on aspects of the history that have merely been overlooked, and on fresh perspectives which help better to interpret the denomination's life. Finally, this book attempts to comprehend the whole, in a broad view that encompasses present and past; for this, in a concluding essay, Donald G. Mathews invites observers and readers to listen to the distinguishing voices of the people(s) called Methodist and to echo their message in public and private practices of faith.

This volume attempts to describe the character of United Methodism in American culture, not its caricatures. It aspires to be accurate but makes no claim to be exhaustive. Within its pages are efforts to be honest about who the United Methodists are, who they have been, and who they are in the process of becoming.

It will not surprise anyone acquainted with the United Methodist Church that a General Conference of the denomination in the twentieth century gave considerable attention to declines in membership and difficulties in its financial affairs. What may be surprising is that those issues aroused the anxiety of delegates to the General Conference not merely at the end of the century, but at the beginning. Already in 1912, the bishops of the Methodist Episcopal Church warned the General Conference about a loss in church membership.[7] At that same General Conference the delegates had to cope with appeals from across the country for some sense of order in the denomination's financial systems. As a result, the Commission on Finance was instructed "to make a thorough study" of church finances "and to report their findings" to the 1916 session of General Conference.[8]

This is simply one illustration of the dangers in trying to be descriptive of the denomination on the eve of the twenty-first century. Is the current condition of the church aberrant from, or consistent with, its history? Does not the answer to that question depend on who reads the present and who writes the history? Is there some way to comprehend the people(s) called United Methodist apart from the polarities of despair or triumphalism?

A number of observers, obsessed with the contemporary institutional condition of the United Methodist Church in the United States, conclude from the statistics reporting membership and financial declines that the church is rusting away.[9] Their comments are voluminous, and some are even valid. Other observers celebrate triumphant periods in the history of American Methodism and complain that the church in recent years has sacrificed its evangelical edge on the altar of ecumenical agendas or its prophetic passion to the pursuit of economic comfort. They tend to conclude that the church has lost its way, and they cry for it to return to some former patterns so that United Methodists can be successful again.[10]

But what might constitute "success"?

Instead of re-visiting the arguments of such observers and advocates, this volume proposes a different approach. It seeks to assess the forms in which United Methodists, through their present and predecessor bodies, have connected their lives with one another and with the American culture in which they flourished. It seeks to examine the critical transformations that have occurred, are occurring, and will occur in the connection.

By way of introduction, this essay proposes three theses about the forms and reforms of United Methodist life in America.

First, the people(s) called Methodist could be described as a "**settled movement**." Linked to a founder who looked upon the world as his parish, Methodism still uses language to define itself as people moving in mission on a global scale. Its bishops are constitutionally known as an "itinerant general superintendency."[11] Its ordained elders are known constitutionally and legislatively as "traveling preachers."[12] Its clergy who exited from the itinerancy have been, at best, subordinated and pejoratively labeled "located." Its units of governance are the gatherings of people who meet for conference. Even its local churches have responsibility for their members "wherever they live."[13]

In short, to be in motion is to be most characteristically Methodist in form. Begun as a movement to renew the Church of England and its geographical parishes, Methodism came to America as a movement among people who felt led or called to bear witness to the gospel without waiting to be told that they had some authorization to do so: laity in Maryland and New York set things moving before any licensed or commissioned or ordained ministry arrived to settle matters into some order. The boundaries of that motion, if originally understood to be as broad as the boundaries of the planet, were at least understood in America to stretch from sea to sea. Methodism moved every place because it was limited to no place.

Along the way, the people(s) called Methodists settled in many places and accomplished a presence across the land. In the nineteenth century, they began to settle into fine buildings and to found formidable institutions. In the twentieth century, they began to settle into ecclesial language that was more familiar to non-Methodist traditions. They began to conceive of themselves as congregations with local independence, rather than as societies within a larger connection. They began to imagine their pastoral ministry more in terms of its links to a city, county, or community than to a conference. Whereas the *Discipline* of the Methodist Episcopal Church in 1904 had understood that the people(s) called Methodists "were members of the whole connection first, then affiliated with local societies served by a pastor,"[14] the *Discipline* of the (United) Methodist Church since 1964 has placed membership in the local church with extension to the whole connection.[15]

The language for ministry still includes the pejorative possibility that a traveling preacher could be "located." But the language for ministry also affirms the status of a non-ordained "local pastor," who is neither an itinerating nor a traveling preacher but is still a clergy member of the annual conference. The language for local church organization through the middle of the twentieth century referred to a Committee on Pastoral Relations, but in 1968 that was changed to a Committee on Pastor-Parish Relations—not understanding the world as the preacher's parish, but understanding the congregation as the parish. The language for the episcopacy assigns bishops to "areas" in which they "reside," thus conveying the impression that they are the equivalent of diocesan bishops in other church bodies. Members settle into local congregations, clergy settle into communities, and bishops settle into areas.

Hence, the people(s) called Methodist have become a settled movement. Under rubrics that combine traveling preachers with local pastors into conference membership, that use Anglo-Catholic place terms like parish in combination with non-geographical descriptions of church, and that place bishops in assigned regions, United Methodists have evolved into a system that tries to yoke congregational and connectional forms of life.

Second, the people(s) called Methodist could be described as "**reformers of the nation**." At about the same time that Methodism began to stir as a lay movement in America, John Wesley published the first edition of his "Large" *Minutes*, which gathered the data from his conferences with preachers up to 1763. God's purpose in raising up the Methodists, Wesley said, was "to reform the nation . . . ."[16] The initial devices for doing this, in England and America, were evangelical preaching by people in conference with one another and mutual discipline exercised in societies of people who were spiritually committed to God and one another.

American Methodists, in particular, developed other devices for reform. In the nineteenth and twentieth centuries, cries for temperance became clamor for abstinence followed by crusades for prohibition of the sale and use of beverage alcohol. Public preaching and personal piety found avenues to political power. Voices and forces in the church found allies in the culture, and vice versa. The great crusade reached a crescendo with the approval of an amendment to the United States Constitution establishing prohibition in the land. In Washington, D.C., across one street from the Capitol where the amendment was first adopted and sent to the states, and across another street from the Supreme Court where the amendment would reign, the Methodist Building stood as a symbol of the denomination's power to reform the nation.

Other reforming efforts arose. As the people(s) called Methodists increasingly found themselves to be part of the rising middle class, they resonated to the causes of some who sought to be there. Laborers seeking to be unionized and women seeking to be franchised motivated some Methodists to do what they seem to do best—organize. At times, the causes affirmed by some of the people(s) called Methodists conflicted with the interests of other people(s) called Methodists. At times they conflicted with the interests of others in the culture. Still, the impulse to reform the nation endured.

The more that the people(s) called Methodists felt compelled to seek reforms, and the more they found themselves with access to places of power in the culture, the more they used the establishments of power to effect change. However, they also became more inclined to protect their established power. Hence there were occasions, such as the time when Martin Luther King Jr. wrote his "Letter from Birmingham Jail,"[17] that Methodists in power were perceived as obstacles to reform, not agents of it.

Their power established, the people(s) called Methodists discovered that the forms of their life had to be reformed along with the nation.

Third, the people(s) called Methodists have been committed to "**spreading scriptural holiness over the land**." Echoing again the initiatives of John Wesley in his conferences with preachers, American Methodists developed forms for shaping personal and social holiness as expressions of grace at work, as manifestations of piety in practice, and as articulations of doctrine in the disciplines of life.

Methodism has always had a societal, or connectional, character. Publics, that is, groups of people, formed social entities for shaping spirituality. God's transforming grace has always been understood as a dynamic process rather than as a defining instant. Persons who, like Mr. Wesley at his Aldersgate Street experience, found that they "did trust in Christ, Christ alone, for salvation" had the assurance that they were embarking upon the scripture way of salvation, not that they had arrived at the destination.

Spiritually, the journey is not a private one, but one in the company of other Christians. Corporate forms became instruments for shaping piety under the principle of sanctifying and perfecting grace. Laity in differing eras formed societies, classes, bands, covenant discipleship groups, Bible studies, fellowships, Sunday school classes, and more. Circuit-riding preachers traveled together, as well as conferenced together.[18] Individuals who felt a call to preach have been variously apprenticed, mentored, monitored, supervised, entered into probation, educated, and otherwise viewed as persons to be formed in the faith rather than merely provided with knowledge or technical skill. And in the present form of denominational polity, United Methodist clergy still hold one another accountable for spiritual disciplines when in conference they are asked, "Are all the clergy members of the conference blameless in their life and official administration?"[19]

It is worth asking whether such forms of life still succeed in spreading scriptural holiness. In an age that values the entrepreneur in ministry and that affirms an individual's choice to design her or his own journey of faith, the devices that the people(s) called Methodists have used for spreading scriptural holiness are under review.

So the people(s) called Methodists made their presence known in America as a settled movement, seeking to reform the nation and to spread scriptural holiness over the land. They created forms of life and ministry for accomplishing these goals. They have variously revised, renewed, rejected, re-created, and relinquished those forms. They have at times done so without realizing the connection between their doctrines of faith and their disciplines of life. They continue to engage in debate, to fret over decline, and to seek new designs for their enduring traditions.

Some United Methodists love to think of a golden era, perhaps back in the gilded age, when all the churches were strong, all the preachers full-throated, and all the Sunday school children above average. Alas, it was never so. The people(s) called Methodist were a diverse lot and still are.

A Settled Movement

The image of a solitary circuit rider is central to the Methodist myth. Celebrated in preaching and teaching, in art and commerce, the circuit rider conveys a vision of dedicated ministry. In a sense such preachers were the interchangeable parts of a growing connection. They could travel in their assigned regions for three months, six months, or a year, and then they could be appointed to other circuits. People moved, and preachers moved. Where people settled, preachers were sent to reach them, delivering a simple evangelical message about what to believe and how to live.

The people called Methodists were physically mobile. They were also a social movement. They built connected networks through preachers who traveled and people who gathered, through camps and conferences, through common hymns, and through commercial publishing. They fostered education, founded missions, and fought with one another over slavery, gender, and political control of church governance. Yet one support system served to sustain them, and that was the itinerant ministry, which structured itself through the conferencing process that kept it going. Preachers with Bibles, hymnals, and books of "Doctrines and Disciplines" in their saddle bags had everything they needed to keep the popular movement in motion. They rode, sometimes to be received and sometimes to be rejected. Then, in conferences of various kinds, these people called Methodists renewed their vigor for the movement, and the preachers rode again.

Such pioneering efforts managed to accomplish a Methodist presence in all sorts of places across America. Homesteaders in their isolation and slaves in their bondage heard Methodists preach, held Methodist conferences, and sang Methodist hymns. So did laborers, landowners, homemakers, farmers, and shopkeepers. In small towns around mines and mills, in cities around foundries and factories, and at the crossroads of adjacent farms, these Methodists connected with one another.

The consequence of all this motion was that American Methodism accomplished something rather remarkable. It stretched across the continent and could be found almost everywhere throughout the United States. As a result, if one traveled to nearly any county in the country, one could meet Methodist people.

The customary form of that Methodist presence in the twentieth century was a small congregation meeting in a small building which housed its worship, fellowship, and educational activities. In the nineteenth century, says Kenneth Rowe,[20] Methodist church buildings had begun to appear on Main Street as well as on the back streets. In the twentieth century, they surely began to appear in the growing suburbs around great cities. But in terms of sheer numbers, most Methodist church buildings were neither the glorious Gothic ones in urban centers nor the stately stone ones in suburban subdivisions; they were more likely to be the small wooden structures scattered around the countryside and in small towns, housing worship for a few score members. When a merger brought the Methodist Church and the Evangelical United Brethren together as the United Methodist Church in 1968, the new denomination had 41,901 of these local churches and claimed that more than eleven million members had settled into them.[21]

In the three decades following that merger, both the number of members and the number of congregations declined.[22] What remains unchanged is that these congregations were then, and are now, primarily small churches with relatively few members. Current statistics indicate that only 605 (or 1.6% of) United Methodist churches have an average worship attendance of 500 or more persons on Sunday. Meanwhile, 22,344 (or 61%) of the denomination's local churches have an average worship attendance of 75 or fewer, and among that group as a whole, the average worship attendance is about 36. As Wade Clark Roof and Jackson Carroll demonstrate in their chapter, the size of congregations is crucial. Congregations are the primary bearers of tradition. And church size tends to be the single most important variable in determining how they bear the tradition. United Methodists attempt to carry their traditions mainly through a huge number of small congregations.

Thus, the primary form in which United Methodism has accomplished a presence in American culture is through little groups of people. This is a church of many tiny churches.

It is also a church which underrepresents certain segments of American culture. About 94% of United Methodists in the United States are of Anglo-European descent. So 6% of United Methodists are non-white. But almost 27% of the American people are non-white.[23] Simply put, United Methodists have accomplished a presence among English-speaking white persons far more effectively than among African Americans, Asian Americans, Latino Americans, Native Americans, and other ethnic minority groups. Certain age groups are also under-represented, namely those born after 1945. The median age of all Americans is 34.5, while the median age of United Methodists is 56. Only 13% of the American people are 65 and older, but nearly 33% of United Methodists are.[24] United Methodism is whiter and older than the American culture of which it is part.

Yet in terms of economic status, the United Methodist presence is situated right in the middle of American life. By and large, this is a middle-class denomination. Its members aspire to property ownership, support public education, and live according to a standard made possible by their current incomes. For the most part, they are not people of inherited, unearned wealth or chronic, grinding poverty.

Similarly, in terms of civic values, United Methodists occupy a presence in the middle of America. To be sure, some of the church's members are aligned with the extremes of the theological, ideological, and political spectra. Nevertheless, as John Green and James Guth show in their chapter, the defining perspective of United Methodists looks at issues from the center of American public opinion.

One of the ways in which this "centrist" tendency has been expressed in the twentieth century is in the church's slow pace toward achieving social and ecclesiastical reform. The denomination acceded to the national pattern of racial segregation in 1939 with the creation of the Central Jurisdiction, and it did not end this racist system until 1968, by which time the cultural perspective had shifted toward an integrationist point of view. This suppression of a portion of the people(s) called Methodist was not a unique moment in American Methodism. It has been characteristic of the denomination's history, and of the way that the denomination's historians have written about that history. The chapters by James Shopshire and Will Gravely make that clear. What is also clear is that, in matters of race, the church behaved like the center of the culture into which it had settled.

Another example involves the denomination's struggle with the issue of homosexuality. The center of the American culture has found ways to affirm the civil rights of gay and lesbian persons while resisting full access of homosexuals to social institutions such as marriage or iconic institutions such as the military. Likewise, although United Methodists have declared that homosexuals are persons of "sacred worth," the church has also adopted legislation to prohibit these people of holy value from entering marital covenants or exercising the pastoral office.[25]

Still a third example of United Methodism's affinity with the middle of American culture involves the presence of women who occupy positions of leadership in society and church. Here, too, a portion of American Methodist history must be recovered, as the chapter by Barbara Troxell and Patricia Farris urges and offers. Moreover, as with other features of American Methodist life, the institutional changes with regard to leadership and ordination of women occurred as the culture shifted. The number of women in United Methodist pulpits began to increase about the same time as did the number of women in corporate executive offices, law partnerships, university professorships, and other defining institutions at the center of the society.

Debates, decisions, and dissent in the United Methodist Church have mirrored those in the cultural middle of America.

It is not that United Methodism yields to the opinion *of* middle America. It is that United Methodism is primarily present *in* middle America. Its mission history, according to the chapter by Stephen Kim, is more about culture than it is about church. As a "popular" movement—that is, a movement of people—it has accomplished a presence within the midst of a broad middle of the culture. And yet it has a character that is identifiably different from the middle of the culture ethnically, racially, and generationally.

To say that the forms and reforms of United Methodist life are "popular" is to recognize those descriptive limitations. The denomination is "popular" in the sense that it is a movement of people. But that does not suggest that it has popularity. In fact, the evidence clearly shows that the younger generations of Americans, as well as ethnic minorities of Americans, have not celebrated, affirmed, or embraced American United Methodism in anything close to their proportion in the population.

The people called United Methodists have accomplished a presence in America. That presence is in the form of a settled movement which is geographically dispersed, economically potent, and morally in touch with the broad center of American life. But that presence is also overwhelmingly of a certain size, class, color, and age. Do the forms of that presence at the close of the twentieth century have any actual or potential power to impact the forms of the American culture? Are there reforms in the life of the church that might enable this United Methodist presence in the United States to be an influence for reforming the culture in the continent?

Reforming the Nation

There are certain settings within American society where particular religious groups have established a dominating power over the culture. An obvious example would be the Mormons in Utah. A possible example would be Baptists in North Carolina. In such places, moral standards, political decisions, and commercial opportunities are driven by the prevailing ecclesiastical ethos. Churches could reform the nation, or at least their controlled segment of it, by imposing their values and priorities upon it. In twentieth-century America, there have been at least a few locations from coast to coast—for instance, Ocean Grove, New Jersey; Evanston, Illinois; Pacific Palisades, California—where Methodist municipalities were established. None remains in its original form. Though there may be some communities where United Methodists are pre-eminent today, they have no large regions of comparable controlling influence.

Yet, establishing power does not necessarily require establishing control. Nor does reforming the nation require exclusive power. In the twentieth century, United Methodists and their institutional forbears have been broadly ecumenical in spirit and practice. As one of the seven mainstream Protestant[26] denominations, Methodism demonstrated a capacity to exercise influence through commercial, judicial, legislative, educational, and other institutions by the networks it could create with Protestant peers. After every Congressional election, for instance, someone would count how many members of the House of Representatives and Senate were members of each denomination. It was not unusual for Methodists to have a plurality. More important, though, was the affinity that mainstream Protestants had for one another and for the cultural center of American life that they tended to share.

As a result, such churches served as mediating institutions in the larger society. A common vision seemed to be kept in view by various forces with an eye on the community: public schools, civic clubs, youth organizations, and Methodist (as well as other mainstream Protestant) churches. Clergy and lay leadership of congregations could move readily across social as well as ecclesiastical organizations in the community, influencing if not controlling programmatic priorities of the group. A moral and ethical design for reforming the community could arise from a shared vision of life. Sports clubs for youth, for example, would practice and compete according to a schedule that did not conflict with church schedules.

That changed in the twentieth century. United Methodists (like other mainstream Protestant bodies) increasingly lost the loyalty of younger American generations. Pluralizing changes in the society offered alternative access to influence. Pursuits of power, as well as truth, grew increasingly decentralized in the last years of the century. The latest innovation to threaten church power, according to journalist Howard Fineman, is the internet. "What musty academics call 'mediating institutions'—from party conventions to network news—have been declining for a host of reasons. The digital future could kill them off entirely. In the digital world, every unchecked 'fact' is all too available, every opinion equal."[27]

Meanwhile, those whom the church had been neglecting, ignoring, or failing to reach found other ways to establish their power.

True, American Methodists had exercised some clout to generate racial justice in the United States. A few white preachers took leave from their parishes and traveled south to join marches. And occasionally a Methodist symbol served as a beacon for change. Until the 1960s, for instance, if black tourists who were visiting Washington wished to see the Supreme Court building or the halls of Congress and then have lunch before resuming their journey, there was only one integrated restaurant where they could buy a meal on Capitol Hill. It was across the street from those segregated citadels of American justice, in that church facility constructed to symbolize the denomination's presence amid the towering political institutions of the nation. It was in the Methodist Building at 100 Maryland Avenue.[28]

But power generally has been established by, and exercised for, the primary white Methodist constituency at the center of American culture. The church was about as slow as the society to change. United Methodism was more likely to experience reform along with the culture than it was to be the body bringing about reform of the culture. Thus, it was only in the year of Martin Luther King's death that the Central Jurisdiction ended.

Meanwhile, internally, United Methodism in the latter years of the twentieth century looked for ways to help the heretofore neglected and overlooked people among the peoples called Methodists.

One form of this empowerment was to secure an over-representation of racial and ethnic minority persons on the governing bodies of the denomination's program bureaucracy, among its pastoral ministry, and in its Council of Bishops. The entire membership of the United Methodist Church remains about 6% non-white. But, with the selection of directors for the church's general boards and agencies during the last three quadrennia of the century, persons from racial and ethnic minority groups have held about 35% of the seats. With decisions about the episcopacy, another visible change occurred. More than one-fourth of the active bishops in the United States are ethnic minority persons. Still another change involved a new priority for that oldest of Methodist devices, the itinerant ministry. A policy of "open itinerancy" was legislated by the General Conference and adopted, at least in principle, by many Annual Conferences.

What remains unclear for United Methodists is whether these efforts at establishing power with and among such constituencies are working. The strategies may be signs that serious renewal is occurring. However, they may also reinforce suspicions that the governing boards of the bureaucracy, the bishops, and the itinerant system are at such distance from most United Methodists that they are out of touch with the needs and priorities of the existing congregations. The chapters by Daniel V. A. Olson and William McKinney and by John Green and James Guth show some evidence of a gulf separating denominational leaders from church constituents. These insights provide further support for the argument that a strategy of empowerment at the upper levels of the church's structure has not succeeded in sharing power among all the people(s) called Methodist at the level of the denomination's local churches.

Among the ways to measure power, of course, is money. And the evidence shows that power still resides in the existing local churches, because local churches are finding ways to control more of their money. The portion of every dollar which is given to each local United Methodist church and which remains in that local church is growing.[29] To put it another way, fewer pennies of every church dollar are reaching the places in the structure that the bishops and the bureaucracy control.[30] Trying to empower, or establish the power of, those who have been neglected, overlooked, or unreached is a compelling cause. But so far, such empowerment has only occurred at those places in the system that are perceived by the church body to be less powerful.

Externally, the church's capacity to reach younger generations and underserved constituencies is being tested by a change in the culture. It appears to be the larger churches that are growing in America, often because they are more effectively reaching baby boom and subsequent cohorts. Though widely deployed—and thus geographically positioned—to evangelize and serve the American people, United Methodists are apparently configured in the wrong form to do it. This is a denomination of small-membership local churches. Average Sunday worship attendance for all United Methodist congregations in 1994 was 3,401,468. Of that total number, 810,942 attended the more than 22,000 churches whose average worship attendance was 75 or fewer. For the same year, there were about six hundred local churches whose average attendance exceeded 500, for a total of 466,327 worshipers. To put these statistics in some perspective, about 14% of United Methodist worshipers are in large congregations (with an average attendance of 771), and about 24% of all worshipers are in small congregations (with an average attendance of 36).

This appears to be a significant imbalance. It requires more than 22,000 buildings, local church boards or bureaucracies, and part-time or full-time pastors to serve one-fourth of the denomination's worship participants. It only requires 600 properties, governing bodies, and pastoral teams to serve one-seventh of its worshipers. At that rate, it would take about 625 new large-membership churches (plus local bureaucracies and pastoral leadership) to increase worship attendance by one-half million persons per year, but it would take almost 14,000 new small-membership churches (with their governing systems and pastors) to achieve the same thing. If the denomination is interested in reasserting missional power in the culture, the preferred strategy seems clear: strengthen support for larger churches.

Yet that could be an over-simplification. The obvious way to establish powerful large membership congregations is to found new ones where demographic trends are favorable. Usually that means finding a tract of land where new housing is being developed and getting new ministries in place. In fact, several annual conferences are planting churches in fresh suburban subdivisions, providing salary support for three years of ground-breaking pastoral work, and hoping that growth will make the congregation self-sustaining in that time.

This does two things. It commits the denomination even further to the middle class of American culture, to the constituency that can afford to be United Methodists. It also signals that United Methodists will await the arrival of more ethnic minority persons in the middle class, rather than evangelizing them in the crowded urban areas or dusty rural areas where they now gather. It is what Justo González calls the "Kentucky Fried Chicken" approach to evangelism.[31]

The accomplished presence of United Methodism in American culture is not necessarily a basis for claiming that the church has the resources for establishing power. There are too many underrepresented groups, too many underserved generations, and too many undersized congregations for United Methodists to exercise power in the coming century.

On the other hand, the denomination has some devices at its disposal for reforming its life in an effort to reform the nation. Among them is its use of caucus groups to connect isolated or dispersed Methodist people(s) who share a common history, a common identity, or a common goal. In the nineteenth century, Methodist women found ways to connect when they were excluded from the decision-making centers of the denomination and from the orders of ministry in its leadership. Social activists formed the Methodist Federation for Social Service almost fifty years before the denomination established an official Board of Christian Social Concerns.[32] More recently, minority groups have formed ethnic caucuses (Black, Hispanic, Native American, Asian American, and Pacific Islander), have fostered intra-ethnic and inter-ethnic conversation, and have lobbied the denomination's leadership under the rubric of empowerment. Efforts directed at younger generations of people(s) called Methodists are also in evidence: a new United Methodist Student Movement has been launched, a youth renewal movement called Chrysalis is spreading, and an episcopal initiative focused upon children has begun.

Even more widespread than such ethnically or generationally focused efforts have been the denomination's educational, spiritual, and missional groups to energize its members and extend their outreach. Generations of women, for example, have been linked beyond local churches to one another and to global mission causes through a movement of Methodist women. In earlier eras, they were known as the Ladies' Aid Society, the Women's Society of Christian Service, and the Wesleyan Service Guild, all of them predecessors of the United Methodist Women today. Rooted in the self-initiated efforts of the Women's Foreign Missionary Society and the Women's Home Missionary Society of the nineteenth century, these organizations assembled women for mission education and channeled their funds directly to overseas missionary programs. They served as a link between the women and the world.

Yet, in their current form, do these efforts actually acquire clout with the constituents for whom they seek to speak and upon whom they seek to exercise influence? Do the faith and mission education efforts truly have an impact? Are they viable vehicles for reforming the nation?

The United Methodist Women (and their predecessors) have been enormously effective in their history. Yet their members represent a rapidly aging constituency, one that is in many cases out of touch with the younger women who have single-parent responsibilities, career goals, and educational needs. Their financial contributions to the connectional mission work of the denomination are in steep decline, down ever eighteen percent in unadjusted dollars during the past decade.[33] This suggests either that their gross revenues are falling, or that more of their revenues are being used to prop up their local church needs, or both.

In short, some old institutions remain, some venerable devices are being renewed, and some new endeavors are underway to establish the power of a church with such a visible presence, to reinvigorate this settled movement for reforming the nation.

Will such empowering activities impact a sizable share of 36,000 congregations? Will the money, which is one way to measure power, move from the maintenance of ministers and buildings toward the people and places where the church lacks influence, impact, inspiration? Will the forms of leadership and ministry which the church adopts serve effectively? Will the patterns of piety, in which the people(s) called Methodists are shaped, have anything distinctively Methodist about them?

Spreading Scriptural Holiness Over the Land

Presence and power are important social indicators of a church's role in culture. But what is the content of that presence? To what end is the exercise of that power? With what theological understanding is it given purpose? Through what forms of ministry and leadership is this settled movement for reforming the nation and spreading scriptural holiness over the land symbolically demonstrated and substantively exercised?

In earlier eras, American Methodists used a number of devices to form one another's lives according to Christian discipline. Class meetings, camp meetings, and revivals were among the classic forms. From the late nineteenth century and into the twentieth, nothing was deemed more important than the Sunday school. In nineteenth century America, the Methodists were leaders of the interdenominational Sunday school movement. George Albert Coe, John Heyl Vincent, and others fashioned the philosophy, the architectural environment, and the curriculum for Christian education through Sunday schools. There were certificate programs for training teachers, awards in the form of banner pins for any who achieved perfection (at least in attendance), fellowship activities to sustain groups and supplement their Sunday morning studies, and whole buildings constructed by local churches to serve as space for Christian education. Add to this a huge commitment to writing and marketing curriculum materials, and the Methodist

Sunday school represented an immense investment of time, talent, and treasure.

At the time of the 1968 merger, United Methodists had an average Sunday school attendance of 3,503,146 each week. By 1994, average Sunday school attendance had fallen to 1,775,722. So, in 26 years, while worship attendance decreased by about 20%, and while the number of United Methodist congregations decreased by less than 13%, Sunday school attendance decreased by almost 50%.[34] The primary vehicle for inculcating Christian piety was reaching half as many persons as it had barely a quarter century earlier.

It is not that the denomination has done nothing new in the area of spiritual formation. The *Disciple* Bible study program has reached more than one-half million United Methodists in a structured, demanding, disciplined approach to encountering Scripture. Covenant Discipleship groups have been formed in countless congregations. The Emmaus Walk program has fostered small networks connecting people of renewed faith together. And there have been other instruments for spreading scriptural holiness. Yet nothing approaches the impact of the Sunday school movement in its breadth, age-level diversity, or comprehensiveness.

The consequences for failing to inculcate piety are spiritual and temporal. Any decline in faith formation makes the denomination even more reliant upon the values and priorities of the culture in which it is invested. There was a time when Methodists could count on the culture to be faith-affirming. But that was, in part, because Methodists (along with peer Protestant mainstream bodies) had established power in the culture, had helped form the nation. Now the church has to be more focused upon inculcating piety if its congregations and connections are to be effective as bearers of the faith in reforming the nation. There are fiscal, as well as faithful, considerations. As Charles Zech concludes in his chapter, a sense of belief and a sense of belonging are among the primary factors shaping members' giving patterns. Stewardship, in other words, is not merely a decision about money; it is an expression of the faith in which one has been formed and the feeling that one has a place in the community.[35]

A commitment to faith and a sense of community can be formed in many ways. United Methodists, in overlooking or neglecting the presence and contributions of some of their people(s), have denied themselves access to some important patterns of personal formation. Justo González, for example, describes the concept of *familia de Dios*, or the great family of God, in his chapter. It is a sense of belonging which transcends the local congregation, which is expressed wherever Latino or Latina folk gather, and which has some promise for a connectional church like United Methodism in American culture. Yet it will require an affirmation of one of the people(s) called Methodist who, in the denomination, have been so underrepresented.

Inevitably, the responsibility for spreading scriptural holiness becomes a matter of leadership. Who teaches Sunday school classes, leads Disciple Bible study groups, and guides youth ministries? Who trains the persons who do these things? Who comes forward to declare himself or herself as a candidate for ordained ministry? Who mentors, supervises, nurtures that person? Who embarks on behalf of the church in prophetic new ventures of justice and service? Who fulfills the pastoral office through preaching, teaching, sacramental administration, and pastoral care? And how does the denomination value those who exercise such forms of leadership?

At its 1996 General Conference, the United Methodist Church made major changes in ordering its ministry. These legislative actions represent the latest, and perhaps most dramatic, event in a long series of studies and decisions over the past fifty years.[36] The offices of deacon and elder are now separate orders of ministry. The pastoral office is now to be entrusted to non-ordained persons as standard practice. The ministry of ordering the church is now assigned to persons who are not ordained to that form of ministry.[37]

United Methodists will enter the twenty-first century with a structure of ordained ministry that was adopted in the hope that God was doing a new thing through the church. But that hope has been given institutional expression before, only to abandon the experiment and try something else.

The denomination has had a particular problem trying to decide what to do with the concept of servant ministry. The ecumenical Christian community has affirmed that all who are baptized have a call to serve, yet has vested a particular responsibility for servanthood in the office of deacon. American Methodism has, since its inception, followed the Anglican practice of ordaining persons first as deacons and later as presbyters, or elders.[38] Thus, all ordained ministers were authorized first to serve.

But in the twentieth century, United Methodists have frequently tampered with the diaconate. Persons who were elected to associate membership in an annual conference, for instance, could be ordained deacon with no prospect or expectation that they would move toward ordination as elders. They could be, in effect, permanent deacons, though they would be functioning in ministries as if they were elders.

In 1976, the denomination created a consecrated lay office called "diaconal ministry" which co-existed with the ordained diaconate, albeit under differing forms of supervision and with differing vocational objectives. Then, in 1996, the General Conference eliminated both the diaconal ministry and associate membership for any future candidates. Hereafter, or until the church's legislature changes the rules again, deacons and elders will both be ordained, but to different forms of ministry. A form of non-itinerating ordained ministry has been created to embody servanthood, while those who are ordained elder will be assumed also to exercise the ministry of servanthood but not be ordained to it. Both deacons and elders are, by legislative fiat, to be servant leaders.

How all of this will enhance the effectiveness of those who are authorized to lead in spreading scriptural holiness of the people called United Methodists remains unclear. The nature of the annual conference as a membership body of clergy and laity will change. The character of the ordained ministry as separate, at least in part, from itinerancy will mean a major change. The decisions about ordering the life and ministry of the church will be entrusted, at least in part, to persons not authorized by any ordaining act to make those decisions. In short, United Methodists have further weakened (if not cut) the link between ordination and the authorization to engage in ministry. Perhaps they have weakened (if not cut) an important link between ordination and leadership.

Beyond the structure of ministry, the denomination faces questions about the practice of ministry. Reports of clergy sexual abuse and misconduct have made headlines in recent years. Debates over the content of theological education for ministry continue to engage scholars, bishops, boards of ordained ministry, and the laity who are served by the clergy they are sent. Worries about the financial burden of theological education, about the willingness of the denomination to sustain its Ministerial Education Fund at current levels, and about the capacity of the denomination in its current configuration to support its clergy economically, trouble many in United Methodism. One study has indicated that more than half of the expenditures of a small-membership church are likely to go for supporting the pastor.[39] For an individual congregation, given the service and programmatic leadership it expects to receive from its pastor, that may be legitimate. For a denomination of more than 22,000 small-membership churches, that is a significant allocation of resources.

Clergy compensation, of course, is not the fundamental issue for ministry. The content and quality of that ministry in exercising leadership is a far more crucial consideration. For leaders, clergy and lay, must conceive and communicate the vision that will enable a settled movement of people(s) called Methodists to reform the nation and spread scriptural holiness over the land. At one level, that involves ascertaining the fitness of the persons who step forward as candidates. At another level, it involves sustaining the spiritual commitment and theological insight of the persons who are in ministry.

In his chapter, Rolf Memming looks at data regarding those ordained persons who do not stay in the pastoral ministry. In her chapter, Patricia M. Y. Chang looks at the women who are continuing in ministry while coping with quantitative and qualitative concerns about their vocation. From both, one could conclude that there are personal and professional risks to be faced by individuals who receive, accept, and follow a call to Christian ministry in the United Methodist Church. Of course, taking risks should not be a deterrent. The circuit riders did. And if their prototypical image still has value for the people(s) called Methodist, then some sense of risk will be understood as endemic to ministry.

Of abiding concern is the theological center of the piety formed in church leaders, including clergy, and the piety shaped by those church leaders in the constituency. Is it the work of sanctifying and perfecting grace? The United Methodist Church is not heir to a tradition that affirms a rigid doctrinal code. It embraces theological diversity. But it is heir to a theological commitment that values practicing the faith above all other considerations. Not only is holiness both personal and social. It is a disciplined pursuit made possible solely by the gift of God's grace. It is a sacred trust.

On the verge of the twenty-first century, the United Methodist Church must find new vehicles to shape that faith and practice it. Not for the sake of institutional survival, let alone success. But because a practiced faith is what forms the identity of the people and the peoples called Methodist.

PART ONE
A Portrait of American Methodists and Their Leaders

John C. Green and James L. Guth

If it were possible to assemble in one place every United Methodist in America, how would the group photo look? And if one were to take advantage of such an opportune gathering and collect their views on a variety of theological, political, and social issues, what might be the range of their attitudes?

Political scientists John C. Green and James L. Guth have developed such a portrait by taking data from a variety of social science resources, putting the pieces together, and providing a connected composite. What emerges is a picture of persons who are older, whiter, and more disproportionately female than the denomination likes to imagine itself, and certainly more so than the American people as a whole. What also emerges is that more individuals consider themselves to be in the picture than the denomination can actually count.

Most interesting, though, are the attitudes of Americans who define their religious affiliation as United Methodist. On the one hand they occupy a place near the center of the social and political spectrum; according to Guth and Green, this is "the church of the golden mean." On the other hand, the middle position that United Methodists occupy is a very wide berth; so, say the authors, this is "the church of the large standard deviation." In short, it is the very nature of the denomination to live in the middle of American life and, therefore, at the intersection of America's great controversies rather than at the extremes of opinion. For good or ill, the United Methodist Church is not a sectarian body with sharply defined counter-cultural views; it is an incarnational body, which takes on the form of the vast middle of the culture wherein it lives and serves.

As Green and Guth demonstrate, differences of opinion characterize this household of faith. There are pronounced divisions: between clergy and laity; between laity who are marginally involved and laity who are actively committed; between the committed laity who hold traditional views and those who hold moderate views; between those who feel strongly attached and those who feel loosely attached to the denomination. And for a church with Methodism's evangelical heritage, less than half of today's United Methodists consider themselves "born again."

Can a community with this sort of fragmented family find ways to remain connected? Can it make room in the group photo for everyone who wants to be in the picture? If so, can it develop sufficient consensus around goals and objectives to act in a concerted and effective fashion? Can it constructively and prophetically serve a culture whose center it occupies?

United Methodists and American Culture: A Statistical Portrait

John C. Green and James L. Guth

The public role of religion in America is a source of considerable confusion. On the one hand, religion's impact is routinely dismissed because of the constitutional separation of church and state, but on the other hand, observers regularly search for common religious values that undergird public life and give it coherence. Of course, as Tocqueville (1945:10–15) recognized long ago, both realities exist side by side in America: having no official sanction, religion still exercises enormous influence through the attitudes and activities of believers. Indeed, some scholars argue that the absence of official sanction has enhanced this informal influence (Finke and Stark 1992).

The impact of United Methodism on public opinion is a good example of these tendencies. Although hardly the "official church of America," Methodists have long been central to American public life. Indeed, many observers have assigned Methodists a key place in a *de facto* religious "establishment" that included the other mainline Protestant churches and reached its zenith at the end of the nineteenth century (Hutchinson 1990). This key role came in large measure from the great size and diversity of Methodism, characteristics that led Roof and McKinney (1987:87–90) to classify Methodists as "moderate" Protestants and the chief occupants of the "center" in American religious life.

The twentieth century and its manifold changes have put great strains on this Protestant "establishment" and the religious "center" it upheld, and not surprisingly, United Methodists have suffered greatly from the attendant stresses and tensions (Bellah et al. 1991), and figure prominently in possible responses to them as well. Some observers see Methodism and the rest of the "residual establishment" (Campbell 1995) as a key building block for reconstruction of a "public church" and a new center in public life (Marty 1981). But other observers are less sanguine, arguing that a fundamental "restructuring" of American religion is dividing the mainline churches, including United Methodists, into rival "liberal" and "conservative" camps, making them less capable of fulfilling their traditional integrative function (Wuthnow 1988). Even less optimistic writers see public life as degenerating into "culture wars"

27

as the fraying center parts (Hunter 1991). There is thus much at stake in understanding the role of United Methodism in public life as the millennium approaches.

The purpose of this chapter is to assess the attitudes of the United Methodist laity and their connection to American public opinion. We will begin by considering the size of the Methodist communion, its internal divisions, and the religious and social characteristics of Methodists. Then, we will use these findings to structure a detailed consideration of Methodist attitudes on a wide range of social, domestic, and foreign-policy questions. Finally, we will compare the attitudes of the laity to the official positions of the Methodist church, the views of its clergy, and the perspectives of Methodists active in national politics.

Our findings are straightforward. In the closing years of this century, United Methodism is best described by statistical metaphors: it is both the "church of the golden mean," and at the same time, the "church of the large standard deviation." Overall, United Methodists hold a middle ground on many theological and political issues, serving as a sort of linchpin for Protestantism, and often, the entire country. This central position does not result, however, from consistent moderation. Rather, United Methodism usually encompasses a wide diversity of attitudes, so that there are often greater differences within the denomination than between it and other religious groups. These internal divisions are tied to differences in religious commitment and belief, and are reinforced by demographic factors.

We find only limited evidence for a unique impact of Methodism on the public opinion; indeed, Methodists may as often be influenced by public attitudes as the other way around. Instead, the distinctive contribution of Methodism may well lie in its potential to both contain diverse social stands and knit together gaps within the social fabric. On the first count, Methodism's internal divisions are amply reflected in the opinions of Methodist church leaders and political activists. But on the second count, these groups appear to act as echo chambers, magnifying and intensifying the divisions within the church rather than building unity among its disparate elements. Thus, United Methodism is often the vortex of controversy rather than the center of consensus-building.

Measuring Methodism

Unlike many other denominations, United Methodists are relatively easy to study by means of survey research. The denomination's name is clear, related denominations are few and small, and its membership is large, producing many easily identifiable respondents in national surveys. Here we will rely on information from three large national studies: the General Social Surveys (GSS), cumulated from 1984 to 1993, the 1992 National Election Study (NES), and the 1992 National Survey of Religion and Politics (NSRP). A host of other surveys from this same time period support the patterns reported below.[1]

How large is the Methodist constituency, most broadly defined? These studies typically show that between 7.5 and 8% of the adult population claim to be United Methodists, which translates into 14 or 15 million people. These figures far exceed the 8.8 million reported in the 1990 Census of Churches and Church Membership (Bradley et al. 1992), based on official denominational statistics. This disjunction reveals an important point: many more people identify with United Methodism than officially belong to its local churches. In fact, most denominations have a large "alumni society" of marginal, inactive, or former members. Indeed, differences between survey results and official figures can be resolved in part by considering only those respondents who also claimed formal membership in a local United Methodist church, about two-thirds of those identifying as Methodists. This strategy reduces United Methodist numbers to perhaps as few as 9 million, much closer to the official count. No doubt these differences reflect both the amorphous quality of religious affiliation in America and the penchant of United Methodist institutions for precise head counts.

How do United Methodists compare to other religious groups in size? United Methodists are clearly the largest mainline Protestant denomination, the second largest Protestant body (behind the Southern Baptist Convention, the largest of the evangelical Protestant churches), and the third largest Christian denomination (after Roman Catholics and Southern Baptists). Looked at another way, United Methodists account for some two-fifths of all mainline Protestants (who together make up about one-fifth of the adult population) and are equivalent to just under one-third of evangelical Protestants (who account for about one-quarter of the population).[2] Or looked at still another way, United Methodists include one-sixth of all white American Protestants and one-twelfth of all Americans who affiliate with a denomination. Thus, United Methodists are a fairly significant religious group in American society, operating within the broader Protestant and Christian communities.

At every turn, survey evidence reveals considerable religious diversity among United Methodists. To illustrate these differences, we divided those claiming United Methodist affiliation into three groups,

"Nominal," "Moderate," and "Traditionalist." These groups were defined by two procedures.[3] First, to distinguish the United Methodist "alumni society" from more active Methodists, we assigned individuals with very low levels of religious commitment to the "Nominal" category. The remaining respondents included all those with at least a minimal level of religious commitment. We then divided these more committed Methodists according to their religious beliefs, putting the most orthodox in the "Traditionalist" category, and less orthodox respondents in the "Moderate" category, which includes various kinds of theological moderates and liberals.[4] The three categories are of about equal size: Moderates constitute almost exactly one-third of the whole communion, with the Nominal category slightly smaller and Traditionalists slightly more numerous. Although this division is admittedly crude, these three groups provide a useful means of illustrating the denomination's internal divisions.

Religious Commitment and Belief

Two aspects of religiosity are particularly important in assessing the opinions of United Methodists: religious commitment and belief (Stark and Bainbridge 1985). Religious commitment matters because the most religiously active people are the most likely to exhibit the distinctive values of their church. Religious belief has a more direct impact, since individuals' beliefs may well be related to their attitudes on other matters. Thus, an assessment of the religious commitment and beliefs of United Methodists is a necessary first step in an analysis of their opinions.

Here we find a consistent pattern: United Methodists stand between other mainline and evangelical Protestants in religious commitment and attachment to core elements of Christian orthodoxy, slightly ahead of the country as a whole. In addition, this wide spectrum of opinion is replicated within Methodism. As might be expected, Nominals show low levels of commitment and orthodox belief, and Traditionalists are high on both counts, while Moderates occupy the middle ground on commitment, but veer towards the Traditionalists on doctrine.

Table 1 reports on levels of religious commitment, first comparing United Methodists to other mainline Protestants, evangelical Protestants, and the entire country (these comparison figures appear as first line of each item entry), and then reporting on three Methodist subgroups (the bracketed figure in the second line of each entry; "Nom.," "Mod.," and "Trad.," represent the Nominal, Moderate, and Traditionalist subgroups, respectively). In this and the following tables, the items on the left are arranged in descending order for United

Methodists as a group (always located in the middle column); differences of more than four percentage points are statistically significant and thus worthy of attention. Thus, on formal church membership (Table 1) the first line shows that two-thirds of all United Methodists claim to be formal church members, roughly matching the figures for other mainline Protestants (67%), evangelical Protestants (71%), and the entire country (69%). The second line of the top entry [in brackets], however, shows that great differences exist among United Methodists: just two-fifths (41%) of the Nominals are formal church members, compared to four-fifths of the Traditionalists (81%), and two-thirds (68%) of the Moderates.

TABLE 1
United Methodists and American Culture:
Religious Commitment

	Other Mainline Protestants ALL	United Methodists ALL [Nom. Mod. Trad.]			Evangelical Protestants ALL	Entire Country ALL
Formal member of a church*	67%	67% [41%	68%	81%]	71%	69%
Private prayer daily#	51%	58% [17%	72%	86%]	72%	50%
Attends worship weekly#	30%	43% [6%	58%	66%]	54%	38%
Shares faith weekly#	32%	41% [13%	43%	65%]	51%	37%
Private Bible reading weekly#	30%	39% [6%	45%	64%]	56%	31%
Religion "very important"#	30%	36% [7%	34%	67%]	50%	35%
Abstains from alcohol for religion#	28%	32% [19%	26%	48%]	40%	30%
Gives 10%+ of income to church#	16%	22% [8%	26%	34%]	42%	24%

Key: Nom.-Nominal; Mod.-Moderate; Trad.-Traditionalist
Sources: *National Election Studies 1992; #National Survey of Religion and Politics 1992

Formal church membership is a modest exception to the overall pattern in Table 1, which puts Methodists squarely in the middle of Protestantism and accents the internal differences between the

Nominal and Traditionalist subgroups. As we might expect, participation in these various forms of religious commitment falls as the difficulty of the practices increases. For instance, just under three-fifths of all Methodists claim to pray in private at least once a day, a relatively easy activity. This number exceeds that of mainline Protestants and all Americans but falls below that for Evangelicals. Note, however, the range of prayerfulness within Methodism: less than one-fifth of the Nominals claim to pray daily, compared to almost nine-of-ten Traditionalists. On the other hand, consider the last entry in Table 1, the much more strenuous activity of financial contribution. About one-fifth of all Methodists reported giving at least 10% of their income (a "tithe" or greater), matching the population as a whole and falling between other Mainliners and Evangelicals. Once again, Nominals are the least supportive of their churches' budgets and Traditionalist the most.

Activities that require modest levels of effort but that are linked to historic Methodism, such as attending worship services, sharing one's faith with others ("witnessing"), and private Bible reading, are undertaken by about two-fifths of all Methodists on a weekly basis. In these regards, Methodists are more pious than the rest of the mainline Protestants and the country as a whole, but less committed than Evangelicals. As before, these numbers mask great internal diversity, with less than one-fifth of Nominals regularly engaging in such activities, compared to three-fifths of Traditionalists. Very similar patterns hold for religious salience, where over one-third of all Methodists claim their faith is very important to them, and also for abstaining from alcohol for religious reasons, where about one-third of all Methodists report practicing this form of "personal holiness" strongly linked to Methodist history. Overall, then, United Methodists show a middling level of religious commitment compared to non-Methodists, and there is considerable internal disparity in the proportion fulfilling their promise to support their church with "prayers, presence, gifts, and service."

These figures demonstrate that United Methodists represent the center of both the Protestant Mainline and the entire country in religious commitment, but that averages often hide important differences within the group. The Methodist "alumni society" clearly makes few contributions to the life of the local church, while Traditionalists are disproportionately prone to cultivate both the personal piety and institutional contributions that foster the religious life of the denomination. Moderate Methodists trail the Traditionalists but still exhibit considerable commitment compared to the Nominals.

What about the religious beliefs of Methodists? Many observers of American Christianity have stressed that the relevant divisions no longer break along denominational lines, pitting, say, Arminian Methodists against Calvinist Presbyterians, but rather are between "orthodox" believers in all Protestant churches against their "modernist" or "liberal" co-parishioners (Wuthnow 1988; Hunter 1991). Although such divisions date from at least the turn of this century, the recent struggles among Methodists over theological pluralism and doctrinal "boundary-setting" may reflect the culmination of this process. To what extent are Methodists divided over such doctrinal disputes? Some answers to this question are presented in Table 2.

TABLE 2
United Methodists and American Culture:
Religious Beliefs

	Other Mainline Protestants ALL	United Methodists ALL [Nom. Mod. Trad.]			Evangelical Protestants ALL	Entire Country ALL
Bible Inerrant Word of God*	60%	70% [25%	75%	100%]	93%	56%
Believe in God without doubt+	58%	60% [35%	72%	82%]	83%	59%
Believe in Heaven+	52%	59% [29%	79%	84%]	82%	60%
Jesus the only way to salvation#	41%	57% [22%	70%	81%]	76%	45%
A "born again" Christian*	20%	46% [20%	56%	62%]	67%	31%
Believe the Devil exists+	35%	46% [17%	56%	62%]	68%	43%
World will end at Armageddon#	23%	39% [25%	42%	50%]	53%	29%
All religions equally true#	40%	42% [20%	41%	48%]	25%	41%

Key: Nom.-Nominal; Mod.-Moderate; Trad.-Traditionalist
Sources: +General Social Surveys 1984–1993; *National Election Studies 1992; #National Survey of Religion and Politics 1992

As before, Methodists stand between other mainline Protestants and Evangelicals on core Christian beliefs, whether on the authority of the Bible, the unique role of Jesus in providing salvation, or religious universalism. And once again, Nominals tend to pull these figures down, while the Traditionalists push them up. For example, seven-tenths of all Methodists have an "inerrant" view of biblical authority ("the Bible is God's Word and all it says is true," a position that includes both literalist and slightly less stringent interpretations), compared to about two-fifths of other Mainliners and nine-tenths of Evangelicals. The Nominals differ sharply from the Traditionalists in this regard.[5]

This high view of Scripture is mirrored in other doctrines, such as a firm belief in the existence of God and Heaven, and that Jesus is the "only way to salvation." In each case, over one-half of all Methodists agree with these doctrines, exceeding the rest of the Mainline, often by large margins, but falling behind the Evangelicals. Not unexpectedly, Nominals are the most skeptical of doctrinal orthodoxy and Traditionalists are the most accepting, but in these matters the Moderates lean toward tradition rather than the middle ground. Other ideas often associated with historic Methodism are less popular. For instance, fewer than one-half of all Methodists claim to be "born again" (to have had a "heart warming" conversion experience) or believe that the Devil exists, and only two-fifths hold the premillennialist conviction that the world will end in the battle of Armageddon. All these beliefs are much less common among other Mainliners and more prevalent among Evangelicals, although there is some attenuation there as well, reflecting the internal differences among Evangelicals on these matters. Note, however, that the usual differences between Nominal and Traditionalist Methodists persist on these items.[6]

Perhaps one of the most revealing questions involves the assertion that "all religions are equally true and good," a clear rejection of any kind of denominational or even Christian "particularism." Two-fifths of all Methodists and other mainline Protestants endorse this popular version of an important tenet of theological modernism. In some sense, this "lay liberalism" (Hoge, Johnson, and Luidens 1994) is the other side of responses to the "Jesus only" item earlier in the table. Evangelicals— and Traditionalist Methodists—soundly reject this position. Hence, if one includes all United Methodists in the analysis they are squarely in the middle of Protestantism; if one excludes the Nominal identifiers, the bulk of the denomination is on the side of a more traditional understanding of "Scripture, tradition, reason, and experience."

How do United Methodists feel about their denomination? The little evidence we have on this point is consistent with our previous findings. Only one-third of all Methodists report a "strong" attachment to the United Methodist Church, less than for the other Mainliners (about two-fifths) or Evangelicals (about one-half). Nominal Methodists contribute substantially to this modest loyalty: just three percent report a strong attachment. However, Moderate Methodists equal the rest of the Mainline, and Traditionalists exceed the Evangelicals in this regard.

When asked to "grade" their own church, all Methodists resemble other Mainliners in awarding a grade of "A" (around one-quarter), but fall behind Evangelicals (two-fifths). Here Nominals and Moderates differ little from the denomination as a whole, while Traditionalists resemble Evangelicals.[7]

Demography

Religious commitment and belief are only two of many factors that influence individual attitudes on social and political issues. We also need to assess the demographic characteristics of United Methodists before turning to their opinions. Table 3 reports on the most important demographic factors, and reveals a familiar pattern.[8] Just as Methodists stand in the midst of Protestantism religiously, they hold the middle ground demographically as well, and their internal religious divisions are paralleled by social differences. Overall, Methodists are disproportionately older, white, middle- and lower-middle-class, female, residents of the Midwest and South. These social characteristics are most evident among Traditionalists and least descriptive of Nominal Methodists. Indeed, the internal differences between these two subgroups are often quite striking.

TABLE 3
United Methodists and American Culture:
Demography

	Mainline Protestant	United Methodists All [Nom. Mod. Trad.]				Evangelical	Entire Sample
GENDER							
Female	59%	62%	[46%	67%	71%]	59%	57%
RACE							
White	95%	94%	[98%	95%	91%]	96%	82%
AGE							
To 35 yrs	31%	28%	[35%	28%	23%]	32%	37%
36–50 yrs	27%	26%	[31%	27%	22%]	28%	28%
51–65 yrs	20%	20%	[20%	21%	20%]	20%	18%
65+ yrs	22%	25%	[15%	25%	35%]	20%	18%
REGION							
Northeast	21%	14%	[17%	13%	11%]	7%	20%
Midwest	36%	33%	[32%	34%	34%]	25%	27%
West	20%	11%	[15%	10%	9%]	14%	19%
South	24%	42%	[36%	43%	47%]	54%	35%

	Mainline Protestant	United Methodists			Evangelical	Entire Sample
		All	[Nom.	Mod.	Trad.]		
SIZE OF PLACE							
Major Metro:							
City	25%	21%	[22%	22%	18%]	21%	30%
Suburbs	44%	38%	[47%	37%	30%]	34%	40%
Non-Metro:							
Urban	15%	17%	[11%	19%	21%]	16%	14%
Rural	17%	24%	[19%	21%	30%]	28%	16%
OCCUPATION							
Professional	43%	34%	[42%	38%	24%]	24%	31%
Managerial	12%	14%	[15%	16%	12%]	12%	13%
Blue collar	26%	28%	[28%	22%	33%]	28%	34%
Housewife	20%	24%	[15%	25%	31%]	26%	22%
EDUCATION							
Less than HS	14%	18%	[12%	14%	25%]	30%	24%
HS graduate	50%	56%	[58%	57%	54%]	55%	52%
College	27%	21%	[24%	23%	17%]	12%	18%
Graduate	9%	5%	[6%	6%	4%]	3%	6%
ANN. INCOME							
To $15,000	39%	43%	[38%	37%	54%]	49%	47%
$15-$25,000	16%	18%	[18%	20%	18%]	18%	18%
$25-$35,000	17%	13%	[14%	14%	11%]	14%	14%
$35-$55,000	16%	17%	[19%	13%	13%]	12%	13%
$55,000+	12%	9%	[11%	11%	4%]	6%	8%

Key: Nom.-Nominal; Mod.-Moderate; Trad.-Traditionalist
Source: General Social Surveys 1984–1993

To begin, like other Protestants, Methodists are disproportionately female, more so than the country as a whole. On this characteristic, there are striking differences among Methodist subgroups: less than one-half of Nominals are women, compared to seven-of-ten Traditionalists. Similar patterns emerge for race and age. Like the rest of historically "white" Protestantism, the United Methodists have attracted few racial minorities: only about one-twentieth of all Methodists are of African American or other non-white heritage. Nominal Methodists are the most "lily white," while non-white Methodists are concentrated among Traditionalists, making up almost one-tenth of this subgroup. While the age structure of United Methodists as a whole parallels other Protestants (and is somewhat older than the country as a whole), there are major differences within Methodism. These data shows a clear "graying" of the active church: more than one-third of Nominals are less than 35 years old, and two-thirds are under 50, while fully one-third of Traditionalists are over 65 years old, and more than one-half are over 50 years.

Methodists have historically been concentrated outside of the major metropolitan areas of the Midwest and South; these patterns still largely hold. As one moves from the Northeast to the South, other mainline Protestants decline in number and Evangelicals increase (with a decline for both groups in the West). Overall, Methodists stand in the middle of this progression, a pattern that extends to the Methodist subgroups: Nominals are least Southern, and Traditionalists, the most. A similar progression is evident for place of residence. Methodists are less concentrated in metropolitan and suburban areas than the other mainline Protestants, but are more urban than Evangelicals, who populate rural and small urban areas. Among Methodists, the Nominals have more than two-thirds of their number living in major metropolitan areas, while a majority of the Traditionalists reside in non-metropolitan cities and rural areas.

What about socio-economic class? Like other mainline Protestants, and increasingly Evangelicals as well, Methodists are basically a middle- and lower-middle-class church. For example, one-third of Methodists have professional occupations, a figure that expands to one-half if managerial jobs are added in. The remaining Methodists are roughly divided between blue-collar workers and homemakers.[9] Once again, the rest of the Mainline stands to one side of all Methodists, with more professionals, and Evangelicals stand on the other side, with fewer. These divisions also split Methodism in the usual way: two-fifths of Nominals have professional or managerial occupations, while nearly two-thirds of Traditionalists are blue-collar workers or housewives.

The same situations occur for education and income. As Robert Wuthnow (1988) has pointed out, education is a major source of the theological, social, and political divisions afflicting American Protestantism. We see evidence of this pattern in our figures. On both education and income, Methodists are in the middle compared to the two other Protestant groups, being somewhat less educated and affluent than the other mainline Protestants, but better-off than Evangelicals. Indeed, on both measures United Methodists look much like the rest of the country. Internally, however, the usual differences are evident: Nominal Methodists are the best educated and most affluent, and Traditionalists, the least.

So the religious differences in commitment and belief noted above are reinforced by differences in social status. The most committed and orthodox Methodists tend to be women and blue-collar workers with relatively modest education and income. Indeed, this link between lower social status and traditional religiosity is almost a truism among sociologists of religion (Roof and McKinney 1987).

Social and Political Attitudes

This brief assessment of the religious and social characteristics of United Methodists sets the stage for a review of Methodist social and political attitudes, presented in Tables 4 through 7. In these tables, we take religious factors into account by means of our three subcategories (Nominal, Moderate, and Traditionalist). To isolate the specific effects of religious factors on social and political attitudes, we "control" for the impact of the demographic variables reviewed in Table 3. To keep the following tables from becoming too complex, we account for the independent effects of demography by adjusting the table entries statistically. In effect, the percentages presented assume that "everything else is equal," providing a clearer picture of the independent impact of religion on attitudes.[10]

To summarize in advance: United Methodists tend toward the right of center ideologically and lean toward the Republican Party, basically resembling other Protestants. Their conservatism is strongest on social issues, and less visible on economic and foreign-policy matters. There is, however, considerable nuance from issue to issue in each policy area. Internal divisions among Methodists present a clearer pattern, however. Nominal Methodists combine strongly liberal positions on social issues (and some other domestic and foreign-policy matters) with conservatism on economic questions. In contradistinction, Traditionalists are conservative on social issues and consistently more liberal on some economic questions, particularly those involving living standards and social programs. We find only a little evidence for a unique contribution of Methodism to these attitudes, although the great diversity of Methodist opinion may itself qualify in this regard.

Table 4 reports on general political assessments. The first of these, self-identified ideology, shows Methodists as a whole to be on the political right, with almost two-thirds claiming to be some kind of "conservative." In this respect, Methodists are more conservative than other Mainliners and the country as a whole, and look very much like Evangelicals. The reason for this pattern is clear: three-quarters of Traditionalists are conservatives, as well as more than one-half of both Nominals and Moderates. A plurality of Methodists identify as Republicans, but here they lag behind both other Mainliners and Evangelicals, resembling the country as a whole. This data reflects great internal differences: Nominals are the least Republican, and Traditionalists the most.[11]

TABLE 4
United Methodists and American Culture:
General Political Assessments

	Other Mainline Protestants ALL	United Methodists ALL [Nom. Mod. Trad.]			Evangelical Protestants ALL	Entire Country ALL
Ideology Conservative*	57%	64% [57%	58%	75%]	67%	56%
Partisanship Republican*	47%	42% [34%	40%	48%]	48%	37%

Key: Nom.-Nominal; Mod.-Moderate; Trad.-Traditionalist
Source: *National Election Studies 1992

Thus, self-identified conservatism and Republican preferences are clearly linked to traditional religiosity, even when other influences are taken into account. How does this pattern play out on specific issues? We first turn to social issues. Even casual observers of American religious politics have noted the divisive impact that social controversies in the major denominations (Reichley 1985), and Table 5 contains United Methodists' positions on a variety of such questions. Although there are some important exceptions, the overall pattern is for all Methodists to hold modestly conservative positions, usually close to the country as a whole, standing between the other mainline Protestants and Evangelicals. As before, Nominals lean notably to the left and Traditionalists to the right. Positions on school prayer, abortion, and gay rights are the clearest examples of this pattern, although Methodist Traditionalists are never more conservative than Evangelicals.

There is, however, more nuance on other issues, such as making divorce harder to obtain, on policies favoring the traditional nuclear family, and on banning pornography. Here, all Methodists look more like the rest of the Mainline, and Traditionalists are substantially farther to the right than their co-religionists. But there are also some issues which reveal few differences, such as support for tuition tax credits for religious schools and capital punishment for convicted murders. Methodists as a group reject tuition credits and endorse capital punishment, like other Protestants and all Americans. Traditionalists are somewhat more supportive of tax credits than the other two groups, but display a modest anomaly on the death penalty, where they are the least supportive.

TABLE 5
United Methodists and American Culture:
Social Policy

	Other Mainline Protestants ALL	UnitedMethodists ALL [Nom. Mod. Trad.]			Evangelical Protestants ALL	Entire Country ALL
Pro Capital Punishment+	78%	78% [83%	80%	72%]	80%	77%
Pro School Prayer+	52%	62% [56%	62%	69%]	72%	58%
Make Divorce Harder+	54%	56% [49%	58%	62%]	65%	53%
Pro Choice Abortion*	55%	51% [76%	48%	40%]	26%	46%
Pro Gay Rights#	61%	51% [64%	47%	40%]	38%	53%
Pro Trad Family*	38%	42% [32%	31%	56%]	62%	47%
Regulate Pornography+	39%	38% [30%	38%	54%]	53%	41%
Pro School Tax Credits*	29%	33% [22%	35%	46%]	35%	42%

Key: Nom.-Nominal; Mod.-Moderate; Trad.-Traditionalist
Sources: +General Social Surveys 1984–1993; *National Election Studies 1992; #National Survey of Religion and Politics 1992

What about other domestic policies, including economic questions, long the principal axis of political conflict in American society? Table 6 presents evidence on these matters and the picture is quite mixed. First, attitudes on the environment and women's rights are similar to the patterns for social issues. (Indeed, some analysts would argue that these are social issues). Here all Methodists resemble the rest of the Mainline and the country as a whole, while holding more liberal positions than Evangelicals. And as might be expected, Nominals are very liberal and Traditionalists farther to the right, although in absolute terms, even Traditionalists are quite supportive of environmental protection.

Different patterns appear on more conventional economic issues, however. Methodists as a group are the most supportive of economic policies designed to maintain living standards (for example, by reducing unemployment), and stand above other Protestants in this regard. Additionally, all Methodists show some support for related social programs, usually siding with other mainline Protestants rather than with Evangelicals on support for welfare and aid to minorities, and reluctance to cut domestic spending. On the other hand, they join with all other Protestants in resisting major government initiatives designed to equalize incomes, and with Evangelicals in resisting an expansion of the government's role in health care. On all these social welfare questions, Methodists as a group either match or trend modestly to the right of the country as a whole. But the Methodist subgroups show a striking pattern across all these issues: in contrast to the situation on general ideology and most social issues, Nominals are consistently the most conservative, and Traditionalists, the least. This pattern is particularly dramatic on welfare and domestic spending, where Traditionalist Methodists are far less willing to reduce the commitment of public resources to these programs, making them more liberal than the rest of the country.

TABLE 6
United Methodists and American Culture:
Domestic Policy

	Other Mainline Protestants ALL	United Methodists ALL [Nom. Mod. Trad.]			Evangelical Protestants ALL	Entire Country ALL
Oppose Income Equalization+	58%	63% [62%	69%	60%]	61%	56%
Pro Environ. Protection*	59%	63% [68%	58%	54%]	55%	62%
Maintain Living Standard*	46%	58% [50%	56%	60%]	48%	54%
Pro Welfare Spending*	50%	47% [42%	59%	64%]	40%	52%
Pro Equal Rights Women*	50%	47% [51%	52%	40%]	40%	52%
Pro Gov't. Aid to Minorities*	47%	47% [45%	42%	51%]	44%	47%
More Gov't. in Health Care*	50%	41% [34%	38%	43%]	40%	51%
Decrease Domestic Spending*	32%	31% [36%	38%	20%]	39%	31%

Key: Nom.-Nominal; Mod.-Moderate; Trad.-Traditionalist
Source: +General Social Surveys 1984–1993; *National Election Studies 1992

Table 7 shows an even more complex pattern on foreign-policy issues. Some scholars have argued that of all major policy areas, foreign policy is least likely to show the impact of religious factors (Jelen 1994). So it is not surprising that on most issues, United Methodists do not look very different from other Protestants or the country as a whole. Few differences appear, whether on support for the Persian Gulf war, US involvement in foreign affairs, maintaining American military power, support for foreign aid, or willingness to use force abroad. As a denomination, then, United Methodists do not have distinct opinions, despite the considerable attention devoted to issues of war, peace, and international affairs by denominational leadership, whether in the form of the 1986 "Peace Letter" of the Council of Bishops or the more routine actions of the General Board of Global Ministries. Although Methodists may not be distinct from their neighbors on such issues, they sometimes differ among themselves, with Nominal Methodists tending to be slightly more liberal, and Traditionalists, more conservative.

TABLE 7
United Methodists and American Culture:
Foreign Policy

	Other Mainline Protestants ALL	United Methodists ALL [Nom. Mod. Trad.]			Evangelical Protestants ALL	Entire Country ALL
Support Gulf War*	78%	76% [70%	76%	78%]	82%	78%
Want U.S. Involved in Int'l Affairs+	74%	72% [70%	74%	73%]	72%	71%
Maintain Top Military*	63%	65% [60%	64%	70%]	68%	62%
Decrease Defense Spending*	55%	47% [51%	57%	34%]	33%	46%
Secure Energy Abroad*	43%	37% [44%	35%	30%]	48%	47%
Support Foreign Aid*	28%	28% [20%	23%	33%]	28%	28%
Defend Weaker Nations*	22%	25% [15%	23%	39%]	33%	28%
Willing to Use Force Abroad*	21%	23% [12%	23%	29%]	28%	24%

Key: Nom.-Nominal; Mod.-Moderate; Trad.-Traditionalist
Source: + General Social Surveys 1984–1993; *National Election Studies 1992;

When differences do appear, however, such as on decreasing defense spending and defending weaker nations from aggression,

Methodists as a group once again occupy the middle ground, and the gap between subgroups grows, with the Traditionalists taking a more hawkish position. Yet another anomaly appears on the issue of securing energy supplies abroad. Here all Methodists express the greatest skepticism toward this American foreign-policy goal, and Traditionalists lead the way.

Methodist Distinctiveness

After this lengthy review of social and political survey data, what can we say about the distinctive contribution of United Methodism to American public opinion? For the most part, these findings provide only modest evidence for a unique Methodist dimension to political and social attitudes. Indeed, on most issues Methodists look much like other Protestants. More striking are many of the differences within the denomination, with the Nominal Methodists usually leaning to the left (except on some economic issues), and with Traditionalist more inclined to take conservative positions (except on some welfare questions).

If there is a distinctive aspect to Methodists' attitudes, it probably appears among the Traditionalists. First, their more modest support for capital punishment and environmental protection, greater backing for social welfare policies, willingness to aid minorities, and reluctance to employ foreign policy to secure energy may well represent examples of the unique impact of Methodist teaching. In each case, the Traditionalists' position is consistent with churchwide pronouncements and runs counter to their tendency to hold conservative views. In this sense, the denomination's commitment to the "Social Gospel" may be seen in its most faithful adherents. Denominational influence may also appear in another, more historic, guise: the Traditionalists' adherence to conservative positions on almost all social issues probably reflects the former Methodist preoccupation with personal morality. Finally, the Traditionalists' unusual combination of conservative social positions and liberal economic attitudes may represent an echo of the historic Methodist emphasis on both personal *and* social reform. Indeed, it is hardly surprising that such examples would occur among the internal faction most committed to the local church and most imbued with Methodist tradition.

Clergy and Elite Opinion

Over the past thirty years, a constant theme of students of mainline Protestantism has been the disjunction between the social and political attitudes of the laity and the official positions of the mainline churches, often produced by liberal bureaucracies and clergy (Hadden 1969; Quinley 1974). Although many analysts now dismiss the cruder versions of this theory which identify these conflicts as the cause of membership decline, others see this divergence as one factor which has eroded the grassroots base of the mainline denominations. We cannot begin to assess this contention in detail, but we can determine the extent to which a disjunction actually exists.

Overall, we find that the diversity of the laity is often reflected in a similar division in church and elite opinion, and more often than not, the differences are magnified and intensified among them. We can see this pattern by comparing lay opinion to the official resolutions of the United Methodist Church and to survey data on the Methodist clergy and Methodists active in national politics.

We made an extensive comparison of the contents of *The Book of Resolutions of The United Methodist Church* (1992) on all of the topics listed in Tables 5, 6, and 7. Although the discursive quality of many resolutions and narrow focus of most survey questions made this inquiry difficult, the comparisons that could be made produced very mixed results. On several issues, such as on environmental protection, lay opinion and the resolutions are closely matched; in other cases, as on the issue of capital punishment, lay opinion took exactly the opposite position from the resolutions. On some questions, like women's rights, the resolutions reflect positions more in line with nominal and moderate Methodists, while others, like welfare spending, represent well the positions of Moderates and Traditionalists. These disparate results may reflect the political process by which the resolutions are proposed, negotiated, and adopted. Dubbed the "caucus church" by one set of observers (Bellah et al. 1991:203–6), the denomination maintains a decision-making process which emphasizes mobilizing sympathetic supporters as much as accurately representing denominational opinion.

As is true in most Protestant denominations, the clergy have a disproportionate influence over the official positions of United Methodism. And previous studies have demonstrated that, at least in the past, the higher one moves in the United Methodist hierarchy, the greater the theological, social, and political liberalism (Reichley 1985:272–274; Miller 1983). How does lay opinion compare to that of Methodist clergy today? Table 8 depicts lay and clergy opinion on a variety of issues. First, all Methodists are compared to the clergy as a whole, and then Moderate and Traditionalists are compared to their clerical counterparts. Since there is no counterpart to the Nominal laity among the clergy (we hope), this group was excluded. There is also a good practical rationale for this decision: the clergy are likely to confront (and have confrontations with) only those who are sometimes in the pews.[12]

TABLE 8
United Methodists and American Culture:
Laity-Clergy Comparison

	LAITY ALL	[Mod.	Trad.]	CLERGY ALL	[Mod.	Trad.]
Conservative	64%	[58%	75%]	36%	[11%	74%]
Republican	42%	[40%	48%]	44%	[26%	71%]
Pro Capital Punish	78%	[80%	72%]	43%	[31%	62%]
Pro School Prayer	62%	[62%	69%]	33%	[14%	60%]
Pro Choice Abortion	51%	[48%	40%]	51%	[75%	14%]
Pro Gay Rights	51%	[47%	40%]	61%	[78%	35%]
Pro Trad Family	42%	[31%	56%]	79%	[69%	94%]
Anti Pornography	38%	[36%	54%]	82%	[72%	97%]
Pro School Tax Credits	36%	[37%	46%]	35%	[24%	58%]
Pro Environment	63%	[56%	54%]	84%	[92%	73%]
Maintain Stand. Living	58%	[56%	60%]	51%	[65%	30%]
Pro Social Spending	47%	[59%	64%]	84%	[90%	75%]
Pro Women's Rights	47%	[52%	40%]	53%	[72%	24%]
Pro Aid Minorities	47%	[42%	51%]	69%	[80%	52%]
Decrease Budget	31%	[38%	20%]	58%	[45%	77%]
Cut Defense Spending	47%	[57%	34%]	75%	[85%	59%]

Unlike the official resolutions, the laity-clergy comparisons yield clearer results. For example, the laity as a whole are nearly twice as likely to identify themselves as "conservative" as the clergy, but the two groups are quite similar in partisan leanings. The clergy as a group are to the left of the laity on many issues, including capital punishment, the environment, school prayer, social welfare spending, aid to minorities, gay rights, and cutting defense spending, but are occasionally to the right, as on regulating pornography.

Whatever differences exist between clergy and laity, there is a strong and consistent pattern within the clergy. Not only are Traditionalist clergy strongly conservative in ideology and Republican in partisanship, but the Moderate clergy present almost a mirror image. And on almost every issue Moderate (and liberal) clergy show dramatic differences from their Traditionalist colleagues. On abortion, for instance, three-quarters of the Moderates hold a pro-choice position, compared to less than one-sixth of the Traditionalists. Similar gaps appear on many of the issues which have agitated recent General Conferences, such as gay rights, women's rights, and public policy toward minorities. No doubt these differences result from the diversity of Methodist congregations, but in addition, they may reflect the high levels of issue constraint that characterize religious professionals. Divisions over important issues are not cross-cutting, with alignments shifting from issue to issue, but have become cumulative, with theological, social, and political lines coinciding (Guth et al. 1991). In such situations, consensus-building becomes ever more difficult.

Of course, such global comparisons tell us about the differences between Methodist laity and Methodist clergy as a whole, but nothing about the "match-up" that really matters: that of each minister and his or her congregation. There are reasons to suspect that the differences we see in the overall figures may be magnified at the congregational level, because, as we have seen, the Traditionalist laity tend to be most active and committed to the affairs of the local church. In our survey of Methodist clergy, we asked ministers not only for their own stand on a wide variety of issues, but also for their perception of where their congregations stood. Of course, clergy may be more or less accurate in such judgments, but whatever their acuity, most will act on the basis of their perceptions.

As a group, the clergy perceived consistent differences between themselves and their congregations, although collectively these gaps are not as wide as those seen by ministers in some other mainline churches (Guth et al. forthcoming). As the pastors see it, the largest divergence was on racial issues, followed by environmental policy, defense spending, gay rights, prayer in school, and the death penalty; on all of these matters the clergy saw themselves substantially more liberal than the people in their pews. Ministers also perceived themselves as somewhat more liberal on other contemporary questions, including the Equal Rights Amendment and a variety of Cold War foreign policies. On several other issues, the differences were minor, as on abortion and tuition tax credits. On two issues the clergy actually perceived themselves to be more conservative: on regulation of pornography (by a small margin) and on the abolition of state lotteries (by a large margin).

As might be expected, however, these aggregate figures hide very different patterns for Traditionalist and Moderate clergy. Traditionalist clergy perceived far fewer—and generally smaller—differences between their own views on issues and those of their congregations. Indeed, only on a handful of issues were there any significant differences, and most of these were in the liberal direction: traditionalist clergy were significantly more liberal than their congregations on the environment and affirmative action, but were more conservative on regulating pornography.

The situation facing Moderate clergy is quite different, at least as they see it. Such ministers rate themselves as much more liberal than their congregations on a host of issues, such as (in descending order) gay rights, defense spending, affirmative action, school prayer, environmental policy, the death penalty, the Equal Rights Amendment, support for free enterprise, and a series of foreign-policy questions. Only on tuition tax credits and pornography do they resemble their congregations.

Thus, the much discussed "gathering storm in the churches" (Hadden 1969) has indeed produced tension between liberal clergy and conservative laity in the United Methodist Church. While Traditionalist clergy operate in church environments that are basically supportive of their theological, social, and political perspectives, the majority of Methodist clergy with more liberal views often find themselves in less congenial surroundings. And of course, a portion of the Methodist constituency sympathetic to Moderates on many issues, namely the Nominals, is much less active in the local church.

Nevertheless, the Moderates report more encouragement on social and political matters from their denominational superiors, usually in a liberal direction. Indeed, the more liberal the minister, the greater the encouragement he or she senses from the denomination for social and political involvement: 54% of the Moderate clergy report such denominational encouragement, while 60% of the Traditionalists report feeling the opposite, namely discouragement from such engagement. As a liberal political perspective tends to dominate United Methodist decision-making, the situation is ripe for at least two types of conflict: first, between more traditional clergy and more liberal clergy, and second, between a more traditionalist clergy and more liberal denominational leaders.

These divisions among United Methodists are most noticed when the church petitions the government for changes in policy. This raised an important question: What about the opinions of Methodists active in national politics, the natural targets of denominational pronouncements and church lobbying? After all, a good bit of the power of the Protestant "establishment" is reputed to have come from the greater

The People(s) Called Methodist

presence of its laity in political institutions and the corridors of government (Roof and McKinney 1987:73–76). Table 9 addresses this question by comparing the entire Methodist laity to co-religionists who are involved in Republican and Democratic party politics.[13]

TABLE 9
**United Methodists and American Culture:
Laity-Political Activist Comparison**

		ACTIVISTS	
	LAITY ALL	REPUBLICANS ALL	DEMOCRATS ALL
Conservative	64%	85%	—
Liberal	20%	—	40%
Pro Sch Prayer	62%	31%	12%
Pro Choice Abortion	51%	35%	67%
Pro Gay Rights	51%	25%	47%
Pro Trad Family	42%	61%	37%
Pro Environment	63%	45%	68%
Maintain Stand. Living	58%	40%	78%
Pro Welfare Spending	47%	26%	63%
Pro Women's Rights	52%	50%	61%
Pro Aid Minorities	47%	34%	63%
Decrease Budget	31%	84%	35%
Cut Defense Spend	47%	28%	64%
Pro Foreign Aid	28%	27%	39%

Source: Laity: see previous tables; Activists: surveys by authors.

Like the clergy, Methodists political activists magnify and intensify differences within the church. The overwhelming conservatism of Republican activists and the liberal plurality among Democrats is to be expected, but these differences prefigure the overall pattern: Republican activists are far more conservative than the United Methodist laity as a group and Democratic activists are more liberal. These differences are even sharper on most of individual issues, with the Republicans strongly to the right and the Democrats strongly to the left. There are some exceptions, of course. Neither set of activists is much in favor of school prayer, Republicans are hardly more conservative than the laity on women's rights, and the Democrats are farther to the left on environmental protection. These patterns are much stronger if Nominal and Traditionalist Methodists are separated out among the party activists (data not shown). This tendency for political activists to have more extreme views than the public is well documented (McCloskey et al. 1960).

Conclusions

Our review of survey data on United Methodists provides a vivid portrait of a denomination that spans the center of the country not only in its religious and demographic diversity, but also in social and political attitudes. In many ways, the assignment of United Methodism to a "Moderate Protestant" category by Roof and McKinney (1987) is apt, for on many traits and attitudes United Methodists do fall between other mainline and the evangelical Protestant churches. It is in this sense that Methodism is still the "church of the golden mean," standing close to the center of American public life. However, this seeming "moderation" is often a statistical artifact, hiding deep divisions between Nominal Methodists, who on many (but not all) issues are quite liberal, and the more committed and orthodox Traditionalists, who tend to resemble their evangelical cousins on most (but not all) matters. Thus, Methodism is also the church of the "large standard deviation," containing many of the tensions that threaten consensus in American society.

These differences within the broader United Methodist constituency are exacerbated by ideological polarization among the clergy, who differ profoundly on theological, social, and political issues. Traditionalist clergy are no doubt energized in part by relatively supportive congregational environments, while more liberal clergy find a more supportive organizational environment in the denominational hierarchy (Guth et al. forthcoming). In this context, the "caucus church" speaks with contradictory voices on public affairs, differences which are further magnified by the stark divisions between Methodists active in national politics.

What are the prospects for the future of United Methodism as the "church of the large standard deviation"? And can it make good on the opportunity to bridge the differences among its many constituencies and become the "church of the golden mean" in fact rather than by virtue of statistics? Several possibilities come to mind. Given the growing polarization of laity and clergy along ideological lines, one solution is a moratorium on social and political involvement. Of course, this possibility not only runs against many strands of Methodist history and tradition, but would also contravene the dictates of many contemporary social theologies, whether of the "social gospel" of the left, or the emerging "civic gospel" of the Christian Right. In any event, these controversies are so tied to theological divisions that it seems highly unlikely that they could be banned from denominational debates. And such a decision would mean abandoning any attempt to serve as a consensus-building institution.

Another solution is decentralization. If critical theological, social, and political questions were left in the hands of local churches or annual conferences, the great diversity of United Methodism might prove less divisive. Such devolution would involve substantial changes in Methodist connectionalism, of course, and would face concerted opposition from denominational loyalists. Of course, even in congregational polities controversy seldom remains at the local level, as the recent experience of the Southern Baptist Convention attests. This solution would defuse some conflict by reducing the confrontations in central denominational forums but would also abandon the goal of consensus-building.

In the absence of a moratorium on social and political issues, or of major changes in Methodist organization, it seems unlikely that many of the controversies over social and political issues can be avoided. Perhaps the best that can be expected is for policy-making procedures to be redesigned to encourage the development of genuine agreement rather than simply the expression of competing points of view. For example, Methodists might require super-majorities for passage of official resolutions or lengthen the period of time involved in adopting them. But whatever the technique, Methodists must realize that consensus does not emerge from diversity by magic, and that it requires great institutional and personal commitment to achieve.

If such a strategy of improved decision-making were to succeed, United Methodists might well contribute to the formation of a new "center" in American public life. But if it were to fail, a final option comes to mind, and that is some kind of division of the United Methodist Church. This possibility should not be taken lightly. Even a casual observer could not have missed the outlines of potential "Liberal Methodist" and "Evangelical Methodist" churches in the above description of the denomination's subgroups. Such an occurrence would be a tragedy of extraordinary proportions, both for Methodists and the nation as a whole.

References

Bellah, Robert N., Richard Madsen, William M. Sullivan, Ann Swidler, and Steven M. Tipton. 1991. *The Good Society.* New York: Alfred A. Knopf.

Bradley, Marin B., Norman M. Green, Jr., Dale E. Jones, Mac Lynn, and Lou McNeil. 1992. *Churches and Church Membership in the United States 1990.* Atlanta: Glenmary Research Center.

Campbell, Dennis M. 1995. "United Methodism in the United States: Retrospective and Prospective Considerations." *Quarterly Review* 15(1): 5–22.

Davis, James Allen, and Tom W. Smith, eds. 1993. *General Social Surveys, 1972–1993.* National Opinion Research Center, University of Chicago. Storrs, Conn.: The Roper Center for Public Opinion Research, University of Connecticut.

Finke, Roger, and Rodney Stark. 1992. *The Churching of America.* New Brunswick, N.J.: Rutgers University Press.

Green, John C., James L. Guth, and Cleveland R. Fraser. 1991. "Apostles and Apostates? Religion and Politics Among Party Activists," in *The Bible and the Ballot Box,* ed. James L. Guth and John C. Green. Boulder, Colo.: Westview.

Griffith, Merle L. 1995. "A Profile of United Methodists." Dayton: General Council on Ministries, The United Methodist Church.

Guth, James L., John C. Green, Corwin E. Smidt, and Margaret Poloma. 1991. "Pulpits and Politics: The Protestant Clergy in the 1988 Election," in *The Bible and the Ballot Box,* ed. James L. Guth and John C. Green. Boulder, Colo.: Westview.

Guth, James L., John C. Green, Lyman A. Kellstedt, Corwin E. Smidt, and Margaret Poloma. Forthcoming. *Confronting Caesar: The Politics of Protestant Preachers.* Lawrence, Ks.: University of Kansas Press.

Hadden, Jeffrey. 1969. *The Gathering Storm in the Churches.* Garden City, N.Y.: Doubleday.

Hoge, Dean R., Benton Johnson, and Donald Luidens. 1994. *Vanishing Boundaries.* Louisville: Westminister/John Knox.

Hunter, James Davison. 1991. *Culture Wars.* New York: Basic Books.

Hutchison, William R., ed. 1990. *Between the Times: The Travail of the Protestant Establishment in America 1900–1960.* Cambridge: Cambridge University Press.

Jelen, Ted. 1994. "Religion and Foreign Policy Attitudes: Exploring the Effects of Denomination and Doctrine." *American Politics Quarterly* 22:382–400.

Kellstedt, Lyman A. 1993. "Religion, the Neglected Variable: An Agenda for Future Research on Religion and Political Behavior," in *Rediscovering the Religious Factor in American Politics,* ed. David C. Leege and Lyman A. Kellstedt. Armonk, N.Y: M. E. Sharpe.

Kellstedt, Lyman A., and John C. Green. 1993. "Knowing God's Many People: Denominational Preference and Political Behavior," in *Rediscovering the Religious Factor in American Politics,* ed. David C. Leege and Lyman A. Kellstedt. Armonk, N.Y.: M. E. Sharpe.

Kellstedt, Lyman A., John C. Green, James L. Guth, and Corwin E. Smidt. 1994. "Religious Voting Blocs in the 1992 Election: The Year of the Evangelical?" *Sociology of Religion* 55:307–26.

Marty, Martin E. 1981. *The Public Church.* New York: Crossroad.

McCloskey, Herbert, Paul J. Hoffman, and Rosemary O'Hara. 1960. "Issue Conflict and Consensus Among Party Leaders and Followers." *American Political Science Review* 54:406–27.

Miller, James Foyle. 1983. *A Study of United Methodists and Social Issues.* Dayton: General Council on Ministries, The United Methodist Church.

Miller, Warren E., Donald R. Kinder, Steven J. Rosenstone, and the National Elections Studies. 1993. *American National Election Study, 1992.* Center for Political Studies, University of Michigan. Ann Arbor, Mich.: Inter-university Consortium for Political and Social Research.

Quinley, Harold. 1974. *The Prophetic Clergy.* New York: Wiley.

Reichley, A. James. 1985. *Religion in American Public Life.* Washington, D.C.: The Brookings Institution.

Roof, Wade Clark, and William McKinney. 1987. *American Mainline Religion.* New Brunswick, N.J.: Rutgers University Press.

Stark, Rodney, and William Sims Bainbridge. 1985. *The Future of Religion.* Berkeley: University of California Press.

Tocqueville, Alexis de. 1945. *Democracy in America.* Vol II. New York: Vintage Books.

United Methodist Church. 1992. *The Book of Resolutions of The United Methodist Church.* Nashville: The United Methodist Publishing House.

Wuthnow, Robert. 1988. *The Restructuring of American Religion.* Princeton, N.J.: Princeton University Press.

Jackson W. Carroll and Wade Clark Roof

While Guth and Green take an aggregate look at United Methodists and offer a macro-Methodist portrait of the denomination, sociologists Jackson W. Carroll and Wade Clark Roof offer a portrait of micro-Methodism. It is congregations, according to Carroll and Roof, that carry religious cultures. So they have conducted ethnographic studies of several United Methodist congregations. Their method is to examine local churches in different regions of the country—churches of different size, history, and ethnic blend—seeking answers to two questions. First, how much does "region" matter in shaping the identity and ethos of a United Methodist congregation? Second, how much does "region" matter with regard to generational differences and the transmission of tradition from one generation to the next?

For this purpose, Carroll and Roof selected six congregations within American culture—three from the most Methodist region of the country (the southeast), and three from the least Methodist region (the west coast). What they discovered is that region proves to be relatively insignificant compared to other issues, such as congregational size, which have nothing to do with region.

Even beyond that, however, they have discovered in local United Methodist churches some practices that may help answer other questions. First, why is the average age of members of the denomination older than the average age of people in the American culture? Second, why is the sense of identity and denominational loyalty among United Methodists not particularly strong? Third, are congregational efforts to form denominational identity compatible with congregational efforts to foster denominational loyalty? Fourth, is there something about United Methodist doctrine that shapes in a particular way a United Methodist congregation?

United Methodist Congregations in North Carolina and California: Regional and Generational Trends

Jackson W. Carroll and Wade Clark Roof

Of the many American religious traditions, Methodism is the most widely dispersed. United Methodist congregations are found in 97% of the 3,043 counties in the United States.[1] For a denomination so scattered across the country, it follows that there are likely to be significant differences in religious and cultural styles from one geographical area to another. Yet, it is also true that many of the historical differences in regional cultures appear to be declining in an age of rapid social change, television, and mass media, and what is sometimes described as the "McDonaldization" of American life.

In this chapter we address the following questions: Are there differences in identity and ethos of United Methodist congregations attributable to region today? And related to this, do these regional differences hold among young generations within United Methodist congregations? In examining these questions, we conducted descriptive case studies in six congregations in two regions, in the Research Triangle area of North Carolina and on the Central Coast of California. North Carolina congregations included Edenton Street UMC, Raleigh; Glendale Heights UMC, Durham; and Genesis UMC, Cary. California congregations included North Oxnard UMC; First UMC, Ventura; and St. Mark's UMC, Santa Barbara.[2] While we can hardly claim that these locations or congregations constitute a representative sample of United Methodist congregations, the choice of settings does allow for a sharp contrast in cultural and religious ethos.

Focus on Congregations

Congregations are important to study because they are the carriers of religious cultures—that is, constellations of values, practices, and webs of meaning as shaped partly by denominational history and heritage, but also by a myriad of social factors such as social class, ethnicity, region, generation, and so forth. In this sense, each congregation has a distinctive ethos that is part of its identity, independent of any ties to a larger religious body. Furthermore, as R. Stephen Warner maintains, religious bodies in the United States—no matter what their stated polity—generally reflect what he calls "*de facto* congregationalism."[3] This is to say that religious denominations, including the United Methodist Church with its strong connectional emphasis, have converged more or less towards the Reformed model of the congregation as a voluntary religious community. Recent moves within United Methodism, including proposals for a "new connectionalism,"[4] have pointed to this *de facto* congregationalism.

The dual focus implied by these observations—congregations as carriers of a denominational heritage and of local religious cultures partly shaped independently of the denomination and becoming increasingly "congregational"—raises important questions for a strongly connectional denomination such as the United Methodist Church. Just what goes on in Methodist congregations? How "Methodist" are they in their beliefs and practices? How well do United Methodist congregations function as part of what some have called the "ecosystem" of faith and practice,[5] nurturing new generations of members in Methodist beliefs and practices? These broader questions about Methodist congregational life lie behind our more specific focus on region and generation. To what extent do regional and generational differences impact the role of congregations as carriers of a denominational heritage?

Region

As is well-known, the South continues to be religiously exceptional in its relative homogeneity and strong cultural support for religion. Despite changes, especially in the post-World War II period and particularly evident in the Research Triangle area of North Carolina, our southern research site, the region continues to be highly Protestant and dominated by a popular, evangelical religious ethos. Samuel S. Hill Jr. (1972) has argued that the region has two cultures, "southernness" and "religiosity," and that the bonds between them historically have created a strong unity.[6] While the South has obviously changed since Hill made this observation, especially as a result of a considerable immigration from other parts of the United States and elsewhere, we believe that his generalization still holds for much of the South. More recent research shows that, when compared with people elsewhere in the country, southerners are far more likely to identify with their region, southern Protestants are almost twice as likely as non-Southern Protestants to look upon church-going as essential to the Christian life, and they are more likely to attend church services. Likewise,

Methodists in the South are more traditional in beliefs and practices and more likely to "feel close" to other members in their churches, than is true of Methodists in other regions.[7]

In sharp contrast, California offers a much higher level of religious pluralism and is known for its individualism, its mobility and rootlessness, and its lack of strong traditions. It is a context that has long been receptive to unconventional beliefs but is characterized by low rates of church membership and religious attendance. In spite of being one of the few states that was culturally Catholic before Protestantism came on the scene, California lacks a strong culturally shaped religious establishment. This, some commentators have argued, has opened the way for sects, cults, and religious movements of all kinds to flourish.[8] Generally, the religious climate has been one described as a "contented indifferentism" where "custom does not keep the ministry." California, like the West coast as a whole, does not have as strong a Christian cultural base as is found in some other regions.[9] West coast denominations, Methodists included, cannot rest on the culture and its support as their counterparts can in the South.

Generation

The generations born after World War II (the so-called "baby boomers" and "Generation Xers") have grown up in a world of television and visual media, increased consumption, and culturally-sanctioned choice, but also a world marred by the shadow of the Holocaust, assassinations of national leaders, ecological disasters, nuclear threats, and the agonies of an unpopular war. They have known pluralism—including lifestyle pluralism—far more than any previous generation, they have experienced disruptions of traditional family life and carved out new styles of family and intimate relations, and they have enjoyed higher levels of education and expanded scientific and technological approaches to learning; they have been deeply touched by a popular culture.

With these cultural changes have come declines in traditional beliefs and religious practices. Loyalty to religious institutions has eroded. Knowledge of denominational heritage has weakened for members of these generations. Many of them dropped out of active religious participation when they were growing up, but in more recent times many have also returned to church. By and large, younger Americans are drawn to expressive, experiential styles of faith. The trend toward the more expressive holds across regions and across religious traditions.[10]

The Churches

We turn now to the six congregations, beginning with those in the Research Triangle area of North Carolina. For each, we present case descriptions based on participant observation of worship services and other church events and focused interviews with twelve members and the pastor of each congregation.[11] Limitations of space have required that we keep the case descriptions brief. We have tried, however, to provide enough comparable information to capture the "flavor" of the six churches with particular attention to the congregations' and members' sense of United Methodist identity.

Glendale Heights United Methodist Church

Glendale Heights United Methodist Church (GHUMC) is a "two-celled church," says the pastor who has completed his first year at the church. One cell is "the pioneers, fifty of them, [who] joined this church in the first six years [of its existence]; all others after that were settlers or squatters. The pioneers include each other, but they exclude all others." The squatters, many of whom are young adults, are not well organized and are struggling to develop leadership. A lifelong member, now in his early thirties, says that he relates well to both groups and often finds himself in the middle of "controversy between the young adults and the older people." A lay woman, also in her thirties, speaks of resistance to change: "They [older members] can't accept that you've got these young adults coming in here and 'trying to take over.'"

GHUMC was founded in 1950 to serve what was then a white, solidly middle-class suburb that developed in post–World War II Durham, North Carolina. Many of the nearby houses are one-story ranch style houses typical of that era. In recent years the neighborhood has undergone change. Though still middle class, it is now racially mixed. The church's ZIP code area was 60 percent white and 40 percent African American in 1990. Blacks are the majority in an apartment complex down the street from the church. The congregation remains all white, and many members no longer live in the church's immediate vicinity. Membership stands at 460, which includes some transfers from another United Methodist congregation that closed in 1988. Average worship attendance is 110, with an average Sunday school attendance of 65. "If there is a 'demographic hole' in the congregation," one person said, "it would have to be the absence of people in the 18 to 25 and 40 to

50 age bracket. There are a lot of young adults who are beginning families. The church's nursery is always full."

Originally meeting in a school, the congregation built its facilities in two stages. The first building contained Sunday school classrooms, offices, and a fellowship hall used also for worship. A new sanctuary was added in 1986. Heavy indebtedness on the new sanctuary is a major issue facing the congregation. References to the debt and to fund raising events to aid in debt retirement are regular features of the newsletter. Fund raisers include fish fries and other dinners, food sales, and more recently operation of a refreshment stand at Durham Bulls' baseball games. Fundraisers, says the pastor, are important not only for the debt but for increasing communication and cooperation across congregational divisions. They "take people from all the little cells and force them to work together." The ballpark venture, however, may have the opposite effect. Some older members oppose it because beer is sold at the games.

The new sanctuary has "wrap around" seating, with four sections of cushioned pews arranged around the chancel area. Younger members tend to sit toward the left side of the sanctuary; a group of older members to the rear of the center section, with the members who transferred from the closed congregation sitting together on the right. The central pulpit stands behind the communion table, which is "fenced" by a padded communion rail. Choir members sit on tiered seats directly behind the pulpit, making them the center of attention. A cross hangs on the wall over the choir, with another on the communion table. Bibles and United Methodist hymnals are in the pews. In the hallway of the church school building are photographs of former pastors and tables and bulletin boards with local and denominational program announcements and promotional material. In addition to classrooms and a fellowship hall, the church school building houses a parlor named in memory of a much-loved matriarch of the church. An older adult Sunday school class, named in memory of a male member of the congregation, meets in the parlor. No rooms or Sunday school classes are named for Methodist "worthies" or bear distinctive Methodist names.

Morning worship usually follows the "Basic Pattern for Sunday Worship" from the hymnal and was introduced without much consultation by a pastor during the late 1980s. It is too formal for some of the older members, who, as one said, prefer the "old fashioned way . . . where we come in, sit down, sing a few hymns, listen to a sermon, and go home." An announcement period before the formal service has a familial feeling. Laity join the pastor in making announcements and sharing information about fellow members. Following announcements, acolytes, choir, and the robed pastor process to the chancel area. Sermons, preached in a "folksy" style, are usually based on the lectionary text and often have grace as a central theme. The pastor, a former farmer who often refers to himself as "a farmer called to preach," frequently uses agricultural references in his sermons. Communion is celebrated monthly. Members "dress up" for worship. Most men wear coats and ties, and women wear their "Sunday best." The music program is quite strong, with four choirs (adult, youth, and two for children) and a forceful choir director who has held the position for 25 years. The pastor indicated that he was soon instituting a week night alternative worship service on a trial basis: "There will be quite a bit of singing, an open kind of [service] where people are free to speak out if they choose. . . . It will be very Spirit led."

In addition to Sunday school, the church has an active United Methodist Men's organization with about 30, mostly older, members who meet monthly for dinner and sponsor various projects. A United Methodist Women's group involves roughly one-third of the women and sponsors occasional missions studies. Popular, especially among some of the younger members, is church involvement in two local outreach activities: an Interfaith Hospitality Network through which local churches provide temporary housing for homeless families, and serving dinner at a local homeless shelter six times each year. The church also makes space available at no charge to several twelve-step groups. A church-sponsored aerobics group also meets at the church. One younger member lauds the group for helping her keep both spiritually and physically fit.

When asked what attracts them to the church, most, old and young alike, emphasize the church's family-like, friendly character. They like its feel of a small church and worry about getting too large. There is "a lot of energy among the younger members," one member added. A number of the younger members were attracted by a popular pastor during the late 1980s. When he was appointed to another church in Durham, some younger members left to join the other congregation. The exodus created tension in the congregation and anger at denominational officials for moving the pastor to such a nearby church. Several who were tempted to leave reaffirmed their commitment to GHUMC rather than to any single pastor. "I will support this charge and the pastor who is here," said one 30-year-old male who was close to the former pastor. "That's the itinerant ministry and that's why I am a . . . United Methodist."

Among younger members, Methodism's more formal style of worship and its openness to diversity are especially valued. They contrast it with the narrow fundamentalism that they see in many Southern Baptist and other conservative churches. Most members, however, both young and old, wear the church's Methodist identity lightly. As the pastor sees it, "probably 50 percent of them wouldn't care what name was on the 'marquee' out front." "My decision to become United Methodist," said a member in her thirties, "didn't have anything to do with the [congregation's Methodist] background. It had to do with *this* congregation, with *this* church, and with *these* people." Another younger member indicated that being Methodist "is just what comes with joining this church. I've never been particular on what denomination someone belongs to, so long as they are Christian." According to an older male, many of his friends in the congregation "wish we could just have our own little church" [instead of being part of the denomination]. Forget about the big church with all its rules and regulations! But, I really think," he added, "that it is an advantage to being bigger and an organized church." As the pastor puts it, "It's sort of an 'us' and 'them' type thing, and we don't hold paying our apportionments high on the list of things to do. . . . We like it when [the denomination] is giving us 'stuff,' but we don't care too much for it when it comes to giving something back."

With few exceptions, interviewees, all of whom were active in the congregation, had only limited knowledge of Methodist history, beliefs, social positions, or organization beyond the local church. One said that the practice of baptizing infants reflects Methodist belief in "prevenial grace"! Several who had not been raised Methodist indicated that they had received no instruction in Methodist beliefs and practices when they joined the congregation.

As the pastor reflects on the future, he sees his primary goal as helping the congregation grow spiritually. "They are in a spiritual winter," he says, noting that spiritual growth involves the healing of the divisions. Beyond this, "the program that I really want to build on is the children . . . to the point that we become known as a church that does children's ministries. . . . If [a church does] one thing really well, it usually helps everything else."

Genesis United Methodist Church

"Rookies." "Young in faith." These are phrases the pastor uses to describe members of his congregation. Genesis United Methodist Church, located in Cary, North Carolina, is itself a "rookie" congregation, founded in 1987 when Wilkerson [the founding pastor] went door to door inviting mostly unchurched young couples to join him in doing something important. After meeting in a school cafeteria and a local YMCA, the congregation, which now numbers approximately 200 members, moved into its new facilities in September 1994. Appropriate to its rookie members, Genesis's bulletin and newsletter carries the motto, "A Place for Beginning, a Place for Belonging, a Place for Becoming."

Though primarily a suburb of Raleigh and near the Research Triangle Park, Cary's rapid growth has made it the eleventh largest city in North Carolina. It is home to an affluent, highly educated, predominantly white population with many young families. Seventy-five percent of the residents of the ZIP code area in which the church is located were under 44 at the time of the 1990 census.

One reaches Genesis by driving down a major thoroughfare, past new housing developments advertising homes in the $200,000 to $300,000 price range, two churches under construction, and a new shopping center. A sign with the United Methodist cross and flame marks the entrance to the church property. On a typical Sunday morning, one might mistake the church's gravel parking lot for a minivan dealership.

The new brick facilities include a sanctuary (that doubles as a fellowship hall) and a church school building containing classrooms and offices. The sanctuary and church school are separate structures connected by an atrium-like narthex. The sanctuary, roughly square with small, high, clear glass windows on three sides, resembles the inside of a boat (Genesis's logo is an ark and rainbow). Over the chancel area, there is a large clear window etched with a circle. Intersecting bars form a cross in the window. The chancel is a low platform with a pulpit-lectern, baptismal font, and communion table. A large wooden cross stands to one side of the space. The choir sits to the right of the chancel area. There is a piano but no organ (a fact that a number of members noted favorably as being less formal). Windows are sufficiently high that only trees and sky are visible. Cushioned chairs are movable. Racks in the back of the chairs contain United Methodist hymnals. A table in the entry holds various brochures describing Genesis program offerings as well as other program and social ministry opportunities available in the area. Signs announce group meetings, many of them having to do with parenting issues.

Many Genesis members come from other denominations, and often from mixed Protestant-Catholic marriages. Most were functionally, if not actually, unchurched before joining. Of the twelve members interviewed for this project, ten were raised in denominations other than United Methodist. The pastor, himself raised as Presbyterian, estimates that at least half come from other denominations. Whether they grew up Methodist or not, few know much about Methodist history, beliefs, or positions on social issues. When asked about knowledge of Methodist history, one woman mentioned the Wesleys and added that there was also some relation to Martin Luther, "but," she continued, "I guess that is my Presbyterian background." When asked about Methodist positions on social issues, another commented that she didn't know "if Methodists were republican or democratic." Few know that they are joining a connectional church. When they find out that this is the case, some (especially former Baptists) see the connectional system as a safeguard from "wacko independent ministers." Others tolerate it as a burden to bear. "United Methodist identity is very low," says the pastor. "It's not a 'biggie.'" "How a church feels, rather than its denomination, is what is important to me," one member said.

What is most important to those who join Genesis is the church's friendly, caring atmosphere, symbolized especially in the "celebrations and concerns" period during Sunday worship, when members can share joyful events in their lives or lift up personal, family, and social concerns for prayer and support. Members say that "C & C," as they call it, connects them to each other and to the world. A particularly important symbol of caring—mentioned in several interviews—was the baptism of an infant whose mother had almost died following childbirth. The baptism moved the entire church family to tears as the mother and father used the event to thank the church for the support they had received from the congregation.

Also valued is the church's casual style, a carryover, perhaps, from its early days in the school cafeteria. One doesn't have to "dress up" in Sunday best. When one of the authors attended a Sunday service, he was the only one wearing a jacket and tie. Members worry that the new building will lead to greater formality in style and dress. So far, this is not the case.

Another valued attribute of the congregation—and of United Methodism generally—is its open-mindedness and tolerance of diversity. Several interviewees mentioned the denomination's openness to gays and lesbians as especially appealing: "We are all equal in God's eyes in the Methodist Church," said one young woman who was raised as a Free Will Baptist. (Genesis, however, has no openly gay or lesbian members.)[12]

Most members also enjoy and value being connected to others who are like them—young, family-oriented (and highly mobile) professionals. In contrast to most, one woman interviewee in her late sixties confessed that she feels out of place in the congregation: "Maybe I should have joined a church with more old people."

Sunday worship services—there are two (8:30 and 11 a.m.)—are the most important weekly gatherings, and the opportunity to gather together, deepen their commitment, and find renewal for the coming week are the most important reasons given for participation. Average attendance at the two services is over 200, including children. Members look for a practical, take-home message from the sermons. For the most part, they appreciate the pastor's emphasis on love and his use of life-experience stories to illustrate his points. Sermons regularly encourage people to engage in local mission activities—and some do, but members see this as more the pastor's emphasis than that of the membership.

A minority of adults participate in the Christian education program. They view it as being primarily for children. The children's program uses a newly approved United Methodist curriculum, based on the lectionary, that integrates education and worship. For adults who do participate in Sunday school, adult classes include a Searchers class for in-depth Bible Study (several of its members have completed Disciple Bible Study), a Back-to-Basics class that serves as an outlet for more conservative members, a Putting Faith into Practice class focusing on issues of personal growth, and a Family class discussing family-life issues. The Family class regularly uses books written for general audiences; God is rarely mentioned as the class engages in problem-solving about issues they face. There are also Sunday evening and weeknight classes, including one on parenting, Disciple Bible Study, and New Member classes (led by the pastor). Some members are involved in the Walk to Emmaus program.

A United Methodist Women's group is active and growing. There is also a small, less active men's group. Occasional activities include pot-luck suppers and picnics, participation in a church softball league, and an annual Blessing of the Animals service. Members do little formal evangelism, but the pastor regularly encourages them to invite their friends.

Because of the busy lives led by the members, volunteer time is at a premium and is a serious problem for the church. In a summary of concerns as part of the church's "Goals for 1995," volunteer issues figured in ten of the twenty concerns listed.

Edenton Street United Methodist Church

"Tradition," says the pastor, "is firmly entrenched at Edenton Street United Methodist Church—respect for what is already in place. . . . When there are conflicts between the traditionalists and visionaries, the traditionalists generally win out. Change takes time . . . because we tend to get 'infected' with tradition like it is some kind of plague."

This respect for tradition is perhaps understandable. With ties to Francis Asbury and Jesse Lee, both of whom were instrumental in bringing Methodism to the Raleigh area, Edenton Street United Methodist Church (ESUMC) has a long and proud heritage. It has been an influential voice in the public life of the city and state, the North Carolina Annual Conference, and the United Methodist Church generally. The church was founded in 1811, eleven years after Asbury preached in Raleigh. The church's pastor, Melville Cox, left in 1832 to go to Liberia as the first foreign missionary of American Methodism. Recently, when the United Methodist Church introduced its new hymnal, Edenton Street hosted the national celebration.

The congregation has a membership of just over 3000 and an average worship attendance of between 750 and 800. Membership fell to 2500 in the early 1980s but has subsequently recovered. Members are from all age groups, though leaning towards middle age and older. In recent years a growing number of younger families have been joining, leading the church to add nurseries and renovate church school facilities for children. As recently as the late 1950s, over 90% of the members lived within two miles of the church. Few are any longer that close but are spread throughout the city and its suburbs. Professionals, especially lawyers, make up a significant proportion of the membership. Because of the church's proximity to the annual conference headquarters, clergy and other church professionals are also numerous. Some Good News Movement sympathizers are members—a lay member is a member of the national board of directors, but they are joined by liberal activists. While there is limited racial and ethnic diversity, the congregation is overwhelmingly white. A professional staff of nine leads the congregation.

The church is in its fourth building on the same site in downtown Raleigh near the state capitol and is surrounded by state office buildings. The sanctuary is a red brick Gothic structure with a tall spire topped by a cross. A large education building stands to one side, connected to the sanctuary by a cloistered walkway. The education building houses offices, a Child Development Center, Sunday school classrooms, fellowship hall, and a chapel. A Korean Methodist congregation with no formal ties to ESUMC meets in the chapel. Several Sunday school class names reflect the church's Methodist heritage: Cokesbury, Foundry Fellowship, and Wesley Covenant Class. The center hall of the education building is flanked with maps and photographs important to the church's history. Ample off-street parking is nearby in church- and state-owned lots (the lots, as one person noted, are where many members' houses once stood).

Rebuilt following a fire in the 1950s, the sanctuary has a center aisle, divided chancel, ornate reredos and marble altar over which is a stained glass rose window. Additional stained glass windows depict Jesus and other major figures of the Old and New Testaments. The choir sits in the chancel on both sides. Pews of light oak hold United Methodist hymnals and RSV Bibles. There is a four-manual pipe organ with a full set of antiphonal pipes, a grand piano, and an electronic inside-outside carillon. On one of the Sundays we visited the church, a timpani was also used for musical accompaniment. A handbell choir played from a balcony at the rear of the sanctuary. The formality of the sanctuary is "warmed up" by the use of seasonal banners.

Worship services at ESUMC (two essentially similar services each Sunday morning) are "high church, formal, and elegant," as one member described it. The two services follow the "Basic Pattern of Worship" as found in the hymnal. As members gather a pianist plays various familiar hymns such as "How Great Thou Art" and "What a Friend We Have in Jesus." Announcements follow. Choir and ministers process, led by a crucifer and two acolytes. Sermons generally are based on the lectionary text. Politics and social issues are rarely discussed from the pulpit. On a Sunday that one of us attended, the sermon was based on the parable of the Prodigal Son and emphasized both human freedom and a waiting God who gives us freedom but who also receives us back, just as we are. The preacher, the senior minister, used numerous stories to illustrate his points. A children's sermon precedes the main sermon. Children then leave for children's church. Choir anthems are professionally rendered by the Chancel Choir. Communion is celebrated monthly at the 8:45 service and quarterly at the 11 a.m. service. Members kneel at the altar to receive the elements (individual cups and wafers). As one member put it, there seems to be a feeling that "Methodist communion that doesn't involve kneeling at the altar is not communion at all." Leaders find it difficult to try new things in worship. Such acts as passing the peace are perceived as not orderly. Prayers tend to be "generic." "People don't feel comfortable having specific names mentioned. They . . . prefer it more anonymous," reports the pastor. Until recently, ushers were always male. Member attire at worship is relatively formal: Most men wear coats and ties. Even young people wear shirts and ties, often with baggy Bermuda shorts.

Program options at ESUMC are extensive, varied, and generally positively evaluated by those we interviewed. The music program is especially valued. The church also has strong children and youth programs. Multiple opportunities are available for adult study, including Disciple Bible Study. A Stephen Ministry program involves laity in doing pastoral care. Service and outreach programs attempt to address needs in the urban setting, including an Adult Day Care Center, a prison ministry, a summer day camp for inner city children, and participation in a countywide Faith Hospitality Network (providing temporary housing for homeless families). One ministry singled out as important is the ESUMC Care Team, whose goal is to provide "compassionate support, friendship, and care to persons with AIDS." Although the congregation supports overseas mission efforts and has a long history of mission involvement, missions did not surface as an important issue in member interviews. Because of the church's downtown location and its distance from most members' residences, many programs and business meetings are scheduled on Sundays and on a "meeting night" to minimize travel.

Being part of a viable downtown church with capable staff and quality programs is important to members, many of whom drive by several other United Methodist congregations to come to ESUMC. The size of the congregation and its diverse programs are also attractive to some, if for no other reason than, as one member put it, "you can hide and get lost in it." For others, family and friendship ties were important factors in their membership in the congregation. Some grew up in the congregation; their parents and often grandparents did also.

How important is ESUMC's Methodist identity for those who join? In the pastor's view, it makes little difference for most members. Several interviewees agreed: "I'm here because [my parents] are here. My attraction to this church is the people. . . . The importance of being a United Methodist lies with my parents" (19-year-old male). "The reason I am a United Methodist is that this [church] is where I grew up" (female, late-20s). "I was born into this church. It feels like home to me. . . . Being Methodist isn't particularly important to me at this time" (male, early-30s). "I'm a United Methodist because I am connected with ESUMC. . . . My local church is what it's all about" (female, mid–40s). Nonetheless, eight of the eleven interviewees grew up Methodist and sought out a Methodist church rather than some other. In addition, all commented positively about features of

Methodism that are important to them, especially the denomination's inclusiveness, openness to diverse theological and social views, emphasis on lay ministry, and connectional character. Itinerancy is particularly valued: "If you get one preacher you don't like, you don't get stuck with that one forever" (female, early 70s). Interviewees were also relatively well informed about Methodist history and polity, but somewhat less knowledgable about doctrine. Most could imagine themselves as Presbyterians if they were not United Methodists. They would not, however, be Southern Baptist because of a perceived narrow-mindedness and intolerance of the current SBC leadership.

North Oxnard UMC

Located at the entrance off a major thoroughfare into a residential development, the North Oxnard United Methodist Church gives the appearance of a being a middle-class, suburban church. And to some extent, it is. Twenty years ago the church was constructed on this site in hopes it would draw members from this community, and a few local residents have joined. But most of the congregation's members still live "in the old neighborhoods," which are more downtown and a couple of miles away. These are the longstanding, faithful members, who have weathered 25 years of struggle in keeping the congregation alive and together. They are electricians, retailers, nurses, homemakers, and retired Navy personnel largely from a working- and lower-middle-class background. Young recruits have come from the nearby military base; a few have stayed with the church over the years, most have left. All are Anglo except for two or three who are Asian. Total membership is about 65, about 40 of whom are active. The small size of the congregation gives it a cozy, friendly, supportive atmosphere—a "small church with a big heart," as members describe it.

The church facilities include a sanctuary, fellowship hall, pastor's study, several classrooms, playground, and parking lot. In the entryway, there is a table with books, pamphlets, and materials provided by Cokesbury, some for sale but mostly free of charge, and a bulletin board with a description of upcoming events. The sanctuary seats about 150 people and has blue cushioned pews. The walls are paneled with wood rising to meet the vaulted ceiling. Above the altar is a banner on the wall with large letters "Follow Me" in English, Spanish, and Japanese. On the left wall is a small sign made by a home computer: "God made me, and God does not make junk." The right side of the sanctuary opens into a garden area which is visible through sliding glass doors. The chancel area is elevated one step above the sanctuary floor and houses the choir loft, piano, lectern, and altar. The chancel is separated from the pews by a wooden rail. Racks underneath the pews carry United Methodist hymnals. Bulletins for the worship service on Sunday morning carry a Cokesbury imprint, which, along with the hymnals, gives the service a Methodist flavor.

Yet as the pastor says, it is an "open, exploring" style of Methodism, marked more by curiosity and willingness to learn about the tradition than by a firm understanding of it. The older members of the church know the most about the Methodist heritage: they know about the Wesleys, the connectional system, concern for the poor, emphasis upon both personal faith and social concerns, and the importance of traditional values and belief. The pastor, new to the congregation, has initiated a "Vision Workshop" exploring Methodist heritage and the meaning of Christian faith and life today. People appear to be drawn to an understanding of Methodism that makes room for those who have honest doubts in their faith, and they are quite taken when learning that John Wesley himself struggled with his beliefs throughout his life. Members of the congregation know about the social teachings of the United Methodist Church, but not much is said about them. Important in the congregation are what might be described as Golden Rule values—respect for people and property, good moral character, family life, treating others as you would like to be treated.

Younger members know far less about Methodism and are not particularly interested in the heritage. Their language of faith is informed less by history and the theology of Wesley, Asbury, and others than by popular culture. A young, female transfer member from a Baptist church could not name any founders, relate any history, or describe the organizational structure of the church. As for beliefs, she offered the following as a creed: "Be good. Follow the 10 Commandments, I guess. And worship Jesus." She could not comment on the church's position on any social issue. Historic differences among the denominations seem not to be very important, as was evident in the comment of a 29-year-old, lifelong Methodist woman: "Potatoes. It's all about potatoes. Baked potatoes, mashed potatoes, French fries, potato chips—regardless of what you eat, you're still eating potatoes, right? Well, that's how it is with church." A young man likes the fact that the church is "not hung up on 'no women ministers'" and, when asked about the church's past, spoke of "a man named Wesley who started a new church for some reason because he was mad at somebody" and who had a brother who was "big in music." This same young man, who works as an electronics technician, now attends the Bible study group, and after having read the book of Romans for the first time, he decided "God is pretty cool."

Young and old alike, however, are attracted to the congregation largely because of its diversity of belief—a theme expressed in just about every interview we conducted. "It's so neat that the church doesn't tell you certain and specific beliefs," commented a 62-year-old woman. "United Methodism is "more accepting of people who don't have a strong sense of religious beliefs," comments a 41-year-old man. Many members told us that the United Methodist Church is "open-minded." This sense of openness and diversity of belief arises partly out of the fact that the church has had two women as pastors—"those who couldn't stomach that left, and the rest got used to it," as one longtime member put it. Also, the social and religious context of a place like Oxnard is a factor. Members in the congregation like the fact that the church is open in what you can believe and liberal on sexual issues (birth control, abortion), unlike fundamentalists, Mormons, Jehovah's Witnesses, and Roman Catholics. Methodist identity is defined partly in relation to who they are *not* in Oxnard's pluralist religious environment.

Just about everything in this church is done in a small way. On Sunday mornings only six or seven children are in church school. There is no adult class. But a small size has its positive features. Often on Monday night at Bible study three-fourths of the congregation are present. This allows the pastor to connect the Bible study with his preaching. And during the morning worship service they spend about fifteen minutes sharing news, discussing what will be happening in the week ahead, and asking for prayers for themselves and for others. As a result, there is a strong sense of supportiveness and family atmosphere. "We are known more for the quality of our church than for its quantity," says an older man quite pleased about the direction the church seems to be going these days.

Because of its size and networking, the congregation has been largely turned in upon itself. Mission, or a sense of outreach, has been, and still is, largely undeveloped. But this may be changing. The pastor has hopes that the Vision Workshop and ongoing Bible study will open up new horizons of ministry to the local community and the larger world. Already there is a successful preschool for children of migrant workers, and the pastor is closely identified with Revival of Hope, a ministry to those affected by alcohol, tobacco, and violence. One senses in the congregation an openness to new visions and ventures—the possibility that this "small church with a big heart" might do more mighty things in the days that lie ahead.

St. Mark's UMC, Santa Barbara

On a Sunday morning at St. Mark's United Methodist Church, activities begin with a praise service about nine o'clock. It is a time of singing and sharing led by lay members of the church and complete with guitar, flute, and drums. Using lyrics projected onto a screen in the front of the sanctuary, members sing as the congregation slowly gathers. Next come praise reports or events in people's lives to be celebrated, then prayer requests. One person after another speaks of someone who is currently ill, facing a personal hardship, or for some reason is in need of prayer; prayers are offered, and the congregation responds with a warm "amen." Then, following a final lively and rejoicing praise lyric, the pastor and choir process into the sanctuary—a signal that the morning service as printed in the church bulletin is ready to begin.

The St. Mark's congregation was organized over 30 years ago, when a group of people decided that the larger UM church downtown was "too large, and too socially conscious," as one longstanding member put it. Its membership is white and middle-class, consisting of building contractors, small business owners, sales people, most of them over the age of 50. There are 290 members currently, of which about 130–150 are active. The church is located in a suburban community within Santa Barbara. One senses among old-timers, however, that the congregation hasn't grown as they had hoped, plus some members have left; once there were about 500 members, with many young people and children, and now there aren't as many.

But there is a new minister who brings lots of energy and new possibilities, and hopes are riding high again. The new pastor, a member of the Order of St. Luke, has moved the congregation toward a more liturgical service in the Wesleyan tradition in the short time that he has been there. He hopes to institute the "Word and Table" liturgy, which is a far cry from what the congregation has had in the past ("more a Sunday school assembly than a worship service," the pastor says). While he likes the informal praise music that was already in place before he came, he is now, slowly, trying to combine it with the liturgical service. He has also introduced a healing service after regular worship, which is creating curiosity and interest at present. New people are showing up at church, mainly from evangelical Protestant or Catholic backgrounds. "The Catholics like the liturgical style, and Baptists are okay with the personalized, informal moments before the service begins," says the pastor. The pastor is also a certified aerobics instructor and has organized a weekly aerobics class, which is proving to be a good means of recruiting new members and, he hopes, for cultivating a deeper spirituality.

The church facilities include a sanctuary, a fellowship hall and offices, and a church school building, each physically separate from one another. The sanctuary, contemporary in design, has red-cushioned pews and seats about 300. Above the chancel area is a large cross on the wall. The choir sits to the right of the chancel area. There is also an organ to the right. On the left side is a movable screen that is used for projecting praise lyrics, then pushed aside during worship services. Racks in the back of the pews carry both United Methodist hymnals and a contemporary Christian songbook. In the entryway to the sanctuary one finds literature on opportunities for ministry, such as the Walk to Emmaus, the Transition House (for the homeless), the Rescue Mission (for the hungry and needy), and visits to the prison.

Open communion and lack of strict belief necessary for church membership are very important to the congregation's sense of United Methodist identity. For a moderate-sized congregation, it is also a very busy one. The weekly events as listed in the church bulletin portray a mix of activities aside from the Sunday morning worship and church school: morning prayer group, power and praise group, Bible study, step aerobics, Early Birds, Covenant Discipleship, miniatures unlimited, choir practice, and youth group. In addition, the congregation "loans" its facilities to the Korean Methodists and to the Santa Barbara Community Church, and both hold services on Sunday.

Personal ministry is very important at St. Mark's. "We're more evangelical than Methodism as a whole," comments on older man and longstanding member of the congregation; "we stress a personal relationship with Christ." Emphasis is upon reaching out to others, helping people in times of need. To be Christlike, "one has to rise out of love and prayer, and a sense that Christ is in your life," adds another member. Older people especially talk about the prayer group and the many years that they have had a prayer chain in the congregation. During times of illness, accidents, war, deaths, hardships of whatever kind, people feel pulled together as a family and the support that only God can provide. "Because we are a praying church," says a 60-year-old woman, "we are also a spirit-filled church." A few members are openly charismatic; most simply call themselves evangelical. Lay leadership is emphasized, as is the importance of cultivating a strong spiritual life through prayer and Bible study.

Holding to a strong personal view of Christian faith and life, and generally conservative in outlook, many members within the congregation find themselves at odds with the social stands taken by the UM

Church. An anti-Methodist-hierarchy sentiment widely prevails. "What happened to the faith of our fathers?" a 65-year-old woman asks, admitting her disenchantment with the views of the church regarding social ministry. Older members, more than the younger ones, feel that the bishops take, as one middle-aged man put it, "a left-wing position on everything and don't reflect how people in the pew think." Aggressive leadership on the part of women within the conference, abortion, and most controversial of all, homosexuality, have many of them fired up. Consequently, some of the committees that the conference asks St. Mark's to organize for programming never get organized. An example is the committee on race and gender: "Helping people in need is one thing, and that's important to us," says one of the lay leaders, "but trying to change the country the way some of these people want to today is not for us." Another person, more knowledgeable of the church's theological heritage, noted that the Methodists were always evangelical and concerned about social conscience, but then added, "trouble is, Methodists don't evangelize any more." At St. Mark's, people are pleased that they are holding true to the teachings, even if many other Methodists aren't.

Younger members of the church don't have a very clear understanding of what it means to be a United Methodist. Some share the views of an older generation about the centrality of evangelism and personal faith; a few quietly acknowledge that their views on women, gays, and lesbians are different but they try not to make an issue of it. Asked about distinct Methodist beliefs or positions of the church on social issues, they have little to say. A young man says that the major belief of the Methodists is "to be as close a disciple of Jesus as you can." A young woman says simply that "it's a church [in which,] no matter who you are, you're accepted." Openness to different points of view, "peppier" hymn singing than in most churches, and "letting anyone take communion" are the more social behaviors that shape a United Methodist identity for younger members. At the same time, these younger members worry that others their age are not sticking with the church and that "the faith of the fathers" may not give the church sufficient direction for the years ahead.

First UMC, Ventura

"Diversity—that's what we got going for us here," comments the pastor when asked what makes First UMC Ventura different. To newcomers, diversity is apparent in the choice of worship services: there's a traditional service, which some members say is "the most

Methodist"; a Hispanic service, which is bicultural and not just bilingual; and a new contemporary praise service just started two years ago. More than just trying to provide a choice, the pastor takes some pride in how the church works at creating services that "retain tradition and depth of good theology," something often lacking in the "trendy" evangelical churches. This consciousness about tradition and theology no doubt reflects the fact that both the pastor and the Director of Youth were greatly influenced in Wesleyan thinking by their earlier connections with the Free Methodist tradition. In addition, there is a large, diversified menu of activities available: a pre-school and day care program, a church school with teacher training opportunities for both children and adults, an active UM Women's group and Methodist Men, chancel choir, Bible study class, prayer group, and Questers, which as the title implies, is open to those seeking to explore religious and spiritual life.

Located in an older part of downtown Ventura, the congregation was organized in 1874. The present sanctuary was erected in 1928 and is something of an architectural landmark in the city with its beautiful stained glass wheel/rose window in the arch above the narthex entrance. Recently, a modern organ was added to the original organ to enhance its capabilities. This addition has given the church the reputation of having the best music in town. Membership in the congregation is approximately 600 today and represents a diverse mix of people coming from professional and non-professional backgrounds. About 250 people attend the traditional service on a Sunday morning, about 40 are present at the Hispanic service, and a small number— perhaps 25–35—attend the contemporary praise service. Attention at present is focused upon how to improve the praise service and to attract younger members. Already the sound system in the sanctuary has been revamped and a screen installed for projecting lyrics (in order to eliminate the need for holding a songbook), but there is still a need, as the youth minister says, "to file down the rough edges" and cultivate a better understanding of worship.

Facilities at First UMC Ventura are conducive to a "California-style Methodism," as one woman puts it. The sanctuary seats 250–300 comfortably; while seldom packed, the church is usually full of congregants from front to back. Worship services have a somewhat grand and dignified quality about them. Beginning with the choral introit in the back, the choir processes to the front and take seats to the right of the altar, which is free-standing at the center of the chancel. On the altar are two candles. Above the altar hangs a simple cross, and above that, a large, round stained-glass window depicting Jesus blessing the children. The lectern is to the right and the pulpit, slightly raised, is to the left. The processional cross is placed to the far left, next to the Christian flag. Close by is a banner with the words "Follow Me," next to the American flag. A chair for the pastor is against the left wall. The congregation has a strong music program, and congregational singing is usually enthusiastic. United Methodist hymnals are found in the pews. Copies of *The Upper Room* and other Methodist materials are available on a table in the entryway to the sanctuary.

In addition to the sanctuary, the church has an educational building (with offices) and a small chapel. All three buildings connect to an open courtyard with two bulletin boards for announcements, tables for coffee, and plenty of room for conversation. Coffee hour is held every Sunday between the 9 a.m. and 11 a.m. services; it is usually well-attended and can be quite lively. "Here's where we get things done," says a 45-year-old male baby boomer; his comments reveal not just the importance of the courtyard but the fact that things do get done through social interaction and networks. This way of "doing" church comes easily to a younger adult generation and, as it turns out, is a somewhat sensitive issue within the congregation at present, since growing numbers of people in their 40s and 50s are becoming more involved and taking on tasks and responsibilities within the congregation at a time when some older members are stepping aside.

It is a friendly and easy-going place, reflecting in no small part the pastor's style. He insists that he doesn't try to put people on a "guilt trip" or to make people get involved without knowing why or for what purpose. He also acknowledges that, for him, the sermon is the most important thing: "The sermon is the center of the service because that's where we proclaim Jesus Christ." Morning worship follows the "Basic Pattern for Sunday Worship" with a few slight modifications, blending informality (including a time for the sharing of "joys and concerns") with a sense of dignity and style fitting to worship. Sermons are somewhat "folksy" (the pastor loves to talk about his surfing), are based upon a salvation theology, and advance as a general theme the "good news" of Christ, a message made applicable to all kinds of human situations. There is a passionate quality about the preaching, yet an open and inquiring stance as well—"pretty much mainstream, not evangelical," as one person described the content of the preaching. A similar theme is evident in the church's newsletter (also called "Good News"), a biweekly publication that carries an inspirational message from the pastor and stories with messages about helping people and about how God reaches out to people in the most ordinary of life circumstances.

First UMC's identity is that of an open Christian community that is growing in faith and love. Its Methodist heritage is seen as encouraging freedom, diversity, openness, inclusiveness, and social involvement within the community. "We're not a legalistic church," as one member says. "There's nothing I have to believe," says a 50-year-old woman. At the same time, there's an openness within the congregations about social issues. The pastor has been quite vocal, for example, in opposing the war in the Persian Gulf, in dealing with issues of human sexuality, and in encouraging church members to divest themselves of any stocks or bonds in companies with poor ecological policies. Though there are sometimes disagreements, the congregation has been reasonably able to resolve them. Both in informal settings such as the coffee hour and in church committees, there's plenty conversation—"a dialogue process" which the church staff has tried to encourage. As long as some people can remember, members of the church have been able to disagree over issues but also to extend hands to one another and "still be Methodists." Several people singled out the "connectional system" of Methodism as a catholic spirit that carries over in many different ways.

Important as these features of Methodism are, still many First Church members are concerned that people don't really know much about the heritage. There are questions particularly about Methodist beliefs. Thus, during the time of our study in Ventura, the church initiated a thirteen-week-long session on "What We Believe" looking at the Articles of Religion as explained in Norman P. Madsen's *This We Believe*. Conversations were lively among the fifteen people who attended. There were differences of opinion along predictable age lines: younger persons adhered to a more openly liberal, non-literal approach to the teachings, and emphasized the importance of being affirmed as individuals with questions and wanting to explore; older members were more inclined to take the Bible and Methodist teachings as having final authority, with less room for interpretation. On social issues such as abortion, women's ordination, and gay rights, differing views were expressed in a courteous manner. People in this congregation seem to be able to share their views in a serious way and regard civility and respect for one another as more important than forcing each other to believe in a certain way or to hold to a single point of view on a social issue.

Where the dialogue on Methodism, its beliefs and teachings will lead in the years ahead is unclear. Members take pride in the fact that they are not "rigid" in their views; newcomers who have recently joined the congregation say that they have chosen it because of the "openness" and "tolerance;" the current pastor says it is far more important "to make them Christian than Methodist." It is these looser bonds inherent in a Methodist identity that hold the congregation together, and they are working pretty well at present. It has been said that there is strength in weak institutional ties, and First UMC, Ventura, may be a splendid example of this social principle.

Conclusion and Implications

What can we conclude from these cases about regional differences in United Methodist congregations, about Methodist identity and ethos as reflected in these congregation, and about implications for the United Methodist Church? Obviously, our sample of six congregations is considerably limited, and our focus is only on North Carolina and California, not on U.S. regions generally.

First, what about regional differences? We know from other survey and religious census data that significant regional differences exist between North Carolina and California Methodism;[13] thus, it is not surprising that some differences in ethos are evident in the congregational cases. California churches appear more "laid back" or "easy going," as the member of First Church Ventura put it, and this contrasts especially with the more reserved style of Raleigh's Edenton Street Church. Genesis, among the North Carolina congregations, is most like the California congregations, a result more of its generational profile than its region. Also, a more traditional, Baptist-like style of evangelical piety and ecclesiology seems characteristic of the older members of Glendale Heights in North Carolina. This style is typical of many North Carolina United Methodist congregations that we did not include in our study, especially churches located in small town and rural areas. While St. Mark's, Santa Barbara, is evangelical, it draws upon newer, pentecostal-influenced forms of piety to express its spirituality, but this also is the case for other United Methodist churches in both states. Both Glendale Heights and St. Mark's, however, combine their particular forms of piety with more formal United Methodist liturgical practices. All used some variation of the Word and Table liturgy recently introduced into the denomination.

Among other regional differences, ethnic diversity is more apparent in the three California churches, though not as much as might have been expected given the state's ethnic diversity. Two of the California congregations host ethnic congregations. So also, however, does North Carolina's Edenton Street.

One other regional difference that we can only speculate about derives from the comparative social strength of United Methodism in the two regions. We suspect that the relatively prominent place that traditional religious institutions generally and Methodism in particular occupy in North Carolina and the relatively lower salience of traditional religious institutions, including Methodism, in California make it easier to be an active Methodist in North Carolina than in California. There is greater social support for church involvement. Or, to use Peter Berger's term, the southern religious ethos provides a stronger "plausibility structure" that supports religious involvement by affirming its importance than is true in California. One has to work harder at being an active church member in the California setting.

In final analysis, however, what is really striking is how similar the congregations are in many aspects of their cultures and styles. In one sense, this is not surprising. After all, these are congregations, and congregations, as a distinctive institutional field, have similar characteristics that make them more isomorphic, more like each other than, for example, schools, businesses, or government agencies.[14] The congregations all have buildings that are identifiable as churches, engage in quite similar forms of corporate worship, and have Sunday schools and other similar programs. They also share various Christian symbols and practices, even if they engage in the practices somewhat differently. Furthermore, they all, by definition, share a United Methodist identity. While these similarities seem so commonplace as to be taken for granted, we should not ignore them in our quest for differences. It would have been unusual not to find the similarities. Nonetheless, we had expected that there would be more regional differences than we found, and we were genuinely surprised by their relative absence. In part their absence may be the result of the particular churches we studied. The Research Triangle area of North Carolina, site of the three churches, is not really typical of all of North Carolina. The lack of clear regional differences may also suggest that such things as population mobility, new communications technology, and the continuing impact of technology are making these regional distinctions less important and visible—what we earlier called the "McDonaldization" of American life. While, to be sure, there are differences in the congregations we studied, they are not primarily explained by region. Let us mention two other non-regional factors.

One is congregational size. The small and mid-sized congregations—Oxnard, St. Mark's, Glendale Heights and Genesis—

seem to have a more *gemeinschaftlich* or 'communal' flavor than is true of the two large congregations. Relationships, intimacy, caring, and mutual support are highly valued in these churches. In contrast, First Ventura and especially Edenton Street are what some have called "corporation" churches.[15] Such congregations have multiple staffs. They place more emphasis on doing things well, on quality preaching and music, and on offering a variety of programs as entry points for new members. Relational and intimacy dimensions are not lacking, but they happen in smaller groups that people can choose to join or not. Some individuals prefer the anonymity of the large public gatherings. Contrast the discomfort Edenton Street's members express at having specific names mentioned in congregational concerns and prayers with the high value that Genesis members place on the "C & C" (Celebrations and Concerns) time during their worship or that St. Mark's members place on their praise reports and prayer requests during the informal time before the more liturgical service begins. Size plays at least as important a role in differences in congregational life as region.

The second and most striking non-regional factor that we observed in these congregations is the impact of generation or generational cohort. One example is in knowledge about basic Christian beliefs and practices, and especially about United Methodist beliefs, practices, and polity. There are exceptions: at Edenton Street, knowledge of Methodism was considerable among all whom we interviewed, though this could be partly the effect of the small number of interviews that we were able to conduct. Generally, however, most of the younger generations know less than their elders about these Methodist beliefs and practices. This is particularly true of those in their 30s or younger, but it is also true for many in their 40s. The younger generations reveal, for the most part, limited religious socialization. In this connection, the blame seems to lie with some of the present or past pastors who have done little to provide adequate confirmation training or training for new members.

Generational cohorts also differ somewhat in the expectations that they bring to the church. Perhaps it is most obvious at Glendale Heights in the conflict between the "pioneers" and "squatters" which partly has to do with older members' resistance to sharing leadership. But different expectations and understandings of the church also seem to be present. Younger members seem more calculating in their choice of a church and in what they expect from it. As at Genesis, the congregation most representative of the baby boom generation, younger members are more likely to ask, "what am I, and especially my children, going to get out of this?" And secondarily, "are we doing anything worthwhile to serve the local community; is involvement in this congregation worth my time?"

Finally, generational differences are evident in the decreasing importance that younger generations attach to United Methodist identity. Obviously, this bears some relationship to poor religious socialization, but it seems to reflect a more general decline in the importance of denominations that a number of observers have noted in recent years. Most members of these congregations, but especially younger members, think first about their congregation, its members, and its programs. They accept the denominational label and what it implies about particular practices because, so to speak, the label "goes with the territory." They not only know little but also care little about what the denomination is doing at regional and general church levels. What is most important is how involvement in this particular congregation is meeting their own expectations and needs and how it is serving and meeting needs in the local community.

Let us temper this statement about Methodist identity somewhat. Members of all ages in each of the congregations value some aspects of their congregation's United Methodist identity. Almost without exception, and regardless of region, older and younger members value the openness, tolerance, and respect for diversity that they believe characterize United Methodist beliefs and practices. They don't like fundamentalists. They dislike intolerance. They like it that we seem, rightly or wrong, to encourage a "think and let think" stance. They like our practices of open communion and infant baptism, which they also identify with a general Methodist openness and tolerance. Many, though not all, also like and value Methodism's positions on social issues insofar as they understand them. And many, especially in the two larger congregations, value the itinerancy. Those who do not especially value it at least "stomach" it as generally helpful; while it sometimes means losing a well-loved pastor, the itinerancy also offers diversity of leadership, including not getting "stuck" forever with a poor pastor.

We conclude with reflections about some of the implications that these case studies suggest.

Alasdair MacIntyre has argued that it is through participating in the practices of living traditions that personal and collective identities are shaped.[16] A person's or group's identity and actions are intelligible, MacIntyre argues, in terms of the stories and traditions of which they are a part. Drawing on MacIntyre's perspective, Dorothy Bass considers how congregations are tradition bearers. She writes:

Congregations, as tradition bearers, are arenas within which individual and collective identity can be discovered, in all the local particularity that enables people to experience a deep sense of belonging. At the same time, they are also places where the conflict that characterizes living traditions takes place, and where the larger tradition's challenges to restricted local forms of individual and group identity are encountered. . . . This bearing of traditions has two dimensions, each integrally related to the other. Congregations impart to individuals and families a place in a tradition, and conversely, these same individuals and families, through congregations, give back to a tradition its own being and vitality, constituting and reconstituting it through time.[17]

We agree—both that congregations bear the larger traditions through which individual and collective religious identities are shaped, and that individuals and congregations have an important role to play in keeping the larger traditions vital and living. (Recall our earlier reference to congregations as part of the "ecosystem" of faith.) At the same time, we also recognize that this point of view poses a considerable challenge to United Methodist clergy and lay leaders. If the congregations we have studied are any indication, Methodist congregations are not doing a very effective job of bearing Wesleyan traditions so that they shape the religious identities of members. Partly the blame lies with the leaders who, as we have suggested, are not taking their teaching role seriously enough. There was a clear relationship in the interviews between lack of knowledge of the Methodist heritage or Methodist polity and practices and the lack of confirmation and new member training. But teaching alone is not sufficient. It is only one of the practices through which the tradition is embodied and passed on. Other practices—worship and the sacraments, spiritual disciplines, stewardship, acts of caring, and acts of service or of prophetic criticism—are also powerful teachers of the tradition. These practices, however, must be practiced—often and with seriousness—if they are to be effective. T.S. Eliot once said of tradition, "It cannot be inherited. . . . [I]f you want it you must obtain it by great labour."[18] Or as sociologist Anthony Giddens has written: "The 'integrity' of a tradition derives not from the simple fact of persistence over time but from the continuous work of interpretation that is carried out to identify the strands that bind past to present."[19] Such work includes serious attention to the tradition's practices.

This is easier said than done. The kind of world in which we live today makes bearing traditions much more difficult and problematic than was true in the not-too-distant past. Until relatively recently congregations existed primarily as communal institutions, deeply embedded in their local settings, touching the lives of their members at many points and shaping their religious identities. In increasingly segmented and global societies characteristic of late- or post-modernity, the situation has changed considerably. Social life and relationships have, as Giddens argues, become disembedded, lifted out of the time- and place-bound local contexts in which traditional institutions have had their powerful identity-shaping effect.[20] Rather than being shaped by the traditions or stories of a particular religious community in whose practices one participates—a Methodist congregation for example—one increasingly constructs her or his identity out of the bits and pieces of the practices of various communities, religious and otherwise. In a discussion of the religious identity of United Methodists, Penny Long Marler and C. Kirk Hadaway describe this as "self authoring."[21] Such self authoring is particularly true for the post-war generation who, for most of their lives, have known only the disembedded social life and relationships characteristic of late modern society. Many still look to local congregations for religious nurture and support, but they are much more likely to do so in a kind of "*à la carte*" way. Their religious identities are only loosely coupled to that of the congregation. In sum, all of this means that congregations face an unusual challenge if they are to be bearers of traditions that shape individual and collective identity.

Let us note one other related implication of our congregational comparisons. We noted above several particular characteristics of the United Methodist heritage that most people, young and old, affirmed as positive: its tolerance of diversity, its non-dogmatic stance, its openness to diverse beliefs and perspectives, its "think and let think" stance. Some might argue (and we would agree) that this is a rather truncated version of the classical Methodist heritage. Even if these affirmations do capture some of the openness characteristic of Wesley and Methodism, they create an interesting problem. How can such a protean or boundaryless tradition give any identifiable shape to individual or collective identity? Or to change the metaphor, "Can a sieve hold water?"

Two recent research projects highlight this issue and show that it is not restricted to United Methodists. In their study of Presbyterian baby boomers, Dean Hoge, Benton Johnson, and Donald Luidens identified a religious style that they called "lay liberalism." Here is how they describe it:

> . . . the defining quality of lay liberalism is its wide-open tolerance of diversity in matters of belief and practice. Christian teachings are seen as

one resource among others. Lay liberals believe that individuals today need to chart their own way without external pressure, that children need to be exposed to the main religions today so they can make their own decisions at the appropriate time later. Lay liberals have come to terms with the multiple, often conflicting cultural messages they receive in this world.[22]

More recently, Nancy Ammerman, analyzing a large sample of responses from church members from a number of denominations, found a similar style among about 50 percent of those in her survey.[23] She calls them "Golden Rule Christians." Their expectations for the church and the style of religion they appreciate are akin to the Golden Rule; that is, they care for interpersonal relationships and for persons in need, and they seek to express this care in response to a relationship with God. They want to get in touch with something beyond themselves. The congregations they join make low demands on them and, thus, Golden Rule Christians exhibit lower commitment than, for example, members of high-demand evangelical congregations.

Both lay liberalism and Golden Rule Christianity are examples of self authored religious identities that result from the disembedding of traditional social relationships that we described above. From the perspective of the denominations, it seems safe to say that both represent "weak" forms of religious identity, especially denominational identity. Yet, as Ammerman points out, many of the "low demand" congregations to which Golden Rule Christians belong are thriving. These congregations have worked out practices that nurture the spiritual life and lead to the good life as defined by Golden Rule Christians—care for interpersonal relationships and care for people in need.

We are in no way suggesting that United Methodists should settle for Golden Rule Christianity as the defining characteristic of the Methodist tradition in the late twentieth century. The Wesleyan heritage has much more to commend it than this. Surely Methodist openness and appreciation of diversity are, rightly interpreted, positive and attractive features of the Wesleyan tradition from which congregations can nurture a deeper Christian (and Wesleyan) identity. But to do so will require renewed and imaginative attention to the practices through which the tradition is imparted and through which, in turn, the tradition is revitalized and renewed.

Charles E. Zech

Among all of the ways that one might measure church members' commitment to mission, activity in service, and loyalty to denomination, one of the most widely used standards is money.

American culture often associates such characteristics as personal popularity and political influence with financial status. So it is inevitable that the health of a church include an evaluation of its wealth. Guth and Green, in their statistical portrait of American United Methodists, indicate that the denomination is generally a collection of middle-class to lower-middle-class members. However, economic rank is only one element of the description. Another is the pattern of generosity, philanthropy, and stewardship demonstrated by the membership. How much do United Methodists give to their church? What percentage of personal or household income is contributed to support the ministries of the local and larger church? Why do United Methodists give? To what degree is giving affected by connectional initiatives, congregational needs, and commitment to the faith? What factors might motivate members to contribute less—or more?

Economist Charles Zech has conducted some original research in an effort to answer these questions. Using a set of ten hypotheses and measuring the views of United Methodist laity drawn from a unique national sample, Zech has surfaced some important connectional and congregational insights. They include the earthy (Should a local church conduct an every member canvass?) and the ethereal (Do Methodists give to the church or to God?). And although his analysis focuses upon patterns of regular church giving rather than responses to such special situations as capital campaigns, Zech looks at the issue of church endowments (Does having a substantial endowment inhibit giving by members to their church?).

It will be tempting to read Zech's data and his analysis either for their immediate applicability in a local church setting or their descriptive capability with reference to the denomination as a whole. Might it be wiser to search beyond such temptations and see the delicate financial balance of the whole connection?

Patterns of Giving Among United Methodists: Member Contributions to the Local Church

Charles E. Zech[1]

Stewardship in general, and religious giving in particular, is a hot topic among U.S. churches. Almost no church is totally satisfied with the level of giving that it receives from its members. High-giving, fundamentalist churches recognize that their contributions would be even greater if more of their members followed the biblical imperatives urging them to tithe. Medium-giving mainline denominations look with envy at the success of the fundamentalist churches in generating their level of contributions, and Catholics are keenly aware of the opportunities that are lost to them because their members don't even contribute at the level of the mainline Protestants. As other research indicates, local church financial pressures are the primary cause of denominational mission funding problems.[2] The United Methodist Church is no different. It, too, would like to increase the level of its members' contributions. This chapter examines religious giving among United Methodists and considers ways to increase it.

Figure 1[3] places the relative giving of various denominations in perspective. It shows the portion of income going to religious giving in the late 1980s. Unfortunately, United Methodists rank in the bottom third of that list. While ecclesiological differences probably prevent the United Methodist Church from ever generating contributions at the level of Mormons or the Assemblies of God, it is not unreasonable to expect that United Methodist contributions could be increased to the level of liberal Baptists or Presbyterians. One can only imagine the good the Church could accomplish if contributions increased by just one percent of members' incomes.

There are a number of possible explanations as to why United Methodist giving is low. This chapter considers ten hypotheses concerning religious giving. Each is examined individually to determine its impact on giving in the United Methodist Church. Based on the empirical findings, a series of proposals to increase member contributions is presented.

Methodology

The method used to test the hypotheses was to survey a group of United Methodist Church pastors and Administrative Board members with a questionnaire intended to elicit information on all ten hypotheses. Responses from the survey were grouped by hypothesis. Then each variable was tested for its impact on member contributions, both individually and after controlling for the effect of other factors.

The data were collected from a random sample of 1000 UMC local churches. Most UMC congregations are small, but most church members belong to larger congregations. To account for this the larger congregations (200 or more members) were over-sampled, with two-thirds of the congregations selected from this group. Later, the sample was weighted to reflect the proper size distribution of UMC local churches.

The pastor of each local church in the sample received two types of surveys. One, that she/he was asked to complete, contained questions on local church background (size, ethnic makeup, age and income distribution of members, etc.) and questions of opinion that related directly to the hypotheses. Each pastor also received eight surveys intended for members of the Administrative Board that also contained questions relative to the hypotheses. No claim is made that the Administrative Board members in the sample were randomly selected; rather, pastors were merely requested to distribute the survey instrument to eight members of the Board. Presumably many pastors distributed them to those Board members whom they felt to be most supportive of their own positions. However, it is interesting to note that, of the 20 questions on the two surveys that were identical, correlation analysis showed that for 14 questions there was no significant relationship between a pastor's responses and those of the Administrative Board members of her/his local church; for three questions there was a significantly positive relationship; and for three questions there was a significantly negative relationship. In any event, all of the completed surveys were returned directly to the Principal Investigator so the pastor didn't see individual responses. While this survey method is not perfect, it is cost effective and has been used elsewhere.[4] The survey of the pastors was random. The best that can be stated about the Board surveys is that they are probably representative.

Survey packets sent to eight local churches were undeliverable. A total of 316 pastor surveys (31.9%) and 2243 Board member surveys (28.3%) were returned. To ensure adequate representation, analysis was restricted to only those local churches where both the pastor survey and at least 5 Administrative Board surveys had been returned (n=198).

A word on the statistical interpretation of the data is in order. Some of the giving differences found in the hypothesis testing are not statistically significant. That means that, although differences may occur, there is so much variation in people's giving with respect to that hypothesis that no trend can be ascertained with a high level of confidence. Also, the significance of any relationship must be evaluated in two separate contexts: when the relationship is viewed in isolation, and when it is evaluated in conjunction with all the other relationships simultaneously. In other words, some factors may affect contributions "of and by themselves," while others may only have an impact when the effect of other factors is controlled.

The statistical technique of multiple regression analysis was used to analyze all the determinants at once. The dependent variable was contributions per member for regular offerings (i.e., excluding capital campaigns).[5] Some control variables (a measure of local church racial distribution, educational levels, and median income) were included. A stepwise multiple regression technique was employed which only included those variables from the ten hypotheses that significantly affected per member contributions when the other factors were controlled. The results of incorporating all the control variables and the hypothesized determinants of giving in the analysis are shown in Table 1.

Following is a discussion of each of the ten hypotheses.

Hypothesis 1: Smaller Local Churches Have Greater Per-Member Giving.

This hypothesis is based on the general impression that smaller churches are more personal. People get to know each other and the pastor well. They may feel that they have more of an impact on church matters and take more of an ownership perspective. There is also less of a tendency to "free ride," that is, to assume that other members' contributions will compensate for any shortfall in one's own level of giving.

To consider the effect of local church size on giving, the sample was divided in half: smaller churches of 150 or fewer members, and larger churches with more than 150 members. Figure 2 shows that there is very little difference in the per member giving between the two groups. However, Table 1 shows a significantly negative relationship between local church size and per member contributions when other variables are also considered.

This is not meant to imply that larger churches should be "downsized" or that churches should be discouraged from growing (an alternative that would surely be contrary to the Great Commission).[6]

Rather, churches should be made to feel like they are small, personal communities, where members perceive a sense of ownership.

Hypothesis 2: *Members of Local Churches that Provide a Wide Array of Programs Contribute More.*

The real issue here is the extent to which members' contributions reflect their satisfaction with local church programs. Are members in a marketplace for religious goods willing to pay more for those they believe to be of higher quality? Or, from another perspective, are they searching for a niche that churches with more programs are able to offer?

There were two measures of local church programs in the study. One was a proxy for the number and quality of programs by asking how many full-time equivalent lay staff serve in the ministries of Christian education, music, worship, or youth ministries. The other was the level of enthusiasm board members felt for their local church's programs.

The impact of lay staff members in ministry on contributions is shown in Figure 3. Many local churches have no paid staff. Those who do have paid professional staff receive significantly higher per member contributions than those who do not.

The effect of enthusiasm for programs on giving is shown in Figure 4. Church members tend to exhibit a high level of satisfaction with their local Church's programs. After all, they voluntarily chose to join the church, and can leave at any time. It would be expected that administrative board members would exhibit even greater satisfaction than other members. In fact, on the average, 87.5% of the Board members were satisfied with their church's programs. The sample was divided into two groups: those whose board members' satisfaction was greater than average, and those whose satisfaction was less than or equal to the average. Greater enthusiasm for programs is associated with significantly larger per member contributions.

These results should be interpreted with caution, though, because of possible circularity of reasoning. Is it true that better church programs elicit higher contributions, or are the programs' quality the result of larger member contributions? These results don't give a firm answer to that chicken or egg problem. In fact, neither measure is significantly related to giving when viewed in combination with other factors (Table 1). The most that can be said is that these results are consistent with the hypothesis that better programs are associated with larger contributions.

Hypothesis 3: *Canvassing Members Leads to Greater Per-Member Contributions.*

The conventional wisdom is that contacting members to remind them of their responsibility as church members to support the Church financially will elicit larger contributions among those who have been giving, and induce those who haven't been contributing to start. Figures 5 through 8 contradict the conventional wisdom. Whether every member is contacted in person or by telephone, or only some members are contacted, a negative relationship exists between canvassing members and per member giving. This somewhat surprising result is supported by the experience of many pastors. They have expressed concern that people are contacted too often for money, which turns off both the members doing the contacting and those being contacted. They also worry that in too many local churches, members are *only* contacted for money. There needs to be a regular, ongoing personal communication between the pastor and church staff and the membership on matters other than money (e.g., spiritual concerns). When the only personal contact members receive from the local church is to beg for money or, worse, lay a guilt trip on them, the canvassing is bound to backfire.

Because of the interrelatedness of the various canvassing methods, only one entered the multiple regression analysis in Table 1. Canvassing some members by telephone is negatively related to member contributions.

It should be recognized that, as in the previous hypothesis, there is a causality issue here. Is it the case that local churches that canvass receive lower contributions, or do churches that are already receiving low contributions feel more compelled to canvass? The best that can be concluded here is that canvassing is not consistent with an increase in contributions.

Hypothesis 4: *Local Churches that Emphasize Giving as an Essential Aspect of Christian Living Receive Larger Contributions.*

The issue here goes to the ultimate motive that people have for contributing to their church. Is their motive, as many fundamentalist churches preach, one of returning to God what is God's, or are they prompted by some other objective, such as altruism, support of church programs, or personal satisfaction. The pastors in the sample were asked what the message was that they tried to convey. Figure 9 compares giving in churches that preach the message of giving to God versus other messages. Churches that emphasize giving to God receive lower per member contributions than do those churches conveying a different message. This is true when this variable is viewed in isolation. However, after controlling for other factors, Table 1 shows that the content of the message that is communicated to the membership does not significantly affect member giving.

Hypothesis 5: *Members Who Believe the Local Church Has Serious Financial Needs Will Contribute More.*

This hypothesis centers on the extent to which the membership is influenced by the local church's financial situation. Administrative Board members were asked about the seriousness of their local church's financial needs. An average of 40% responded that their local church had serious or very serious financial problems. The sample was divided into two parts—those where more than 40% of the Board members thought their needs were serious or very serious, and those with 40% or less. Figure 10 shows the difference in giving between the two groups. There is significantly greater giving in those churches where the membership is convinced the local church has financial difficulties. This is true when this factor is considered by itself, and also after controlling for other determinants of giving (Table 1).

Hypothesis 6: *Members Who Believe the Denomination Has Serious Financial Needs Will Contribute More.*

This is similar to the previous hypothesis except that it refers to the denomination. Administrative Board members were asked about their perception of the denomination's financial position. An average of 50% thought the denomination has serious or very serious financial needs. The sample of local churches was divided into two groups: those where more than 50% of the Board felt the United Methodist Church has financial problems, and those where 50% or fewer Board members expressed this concern. The difference in the per member giving to the local church between the two groups is shown in Figure 11. Of and by itself, the perception that the United Methodist Church has financial pressures elicits larger per member contributions. However, when this variable is tested along with the other variables, it has no significant impact on giving (Table 1).

Hypothesis 7: *Members With More Traditional Religious Beliefs Contribute More.*

Administrative Board members were asked about factors that might give a clue as to the nature of their religious beliefs. One question concerned the amount of time they spent reading the Bible, and the other asked them about their attitude toward ecumenical interactions. Reading the Bible tends to be associated with religious orthodoxy. Unlike many other Christian religions, ecumenism is also a traditional belief for United Methodists (one pastor observed that, "Methodists are ecumenical to their toes"). An average of 80% of the Administrative Board members indicated that they spent free time reading the Bible[7]. Similar to the method used in the previous hypotheses, the local churches were split into two groups along those lines. The impact of this orthodox belief on giving is shown in Figure 12.

When Board members were asked about ecumenism, an average of 57.1% supported more efforts in this area. The local churches were split along this line, and the effect of the desire for more ecumenism on giving is shown in Figure 13.

Both Figures 12 and 13 reveal that orthodoxy of belief, taken by itself, leads to larger per member giving. When combined with other variables only the ecumenism measure enters in at a significant level (Table 1), probably because of the close relationship between the two measures of religious orthodoxy.

Hypothesis 8: *Local Churches that Employ Member Pledging Receive Large Contributions.*

The underlying issue here is commitment. Local churches that are successful in convincing their members to make a firm commitment to support the church are likely to receive larger contributions than do churches whose members decide each week or month how much they can afford to give at that time. Figure 14 illustrates the effect on giving when the issue is whether or not local churches use pledge cards. As Figure 14 and Table 1 reveal, pledging is a significant determinant of giving, both of and by itself and even after controlling for other factors.

Hypothesis 9: *Baby Boomers Contribute at Different Levels than do Non-Baby Boomers.*

There has been an emerging literature in recent years that demonstrates that, with respect to religion, baby boomers are qualitively different from members of other age cohorts.[8] They are more apt to view religion as simply another product, which they are free either to purchase or not, and the brand of which they can change if they feel the urge. In short, they tend to be less committed church members.

Nationally, an average of 26% of United Methodists are in the age bracket 35–50 (approximating the baby boomer generation in 1994). The Administrative Board sample contained an average of 28.6% members in that age bracket. As in many of the previous hypotheses, local churches were divided along the average for the purpose of the univariate analysis. Figure 15 demonstrates that local churches with a higher proportion of baby boomers among their Board members receive significantly lower contributions. However, once other factors are controlled, this significance disappears (Table 1).

Hypothesis 10: *Local Churches With Endowments Will Receive Lower Contributions.*

The theory behind this hypothesis is that endowments signal less of a need for regular contributions. In fact, some might feel that the entire religious life of the local church is imperiled by higher endowments since members might become less committed on all levels. The attitude of some members might be that, if a church task needs to be performed, let them hire someone (rather than rely on member volunteerism); they can afford it, they have an endowment.

The effect of having an endowment on per member contributions is displayed in Figure 16. Contrary to the hypothesis, endowments are associated with higher giving, although not on a statistically significant level. But when other factors are controlled, endowments are shown to significantly increase per member contributions (Table 1). It could be that local churches that have been successful in developing a sense of stewardship among the members will see it exhibited both in high current giving, and in bequeathments that build endowments. The two are complementary, rather than competitive, in the local church's financial life.

Discussion

This chapter has considered 10 hypotheses concerning the determinants of local church regular giving. Some of the variables considered proved to be significant determinants of giving of and by themselves, some were significant when combined with other factors, and in some cases, both patterns emerged.

So what are the findings? What kinds of things should local churches be doing to increase their members' contributions? This study found five primary factors:

1.   Pledging is important. Local churches must motivate their members to commit themselves to the church, both spiritually and financially, by making a pledge. Failing to pursue this commitment, and

relying on members' good will in deciding how much they can afford to contribute each month or week, is an invitation to financial stagnation or worse for the local church.

2. In general, canvassing doesn't work. One pastor has commented that he doesn't believe that canvassing shakes loose any money that wouldn't have been contributed anyway. Canvassing is especially ineffective when it is done too often, or when it is the *only* personal contact a member has with the local church.

3. Membership size is important. Whether the local church actually has a small, personal membership or people are merely made to feel that way, the attitude of ownership and personal involvement that a small church can instill will induce members to be more generous with their time, talents, and money.

4. Orthodoxy of belief is significant. People are looking for a concrete set of beliefs that they can refer to. A local church that is preaching an orthodox United Methodist message (the importance of Bible study and ecumenism) will be attractive and members will respond with more generous financial support.

5. Members need to be aware of the local church's financial position. People respond to a need when they are kept informed of that need. A regular dialogue among the pastor, Administrative Board, and membership is critical.

These factors were found to be significant determinants of local church contributions even when controlling for other elements. Other, secondary determinants significantly affected giving only when viewed in isolation. They included:

6. Church programs. While there is some circularity of reasoning here, the provision of high quality church programs is consistent with high contributions.

7. Motivation for giving. Of and by itself, an emphasis on giving as returning to God what is God's is associated with lower giving. United Methodists apparently do not respond well to this as the primary stewardship message.

8. Baby boomers. When viewed in isolation, baby boomers contribute at a significantly lower level than do other age cohorts (or, at least local churches with an above average proportion of baby boomers receive lower contributions). While this pattern disappears when other determinants are controlled (including income and education), it is a phenomenon that deserves attention. The United Methodist Church (along with other churches) must find a more effective way to minister to this group.

9.   Denominational financial needs. As with congregational financial needs, the perception that the denomination has serious financial needs is associated with larger contributions. However, the significance of this factor is greatly diminished when it is combined with other variables including awareness of local church financial needs.

One final element to be considered in the role of endowments. Rather than reducing member contributions, endowments are associated with higher contributions. This is probably an indication that successful stewardship efforts not only generate larger current contributions, but also result in bequests and other large gifts that serve as the basis for endowments.

Table 1
STEPWISE MULTIPLE REGRESSION
RELATIONSHIP BETWEEN INDEPENDENT VARIABLES
AND PER MEMBER CONTRIBUTIONS

Variable	Beta Coefficient
% College Graduates	.19*
% Caucasian	.04
Median Income	-.02
Size of Local Church Membership	-.11*
Church Canvasses Some Members by Phone	-.58*
% Believe Local Church Has Financial Needs	.19*
% Desire More Ecumenism	.64*
Local Church Uses Pledge Cards	.26*
Local Church Has Endowment	.66*

$R^2 = .21$
*p < .01

Variables Not Included Because of Lack of Significance
FTE Lay Professional Staff
% Enthusiasm for Local Church Programs
Pastor Message One of Giving to God
% Spend Free Time Reading Bible
% Baby Boomers
% Believe Denomination Has Serious Financial Needs

FIGURE 1
Giving as a Percentage of Income by Denomination, 1987–89

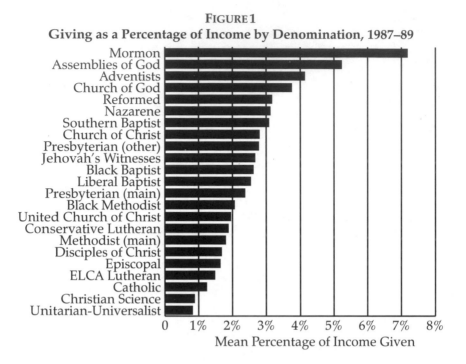

FIGURE 2
Contributions by Local Church Size

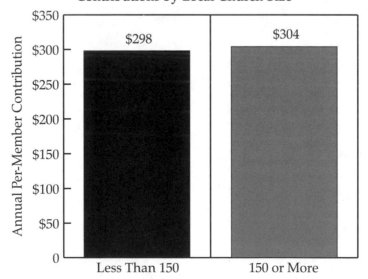

FIGURE 3
Contributions Based on Lay Staffing

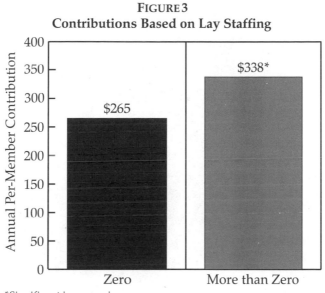

*Significant in regression

FIGURE 4
Contributions Based on Lay Enthusiasm for Local Church Programs

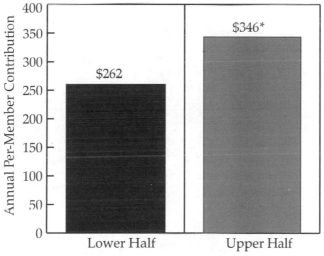

*Significant in regression

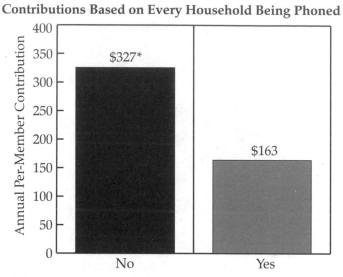

FIGURE 5
Contributions Based on Every Household Being Phoned

*Significant in regression

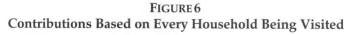

FIGURE 6
Contributions Based on Every Household Being Visited

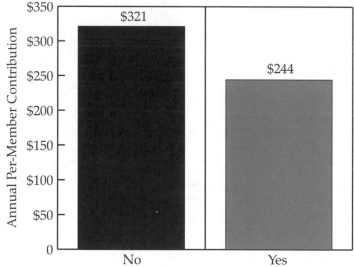

FIGURE 7
Contributions Based on Some Households Being Phoned

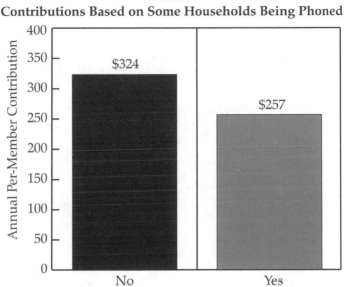

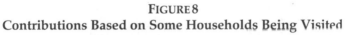

FIGURE 8
Contributions Based on Some Households Being Visited

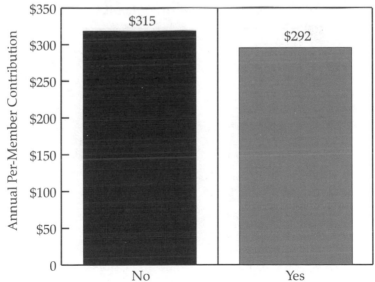

The People(s) Called Methodist

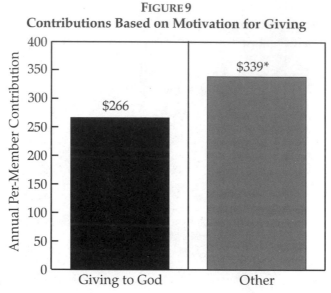

FIGURE 9
Contributions Based on Motivation for Giving

*Significant in regression

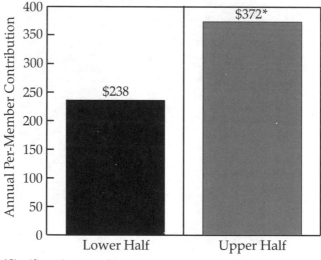

FIGURE 10
Contributions Based on Lay Response
to Serious Financial Needs of Local Church

*Significant in regression

FIGURE 11
Contributions Based on Lay Response
to Serious Financial Needs of Denomination

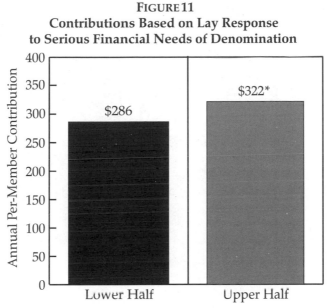

*Significant in regression

FIGURE 12
Contributions Based on Lay Response
to Free Time Spent Studying the Bible

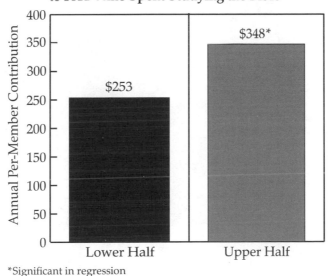

*Significant in regression

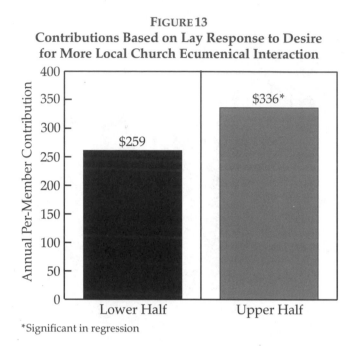

FIGURE 13
**Contributions Based on Lay Response to Desire
for More Local Church Ecumenical Interaction**

*Significant in regression

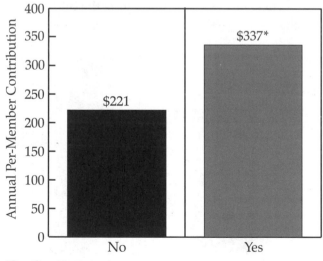

FIGURE 14
Contributions Based on Local Church Using Pledge Cards

*Significant in regression

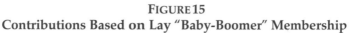

FIGURE 15
Contributions Based on Lay "Baby-Boomer" Membership

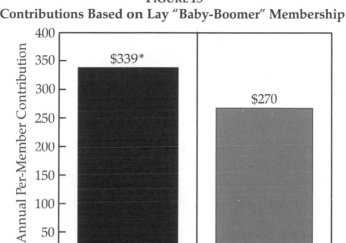

*Significant in regression

FIGURE 16
Contributions Based on Local Church Having Endowment

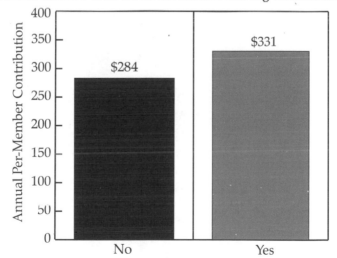

Daniel V. A. Olson and William McKinney

One of the clearly discernible dividing lines within the United Methodist Church lies between the members of the denomination and their denominational leaders. The statistical portrait drawn by Guth and Green showed differences between clergy and laity. Carroll and Roof found that congregational and cultural factors are far more formative in church life than denominational forces, and that church leaders can be faulted for failing to assimilate members into the Wesleyan theological heritage. Zech concluded that an awareness of financial problems at the denominational level produced no significant change in members' contributions. A perception that a huge trust gap exists between members and leaders, between local churches and general church agencies, seems beyond question.

Sociologist Daniel V. A. Olson draws upon a larger collaboration with William McKinney to focus his attention on United Methodist leaders. How do they make their judgments? In what authority do they trust? Upon whom and what do they rely for reaching determinations about moral value? How do they articulate the mission of the church?

The answers to such questions produce a revealing and vibrant image of United Methodist leaders. Any perceived gap between leaders and locals in the denomination cannot be oversimplified into ideological disparities. In fact, the leaders seem to display a diversity of opinion among themselves that is not so different from the diversity (noted by Green and Guth) which characterizes the church as a whole. This pattern of diversity and disagreement has consequences for the ways that leaders express their authority and exercise their leadership. Some, who seek prophetically to lead, are not granted by the church the authority they need to take the denomination in bold new directions. Others, who are granted the authority to lead, retain it so long as they limit themselves to managing a diverse and divisive community.

What are the implications of all this? Will the leaders bring the church to divide over one or more great issues and fall into schism? Or will the leaders feel bound to manage the church's conflicted parts and hold them so skillfully together that the denomination will grind into gridlock? Or is there another alternative?

United Methodist Leaders:
Diversity and Moral Authority

Daniel V. A. Olson and William McKinney

During a phone interview a United Methodist district superintendent from a southern state told us:

> The Methodist Church historically was an evangelical church, but over the
> years and recently, especially in the Northeast there has been a great push
> for social action. These Northeast leaders forget that persons are
> two-tiered, that they have a spiritual dimension. Actions the Church takes
> that forget this are not fruitful and indeed raise the ire of many of the
> grass-roots constituencies.

But such is not the view of all United Methodists. In another
interview, we asked a national-level board member, who incidentally
comes from a northeastern state, what she thinks the top priorities of
United Methodist Church should be. She listed human rights issues,
civil rights, alcohol, drugs, and AIDS. Although she is accepting of other
points of view, she is concerned about the influence that some of the
more evangelically inclined leaders of the denomination are having.
She told us:

> I recently attended a board meeting where the very conservative
> evangelicals, the Good News people, criticized everything that was being
> done. They are doing this all over the church and creating tension. While
> Methodists seek to be inclusive of different points of view, tolerance of
> others' viewpoints has also been important. The Good News people are
> attacking what the church is doing, also saying they will leave the church if
> it doesn't do what they want it to do. In order to keep them there has
> already been some accommodation.

Tensions such as these are common in many Protestant denominations. In the *Restructuring of American Religion*[1] Robert Wuthnow argues
that these tensions are the result of a new division in American religion,
a division that increasingly separates liberals and conservatives within
the same denomination and makes allies among conservatives and
among liberals across lines. Taking up these themes, James Davison
Hunter argues in his book *Culture Wars*[2] that a somewhat similar

liberal-conservative division divides not only American religion, but also American culture and politics.

The data for this chapter come from a larger research project, the aim of which is to examine the potential for cultural and religious tensions among leaders from six Protestant denominations. This chapter takes up three issues. First, we examine the extent to which denominational leaders are divided into two competing groups along a single liberal-conservative, evangelical versus social activist, divide. Second we explore the extent of the diversity within and between denominations. After American Baptists, Methodists are the most diverse denomination in our study. Third, we suggest that the amount of diversity in different denominations is partly the result of denominational differences in the location of religious and moral authority. Social groups, including denominations, differ in the extent to which they locate moral authority in individuals, their reason and experience, versus some collective source that is considered binding on all in the group. While this third section is somewhat speculative, our data suggest that issues related to the location of moral authority may have much to do with the types of problems, tensions, and conflicts faced by denominations like United Methodism.

Data Sources

The study is based on a questionnaire survey of 1,500 denominational leaders and 51 phone interviews with a select group of these same leaders. The leaders are drawn from six denominations, including the United Methodists (UMC), the United Church of Christ (UCC), the American Baptists (ABC), the Baptist General Conference (BGC), the Evangelical Free Church (EFC), and the Assemblies of God (AOG). The study also includes National Council of Churches leaders, and leaders of local and regional ecumenical agencies. Within each denomination our study includes three types of leaders: staff of national-level agencies, staff of state or regional level agencies, and board members of national-level policy-making boards.

Though the questionnaire was 15 pages long, more than half of the approximately 3,000 leaders surveyed completed and returned the questionnaire. At the end of the questionnaire we asked leaders if they would be willing to be interviewed by phone. Based on preliminary analyses of the questionnaire data we selected persons for interviews who represent distinctive leadership orientations, different denominations, and different types of leadership positions. The details of the sampling are described elsewhere.[3]

Although response rates were fairly similar across the six denominations, our study includes many more leaders from the three oldline denominations (the UCC, UMC and ABC) than from the three more conservative denominations (the BGC, the EFC, and AOG). This is because there are many more leaders in the three oldline denominations. The oldline denominations are generally larger and they have many more leaders per member than do the three conservative denominations. Thus while denomination-specific results reported here are reflective of the corresponding denomination, average results based on our entire sample are tilted towards the oldline denominations.

Mission Priorities: Evangelism and Social Action

Is American Protestantism divided into two competing camps? The notion of a "two party" system in Protestantism has long been popular among scholars. The two branches of Protestantism have been given a variety of names, e.g. private and public (Hoge, Marty), this-worldly and other-worldly (Roozen, McKinney, and Carroll), ecumenical and evangelical (Mouw), liberal and neoorthodox versus conservative and fundamentalist (Hadden), political and metaphysical (Cox), modernist and pietist (Pratt), modernist and traditionalist (Quinley), liberal and evangelical (Coleman, Hunter, Quebedeaux, Warner), liberal and conservative (Wuthnow), progressive and orthodox (Hunter).[4]

These scholars emphasize a variety of distinctions, many of them theological. Although we asked leaders about a broad range of issues, we were particularly interested in leaders' views concerning the mission of the church. What is it that the church ought to be doing in the world? For what purpose should the church use its financial and organizational resources? Over the past century, such issues have often embodied, or been closely related to other, theological, cultural, and social differences that have been the source of religious conflict.

In the questionnaire, we presented denominational leaders with a list of eighteen statements describing various activities of the church. We asked respondents to indicate for each item "whether this activity is contradictory to, has no importance, some importance, high importance, or very high importance for *your understanding of the churches' mission* in today's world." We then used a statistical technique known as factor analysis to identify the major factors among the eighteen items. In somewhat simplified terms, a factor is a subset of items that all measure approximately the same thing; that is, an individual tends to give similar responses to all of the items in the subset.

The most important factors to emerge from our analysis are a subset of six items that mainly focus on evangelical activities and another subset of four items that focus on social justice activism. Table 1 lists the items included in each subset and the percentage of respondents from each denomination who placed high importance or very high importance on an item. It also lists, in parentheses, the percentage of persons from each denomination who said that a particular goal was "contradictory to" their understanding of the church's mission in the world.

TABLE 1
MISSION PRIORITIES BY DENOMINATION

Church Activity	Percent in Each Denomination Placing High or Very High Importance on Activity (Percent Viewing Activity as Contradictory to the Church's Mission)						
Evangelical Items	ECU	UCC	UMC	ABC	BGC	EFC	AOG
Supporting evangelistic missions overseas to convert the world to Christ.	27 (15)	12 (18)	40 (3)	65 (2)	98 (0)	100 (0)	99 (0)
Encouraging church members to make explicit declarations of their personal faith to friends, neighbors and coworkers	39 (4)	30 (4)	49 (2)	62 (0)	88 (0)	100 (0)	99 (0)
Establishing new churches	44 (1)	52 (0)	73 (0)	76 (0)	98 (0)	97 (0)	98 (0)
Actively reaching out to members of other religious groups with an invitation to find true salvation	15 (39)	6 (46)	10 (32)	16 (27)	74 (2)	71 (2)	63 (1)
Protecting church members from the false teachings of other religious groups.	18 (20)	16 (17)	18 (12)	27 (11)	65 (2)	72 (0)	76 (0)
Helping church members resist the new life-styles	15 (23)	9 (22)	20 (13)	28 (12)	56 (0)	65 (3)	72 (1)

Social Activism Items	ECU	UCC	UMC	ABC	BGC	EFC	AOG
Encouraging pastors of local churches to speak out in public on social, political, and economic issues that confront American society today	77 (0)	72 (1)	63 (1)	55 (1)	26 (0)	29 (2)	28 (4)
Identifying with political movements of the poor and oppressed even when this challenges the interests of current members.	78 (1)	70 (1)	62 (1)	53 (0)	22 (0)	19 (18)	13 (10)
Promoting social justice in North America and throughout the world by the use of organized, collective action such as lobbying in Congress	77 (0)	75 (1)	53 (1)	55 (2)	22 (0)	18 (12)	10 (11)
Encouraging and inspiring church members, as individuals, to become involved in social and political issues.	89 (0)	81 (0)	76 (0)	76 (0)	51 (0)	50 (0)	37 (3)
Average number responding to items	232	353	359	286	60	68	103

Key to Denominational Abbreviations:
  ECU = National Council of Churches and regional ecumenical agencies
  UCC = United Church of Christ
  UMC = United Methodist Church
  ABC = American Baptist Church
  BGC = Baptist General Conference
  EFC = Evangelical Free Church
  AOG = Assemblies of God

Note the strong differences between the oldline denominations (shown on the left) and the conservative denominations (shown on the right). Contrary to Wuthnow's restructuring thesis, denominational differences remain very strong. Persons in conservative denominations are more likely to place high importance on evangelistic activities and low importance on social activism. The pattern is reversed in the oldline denominations and for respondents from ecumenical agencies.

Note also that Methodist leaders' views towards evangelism and social activism are most similar to those of American Baptists (ABC) and United Church of Christ (UCC) leaders. On almost all the items, the percentages for Methodists fall in between the percentages for these two oldline denominations.

The numbers in parentheses (indicating the percent who feel a goal is "contradictory to" the church's mission) also show an interesting pattern. Among leaders in the oldline denominations significant minorities, from a quarter to almost one-half of the respondents, are opposed to some evangelical goals, especially those that imply that there is one correct belief or behavioral standard to which all should comply. Leaders in conservative denominations, on the other hand, are less likely to say that social activist goals are "contradictory to" the mission of the church, they simply feel they are less important. In no case are there as many as 20% in any of the evangelical denominations who oppose any of the social activist church goals. This suggests that evangelism has greater potential than social justice activism to generate conflicts and disagreements within and between denominations.

One problem with factor analysis as we use it here is that it can only identify factors that are present in the list of items submitted for analysis. That is, it is possible that church leaders have other important mission priorities that we failed to include in our eighteen items. We used the phone interviews to find out if this was true. To prevent us from predetermining their answers, we began the interviews by asking leaders "If you had to point to two or three issues that should be national church mission priorities in your denomination, what would they be?"

Most leaders we interviewed listed two or three different issues. Some listed only one. Altogether, the 51 leaders gave 123 responses to this question. Of these, 47% were characteristic of a social action orientation. Another 24% clearly reflected an evangelical orientation while 22% dealt with institutional concerns such as the need for the denomination to improve its methods of funding or its channels of communication between local and national levels. The remaining 7 percent were issues that we we could not easily classify.

The social activist responses included such things as: "the environment," "children in poverty," "racism," "human rights and civil rights," "justice and peace issues," "women's issues," "AIDS," "the homeless," and "economic justice." Responses characteristic of an evangelical orientation included statements like "evangelism," "a worldwide mission to spread the gospel to those people in countries who have never heard it," "continuing evangelism by both clergy and lay persons," and "evangelizing the world—that is our only mission priority."

Among the responses that we categorized as institutional maintenance were statements such as "stewardship—our church is failing to challenge our people sufficiently," "we need a broader base to support our mission," "developing solutions for the fund-raising crisis," "equipping pastors to deal with the complex issues of leadership and conflict in their congregations."

One reason for the lower number of evangelical issues cited is that leaders with an evangelical orientation tended to list "evangelism" as their first mission priority and then went on to mention one or two institutional concerns and sometimes a social activist concern. However, leaders with a social activist orientation tended to list several different social activist issues such as those listed above. No one said "social activism" should be a denominational priority. In addition to explaining the larger number of social activist responses, this observation also suggests that evangelicals may find it easier to unite around a commonly shared goal whereas the basic loyalties of social activists may be distributed among a fairly diverse range of causes.

Together, the questionnaire and interviews confirm our identification of evangelism and social activism as the two main mission priorities of these denominational leaders.

Two Polarized Camps?

Having identified the two main goals held by denominational leaders we now ask whether these leaders are divided into two opposed groups. Certainly one interpretation of Table 1 (above) suggests that church leaders are divided into two groups of competing denominations. There are major differences (often 20 to 25 percentage points) between the number of leaders in oldline denominations and the number in conservative denominations who agree with the various church goals.

However, the percentages in Table 1 show only the results for an entire denomination. It could be that many leaders within each denomination take moderate positions, even though their denominations (on average) take a more liberal or conservative view. Such persons could serve as valuable go-betweens to alleviate conflicts both within and between denominations. Moreover, Table 1 does not tell us much about whether leaders see evangelism and social activism as mutually exclusive or complementary goals.

Midway through our phone interviews we asked: "Some people feel that Protestantism is divided into two camps: a) the evangelically-minded folk who see the church's mission centering on the conversion and nurture of individuals, and b) the social activists who see the mission of the church centering on the transformation of society. Do you feel this is accurate or too simple?"

We separated their answers into three categories, agreement (those who felt the statement was basically accurate), disagreement (those who felt it was too simple), and partial agreement (those who recognized elements of truth in the description but felt that it was overly simplistic). Of the 51 leaders interviewed only 15 (approximately 29%) felt the description was basically accurate. Eighteen of the leaders (35%) felt that the statement was clearly inaccurate and the remaining 18 leaders (35%) thought it was only partially accurate.

Those who disagreed fully or partially most often pointed out that many people take a middle position supporting both social activism and evangelism. For example, one Methodist leader said he believes "there is a broad continuum ranging between [evangelicals and social activists]. They do exist but on opposite ends of a continuum. It is not just either/or." Another echoed this sentiment, feeling the statement was "too simple. It is not an either/or issue but more of a blend in most groups and people that I know." One respondent, a strong supporter of evangelism, noted that

> You can divide up Protestantism into two camps if you want, but I think there are too many people who actually are both to make this division very meaningful. For example there are many of us who hold evangelical values who also have a deep concern for social issues. Also, I personally know individuals whom others would accurately call social activists; but [those others would] mistakenly categorize these persons [as] acting without concern for the gospel message, which is not true.

One UCC leader, a very strong social activist, pointed out that

> even conservatives who have a strong faith are likely to believe that programs to help the needy are worthwhile—and even that something has to be done about social structures in order to bring real help. Conservatives are probably as likely to be interested in social action as the knee-jerk liberal who jumps on every cause.

Not only did many leaders feel the two camp description was too simple, but when we asked them, "do you tilt in one direction or the other?" 22 of the 51 leaders interviewed, or 43%, saw themselves as incorporating both evangelism and social action in their work. Fourteen of those interviewed (28%) described themselves as social activists, 12 leaders (24%) saw themselves as evangelicals, while 3 leaders (6%) felt they were neither social activists nor evangelicals. Perhaps the strongest statement of the middle position came from a United Methodist leader who said

I list heavily toward the left politically. I have a deep personal commitment to Jesus Christ and spreading the Gospel. I have a strong personal piety. At the same time I am a flaming social activist! My friends know me as an outspoken social activist. Yet I work as editor for a magazine which has as its mission to undergird the personal piety of others. So those who know me in my job, would see me as a very spiritual evangelist.

FIGURE 1

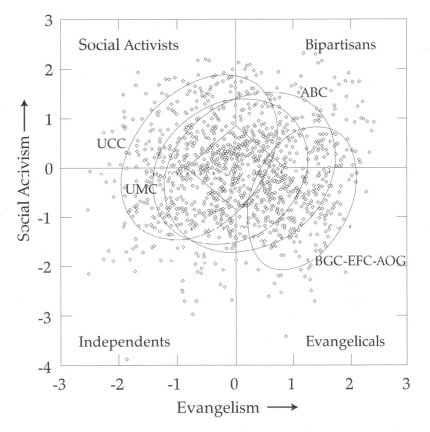

Figure 1 provides a check on the findings from the interviews. It is a scatterplot based on questionnaire respondents' scores on two scales[5] we created from the evangelism and social activism items listed in Table 1. The horizontal axis measures support for evangelism. The scale has been renumbered, or standardized, so that the average evangelism score for all leaders equals zero. Positive scale scores, higher than zero, indicate stronger than average support for evangelism, while negative scale scores, below zero, indicate below average support for evangelism. An arrow pointing to the right shows that higher support for evangelism corresponds to scale values further to the right. Thus, leaders plotted as dots on the right side of Figure 1 give strong support to evangelism, while those plotted on the left side give only weak or no support to evangelism.

Support for church social activism is measured using the vertical scale that is similarly numbered so that zero equals the mean score for all leaders. An upward pointing arrow shows that higher support for social activism corresponds to scale values towards the top of the figure. Thus, leaders plotted as dots near the top of the figure give strong support to social activism while leaders plotted in the lower half of the figure give less than average support to social activism.

Figure 1 can be viewed as a "map" of leaders' mission priorities. Each dot in the figure represents the "location" of one of the almost fifteen hundred leaders in the study. Instead of using latitude and longitude to plot each person's location, we use their scores on the evangelism and social activism scales. For example, leaders plotted as dots in the lower-right portion of the scatterplot give greater than average support to evangelism, but lower than average support to social activism. Figure 1 labels these leaders "evangelicals." Following a similar logic, we call leaders in the upper-left portion of the scatterplot, "social activists." They give strong support to social activism but little or no support to evangelism.

Several important results are apparent in figure 1. The most noticeable is that, just as our interview respondents repeatedly pointed out, lots of leaders are in the middle. One sees no "great divide" separating leaders into two clearly defined camps. Instead, leaders are distributed fairly evenly across the regions of the map. In addition to evangelicals and social activists, there are many leaders in the upper-right portion of the figure who strongly support both social activism and evangelism. We call them "bipartisans." Others, in the lower-left region of our map, give only weak support, or no support, to both goals. We call them "independents." Finally, Figure 1 shows that many leaders give moderate support to both mission priorities. These leaders are plotted in the diamond-shaped central portion of the figure. In order to reduce clutter, we have not labeled this region, but we call such persons "centrists."

Our results suggest that one-dimensional, liberal versus conservative, descriptions of tensions in Protestantism are oversimplified. If leaders were aligned along a single, conservative-liberal dimension, we

might find centrists, but we would not find many bipartisans or independents. Yet our analysis suggests that bipartisans and independents
play an important role in denominational decision making. Figure 1
suggests that Protestant conflicts over the mission of the church take
place on a two- and not a one-dimensional playing field.

Diversity Within Denominations

Figure 1 also shows four ellipses (based on multiple regression).
Each ellipse shows the approximate territories occupied by leaders in a
single denomination, it encircles approximately 75% of the respondents
for a single denomination. We drew a single ellipse for the three
conservative denominations since their respective ellipses are nearly
identical. The United Methodist ellipse is second from the left and is
labeled "UMC."

Consistent with the denominational differences observed in Table
1, there is a clear upper-left to lower-right progression as one moves
from the most liberal of the oldline denominations, the UCC, towards
the three conservative denominations. Leaders from the three
conservative denominations give, on average, stronger support to
evangelism and weaker support to social activism. Thus the ellipse
representing their positions is shown in the lower-right portion of the
figure.

The ellipse representing United Methodists lies near the middle of
the figure, suggesting that the views of Methodist leaders are about
average among the leaders in our sample.[6] It encircles the centrist
diamond and approximately equal portions of the other four regions of
the map. This is consistent with the percentages of Methodist leaders
who fall in each of the five regions of our map. Centrists make up the
biggest group (33%) of Methodists. Independents are the next largest
group at 24%, bipartisans make up 16%, while only 14% are social
activists and 13% are evangelicals. Thus, only 27% of Methodists fall in
the two regions of our map that are most often described as the main
opponents in denominational conflicts. Fully 73% of Methodist leaders
do not fit in the two-camp, evangelical versus social activist picture of
denominational tension.

Figure 1 shows another tendency not apparent in table 1. While the
different locations of the ellipses suggests considerable differences
between denominations, the breadth of the ellipses shows that there is
also considerable diversity *within* denominations. The greater the width
of the ellipse, the greater the diversity of the denomination. The large

size of some of the ellipses suggests that some denominations, like the UMC, include leaders with quite diverse mission priorities. Moreover, this diversity means that there is considerable overlap in the positions taken by leaders in different denominations. For example, some United Methodist leaders have mission priorities similar to some Assemblies of God leaders.

The shape of the ellipses is also suggestive. The ellipse for the three conservative denominations is quite tall, suggesting that they are internally quite diverse with regard to support for social activism, the vertical dimension of the figure. But this same ellipse is also fairly narrow, suggesting that diversity with regard to evangelism is more limited in the conservative denominations. In contrast, the ellipses for the three oldline denominations are almost circular, suggesting a broad range of diversity on both mission priorities. In other analyses not shown here, we found similar patterns for a broad range of theological, economic-justice, and personal-moral issues included in the questionnaire. More specifically, leaders in oldline denominations tend to hold quite diverse opinions on all of the issues examined. Leaders in the three conservative denominations held diverse views on economic-justice issues (e.g., welfare spending, redistribution of income to the poor), but they held consistently conservative views on matters of theology and personal-moral issues (abortion, sexuality, and free speech issues).

United Methodists are, following American Baptists, the second most diverse denomination in the study. Not only was this true for the evangelism and social activism scales, but it was also true for almost every other scale we examined. Thus, while United Methodism is not divided into two clearly defined competing groups, there is more than enough diversity to provide fuel for denominational tensions.

The Location of Moral Authority

Does the great internal diversity of United Methodism mean that it is likely to split apart? While some congregations and members may leave the denomination, we think schism is unlikely. In this concluding section we speculate that United Methodism and other oldline denominations are threatened more by gridlock than by schism.

After comparing scale scores on numerous issues and reading through many hours of interview transcripts, we began to notice another difference among leaders from different denominations, a difference that may partly explain the greater internal diversity of the oldline denominations and the kinds of problems faced by United Methodism. This difference concerns the location of moral authority.

As described by Fred Kniss[7] the location of moral authority "concerns the standard one uses to discern the fundamental basis for ethical, religious, aesthetic, or epistemological standards (i.e., the nature of 'good,' 'beauty,' and 'truth')." Does one look primarily to individuals, to the individual's reason, experience, or intuition, something that may vary widely from one individual to the next? Or, does one look primarily to a collective source of some type (for example, a shared interpretation of religious scriptures, a church or group hierarchy, group written or oral history, or some binding collective decision-making process). Social groups, including denominations, differ in the extent to which they locate moral authority in individuals versus some collective source that is considered binding on all in the group. At stake is the right of the group to make claims upon individual members versus the right of individuals to challenge the legitimacy of group claims.

While this is a complicated issue, the interviews reveal major differences between the orientation of leaders in oldline denominations like United Methodism and leaders in the three more conservative denominations. Denominations like United Methodism appear to grant far greater moral authority to the individual's reason and experience than do the more conservative denominations. Moreover, they do this across a fairly broad range of issues. In fact, many Methodist leaders told us this is one of the things they like most about their denomination.

At the very end of the telephone interviews we asked leaders what their denominational affiliation means to them. Twelve of the 51 leaders we interviewed are Methodists. Of these, seven said that being a Methodist was special because of the the diversity, pluralism, or freedom the denomination affords. For example, one United Methodist minister and national board member told us that she "particularly like[s]" being a Methodist because "this church is broad enough to embrace people from one spectrum to another." Another stressed "the freedom of belief beyond certain core values that is so [much] a part of the Methodist church." One woman, a national board member and social activist hit the nail on the head. She told us, "I am a United Methodist because we have a theology, the Wesley quadrilateral, stressing reason and experience." The two parts of the Wesley quadrilateral that she feels Methodism stresses, namely, reason and experience, both locate authority in the individual, but the two parts of the quadrilateral that she apparently feels are less important to United Methodism, scripture and tradition, locate moral authority in a collective tradition, not the individual. Her statement suggests that she is a Methodist because, as she understands it, Methodism locates moral authority more in individuals than in the collectivity.

The United Methodists in our sample still value the other parts of the quadrilateral, scripture and tradition, but relative to leaders in more conservative denominations, individual reason, experience, and interpretation are granted much greater legitimacy. Thus when we asked a United Methodist leader, a centrist, what it means to be a Methodist, she said:

> [Some time ago] I answered that [question] for a man in my adult Sunday school class. I was talking about what our *Book of Discipline* in the Methodist Church said about war and how to deal peacefully with conflict. He said, "Well, I don't agree; I don't believe we should make peace with the Russians." I said, "Well that is the wonderful thing about Methodism. *The Book of Discipline* is suggestive, you do not have to follow it as law. You and I can disagree in the Methodist Church and still according to its tenets go up to the altar and take communion together. If we accept Jesus Christ as our Lord, we can heartily disagree on other matters." Well, he didn't like my answer at all! He wanted to be able to say what "we" believe, what we as a Church stand for on issues. I am glad to be in a denomination that welcomes diversity.

Her comments indicate a high regard for central elements of the collective tradition, communion, the *Book of Discipline*, and accepting Christ as Lord. But she values Methodism over other denominational affiliations primarily because it gives great freedom to individuals in matters of values and beliefs. According to her, the "wonderful thing" about the *Book of Discipline* is that it is only suggestive, it is not binding. In contrast, the man in her class believes it's important that "we" as a church have something "we" "stand for." He wants the church to invest its collective moral authority in a particular position and thus presumably use this authority to influence members' behavior and opinions.

While many Methodist leaders stress the importance of the individual's right, even need, to question and reinterpret religious authority on the basis of individual experience and reason, few leaders in conservative denominations agree. Perhaps the strongest opposing viewpoint we heard came from this Assemblies of God leader, an evangelical, who described his relationship to his denomination saying:

> My responsibility lies then in my adjusting my philosophies and ideals to conform to [the denomination's] ideals. It is not for me to try and adjust the organization to fit mine. By being supportive and helping to guard against intrusions into its structure of faith, there are great benefits I

receive that are well worth the price of conformation. If the day comes that I can no longer support its ideals and faith, I should withdraw from it, rather than attempt to change it to what I might like.

Although the questionnaire was not originally designed to measure differences in the location of moral authority, some items speak to these issues. For example, we asked leaders to rate the importance of "encouraging church members to reach their own decision on issues of faith and morals even if this diminishes the church's ability to speak with a single voice on these issues." This item lifts up the legitimacy of individual sources of moral authority at the expense of the church's collective moral authority. On average, leaders in the three conservative denominations say this item has between no importance to some importance for the mission of the church in today's world. Leaders in oldline denominations, in contrast, rank this item as having high importance for the mission of the church.

Why does the location of moral authority matter? Although we are admittedly speculating, we think there are at least three important implications for United Methodism. First, the location of moral authority influences the ability of the denomination to undertake collective, coordinated actions. The freedom given to individual members is a two-edged sword. Many Methodists told us they relish the freedom they find in the denomination and they appreciate that their various agenda are given legitimacy. But ironically, it's hard then to call upon the moral authority of the church to persuade others to enact such agenda.

For example, several social activist Methodist leaders say they appreciate the pluralism and freedom the denomination allows individual members but nevertheless tell us they would like to see the denomination take a clearer "stand" on particular social justice issues. They are frustrated that some in the denomination, who presumably also relish the denominations' pluralism and freedom, reject the moral authority of the church to speak and act collectively on social justice matters.

In United Methodism and other oldline denominations, resistance to the collective moral authority of the church is especially strong among leaders in the independent region of our map. Independents are, after centrists, the second largest group within United Methodism. Independents tend not to favor either church-based social activism or evangelism. Instead they are likely to stress the role of congregations in helping individuals to "reach their own decision[s] on issues of faith and morals." Unlike leaders in the other four regions of our map, independents rated this church priority the highest among the 18 church priority items listed in the questionnaire. Many independent leaders told us that they would be happy to see individual members work for social change or evangelism as they see fit, but this should not be the task of the church itself.

Thus, independents are especially likely to resist the efforts of those who want the church to "take a stand." They see it as both inappropriate and divisive. As one independent, United Church of Christ, leader put it, instead of unity in diversity, "what you get are people with diverse viewpoints saying 'if you do not agree with me, we are not in unity.' This results in a low, mean-spirited, autonomy." The freedom oldline denominations give to individuals ends up tying the denomination's hands when it wishes to undertake collective action.

Oldline denominations grant legitimacy to competing and sometimes contradictory "voices." In so doing, it frustrates the church's ability to "speak with a single voice" on issues that matter. While some leaders, especially independents, do not think it is important for the denomination to speak with "a single voice" many want their oldline denominations to make conclusive decisions on issues such as the ordination of practicing homosexuals—despite the fact that any such decision is bound to alienate many. The safe, and common, response is to appoint commissions to study such matters. But without a shared interpretation of a collective tradition to which a commission can appeal, the conclusions are unlikely to be accepted as legitimate by those who disagree.

The *de facto* response to such a situation is to allow individual congregations to go their own way on these issues and allow individual members and ministers to sort themselves out into congregations that share the same views. If we are right, one can expect an increased pressure for designated giving, with each congregation reserving the right to give to those denominational programs that it supports and withholding funds from other programs, a tendency noted and indeed encouraged by Andy Langford and the Western North Carolina Annual Conference in a motion[8] to the 1996 General Conference of the United Methodist Church. In such a situation many denominational "leaders" could become little more than bureaucrats who attempt to keep the peace and make sure that each program receives the dollars sent to it. Individual members and congregations end up setting policy. While such a trend has some compatibility with the congregational polity of the United Church of Christ and the American Baptists, it conflicts with current views of the Methodist connectional tradition and with the traditions of many other oldline denominations such as the Presbyterians and the Episcopalians.

This leads to a second, closely related, implication of where denominations locate moral authority, namely leadership. Judith Smith notes that United Methodism is starving for visionary leaders but instead is beset with a glut of mid-level managers.[9] But this is to be expected in groups where individuals are granted relatively high degrees of moral authority and the group, including its leaders, are granted less legitimacy to make claims upon individual members. Visionary leaders often presume to speak for the group and presume to make claims on individual members. This is exactly what members of such groups do not want them to do. It challenges the individual freedom and diversity that members relish, the very thing that drew them to the group in the first place. Visionary leaders are likely to run into trouble because they claim more authority than members are willing to grant. Managers on the other hand, are successful because they seek only the authority to carry out the will of others. They seek to maximize the multiple and sometimes competing interests of subgroups pursuing diverse ends. So long as the manager can keep competing groups from undercutting one another, the manager's authority is unlikely to be challenged. But this is management, not leadership.

Finally, the location of moral authority affects the types of conflicts denominations are likely to experience. While our research was not specifically designed to study actual conflict events, we did ask leaders about conflicts.

Two patterns emerge. Leaders in the conservative denominations describe few major conflicts. In the Assemblies of God and Evangelical Free Church, the biggest problem leaders report is obtaining the resources they need, staff, money, property, etc. to continue their membership growth. While a few conservative leaders expressed frustration that their denominations are doing little with regard to social activism, these were not considered divisive issues. None reports any significant conflict events dealing with theology, personal-moral issues (except the Jimmy Swaggart affair), or evangelism, issues on which most conservative leaders agree.

Of course, we are aware that this apparently conflict-free situation has its darker side. Denominations that locate moral authority more in a collective source can and do experience quite severe conflicts if and when competing interpretations of the collective moral authority emerge. Such seems to be the case with the recent "battles" between fundamentalists and moderates in the Southern Baptist Convention and similar conflicts in the Lutheran Church: Missouri Synod. Such divisions are not likely to be channeled institutionally and are much more likely to end with one group dominating the organizational structure and with schism or withdrawal being the only viable options left for losers.

In contrast, in oldline denominations like United Methodism, leaders frequently describe comparatively low level, but ongoing tensions over theology, support for evangelism, support for social justice activism, and personal-moral issues such as homosexuality. These are all issues that many oldline leaders consider fairly important, and they are issues on which oldline leaders hold quite diverse views. Thus our questionnaire results show that oldline leaders are much more likely to agree that their denominations contain strong political coalitions that frequently disagree concerning church priorities and directions. The interview transcripts also suggest that oldline leaders are more likely to say there are groups in the denomination with whom they disagree on important matters. But none describes conflicts that are likely to split their denomination in two, though many describe tensions that make them irritated, frustrated, and sometimes angry.

Given the internal diversity of the oldline denominations, one would expect disagreements over mission goals to be quite common, perhaps even continuous. But given the high value that is placed on diversity and tolerance for diversity, one would also expect there to be greater respect and mutual recognition of these differences. Such differences are thus more likely to be institutionally channeled. Thus, it is not surprising that coalitions and caucuses are more common in the oldline denominations and that these organizations often receive official denominational recognition.

Nevertheless, the tensions between various interest groups produce a lot of heat, but not enough to burn down the oldline denominations. Because they have been institutionalized, the heat created by oldline tensions is more likely to be kept in the furnace, where it keeps the whole denomination a little bit warm, sometimes uncomfortably warm. The threat to oldline denominations is less that of schism than of gridlock. The danger is not that United Methodism will split in two. Rather, the danger is that it could become immobilized by an inability to act decisively in a changing religious and social environment.

Rolf Memming

For most United Methodists in America, any discussion of leadership is inextricably linked with the persons who have been appointed as pastors of their local churches. And, for most United Methodists in America, the pastoral office has been associated with the image of a white male who has responded to a call from God and who has made a life-long commitment to ministry as a way of fulfilling that call.

But in the twentieth century, particularly during its later decades, a number of factors are changing that image. The most obvious alterations involve gender and race, with major increases in the percentage of ordinands who are women and with some increase in the ethnic mix of pastors and congregations as a result of open itinerancy. Another is the growing number of persons who pursue the ordained ministry in the middle of their careers and exercise the pastoral office not for a lifetime but for twenty or fifteen or fewer years. Still another is the number of persons who, after ordination, leave the ministry.

Such transitions are of keen interest to Rolf Memming, a United Methodist pastor and researcher. To explore them, he assembled an unusual body of data. He collected information on every United Methodist who was ordained elder between 1974 and 1994, and then he began to analyze what he had amassed. In the process, he discovered some important answers to an array of perplexing questions, and he discovered even more questions that had to be asked.

What do the aggregated data tell us about the numbers of women and men being ordained in these two recent decades? Do women constitute a steadily increasing proportion of the total? Have ethnic minority ordinations increased, decreased, or remained proportionately the same? What percentage of individuals who are ordained elder actually continue to serve as pastors of local churches ten years after ordination? How many of them exercise their ministry in appointments other than local churches? How many of them leave the ordained ministry altogether?

Memming examined the data even more finely. Are women more likely than men to exercise their ministries elsewhere than in local churches? Are women more likely to exit from the ordained ministry than men? Does the age at which one was ordained matter? Does the theological school from which one graduated matter? Are alumni of United Methodist theological schools more or less likely to leave the ministry than alumni of the graduates of schools which are not officially related to the denomination? Are some annual conferences more likely than others to have difficulty retaining their elders? Are ethnic minority elders more or less likely than white elders to exit from local church ministries in particular, or the ordained ministry in general?

Memming's explorations lead him to a straightforward recommendation. But is it a realistic one? And how might the additional data that he hopes to acquire through exit interviews of departing clergy be gathered, disseminated, and used?

United Methodist Ordained Ministry in Transition (Trends in Ordination and Careers)

Rolf Memming

Part One: Ordination Trends, 1974–93

Thoughtful people are aware that "things are not going as they should" in United Methodism. Some are concerned with issues ranging from doctrinal orthodoxy to missional renewal. There is controversy over what is taught in seminaries or done by UM boards and agencies. Yet others are preoccupied with the steady erosion of church membership and resources. Proposals are being made to "re-tradition" the connection. At the same time, voices are being raised over "creeping congregationalism" in the local churches. In the midst of these and other matters just about everyone takes for granted that the clergy are the key to renewing and revitalizing the church.[1]

But what attention, if any, is paid to what is happening in the ranks of the UM ordained ministry? Who is being ordained?[2] What is happening to them?[3] What are some policy implications of these ordination and career trends? By exploring these questions as part of the Duke University Divinity School study of United Methodism and American Culture perhaps this chapter will avert a criticism leveled at the recently concluded Presbyterian self-study. In his review Richard E. Koenig remarked that "there is at least one topic whose omission seems astonishing . . . to pay so little attention to the congregations that make up [the Presbyterian denomination] . . . and *especially to their pastors*."[4] The answer to the question of what is happening among the clergy is not a simple one. It varies according to gender, age at ordination, and ethnicity. It also matters very much what conference ordains and, yes, what seminary trains. These are the basic factors that will frame the findings of this study.[5]

Basic Trends in UM Ordinations

Since 1974, the total number of ordinations has fluctuated between 670 in 1975 and 837 in 1980, slipped to 725 in 1983 and rebounded to 842 in 1988. In 1989, however, this gentle series of fluctuations developed into the beginning of a prolonged six-year slump, and posted a low of

586 ordinations for the class of 1994. This downward trajectory has left some people wondering whether there will be enough new clergy to serve the church in the coming years. Lovett Weems notes, moreover, that "a concern for greater numbers is related to and complicated by our commitment to quality leadership for the church."[6]

FIGURE 1: Ordinations, 1974–94

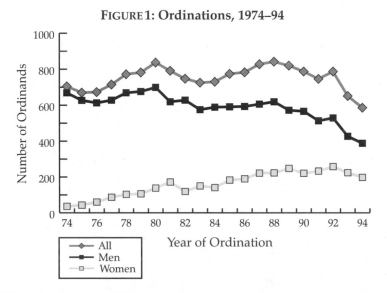

Has there been a shift in who responds and who does not?" Perkins School of Theology professor Schubert Ogden observes that "fewer and fewer undergraduate students who graduated at the top of their classes are coming to theological schools. They are going on to other professions and careers." Ogden adds, "This is *the* problem of a church that is not reproducing the bulk of its leadership from the highest ranks of its young persons."[7] After discussing some of the reasons for the decline in numbers and addressing the danger of a loss in quality, Weems states, "There is no more important task before Christians today than the enlistment and education of leaders for the church."[8] This task, however, contends with a culture that is quite different from that of previous generations.

> Many observers have commented that the trends in youth culture over recent decades have brought a diminished willingness to enter into long-term commitments—in marriage, in vocation or otherwise. With the popularity of such programs as the Peace Corps in view, it is often said that impressive numbers of today's youth are ready to give two years but very few will commit their whole working life.[9]

Returning to ordination trends, a closer look at the male and female components of the overall trend reveals two opposing tendencies. In 1974, men made up 94.9% of that year's class of new elders; a scant two decades later that share had fallen to 65.5%. Some 669 men were ordained in 1974 and their number peaked at 699 in 1980. Thereafter, the annual number of male ordinands fell in gradual stages to 427 by 1993. Women, on the other hand, posted fairly steady gains each year. Thirty-six women were ordained elder in 1974. The gradually increasing annual number of women being ordained reached a plateau fluctuating between 221 and 258 in the early 1990s.[10]

The downward trend in male ordinations may simply be the result of the decline in the number of male live births during the years preceding 1975.[11] The slide in male ordinations also may reflect the fact that mainline churches in general are losing people who are "disproportionately young, male, white, well educated, non-southerners, and frequent movers. They are less conformist on social issues and cultural attitudes and far more open to change." They are in their twenties, thirties, and early forties. "College-educated, cosmopolitan, affluent, middle-class young people who prize individual expression, freedom, autonomy and relativism [have] simply left the churches."[12]

Ultimately, the decrease in the number of new elders and the slide in church attendance must be two sides of the same coin. The slump in ordinations cannot be separated from the prolonged decline in church attendance that in 1995 sank to its lowest level in 20 years, according to research by the Barna Research Group of Glendale, Calif. In his report George Barna states, "increasingly we are seeing Christian churches lose entire segments of the population: men, singles, empty nesters, . . . and people who were raised in the mainline Protestant churches."[13] As goes the macrocosm, the annually falling number of male live births, a trend compounded by men being unchurched, so goes the microcosm, the shrinking annual pool of potential recruits for ordained ministry. And, as Yogi Berra said with reference to falling attendance at Yankee baseball games, "if they're staying away, you can't stop them."

In 1993, women made up 34.5% of everyone ordained that year. If the opposing trends resume, it may not be long, nationwide, before the number of women ordained elder equals or surpasses the number of men ordained. This phenomenon has already occurred in nine Annual Conferences, namely Wisconsin, New England, Northern Illinois, Oregon-Idaho, Northern New Jersey, New York, Kansas East, Pacific Northwest, and Yellowstone. It is also on the verge of happening regionally. In the Western jurisdiction during 1989–93 about 45.6% of the ordinands were women.[14] In other regions the corresponding percentages were: Northeast–37.5%, North Central–35.8%, South Central–27.5%, and in the Southeast–22.5%. Ordination trends suggest the distinct possibility that early in the next century the South will continue to be the bastion of male clergy whereas new women clergy initially may be in the majority in the other jurisdictions. What are the implications of a UM ordained ministry divided along regional gender lines?

Ordinations, By Age Groups

As the number of male ordinations has fallen and that of females has risen, another significant trend has taken place. Between 1974 and 1993, the combined percentage of men and women ordained at age 30 and younger (≤30) fell from 67.9% to 18.2% of the total ordained in those two years. The "30-something" share (ordained between ages 31 and 40) rose from 24.2% to 42.8%. The share of persons ordained at age 41 and older (≥41) rose from 7.8% to 39%. A decisive shift in the ages of successive annual classes of new elders occurred.

FIGURE 2: Number of Ordinations, by Age Group
1974–93

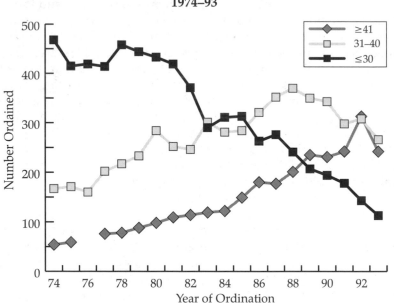

Between 1974 and 1993, the male ≤30 group's share fell from 68% to 19%,[15] the middle group's share rose from 24% to 47.9% and the ≥41 group's share rose from 8% to 29.6%. Like the male ≤30 age group, the corresponding female age group's share also fell, from 65.7% in 1974 to 14.4% in 1993. The class share of the female "30-something" group fluctuated from year to year. It slipped to 20.5% in 1975, rose as high as 43.8% in 1983, and since then gradually fell to 27.9% in 1993. The female ≥41 group's share also fluctuated during 1974 through 1984, but since then its share steadily increased until it made up the clear majority of all women ordained in 1993, with a 51.8% share.

In short, since 1974 each successive class of elders has been gradually "aging." But then, the entire U.S. population has also been doing so, as has the church. The median age in the U.S. in 1970 was 27.9; in 1990 it registered 33. For both male and female UM ordinands the median age in 1974 was 28. For men, by 1993 it rose to 36; for women it climbed to 41.

FIGURE 3: National Median Age of Elders Ordained 1974–93

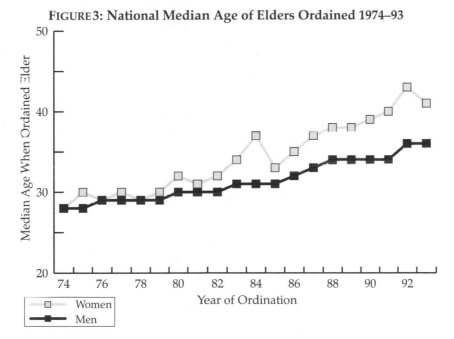

The implications of this "aging" phenomenon as it relates to UM clergy are concisely summed up as follows:

> Policy concerns related to the increased age of seminarians are . . . likely to center . . . on institutional debates about the effect of older candidates on the stability of pension funds or the economics of subsidizing a seminary

education for students who, because of their age, will serve the Church for a relatively short period of time.[16]

Ethnic Minority Ordination Trends, 1974–93

Due to the small number in ethnic minorities who were ordained each year, it is not useful to provide gender and age group ordination breakdowns. However, a few general trends should be noted. In 1974, Whites made up 94.7% of all new elders, Asian Americans 0.6%, Blacks 1.5%, Hispanics 0.4% and Native Americans 0.1%. By 1993, the white share was 88.3%, Asian Americans 3.4%, Blacks 4.9%, Hispanics 1.1% and Native Americans 0.8%. During this twenty-year period, African Americans' highest share (7.4%) was reached in 1986, but since that year their share has been decreasing while that of Asian Americans has shown the strongest growth. If current trends continue, by the late-nineties Asian Americans may attain a decisive plurality among nonwhite ordinands.

Part Two: Career Trends of Elders Ordained 1974–83

Some 7,417 persons were ordained elder nationwide from 1974 through 1983. We will draw some comparisons of their careers ten years out, that is, as of their tenth anniversary.[17] To provide some context for this data, we need a survey of the national, jurisdictional, and conference averages for the ten years as a whole. In Bishop Richard B. Wilke's words, this is accountability time for the leadership of the church: "Leadership must know the numbers." Without solid numbers "we are walking in the dark, ignorant . . . of our most vital enterprises." However, national numbers run the risk of sliding into abstraction. Tables that bring the numbers home, right down to the conference level, will help "tell us where we are and what is happening."[18]

TABLE 1: National and Jurisdictional Averages[19]

	No. Ordained	Retention Rate[20]	ABLC Rate	Termination Rate
Nation	7,417	58.5%	13.4%	7.2%
Jurisdiction				
Northeast	1,565	59.1%	11.7%	6.9%
Southeast	2,135	59.0%	15.0%	8.2%
North Central	1,878	58.0%	13.2%	6.9%
South Central	1,297	57.0%	12.8%	6.9%
West	542	61.6%	14.4%	5.0%

Table 1 may strike some readers as reassuring. The majority of elders ordained between 1974 and 1983 were still in parish ministry as of their tenth anniversary.[21] There are no drastic contrasts between national and regional data. The Western jurisdiction has an above-average retention rate, but not by any great margin. And the Southeastern region has the highest termination rate, but only by one percentage point above the national average. The question of what is happening to clergy becomes more dramatic when conference retention rate data is presented.

TABLE 2: Average Retention Rates (RetRate) of UM Conference Clergy Ten Years Out

Conference	RetRate	Conference	RetRate	Conference[22]	RetRate
Yellowstone	71.4%	Southwest Tex.	60.5%	Troy	54.2%
West Pa.	71.4%	Pacific NW	60.0%	No. Georgia	52.8%
Central Pa.	70.4%	New Mexico	60.0%	Louisiana	52.6%
So. Indiana	68.4%	Desert SW	60.0%	Central Texas	52.3%
So. Illinois	68.1%	Central Illinois	60.0%	W. Michigan	52.3%
Al.-W. Fla.	67.5%	Baltimore	59.8%	Wisconsin	52.2%
Texas	66.9%	No. Arkansas	58.3%	West Virginia	51.9%
Alabama	65.4%	Oregon-Idaho	57.8%	*So. New England	51.8%
Calif Nevada	65.3%	Little Rock	57.7%	No. Central NY	51.3%
Detroit	64.8%	Iowa	57.3%	So. Georgia	51.0%
Florida	64.8%	Memphis	57.0%	So. Carolina	50.9%
Oklahoma	64.2%	Western NY	56.9%	No. New Jersey	50.7%
Kansas West	63.6%	Rocky Mtn.	56.8%	Kansas East	50.0%
Calif-Pacific	63.0%	Tennessee	56.7%	No. Illinois	49.4%
Virginia	62.7%	New York	56.3%	Wyoming	48.8%
Louisville	62.5%	North Texas	55.9%	Nebraska	48.5%
W. No. Carolina	62.3%	NW Texas	55.8%	*Maine	44.4%
Peninsula	62.2%	So. New Jersey	55.8%	#North Dakota	41.9%
Holston	61.9%	Missouri East	55.1%	Kentucky	40.5%
Ohio West	61.8%	Ohio East	54.8%	#South Dakota	40.0%
North Carolina	61.6%	Missouri West	54.7%	*New Hampshire	36.0%
Minnesota	61.2%	Mississippi	54.6%	Rio Grande	27.3%
Eastern Pa.	60.7%	No. Indiana	54.5%	Okla. Indian Conf.	20.0%

Conference-level data displays the broad range of retention rates. For each jurisdiction and conference it is possible to unpack in detail the discussion of retention rates that now follows.

Retention Rates

The average retention rate for all ten classes ten years out was 58.5%. Nationally, the 1974 class led off with 60.7% of their number still serving a local church as of the class's tenth anniversary. The trend fell to 53.3% for 1976. For the following classes the percentage of clergy in local appointment fluctuated around 55%. By the early 1980s this seesawing decreased. The retention rose to 61.4% for 1983, generally maintaining the upward trend.

Analyzing the retention rates by gender reveals that the male clergy's average for all ten classes ten years out was 60.3% over against 47.5% for women clergy. In each class men consistently had the higher retention rate. The difference between male and female rates was as great as 19.4% for the 1980 class when men posted 64.4% and women 45.0%. The percentage of male clergy in each class who were in parish ministry did not fluctuate very much over the ten classes. It began with 61.3% for 1974 and dropped as low as 54.8% for men in the 1976 class. For subsequent classes it rebounded and fluctuated around 61% and settled at 63.4% for 1983.

Women clergy had a somewhat different experience. The 1974 class began with a retention rate of 50.0%. The next class of 1975 registered 55.8% but that was as high as it got for the rest of 1974–83. It plunged to 38.3% for 1976 but gradually recovered to 53.3% for 1983. What age-group subset of women ordinands, by virtue of its growing numbers and career trends, is responsible for this upward inclination?

Do retention rates differ for age groups? Retention rates of persons in parish ministry by age groups do not produce the same clear trends as by gender. As a group, ten years out, men and women ordained elder at age 30 and younger between 1974 and 1983 had an average retention rate of 66.1%; those ordained between ages 31 and 40 averaged 60.8%; persons ordained at ages 41 and older posted a 61.0% average retention rate. The UMC has been ordaining a steady or rising number of people in the very age group subsets that have the lowest retention rate. Is the short tenure of older ordinands due primarily to their being closer to retirement age when they receive elders orders? In fact, a significant percentage of men ordained between ages 41 to 50 leave parish ministry well before their sixties. Older UM seminarians who are men are *not* more likely to stick with parish ministry than are younger men, contrary to trends that may be prevailing in other denominations.[23]

When we plot the trends for these age groups from class to class, we see no graceful tendencies across the ten years. For six of the ten classes, the 30 and younger age group had the highest retention rate, albeit rates that fluctuated by at least five percentage points from class to class, especially from 1979 to 1983. As for the other two age groups, whereas in one class they might have diametrically opposite tendencies, in the next two classes their trends might head in the same direction only to diverge greatly the next year, and so on. The age factor, by itself, does not provide a useful tool for analyzing longitudinal career trends. Only gender or combined gender-age group subsets provide useful comparisons of trends.

This observation is borne out by looking at male and female average retention rates on the national and jurisdictional levels. Nationally, their respective retention rates were 60.3% and 47.5%; in the Northeastern Jurisdiction, 60.9% and 49.2%; in the Southeastern, 60.5% and 43.3%; in the North Central, 59.8% and 48.5%; in the South Central, 59.2% and 40.0%; and in the Western, 61.8% and 60.8%. From these data it is clear that women clergy in the South have had substantially lower retention rates than any other regional gender subset in the country. This becomes clearer when we look at gender-age group retention rates on the national and jurisdictional levels as it pertains to "30-something" women. The disparity of male-female retention rates is most pronounced in this subset.

Nationally, men and women ordained during 1974–83 between ages 31 and 40 had average retention rates of 59.1% and 47.6%, respectively; in the Northeast, 62.0% and 51.3%; in the Southeast, 61.0% and 37.7%; in North Central, 56.3% and 54.2%; in South Central, 55.3% and 34.0%; and in the West, 61.9% and 56.2%. For reasons that perhaps lie deep in the culture of the South, women in their thirties did not long remain in their pulpits.[24] Women in the ≤30 and ≥41 age groups fared better.

Nationally, men and women clergy ordained at age 30 and younger had average retention rates of 62.7% and 48.7%, respectively; in the Northeast, 62.7% and 52.1%; in the Southeast, 61.2% and 52.1%; in North Central, 63.3% and 46.3%; in the South Central, 64.0% and 43.2%; and in the West, 63.4% and 61.5%. The youngest subset of women, whose number was decreasing year by year, had the highest retention rates in the two eastern jurisdictions and in the west.

For men and women ordained at age 41 and older across the conferences, the national averages were 60.1% and 49.7%, respectively; in the Northeast, 57.8% and 42.8%; in the Southeast, 64.7% and 46.6%; in the North Central, 57.8% and 47.1%; in the South Central, 55.0% and 46.8%; and in the West, 66.6% and 69.7%. The retention rates of women by age group noted above suggests that older female ordinands, whose number was increasing, had a higher tendency to remain in parish ministry than their younger sisters. Yet, with such low retention rates overall, especially in the South, it will be a long time before the potential *initial* female majority in ordinations is matched with a long-term majority ten years out.

The growing percentage of female ordinands is not necessarily leading to a correspondingly high percentage of women in pastoral ministry ten years out and longer. If the retention rates given above continue to prevail, women will eventually gain parity with men in parish ministry (just outside of the South?) only when women make up the great majority of new ordinands well into the next century. However, if equality in numbers of male and female clergy is indeed a desired goal, then the church must try to determine the real causes for the lower retention rates of women and resolve them. On the other hand, it may have to come to the realization that the factors which lead to a lower retention rate for women are not likely to change, that women will continue to have abbreviated or interrupted careers, and that in order to achieve eventual gender balance it will have to make the kinds of financial and recruiting changes that will enable more women than men to be educated and ordained for ministry.[25]

Trends in ABLC Ten Years Out

The ten-year average for appointments beyond the local church (ABLC), that is, non-parish ministry, was 13.4%.[26] About 14.7% of the 1974 class was in some ABLC job ten years out; by 1983 the figure was 12.1%, continuing the generally downward trend. Economic conditions might have played a role in the falling number of ABLCs as a percentage of each year's total ordainands. The country went through a serious recession during the early eighties, marked by rising unemployment and high interest rates, thus putting a damper on nonparish employment opportunities.

This might be a good place to try to analyze the women clergy's relatively low retention rates and their high ABLC rates. It may be that women's low retention rates nationwide derive from their having a different sense of ministry than men do. As one former UM district superintendent now serving as a seminary dean has noted, women have a more cyclical sense of calling. Parish ministry is only a place for ministry, not the destination. Their calling is more attuned to relational ministry in chaplaincy or counseling and less concerned with the conference career ladder. Undoubtedly, this insight, perceptive though it may be, vastly oversimplifies the matter. But when this theory is discussed with women clergy it is not dismissed out-of-hand but rather thoughtfully considered.

Another factor that may contribute to abbreviated or interrupted women clergy careers is childbearing and child-rearing; in short, the tension between motherhood and ministry. Caring for elderly parents may also contribute to temporary or long term breaks in women clergy careers. The view that the "husband's career has priority," politically incorrect as it may be, may also affect the appointability and careers of women clergy when the husband's reassignments and promotions call for the wife to move with him out of her annual conference—unless, of course, the clergywoman stays put when her husband takes a new job a significant distance away from her conference and the two of them arrange to commute to one another. Perhaps there is another basic and simpler approach to discovering a reason for women's low retention rate, namely by asking how many women who change careers were United Methodists before they went to a seminary,[27] or what the level of their activity in the local church was prior to enrollment.

Terminations

Next to the retention rates of clergy who remained in parish ministry ten years out and the ABLC rates, terminations made up the next largest category of career trends.[28] Of everyone ordained between 1974 and 1983, an average of 7.2% terminated or had been terminated by their tenth anniversary.[29] The ten-year trend began with 5.2% of the 1974 class, spiked to 8.5% for 1975 then declined to 6.6% for 1980, the low point in the trend. With the 1981 class, the trend began to increase, recording 7.8% for 1983.

The ten-year average of male terminations was 7.6%; for females, it was 4.2%. In each year except 1977, a higher percentage of men terminated than did women. Men in the class of 1974 recorded an exit rate of 5.4%; this figure rose to 8.9% for 1975, bottomed out momentarily at 7.2% for 1977, and gradually climbed to 9.0% for 1983. The women's exit rate posted 2.8% for 1974, peaked at 9.2% for 1977, and after fluctuating between 2% to 5% for the rest of the seventies slipped to 3.3% for 1983.

Overall, of the women who terminated, an equal number either chose to withdraw from UM ministry to unite with another denomination or simply surrendered their credentials outright. The picture is rather different for male clergy. The ratio of men who terminated to unite with another denomination compared with those who surrendered their credentials was 1 to 1.6; moreover, a significant and growing number of male clergy careers were terminated under complaints and charges, for the most part, relating to allegations of sexual misconduct.

What prompted UM clergy to withdraw from ministry to unite with another denomination, presumably as a minister, or surrender their credentials? Would clergywomen's explanations for these choices differ from clergymen's? Do certain regions have higher termination rates than others?[30]

Retention Rates for African Americans

There are too few clergy in most minority groups to track annual retention rates for them. Only for Blacks, who made up 71.5% of all 1974–83 ethnic ordinands, are adequate figures available. The ten year average retention rate for Blacks was 48.4%, compared with 58.5% for all ordinands. Blacks began by posting a career track of 54.5% for 1974 and then plunged to 32.0% for 1976. Their retention rate recovered to 55.0% for 1977 but then began a gradual decline to 43.3% for 1983. What is noteworthy in this decline is that starting in the 1986 class the total number of Blacks ordained elder began to decline. The retention slump for the 1974–83 classes of Blacks anticipated the black ordination slump that started with the 1986 class. Was the twofold decline due to a perception that ordained ministry no longer was the most promising career opportunity for Blacks?

The average African American ABLC rate 10 years out was 18.8%, compared with 13.4% for all ordinands. Annual trends began with 9.1% for 1974 and nearly quadrupled to 36.0% for 1976, offsetting the retention rate slump for that year's class. The next six classes fluctuated around 17.5% and posted 23.3% for 1983. Overall, about half of the total ABLC jobs were in UM connectional boards and agencies and about half in non-UM nonparish jobs.

Other Trends

Transfers. An average 8.3% of the 1974–83 ordinands transferred into another conference by their tenth anniversary.[31] Men and women transferred at the average rates of 8.5% and 7.5%, respectively. The class of 1976 posted the highest percentage of transfers, 10.5%. In subsequent classes this trend went into a gradual downward trajectory; only 4.3% of the 1983 class switched to another conference. Has this been a volitional trend arising out of decisions of the clergy or the result of an unofficial curb by bishops who, after all, have to sign off on clergy transfers? According to Division of Ordained Ministry (DOM) sources in Nashville, no General Conference legislation has been enacted that could account in the early 1980s for the decrease in the number of clergy transfers.[32] As the median age of new clergy has risen, it may be that family ties in the ordaining conference have made transfers a non-option.

The ethnic transfer rates present a different picture. Of the Whites, 8.0% transferred by their tenth anniversary; of Asian-Americans, 19.2%; of Blacks, 15.6%; and of Hispanics, 11.7%. Their career trends in their new conferences differed, also. Based on a random sample of a quarter of the elders in the 1974–83 classes who transferred, about 52.5% of them were serving in parish ministry as of their tenth anniversary. Of the Whites who transferred, 45.7% were in parish ministry ten years out, 23.8% in an ABLC job, and 15.2% had terminated.[33]

Of the Asian-Americans, 50.0% were in parish ministry, 30.0% in ABLC, and 20.0% had terminated. Of the Blacks, 66.6% were in parish ministry, 20.5% in ABLC, and only 2.5% had terminated.[34] The fact that half of the Asian-American and two-thirds of the Blacks who transferred were in parish ministry suggests that transfers provide a useful mechanism for minority clergy to find local appointments in settings that may not be available in their ordaining conference.

Disability Leave, Retirement, Death. Trends of clergy on disability leave, in retirement, or who have died during the first ten years after ordination hint at what may lie ahead in conjunction with the gradually rising median age of clergy. The median age for both men and women ordained from 1974 to 1983 rose from 28 to 33. Of the 1974 class, 1.3% were on disability leave, retired, or deceased within ten years of ordination. For the class of 1983 this figure rose to 3.6%. The ten-year trend in disability by itself fluctuated only mildly, starting at 0.3% for 1974 and hovering around that figure until the 1980 class, for which it rose to 0.5%, before peaking at 0.8% in 1982 and dropping back to 0.4% in 1983. The death rate started at 0.6% for the 1974 class and with gradual upward fluctuation peaked at 2.1% for 1982 and dropped back to 1.4% for 1983. The percentage of clergy who retired by their tenth anniversary showed the steadiest and most consistent growth, starting at 0.4% for 1974 and posting 1.8% for 1983.

The long-range implication of these three trends, if there is any correlation between them and the rising median age of clergy, is at the very least that the denomination will be getting less and less service from classes of increasingly older persons going through the ordination process. If the trend of ordaining older candidates continues for the indefinite future, the denomination faces the prospect of having to ordain larger numbers of older clergy simply to compensate for the increased turnover. This possibility is compounded by the fact that the older ordinands, specifically men, have the lower retention rates. And, surely, short-service clergy will have an impact on denominational pension and health care plans.

UM Seminary Trends

Ordination trends.[35] For the purpose of tracing how theological school affiliations of UM elders changed from 1974 to 1993, we will compare the seminary data for the combined classes of 1974–77 and 1990–93, respectively. (Taking four classes together in the seventies and the nineties helps offset the possibility that either UM or non-UM seminaries might be over- or underrepresented in any year.)

In the classes of 1974–77, about 67% of the ordinands graduated from UM seminaries and 33% from non-UM schools. Of the total number of people ordained during 1974–77, some 41.9% were male UM seminary graduates ordained at 30 years and younger ($\leq$30), 14.6% were male UM seminary graduates ordained between ages 31 and 40 (31–40) and 5.0% were male UM seminary graduates ordained at age 41 and older ($\geq$41). Corresponding data for male non-UM seminary graduates was 17.4% ($\leq$30), 9.6% (31–40), and 3.4% ($\geq$41). Men under the age of 30 who graduated from UM seminaries made up the largest subset of ordinands, and they presumably were also steeped in UM teaching and heritage.

Of the 1974–77 total, some 3.7% were female UM seminary graduates ordained at age 30 and younger, 1.2% were female UM seminary graduates ordained between 31 and 40, and 0.7% were female UM seminary graduates ordained at age 41 and older. Corresponding data for female non-UM seminary graduates was 1.0% ($\leq$30), 0.8% (31–40), and 0.6% ($\geq$41). More than twice as many women clergy graduated from UM seminaries overall compared with those from non-UM theological schools.

A decisive shift in seminary affiliation had taken place by the early 1990s.[36] Only 47.8% of the men and women ordained between 1990 and 1993 were identified as graduates of UM seminaries. About 47% graduated from non-UM seminaries.

Of the total number of people ordained elder between 1990 and 1993, only 8.9% were male UM seminary graduates ordained at age 30 and younger ($\leq$30),[37] 14.2% (31–40), and 8.1% ($\geq$41); male non-UM seminary graduates accounted for 8.3% ($\leq$30), 17.2% (31–40), and 10.2% ($\geq$41). Some 2.7% were female UM seminary graduates ordained at age 30 and younger ($\leq$30), 5.8% (31–40), and 8.1% ($\geq$41); female non-UM seminary graduates accounted for 1.5% (≤30), 3.6% (31–40), and 6.2% (≥41). In short, most of the male ordinands graduated from non-UM seminaries, while most of the female ordinands graduated from UM theological schools.

The growing parity of UM and non-UM seminary background of new elders parallels a telling change in the student constituency. Formerly, as Fisher notes, ministerial candidates emerged from "farm clubs" such as UM camps and youth organizations, church schools, and other programs that helped to guide their spiritual formation. "Now the men and women who are responding to a call into ministry often have little structured experience in the [UM] church . . . [and they are] seekers rather than adherents."[38] Perhaps they were responding more to a conversion experience than to a call.

Adding to this impasse is the fact that, during the 1990s, not only did non-UM seminaries have a growing share of divinity students, they had the largest share of the male age group (≥31) that made up the plurality of all persons ordained in 1994. And of all persons ordained during 1974–83, men ordained at the age of 31 and above had the lowest retention rate. What impact will the ordination of larger numbers of non-UM seminary graduates with predictably lower retention rates have upon the supply of elders for the future needs of UM churches?

Longitudinal Career Trends. There are several positive things to say about the longitudinal career trends of the 1974–83 elders who graduated from UM seminaries compared with the career trends of non-UM seminary graduates. The average retention rate of elders who graduated from UM seminaries was 60.3%, compared with 55.7% of elders who graduated from non-UM seminaries; the average ABLC rates for the two groups were 13.2% and 13.4%; the average termination rates were 3.8% and 9.5%. Class by class, retention rates of UM seminary graduates as a whole were consistently higher than the same data for non-UM school grads. The ABLC rates of the two groups for the class of 1974 were 15.1% and 14.7%, but by the class of 1983 these figures dropped to 10.0% and 12.1%. The termination rates for UM seminary grads as a whole were consistently lower class by class than they were for non-UM seminary grads.

From school to school, however, ten-year-out average UM seminary retention rates ranged from 65.3% to 45.4%. Discussions with officials of several UM seminaries have revealed general unawareness of what has happened in the careers of their graduates.[39] The relevance of these conversations to this project is that the Association of Theological Schools (ATS) is revising its accreditation process, shifting the focus from resource evaluation to "effectiveness." According to Dr. Daniel Alshire, ATS Associate Director for Accreditation, "in the draft of redeveloped ATS accreditation standards due to be released in June, 1996, there is a clear expectation that schools will assess the effectiveness of each degree program they offer."[40] Alshire added that it is no longer assumed that if you have a proficient teacher in the classroom and the necessary library resources, then a student who passes though that classroom and that library comes away with the learning expected of him/her. Alshire agreed that a seminary could include in the assessment of the effectiveness of its M.Div. program a review of the ten-year-out career trends of its ordained graduates.

Some Final Thoughts

As of 1994, the number of persons being ordained has been in a six-year slump. This trend reflects a sharply decreasing annual total of male ordinands, especially younger men. Whether or not one regards younger men as the desired norm for ordination, the fact is that the UM denomination has had only limited success in ordaining enough older men in any given year to level off or slightly reverse the relentless decline in new male clergy. The annual trend of fewer younger male ordinands may confirm the findings of a recent study that some UM elders are reluctant "to encourage someone to enter ministry today."[41] If this finding is accurate, why are clergy "reluctant" to identify and nurture people with evident gifts and grace for pastoral ministry?[42] And if personal encouragement is key to guiding people toward parish ministry, what good is accomplished by national recruitment rallies if there is no follow-through on the parish level?

Although Thomas Oden's critique of theological seminaries[43] may be hypercritical, it is true that some seminaries are out of touch with the needs of the local parish.[44] It is a source of amusement among seminary graduates in at least one jurisdiction that after they receive their Master of Divinity degree and before they start or just after they have begun to serve their first church(es), they are obliged to enroll in a "new pastors school" to learn the practical skills of pastoral ministry neglected by their seminary. The need for this school is especially ironic to deacons who attend such a program on the campus of the seminary from which they just graduated.

Why is there such a wide range in retention rates among the conferences? What is the correlation between the order in which conferences are listed in Table 2 and their respective minimum salaries?

Are salary differentials between men and women clergy who have been in parish ministry for the same period of time in given conferences a key to understanding the lower retention rate of women? Is another reason why women change careers in favor of nonparish ministry tied to their having a lower trajectory in terms of the size of the church after two or three appointments?[45] The appointment in itself can often be the key factor in a male or female pastor's career change. In each conference there are at least a few churches that appear more than once in the pastoral service records of clergy who leave parish ministry.[46]

Ultimately, low retention rates may in general be attributed to a failure of mentoring. As someone has said, "we Methodists do a great job in screening candidates for ordained ministry, but a poor job in sustaining people in ministry." This comment may provide the best clue to understanding the various trends in careers.

One final trend: of the clergy who changed careers within the first ten years of ordination, 30.5% did so by the end of their first year as elder, 53.6% by the end of their third year, and 72.4% by the end of their fifth year.[47]

FIGURE 4: Elders of 1974–83: Interval Between Ordination Year and Initial Career Change

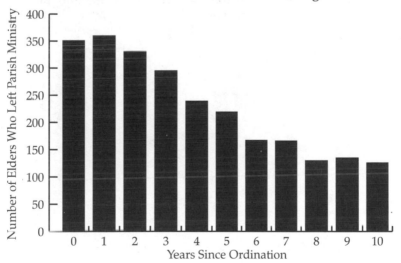

As soon as clergy received elder's orders, they vacated their pulpits. When was it first clear in the minds of career changers that parish ministry was not for them? To what extent is the system for selecting, training, placing, and mentoring UM clergy affected by what at least one author regards as the collapse of national denominational systems in general?[48] Until we better understand the trends of who is being ordained elder and what is happening in clergy careers the ongoing debate about the itineracy will take place in a vacuum.[49]

What's Next?

The general conditions and trends of ordination and clergy career patterns revealed in this research have been shared on a running basis with several UM denominational leaders and nondenominational researchers. The consensus is that the time has come to conduct exit interviews with UM elders as they change careers. Interviews over, say, a four year period of clergy career changes would provide a combined average of results and some trends in decision-making. The four-year process would also even out any tendency for extraordinary results in one year to skew the results.

The point of these interviews would be to ascertain when and why elders decide to change careers or quit ministry altogether. Prudent concern for stewardship of scarce U.M. monies for seminary education alone warrants such a project. It is also likely that the insights gained would enable the selection, training, appointment, and mentoring process to function more effectively.

Bibliography of Sources Cited

Carroll, Jackson, Barbara Hargrove, and Adair T. Lummis.*Women of the Cloth: A New Opportunity for the Churches*. San Francisco: Harper & Row, 1981.

Coalter, Milton J., John M. Mulder, and Louis B. Weeks, eds. *The Presbyterian Presence: The Twentieth-Century Experience*. 7 vols. Louisville: Westminister/JohnKnox, 1992.

Fisher, Neal F., ed. *Truth & Tradition: A Conversation About the Future of United Methodist Theological Education*. Nashville: Abingdon, 1995.

Flaugher, Ronald L. "A Survey of American Clergy." Unpublished report prepared by the Princeton Testing Service, 1990.

Fleet, Bary R. "Leaving the Parish: A Study of the Southern New England Annual Conference, 1977–1984." Unpublished D.Min. project report, Boston University School of Theology, 1986.

Grantham, Dewey W. *The South in Modern America: A Region at Odds*. New York: HarperCollins, 1994.

Jud, Gerald J.; Edgar W. Mills Jr., and Genevieve W. Burch. *Ex-Pastors: Why Men Leave the Parish Ministry*. New York: Pilgrim, 1970.

Koenig, Richard E. "Research and reformation: The Presbyterians' Self-Scrutiny." *Christian Century* (22–29 Sept. 1993), 900–903.

Larsen, Ellis L. "A Profile of Contemporary Seminarians Revisited." *Theological Education* 31 Sup. (1995).

Larsen, Ellis L. and James M. Shopshire. "A Profile of Contemporary Seminarians." *Theological Education* 24, no. 2 (Spring 1988) The Association of Theological Schools.

Maslach, Christina. *Burnout, The Cost of Caring*. Englewood Cliffs, N.J.: Prentice Hall, 1982.

Mead, Loren B. *The Once and Future Church: Reinventing the Congregation for a New Mission Frontier*. The Alban Institute, 1991.

Messer, Donald E. *Send Me? The Itineracy in Crisis*. Nashville: Abingdon, 1991.

Mullin, Robert Bruce, and Russell E. Richey, eds. *Reimagining Denominationalism: Interpretive Essays*. New York: Oxford University Press, 1994.

National Center for Health Statistics. *Vital Statistics of the United States, 1978*, Vol. 1. DHHS Pub. No. (PHS) 82–1100.Public Health Service,

Washington, D.C.: U.S. Government Printing Office, 1982. Table 1–20, "Live Births By Sex. . . ."

Oden, Thomas C. *Requiem: A Lament in Three Movements*. Nashville: Abingdon, 1995.

O'Neill, Joseph P., and Richard T. Murphy. "Changing Age and Gender Profiles Among Entering Seminary Students." *Ministry Research Notes*. Princeton, N.J.: Educational Testing Service, 1991.

Rediger, G. Lloyd. "Clergy Killers." *The Clergy Journal* (August 1993): 7–10.

Roof, Wade Clark, and William McKinney. *American Mainline Religion: Its Changing Shape and Future*. New Brunswick, N.J.: Rutgers University Press, 1987.

Schaller, Lyle. "When Will Women Become A Majority Among UM Clergy?" *Circuit Rider* (October 1993), 17.

Wilke, Richard B. *And Are We Yet Alive? The Future of the United Methodist Church*. Nashville: Abingdon, 1986.

Patricia M. Y. Chang

While Memming looks at only United Methodist elders and explores transitions within that ministerial order, sociologist Patricia M. Y. Chang focuses her attention on a singular item, but uses it comparatively. Drawing upon her major analyses of clergy compensation patterns across fifteen Protestant denominations in the United States, Chang examines some issues regarding salaries paid to women in the ordained ministry: the impact of age, experience, education, and gender; the differences on such matters among the denominations; and the status of gender equality, to the degree that compensation reflects it. She then assesses the levels at which United Methodist clergywomen are compensated in comparison with their male counterparts and the relative levels at which they are compensated in comparison with their female counterparts in other denominations.

Quantitatively the data reveal distressing, if unsurprising, results. Women with comparable education and experience receive lower salaries than men. Nevertheless, the gap between compensation paid to women and men is narrower for United Methodists than for other denominations. Moreover, the level of compensation in absolute dollars is higher for United Methodist clergywomen than for ordained women in other church bodies.

Then Chang examines the data qualitatively. Here the findings, whether or not they are surprising, become disturbing. Compensation patterns are not simple and straightforward bits of objective information. They cloak a variety of interactions and evaluations that lead to specific pastoral appointments, decisions about whether one serves full-time or part-time, and cultural expectations that differ for women and men.

It is important to keep the Memming data in mind while considering the Chang analysis of compensation patterns. Does the combination of a higher incidence of clergywomen's exiting from the ordained ministry and a lower rate of compensation paid to clergywomen mean that women leave because of lower pay? Or does it mean that the subtle, social, sexist forces that persist in ignoring women's experiences conspire to suppress both the opportunities for women to engage in ministries and the level at which they are supported for doing so? What will it take to alter the situation?

Paying the Preacher Her Due:
Wages and Compensation Among
United Methodist Clergy

Patricia M. Y. Chang

On a recent trip, I found myself sitting next to an ordained clergywoman of the United Methodist Church. When she heard about my research on clergy salaries, she shared with me the following story. In one of her previous appointments she served a congregation for four years at a very low salary. In response to her requests for a more livable wage, her bishop replied that because she had a working husband, she didn't need a higher salary. After she left, the congregation received a young male pastor out of seminary and raised his salary by $6000. This story appears to confirm the perception that sex discrimination still persists within the church. It relates the story of a less qualified man getting paid more for doing the same job as a woman.

I mulled over this story for the rest of my journey. I had certainly heard of similar experiences in interviews and personal encounters during my research. This event had happened in 1985, it was now 1995. Could a bishop today still make the same justification for paying a woman pastor less than a male colleague? Would he have been as ready to make the same salary adjustment to a male pastor if he found that his wife had a well-paying job? What factors go into our decisions of how much a pastor's services are worth? Does sex matter? What about education, age, and experience?

The study of clergy wages and compensation is important because it represents a relevant indicator of how an organization values the relative worth of its personnel. In this sense, it is a particularly useful mechanism for evaluating equity between the sexes. As the story above suggests, wage determination is often guided by more than simply experience, training, and qualifications. Subtle, and often unexamined value judgements also determine the dollar amount we place upon a person's time and services. This chapter will focus upon statistical analyses of the reported salary and benefits of clergy from 15 Protestant denominations, including the United Methodist Church. The chief advantage of this kind of analysis is that it allows us to summarize data from a large number of respondents and to understand the contributing factors associated with wage differences in useful ways. However, such analyses offer a general picture of trends that may sometimes obscure individual features of the entire picture. In order to call attention to these elements, this essay will draw upon a variety of sources of information gathered from survey data, telephone interviews with more than 300 clergy, and the research of other sociologists studying gender inequality in employment.

This chapter will seek to answer three questions related to the issue of value in the clergy labor market in general, and the value of women in the clergy labor market in particular:

1. What factors affect clergy salaries; i.e., how do age, experience, education, and gender influence clergy earnings?
2. How does the UMC compare with other denominations in terms of salaries and employment?
3. What do salary analyses reveal, and more important, what do they mask, about gender equality in the UMC and other denominations?

The analyses will use two kinds of data. The first source is based on self-reported earnings and benefits information from the Study of Ordained Clergy conducted by Hartford Seminary in 1994–1995 (Zikmund, Lummis, and Chang 1994). This study collected survey information from random samples of fully ordained clergy, stratified by sex and denomination in 15 Protestant denominations, including the United Methodist Church. Equal numbers of men and women were sampled, resulting in an over-sampling of women. Population weights were used to adjust for correct population distributions in the final analysis. From 9,600 questionnaires we received 4460 valid returns, for a response rate of 46.4%. For this analysis however, we only compared those who reported their salary (an optional question) and who indicated that they were full-time clergy. These two conditions reduce the total usable sample to 2718 respondents (1408 men and 1310 women).[1] Of the 400 United Methodists who responded, only 248 both reported salary information and indicated that they worked in full-time positions (more than 30 hours a week). Of the 20 persons who reported they worked part-time (defined as less than 30 hours a week), all but one were women. The Methodist analysis is thus based on a subsample of 248 full-time United Methodist clergy (128 men and 120 women). Respondents were asked to report their cash salary and a dollar estimate of their benefits (housing, car, education allowance, etc.) for their current job. The amount of salary and benefits were combined for this analysis. The analyses are further supplemented by data collected in structured telephone interviews conducted with more than 300 male and female clergy from various denominations by the research team at Hartford Seminary.

Factors Affecting Clergy Compensation

The first question we examine is: What factors affect clergy salaries overall? This question looks at the determinants of salary for all the respondents from 15 denominations in the Hartford Study (including the UMC). Based on these responses, we use human capital theory (Becker, 1962) to guide the selection of variables used to test the determinants of salary differences. Briefly, human capital theory suggests that salaries reflect rewards for investments in human and social capital. We pay surgeons more than garbage collectors, for example, because the surgeon invests more in years of education and training for his or her profession than the garbage collector. The surgeon must be paid more to compensate for these sacrifices and also to provide the social incentive for others to pursue such difficult and lengthy training. From this perspective, age, experience, and education represent social investments that are duly compensated by salary (Mincer and Polachek 1974, 1978; Polachek, 1981). In this analysis we use multiple regression to look at the effects of these factors plus gender, job type, and denomination.[2] Multiple regression analyses allow one to look at the independent effect each of these factors has on salary while simultaneously adjusting for the presence of all the factors in the equation.

Age: There is a common perception that older clergy suffer from greater disadvantages on the job market. We find support for this hypothesis in Figure 1.

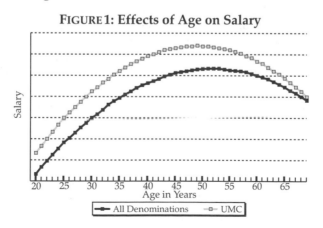

FIGURE 1: Effects of Age on Salary

This graph shows that the trajectory of salary over age increases most rapidly between ages 20 and 50 and then tends to decline gradually. In percentage terms, we find that for full-time clergy, salaries tend to increase approximately 5% per year.

Experience: Rather than measure experience as the number of years since ordination, we calculate it as the number of years a respondent has held an active clergy position since ordination. We have found that holding the year of ordination constant, women tend to have fewer years of experience than men because they are more likely to engage in part-time work, hold temporary positions, and are more likely to be unemployed or employed in secular positions. Yet despite use of this more refined measure, we find that when other relevant factors are considered, labor force experience has a very small (less than one percent) effect on one's salary,. Intuitively, we think that experience should be considered more heavily than age in the consideration of wage benefits. Consequently, there are two possible ways to interpret these results. The first is that employers respond more readily to age needs rather than experience qualifications in setting salaries; i.e., a younger single pastor will be paid less than an older pastor with a family because of anticipated financial needs. The second interpretation is statistical in nature and argues that because age and experience tend to be highly correlated (they tend to increase together at the same rate) these two effects are confounded and should be interpreted together.[3]

Education: Because many clergy have the master of divinity (M.Div.) degree, we seek to distinguish educational differences in the kind of seminary the respondent attended. Using data from the Association of Theological Schools, we divide seminaries into four categories: denominational seminaries such as Garrett, Wesley, or Iliff; university seminaries such as Duke, Harvard, or Yale; interdenominational and non-denominational seminaries such as the Graduate Theological Union, Union Theological Seminary, or Fuller; and all other denominational seminaries, which we categorize "other, non-classified."

The analysis suggests that the seminary one attends pay significant returns in terms of salary differences. Clergy who attended seminary at Ivy League or highly ranked universities have salaries that average 12% over their peers who graduated from denominational, inter-denominational, or "other" (non-classified) seminaries in a given year.[4] There is no significant distinction between the salaries of those who attend denominational, inter-denominational, or non-classified seminaries.

Position: Of course, the most influential determinant of salary is likely to be the position one holds. Position or job type reflects a number of unobserved factors, such as the level of promotion one has received since ordination.[5] In these analyses we compare the salaries of all positions to that of senior pastors as our baseline group. We find that there is no statistically significant difference in the salaries of senior pastors, national staff (ordained), and regional staff (ordained). Assistant or associate pastors come next on the pay scale. They receive about 19% less than senior pastors overall. Sole pastors receive about 22% less than senior pastor salaries overall. However, one must keep in mind that the salary range among sole pastors tends to be more widely distributed than in other categories; i.e., there is a large difference between sole pastors of a large church and the sole pastor of a small, rural church. Copastors tend to make 25% less than senior pastors, but more than interim pastors, who make 35% less than senior pastors in annual income. This may reflect the fact that interim pastors do not always work the full year, depending on the availability of interim positions. Most interesting perhaps is the fact that those ordained clergy in our sample who report that they are engaged in secular work earn the lowest salaries. They report making 58% less than senior pastors. This finding is surprising given that one of the main reasons clergy offer for dropping out of ordained ministry is the lack of adequate financial consideration. However, in looking at the respondents in our sample, we find that a number of ordained clergy appear to move in and out of church work, alternating church calls with secular work. These clergy may be moving between a series of temporary positions including some spells of unemployment. Across denominations, 2–11% of the ordained clergy in our sample appear to have moved into secular work at some time in their careers. This group may represent clergy who are in transition, i.e., have dropped out of church ministries and are doing secular volunteer work, living on savings, or are in temporary employment while making some career transition. One of our interviewees reported that she regularly supported herself walking dogs while waiting for her next interim call.

Table 1 shows the median salaries of men and women for two groups, the total sample and the United Methodist sub-sample.

TABLE 1: **Median Salary of Clergy by Position**
(includes PT and FT)

	Median Salary in Thousands			
	U.M. Men	**All Men**	**U.M. Women**	**All Women**
Senior	48	47	46	43
Associate	46	35	31.5	31
Sole	34	36	30	30
Copastor	26	32.5	32	30
Interim	na	29	na	30
Regional	50	50	53	43
National	5035	4835	na	43
Other	50	43.5	36	31
Secular	33	19	12	10.5

Sex: Finally, the variable we are most interested in is gender, that is, whether or not being a woman makes a difference in one's salary after one accounts for differences attributed to age, education, experience, position, and denomination. We find that when comparing men's and women's earnings in the total sample of respondents, a wage gap between the sexes still exists. Women in the same denomination with equal levels of education, age, experience, and position still earn annual incomes about 9% less than that of men. This news suggests that for our total sample, women are still experiencing wage discrimination compared to their male counterparts in similar positions. In some ways, these analyses represent a very conservative test of wage discrimination. Statistically, we are comparing men and women who are equally matched in terms of age, education, and experience, and we still find evidence of wage discrimination. Such analyses do not explicitly address the factors that make it difficult for women to gain the same qualifications as men. We will address this issue in more detail in the last section of this chapter.

The next section repeats the analyses performed above with a subsample of United Methodist clergy. In this section I ask: *How does the UMC compare with other denominations in terms of salary and employment?*[26]

Compensation in the United Methodist Church

TABLE 2: Average Salary for Full Time Clergy, Ranked by Women's Salaries

Denomination	Gender	Mean Salary
UUA	Women	40,976
	Men	47,276
EC	Women	40,489
	Men	47,173
UMC	Women	38,016
	Men	45,536
SBC	Women	35,022
	Men	48,476
UCC	Women	34,564
	Men	39,242
PCUSA	Women	34,268
	Men	37,923
ABC	Women	34,099
	Men	39,175
ELCA	Women	33,362
	Men	40,152
AOG	Women	32,750
	Men	47,666
Disc	Women	32,459
	Men	36,817
RCA	Women	31,500
	Men	38,000
COB	Women	30,096
	Men	34,652
FMC	Women	28,500
	Men	32,000
COGA	Women	24,818
	Men	37,333
Naz	Women	20,231
	Men	27,114
Wes	Women	20,000
	Men	31,550

Denominations include Unitarian Universalist Association, Episcopal Church, United Methodist Church, Southern Baptist Convention, United Church of Christ, Presbyterian Chruch USA, American Baptist church, Evangelical Lutheran Church of America, Assemblies of God, Christian Church (Disciples), Reformed Church of America, Church of the Brethren, Free Methodist, Church of God, Anderson, Church of the Nazarene, Wesleyan Church.

Table 2 shows that average salary packages (inclusive of cash and benefits) for United Methodist clergy rank third for both men and women among denominations included in the Hartford Study, behind the Unitarian Universalist Association and the Episcopal Church.

As we know, the appointment system creates a unique kind of labor market that distinguishes United Methodists from almost every other Protestant denomination. In this system, the church holds a virtual monopoly on the supply of clergy labor to the churches and thus can theoretically exercise the greater balance of power in negotiations with churches (Bonifeld and Mills, 1980). Ordained clergy have guaranteed employment and can count upon being moved to a different pastoral position within their conference as often as every three to four years.[7] While one often hears complaints about the continual transitions, there are also distinct advantages to the system. It is normative for UM clergy to make a lateral or upward career move each time they are transferred. UM clergy tend to serve a broader variety of parishes and so are more likely to gain valuable ministerial experience or on-the-job training. Likewise, one is more likely to be given the chance to learn from mistakes and the opportunity to start fresh in a new situation. In other denominations a pastor may have a difficult time overcoming a negative evaluation and find it hard to secure subsequent employment. Last but not least, the practice of guaranteed employment offers a degree of job security that is unusual in any organization.

This situation translates into tangible advantages for UM clergy relative to clergy in other denominations. In particular, this system would seem to help women overcome some of the most serious obstacles they experience building a productive career. In our interviews among the larger sample, women report difficulties in getting their first job and even more difficulties in getting their second and third jobs. They also report that once they are tracked into poor-paying parishes in isolated areas they find it difficult to move into the higher-paying jobs that lead to career advancement.

The UM itinerancy system appears to help overcome these problems to some degree, first by guaranteeing employment throughout one's career, and second by ensuring that one moves through a variety of parish experiences. It would be difficult for women to be tracked into a series of dead-end jobs, given that employee circulation is a mandatory feature of this system.

Age: When we compare the effect of age on salary for UM clergy with all respondents in the sample in Figure 1, we find that the overall trajectory is higher, reflecting the fact that United Methodist clergy tend to be paid more than average at almost all ages. However, overall, the general shape of the curve is similar to the larger sample, suggesting a similar rise in salaries with age, peaking at age 50 and declining somewhat thereafter. In general, one's salary tends to increase 6% per year.

Experience: Labor-force experience has a small, yet statistically significant effect on annual salary, less than 1% per year. This result mirrors the pattern we find in the larger population.

Education: Graduating from a university-based seminary again has strong positive effects on one's salary. These graduates earn approximately 15% more than their colleagues who attend non-classified seminaries. Denominational seminary graduates tend to earn about 4% more than the salary of graduates who attend non-classified seminaries, and those who attend inter-denominational seminaries tend to earn about 3% more than those in non-classified seminaries.

Position: The rankings of positions in the UMC generally reflect those in the larger sample. In comparison to senior pastors, national denominational staff (ordained) tend to earn about 2% less than the average senior pastor, while regional staff (ordained) tend to earn salaries about 9% higher. Assistant pastors are paid approximately 17% less than senior pastors. Their salaries are followed by sole pastors who earn approximately 21% less than their senior colleagues. Copastors report earning 30% less than senior pastors. However, this may reflect the fact that a number of copastors are married couples and so may share benefits such as car or housing allowances, thus reducing their individual compensation package. Interestingly, those ordained clergy in our sample who are currently engaged in secular work tend to report relatively high salaries. Their average reported salary is only 4% below that of senior pastors. We also find that on average only 3% of the UM clergy in our sample reported currently being in secular work, which is on the lower end of the scale.

Sex: The wage difference between men and women clergy in the UMC is somewhat smaller than the difference reported in the larger sample. Here women appear to earn 8% less than men, as compared with the 9% difference found in the larger sample. This suggests that the sex gap in the UMC is somewhat smaller than in other denominations. When we also consider that, overall, UM clergy also tend to earn higher salaries than colleagues in other denominations, we realize that in absolute salaries, UM clergywomen often earn substantially more than many of their female colleagues in other denominations, though still earn relatively less than men within their own denomination.

Summary

What have we learned from these analyses? From our sample of 15 denominations we have learned that age, education, experience, and position all explain significant differences in salary among male and female clergy. We have also learned that within this group, women tend to be paid 9% less for the same kind of job even when levels of age, experience, education, and denomination are held to be equivalent. United Methodist clergy appear to fare better than average, both in terms of average clergy salaries and in addressing salary inequities between the sexes. They have the third highest average salaries in our sample, and the wage difference between men and women appears somewhat lower, although not by much. We are persuaded by our interviews that characteristics of the appointment system help women overcome some, but not all, of the obstacles they face in achieving equitable treatment in the labor market. This system helps women get viable employment, a range of pastoral experience, and a degree of financial security. In other denominations none of these can be taken for granted by either male or female clergy.

Beyond Salary: Other Issues Influencing Gender Equity in the Labor Market

The findings of these quantitative analyses are important. They allow us to get a broad statistical portrait of the factors that influence clergy salaries and point to the finding that women still earn significantly less than their male colleagues. While these analyses provide an important benchmark for future discussion, it is also important to caution against the tendency to treat statistical evidence as the only measure of gender relations.

In examining the interview data from male and female clergy in all denominations including the United Methodist Church, we found many stories that reflected sexual discrimination in job opportunities, salaries, and on-the-job harassment. Although qualitative and quantitative methods of analysis are traditionally kept segregated, the stories in these interviews indicate that the voices of clergy persons telling their stories must somehow be given suitable weight in this discussion. Our data is somewhat unique in that we have both qualitative and quantitative evidence from a broad cross section of clergy, and it is our responsibility to seek an integration of these kinds of evidence as much as possible. This section attempts to push such an integration by reflecting on the ways the qualitative material has informed both the analysis and interpretation of the quantitative findings presented in this paper.

It is common to read that women earn a fraction of what men earn, and gross reports of the average earnings of men and women often seem to corroborate this perception. In some cases this is because many women are more likely to work part-time and thus have lower salaries than men. In the initial analysis of earnings data we limited the sample to compare full-time working women with full-time working men. While doing so reduces the sex gap substantially, the interviews reveal that in doing so, such analyses are based on implicit assumptions that make male standards the measure by which we measure women's performance. By excluding part-time clergywomen we exclude a significant portion of women's experience because they are not comparable to the majority male experience. Such exclusion tends to mask the fact that many women are forced to accept part-time work because this is the only employment offered to them, or because this is the best way for them to manage the responsibilities of being a wife, mother, and professional clergy person.

Similarly, in measuring the effects of labor force experience on salary it is important to understand that while many men stay in the labor force for long uninterrupted periods of time, an important factor affecting women's earnings over the span of a career is job interruption. Despite the fact that more women are working today and contributing to household income, they are still more likely than men to quit work when a family crisis emerges (Bergman, 1986). Women are thus more likely to take time out of the labor force, and this action may inevitably have a negative impact on career earnings, lead to a higher drop-out rate among women, or lead to a higher incidence of what is called "under-employment."[8] We find in our larger sample that women are far more likely than men to be employed part-time.[9] Of the 20 respondents in the United Methodist Church who report working less than full time, 19 are women. It is difficult to say whether this is by choice or necessity. This realization caused us to change the measure of "experience" in these analyses from the "number of years since ordination" to the "number of years in active practicing ministry" which excludes periods of leave or absence due to the birth of children, education, etc.

Another form of labor inequality between men and women is found when women are tracked into positions that pay less for the same kind of skills and performance. In our larger sample we often heard the stories of women who could only find work in small churches that could not afford to pay them a living wage. These clergy were often forced to live near the poverty level, pastor multiple churches, or supplement their income with other work. This caused us to return to the data with the following question: "Are women more likely than men to get tracked into poor paying, dead-end jobs such as those in small rural parishes, and from which it is very difficult to move into better paying positions?"

It would seem that the itinerancy system in the United Methodist Church makes it difficult for this to happen among clergy in full connection (fully ordained). Almost all clergy are likely to gain broad experience and training with a variety of church settings, although it has been observed that some clergy are tracked into the kinds of jobs that lead to senior ministries while others are tracked into the kinds of jobs that lead to sole pastorates. In order to examine evidence of possible tracking more closely we examine the percentage of men and women in each of six kinds of clergy positions.

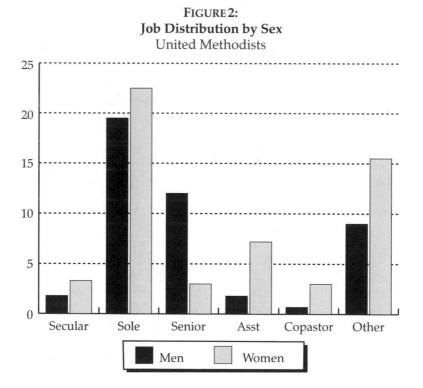

FIGURE 2:
Job Distribution by Sex
United Methodists

As we can see, for the United Methodists, women are more likely than men to have positions as sole pastors, assistant pastors, copastors, and "other" (this latter category includes interim pastorates, regional and national staff positions, and specialized ministries). Men are more likely than women to end up as senior pastors. Women in our sample are more likely than men to take up secular work. One way to interpret secular work is "dropping out" of the church. This figure appears to confirm the perception that women are slightly more likely than men to leave the church.

If we compare this distribution to the total sample (all 15 denominations) we find that the gender composition of positions in the UMC is basically the same as that in other Protestant denominations, with the exception of sole pastorates. In the UMC, there are about 5% more women than men in sole pastorate positions, and in the larger sample there are perhaps 2% more men in these positions.

Since most of our respondents are in sole pastorate positions it is informative to look at this position more carefully. Among our respondents, most expressed an ambition to be the sole pastor of their own church, so it seems a large number of men and women are achieving that ambition in their present position. However, as we also know, there is a big career difference between pastoring a small church, or multiple small churches, and being the sole pastor of a medium or large-sized church.

In order to examine the question of whether women are disproportionately placed in small churches we separated the sole pastorates and reclassified them by size (see figure 3). We define a "small" church as one whose average Sunday attendance is 75 or fewer persons, "medium" as a church whose average Sunday attendance is 76–149 persons, and a "large" church as one whose average attendance is 150 members or more. As we can see, women are more likely to occupy positions in small churches and least likely to occupy positions in large churches. They are slightly more likely than men to be in medium-sized churches. Still, this is more encouraging progress than found in the total sample, where women are most likely to be in small churches, less likely than men to occupy medium-sized churches, and least likely to occupy large churches.

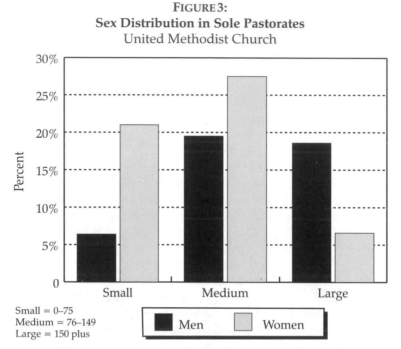

FIGURE 3:
Sex Distribution in Sole Pastorates
United Methodist Church

Small = 0–75
Medium = 76–149
Large = 150 plus

An alarming number of our interviewees told stories of burnout and possible dropout from ministry. The reasons varied, but I was struck by the number that were related to women's positions within the church and society. There were stories of being paid less than male colleagues, of feeling persecuted by colleagues, senior pastors, and executive staff because they did not believe women should be pastors, and failing to find support from congregations hostile to the idea of a female pastor. While these issues are certainly relevant to the ministry of women pastors, our empirical frameworks have been slow to develop adequate measures that will help us incorporate them into our statistical models. In some of these stories, clergy perceive that their negative treatment stems from the fact that they are women. In the healthiest cases, this knowledge provides a useful shield from the criticism which they face. They are able to distinguish between criticism of themselves as women and criticisms of themselves as pastors, and seek positions that are less hostile and where they can practice and nurture their gifts of ministry. These pastors were more willing, and perhaps more able, due to support networks and family situations, to make riskier professional moves until they found a place where their ministry can flourish.

A less healthy approach is exemplified in a second group of women who clearly associate criticisms against women pastors as negative assaults on their own self esteem and professional self worth. One story of a female United Methodist pastor illustrates this case. From objective measures, her career path seemed to be a promising one. She was first placed in an assistant pastor's position to gain experience under a male senior pastor. This man was very hostile to having women on his staff and made her experience both difficult and unrewarding. After this she was placed as the sole pastor of a medium-sized church. Again, this seemed to be a good position but it was clearly an ill-conceived match between church and pastor. She identified herself as a liberal pastor concerned with social justice issues, and she was placed in a very conservative church that was openly hostile to women and change. Her arrival was met with open hostility, and she did not last her full appointment. Finally she was placed in a small rural church of about 10–20 parishioners, which she found to be rewarding but lacking in financial resources and professional challenge. At the time we spoke to her she was beginning to feel that perhaps her call to ministry was a mistake and that she should pursue an alternative career in social work. One felt that she was a potential dropout from the ministry. Her narrative suggests that she blamed herself for her "failures" and did not see that although placed in "good" positions for career advancement, she was also placed in situations where she clearly did not fit and could not readily expect to succeed. Although her narrative is limited, it appears to offer clear evidence that she was intentionally placed in positions that would lead her to drop out or give up her ministry. I came across such themes with such regularity that I began to suspect that patterns of "silent sabotage" extend beyond a few exceptional cases. When this pattern is coupled with anecdotal information that the dropout rate among women is exceptionally high, such suspicions are given greater weight. The insidious feature of such strategies, however, is that without broader information and supportive networks, these women are identifying their situations as personal failures rather than failures of the social or institutional systems in which they are located. Comparative research on the situation of male and female clergy is one step toward overcoming this isolation and personalization of "failure."

The combination of stories, quantitative data, and broader research on issues of gender equality make a convincing argument that denominational leaders need to take proactive steps to nurture and retain female clergy. This is not necessarily interpreted as a case for affirmative action for women, since many of these steps provide

benefits to both male and female clergy. The following recommenda-
tions are offered as suggestive first steps.

1. Until social norms change, denominational leaders need to
recognize that the ordinations of increasing numbers of women make
family issues a central concern for the professional ministry. This issue
should be addressed in a proactive manner. Denominations will benefit
from a clear procedures of guidance, counseling, and planning between
the district superintendent and the clergy person anticipating an
extended leave for the birth of children, the care of sick family
members, or reasons of personal health. Some questions that demand
to be addressed are, "how can men and women who decide to raise
young children remain active and productive members of the clergy?"
"what kinds of productive solutions can be found for women, who for
family reasons, may be required to take temporary leaves or to work
part-time?" and "what can be done, prior to and during one's leave to
facilitate eventual reentry into the labor market?" Rather than let these
valuable members of the community drop out or lose touch with the
church, how can they remain an active, contributing member of the
church community without sacrificing their family's needs?

2. How can district superintendents work more effectively with
churches to protect the professional status of the clergy? The UMC is in
a unique position vis à vis its local churches in that they virtually
control a crucial resource, i.e., the supply of trained Methodist clergy. It
seems that conference leaders can exercise some of that authority by
establishing guidelines that clarify the relationship between
congregations and their clergy. We have heard many stories of how
clergy are unable to protect their private lives from parishioners who
feel that they "own" the pastor and his or her family. Or that small
factions within a congregation have organized to "drive the pastor out."
One pastor shared with us the feeling that because the measure of a
"good pastor" is so ambiguous she continued to work harder and
harder, up to 60 or 70 hours a week, trying to do everything she
thought a "good pastor" should do. All of these stories suggest a need
for active supervision and mentoring in the relationship between pastor
and congregation.

3. There needs to be an effective system of review and arbitration
for complaints regarding sexual harassment and workplace fairness.
Such institutions not only provide an outlet for those who are having
problems with their ministry, but they also serve to publicly clarify
denominational policy with regard to such issues as sexual harassment,
clergy misconduct, and new problems within the church. The slow
progress of women in ministry, and evidence suggestive of high rates of

clergy dropouts, particularly among women, suggest that church leaders need to be more proactive in protecting and retaining the clergy as a valuable resource of the church.

Conclusion

This chapter seeks to answer three questions:
1. What influences clergy salaries?
2. How does the experience of UM clergy compare with other denominations?
3. What do salary analyses tell us and, more important, what don't they tell us about the situation of women clergy?

We find that in our total sample, women still get paid 9% less for the same job even when adjusting for levels of age, experience, and education. We also find that age, experience, education, position, denomination, and gender play important roles in assigning monetary value to clergy positions. Salaries tend to increase with age and experience. Attending a university seminary translates into higher earnings over one's career. Interestingly, those clergy who go into secular work tend to get paid less, not more, than those who remain in the ministry. This would seem to contradict the perception that clergy who drop out for higher financial benefits actually do better than if they stayed in the ministry.

Comparing these findings to the UMC, we find that UM clergy tend to do better than their average colleagues in other denominations. They make the third highest average salary compared to those in our sample, and they tend to have greater job security and opportunities to increase their skill base than clergy in other denominations. Relative to other female clergy, women clergy in the UMC gain distinct advantages from the appointment system, and we find that there is somewhat less evidence of wage discrimination between men and women in the UMC.

In seeking to integrate the qualitative and quantitative evidence we also probe patterns of sex differences in the labor market that indirectly affect women's salaries but may be obscured in the analyses presented above. We find that women are more likely to have part-time positions, are slightly more likely to be in sole-pastor positions, and slightly more likely to be in small or medium-sized churches. Yet there is not enough systematic evidence at this time to suggest that women are necessarily tracked into these kinds of positions. One reason for the lack of this evidence may be that negative work experiences cause a higher percentage of women to drop out of the ministry. This would be consistent with the differing patterns we find in our qualitative and quantitative data. If the women who related negative work experiences are more likely to drop out, then our analyses are more likely to reflect the survivors and less likely to reflect those on the margins. Our interviews taken alone suggest that many more women feel marginalized by their experiences than men and that they are more likely to drop out. This suggests an even more urgent need for systematic research on those who leave the ministry.

For the full potential of ordained women to be realized, one cannot simply apply the same rules and expectations developed from men's experiences to women. Until society changes dramatically, the church must recognize the differences that affect women's lives. Single women require a decent living wage to pursue their ministry, and married women may need to interrupt their careers to have children. Until women are represented in greater numbers in positions throughout the church, leaders need to actively seek a greater understanding of the particular challenges women face in their congregations and ministries. In order to retain women and realize their full potential contribution to the church, denominational leaders must have a greater understanding of women's experiences in the church and develop proactive policies that specifically address the issues that are driving burnout and dropout among both male and female clergy. Perhaps this chapter can make a small contribution in that direction.

References

Becker, Gary. 1962. "Investment in Human Capital: A Theoretical Analysis." *Journal of Political Economy* 70:9–49.

Bergman, Barbara R. 1986. *The Economic Emergence of Women.* New York: Basic Books.

Bielby, William, and James Baron. 1986. "Men and Women at Work-Sex Segregation and Statistical Discrimination." *American Journal of Sociology* 91:759–99.

Bonifeld William C., and Edgar W. Mills. 1980. "The Clergy Labor Markets and Wage Determination." *Journal for the Scientific Study of Religion* 19 (2): 146–58.

Brenner, O. C., and Joseph Tomkiewicz. 1979. "Job Orientation of Males and Females: Are Sex Differences Declining?" *Personnel Psychology* 32:741–50.

Carroll, Jackson W., Barbara Hargrove, and Adair T. Lummis. 1983. *Women of the Cloth: A New Opportunity for the Churches.* San Francisco: Harper and Row.

England, Paula. 1992. *Comparable Worth: Theories and Evidence.* New York: Aldine de Gruyter.

England, Paula, George Farkas, Barbara Stanek Kilbourne, and Thomas Dou. 1988. "Explaining Occupational Sex Segregation and Wages: Findings from a Model with Fixed Effects." *American Sociological Review* 53:544–58.

Lupetow, L. B. 1980. "Social Change and Sex-Role Change in Adolescent Orientations Toward Life, Work and and Achievment: 1964–1975." *Social Psychology Quarterly* 42:48–59.

Mincer, Jacob, and Solomon Polachek. 1974. "Family Investments in Human Capital: Earnings of Women." *Journal of Political Economy* 82 S76–S108.

———. 1978. "Women's Earnings Re-examined." *Journal of Human Resources* 13:118–34.

Peng, S. S., W. B. Fetters, and A. J. Kolstad. 1981. *High School and Beyond: A Capsule Description of High School Students.* Washington D.C.: National Center for Education Statistics.

Polachek, Solomon. 1981. "Ocupational Self-Selection: A Human Capital Approach to Sex Diffeences in Occupational Structure." *Review of Economics and Statistics.* 58:60–69.

Reskin, Barbara F., and Patricia A. Roos. 1990. *Job Queues and Gender Queues: Explaining Women's Inroads Into Male Occupations.* Philadelphia: Temple University Press.

Sorensen, Annemette, and Heike Trappe. 1995. "The Persistence of Gender Inequality in Earnings in the German Democratic Republic." *American Sociological Review* 60:398–405.

Zikmund, Barbara, Adair T. Lummis, and Patricia M. Y. Chang. 1994. "Hartford Study of Ordained Men and Women." Hartford, Conn.: Hartford Seminary.

PART TWO
Methodist Peoples and the Shaping of American Culture

Will Gravely

It is one thing to have social scientists describe the contemporary differences and diversities among the peoples called United Methodist. The assembled data certainly afford us a more candid photo of who we are. It is only on the basis of such a realistic self-portrait that we can then make honest choices about where we are going and what we must do to get there in the future.

Historian Will Gravely reminds us, however, that we also have to be more honest about our past. Most important, says Gravely, we have to acknowledge the choices that have been made in writing the history of American Methodism. Among the crucial choices was the way that most historiography has constructed the issue of race. Some of our story has never been well, or widely, told. Some has only been told as if it were an addendum to, or an aberration from, the main narrative line.

Is the history of the Methodist movement in America essentially an account of the labors expended by white Europeans and their progeny to evangelize the continent and spread scriptural holiness throughout the land? If so, is American Methodist history merely supposed to include, within this framework, a subsidiary report on other peoples, such as Africans and their progeny, who had contact with the normative narrative?

In fact, the history of American Methodism is a complex and multifaceted constellation of stories telling how Wesleyan theology and practical discipline were experienced by, and implemented within, different cultures. Therefore, the question must be asked whether the history of American Methodism has been written under the norms of any particular culture. What realities might be ignored, discounted, or diminished in importance, when one normative view dominates?

Within the context of these compelling intellectual considerations, Gravely revisits the experience of African American Methodists and the way their history has been told. He assesses the limited perspectives within which many noted Methodist historians worked, the occasional accounts of African Americans in the drama of American Methodism that surfaced in various historical accounts, and the rising awareness of multivalent historiography, which has only emerged in the past two decades.

From this reexamination, Gravely invites scholars and observers of the church to evaluate what it means to write an inclusive history. And in so doing, he links the historian's task with the social scientist's analysis and the prophet's voice. Is the fact that we are currently a predominantly white and middle-class denomination perhaps a consequence, at least in part, of the way we have remembered our past? Is diversity essential to the reality of United Methodism in contemporary American culture and in the history of it? Can the writing of history be as expansive as the message of the gospel?

"Playing in the Dark"—Methodist Style: The Fate of the Early African American Presence in Denominational Memory, 1807–1974

Will Gravely

In what public discourse does the reference to black people not exist? It exists in every one of this nation's mightiest struggles. The presence of black people is not only a major referent in the framing of the Constitution, it is also in the battle over enfranchising unpropertied citizens, women, the illiterate. It is there in the construction of a free and public school system; the balancing of representation in legislative bodies; jurisprudence and legal definitions of justice. It is there in theological discourse; the memoranda of banking houses; the concept of manifest destiny and the preeminent narrative that accompanies (if it does not precede) the initiation of every immigrant into the community of American citizens. The presence of black people is inherent, along with gender and family ties, in the earliest lesson every child is taught regarding his or her distinctiveness. Africanism is inextricable from the definition of Americanness—from its origins on through its integrated or disintegrating twentieth-century self.

Toni Morrison[1]

Introduction

On the first Friday in March 1796—a little more than eleven years after the formation of the Methodist Episcopal Church (MEC) as a separate denomination—"the general traveling ministry" in the annual conferences called for "a solemn day of fasting, humiliation, prayer, and supplication." Their Methodist jeremiad listed "manifold sins and iniquities," including "the deep-rooted vassalage that still reigneth in many parts of these free, independent United States." Besides appealing for divine help to end the enslavement of Africans, these "white" (as we say) European-American preachers also petitioned their "societies and congregations" to pray "that Africans and Indians may help to fill the pure church of God."

That same fall, for the last Thursday in October, the Methodist itinerants announced "a day of holy gratitude and thanksgiving," detailing a multitude of blessings that the denomination and the new

175

nation had experienced. The list concluded with thanksgiving for "African liberty," saying "we feel gratitude that many thousands of these poor people are free and pious." Their reference to "African liberty" was to the First Emancipation, which had begun in 1780 and would, by its culmination in 1827, end chattel slavery from New England to Delaware. Their tribute to African piety indicated the early success that the Methodist movement had in the evangelization of black people.[2]

Such an orientation to social reform, combined with a proto-multicultural vision in these earliest years of the denomination, might surprise modern Methodists, who think that our generation was the first to champion social justice or imagine an inclusive church. Those reformist goals, however, eluded the first generation of American Methodism in several dramatic respects, and they still exceed our grasp two centuries later. We might, nonetheless, consider what happened to one constituency of "others"—the "Africans"—in that first generation and beyond, both in the primary records and then as they have been remembered in denominational historical narratives.

Working with the rich manuscript and printed sources of early U. S. Methodism, I have reassessed the presence of black laity (including local preachers, exhorters, and class leaders), of ordained clergy, and of separated congregations in the first generation of the movement dating back to John Wesley's first missionary preachers and lay Methodist origins in New York, Maryland, and Pennsylvania.[3] Examining the diaries, journals and letters, reports, articles, and reminiscences of the preachers, I have drawn four conclusions:

1. The African men and women who converted to Methodism manifested remarkable spiritual power, causing "white" observers to note many cases, individually and collectively, of profound Christian experience that developed to mature faith and practice.

2. Public religious fervor and private spiritual achievement by these African Methodists found structural contexts in the class meetings, love feasts, and watchnights—most of which were held separately from "white" members; in a cadre of lay preachers, exhorters, and local diaconal ministers; and, beginning in 1794, in separate congregations and buildings.

3. Denominational statistics testify to the success of the African Methodist presence in the Wesleyan movement, with black membership totalling 20% of the total membership from 1796 to the period of three racially separate denominations between 1813 and 1822.[4]

4. The logic of this impressive numerical and spiritual presence did not issue in the normalization of conference membership for the early African local deacons. After the final accommodation of the MEC on slavery in 1808, and parallel to the rise of autonomous community institutions for free blacks in the aftermath of the First Emancipation, three separate African Methodist denominations emerged in a nine-year period. Those black Methodists remaining loyal to the MEC, some of whom also called their societies African Methodist Episcopal as late as the 1840s, were a largely invisible presence until the creation of the Washington and Delaware annual conferences during the Civil War regularized their denominational relationship in the North. In the South a significant slave membership resided in the Methodist Episcopal Church, South (MECS) after the separation of Episcopal Methodism in 1845. With the Second Emancipation, they and new converts among the freedpeople found homes in the independent African Methodist Episcopal (AME), African Methodist Episcopal, Zion (AMEZ) and African Union denominations, in the new Colored · Methodist Episcopal (CME) Church formed between 1866 and 1870, or in the MEC mission within the post-war South.

Even though my own findings in the primary sources confirmed some of the conclusions reached earlier in African American Methodist interpretations of the black presence in the first generation, my historical curiosity was still not satisfied. I wanted next to inquire how the story of the early black presence in American Methodism has been interpreted in general denominational historical narratives.[5] In such a historiographical enterprise my questions have been:

— Who remembered, and who forgot the early African Methodists?

— In remembering, how were members represented and leaders featured?

— Who chronicled the African Methodist separations of 1813–1822, of Colored Methodist Protestants (CMP), of the CME Church, of the separate conferences in the MEC?

— Did the biracial nature of the early Methodist constituency impact the subsequent denominational story?

— Were black Methodists always discussed as a secondary aspect of the mainstream "white" story?

My sample became twenty-one histories representing the MEC, Methodist, and United Methodist story and published between 1807 and 1974.[6] All were general surveys, thus eliminating annual conference histories. They were neither chronologically delimited nor regionally based. They were usually popular histories, most often without footnotes or bibliographies. All were written by "white" men—except for some contributors to the multi-authored *History of American Methodism* in 1964. Also aside from it, all but three of the historians—the Englishman George Bourne and southerners Jesse Lee and Holland N. McTyeire—claimed a northern regional base and background. Their histories made the MEC story into the normative account, giving secondary attention to all other traditions.

Essentially, the historical accounts become social texts for contemporary interrogation. The strategy for this analysis parallels the work of historians and social critics concerned with the national cultural construction of race, of scholars who understand how crucial the black-white encounter has been in U.S. religious history, and of historically alert sociologists in the train of H. Richard Niebuhr, who investigated social sources for religious difference nearly seventy years ago.[7]

As a challenge for the Lilly project on mainstream Protestantism, especially for this investigation of the interaction of Methodism and U.S. society, I urge careful attention to the religious dimensions and implications of the ways American Christians, black and white, have constructed race. I advocate an agenda that parallels for religious history, in this case Methodist history, what Toni Morrison has proposed for literary criticism. The Nobel Prize laureate whose nonfiction work, *Playing in the Dark*, gave this essay its unusual title and its first and subsequent epigraphs, shaped my orientation to the twenty-one works in this study. Setting forth an alternative way to read all of American literature, she argues that it should not be possible any more to read that literature without being aware of the African American presence if not directly in the work then in the world, consciously or not, of the author of that work. Since all American writers have existed "in a wholly racialized society, [in which] there is no escape from racially inflected language," readers are forced to recognize "the ways a nonwhite, Africanlike (or Africanist) presence or personae was constructed . . . and the imaginative uses this fabricated presence served."[8]

The need for such a revisionist project in church history was identified—if, finally, incompletely implemented—twenty-five years ago in Sydney Ahlstrom's *The Religious History of the American People*. Asserting that "the basic paradigm for a renovation of American church history is the black religious experience," Ahlstrom included two chapters on black religion. Unfortunately, the chapters were unrelated to his other topics and movements; thus their inclusion had no normative significance.[9] No one has since attempted a similar-scale survey. A Methodist version of the needed reinterpretation, focused on the ways the denomination has contributed to the social construction of race, should encompass how the perspectives of African American historians differ from the authors in this sample in their treatment of the early and later black presence in the MEC-Methodist-United Methodist tradition. It would also need to engage the alternative narratives that are present in the origins and histories of the independent African Methodist denominations and within smaller Methodist bodies where some biracial experience has occurred. Finally, it would have to draw upon the conference and regional histories, especially in the South, which have retained elements of the black Methodist presence. With that larger prospect in mind, and always in dialogue with Toni Morrison, we turn to how the twenty-one denominational narratives have represented black Methodist spiritual experience, leadership, local congregations, and separated conferences and denominations.

I. Spiritual Power Among the Early African Methodist Converts

My project is an effort to avert the critical gaze from the racial object to the racial subject; from the described and imagined to the describers and imaginers; from the serving to the served.

Toni Morrison

The histories in the sample were relatively deficient in rendering the spiritual experience of African Methodists. Given their tendency to concentrate on institutional developments, clerical and episcopal leadership, and popular theological themes, autobiographical or secondary descriptions of Christian experiences of repentance, conversion, sanctification, and spiritual witness for any of the Methodists rarely occurred in the texts. Further, the scarcity of available primary sources and the lack of any one central location for archival material for these historians also help explain the relative absence of reports on African spiritual experience. But there were some hints of a vital African Methodist spirituality.

Nathan Bangs, like Abel Stevens and J. M. Buckley after him quoted Richard Boardman's early letter to John Wesley describing how the large number of black attendants at his preaching affected him.[10] At the same time, Bangs reprinted the Thomas Rankin and Devereaux Jarratt account of the Virginia revivals of 1775–76 without including the many references to the active roles of Blacks which Rankin's manuscript journal contained.[11] Bangs had access to the original Rankin source, which he quoted on another occasion when Whites were inside a Methodist chapel, and Blacks outside for a service—an event that appeared in James Porter's *Compendium* and that William H. Daniels also included in his 1884 *Illustrated History.*[12] Coen G. Pierson in *The History of American Methodism* in 1964 probed Rankin's journal even further, noting that Blacks in the gallery of Boisseau's Chapel on 30 June 1776 were "almost [all] on their knees."[13]

Partly because he was a participant, Jesse Lee narrated some of the features of biracial revivals in Petersburg, Virginia, in 1787, and Bangs reprinted his account.[14] John Atkinson emphasized the Virginia revival, reporting the statistical increase of 817 colored members in one year.[15] Jesse Lee also described the Duck Creek Crossroads Quarterly meeting in Maryland in 1805, at which sixty-eight Methodist preachers ministered to thousands, and where two hundred "whites" and "many other blacks" experienced conversion. He also recounted the biracial mission of early Mississippi Methodism.[16]

Atkinson described the conversions of two African women whose names were not given but who were struggling together to find "liberty of soul" at an Annapolis watchnight service.[17] That kind of detail about the faithfulness of the early African converts, their inner struggles, their deathbed experiences, their spiritual discernment—all of which were richly illustrated in the primary sources of the first generation—was rare indeed among these histories. The general pattern, not entirely atypical of such institutional histories, was not to preserve these more personal stories for the future.

II. African Methodist Organizational Presence

The world does not become raceless or will not become unracialized by assertion. The act of enforcing racelessness in literary discourse is itself a racial act. . . .

. . . American means white, and Africanist people struggle to make the term applicable to themselves with ethnicity and hyphen after hyphen after hyphen.

Toni Morrison

The denominational histories were considerably stronger at the organizational levels, both before and after the rise of independent African Methodist denominations. Beginning with the instructions in 1780 and 1787 for the "white" preachers to give special attention to the spiritual needs of the colored population—which six historians emphasized—there were a dozen specific references to African presence in the social forms of early Methodism.[18] Jesse Lee, followed by three other writers, called attention to the formation of Sunday schools for black and white children. That act was controversial enough in Charleston in 1800 for the "white" preacher, George Dougherty, to be mobbed and dunked in the animal watering trough because his Sunday school for black children was so well attended.[19]

William H. Daniels and Arthur Bruce Moss mentioned the separate classes for black men and women in the Wesleyan system.[20] J. Manning Potts and Willis King quoted Joseph Pilmore's manuscript journal about meeting black members "apart."[21] Frederick Norwood found many references in the unpublished journals of Richard Whatcoat and William Colbert about black classes and separate love feasts. Quoting long passages from Colbert, Atkinson mentioned two special watch-night services for African Methodists—one at Bethel in Philadelphia and the other in Annapolis.[22] Charles Ferguson twice discussed the biracial nature of the camp meeting movement, which also had racially separate services and facilities.[23] John Fletcher Hurst reported that two African slaves were among the eight members of the first Methodist society in Washington, Mississippi, in 1799.[24] A. B. Hyde turned the first-name-only appearance of slave women on the list of John Street Society members who financially supported its first building into an implied commentary on race and social class. He wrote of "African maids—Dinahs and Chloes" appearing alongside "Livingstones and Delanceys, the 'blue bloods' of the time."[25] Buckley more sensitively recorded that "Margaret and Rachel, two slaves hired to take care of the preacher's house," appeared among thirty-five female subscribers to the John Street meeting house.[26] Moss and Frederick Norwood mentioned Peter and Mollie Williams and the slave woman Betty in the first New York city class.[27] Ferguson noted the significant presence of black members in early societies in New York and in Maryland.[28]

The histories paid special attention to the black leadership that appeared in the first generation of Methodist organization, highlighting nine men, but mentioning no African American women by full names except Mollie Williams. Besides Peter Williams—whom two other historians remembered[29]—Harry Hosier and Richard Allen were the most frequently discussed figures, followed by John Stewart and Henry Evans.

Eleven of the histories made Hosier into a somewhat stereotypical illiterate but popular preacher willing to be Asbury's servant and traveling companion. Usually, he appeared in the role of accompanying Thomas Coke in the weeks before the Christmas conference; or he was

Freeborn Garrettson's colleague in opening up New England to Methodism alongside an intended but failed mission to Nova Scotia; or, more generally and less frequently, he was Richard Whatcoat's fellow circuit rider.[30] Two historians recounted Hosier's struggle to regain sobriety, but no one knew of the unsuccessful petition from the preachers, led by William Colbert, to have the recovered Hosier, admitted in 1805 to the ordained ministry.[31] Norwood corrected Hosier's deathdate from 1810 to 1806.[32]

Twelve of the histories featured Richard Allen's ordination to the local diaconate in 1799 by Bishop Francis Asbury and the subsequent legislation at the M.E. General Conference of 1800 authorizing such ordination for the African churches under certain defined conditions.[33] Sometimes, as with Matthew Simpson, the sequence was confused, as if Allen had been ordained after the General Conference action rather than before.[34] Bangs, Porter, and M. L. Scudder referred to Allen as a local elder rather than local deacon, and Bangs explained how that process could occur.[35] Frederick Maser and George Singleton placed Allen with Hosier at the Christmas Conference of 1784 without primary evidence from the period.[36] Called a "southern slave" who was "self-redeemed," Allen otherwise was associated with the congregational, then denominational separation of Mother Bethel AME Church from the ME connection.[37]

John Stewart's career as a missionary to Native Americans, coming in the middle of the second generation of American Methodism, was significant to ten of the historians.[38] Three historians picked up the story of Henry Evans. Originally licensed to preach in Virginia, Evans had a ministry at the African Church in Wilmington, North Carolina, before he founded Methodism in Fayetteville.[39] As with Evans, Stevens used William Capers' autobiography as the source and listed eight other black South Carolina Methodist local preachers active in the evangelization of slaves in the antebellum generation. Stevens also introduced an otherwise little-known black preacher, Father Charles from Montgomery County, Maryland, who was important in the ministerial career of Alfred Griffith.[40] Stevens also was the lone historian who repeated the account of Asbury's conversion of Black Punch in South Carolina, who later had a successful career as a slave preacher in the region.[41] McTyeire preserved the story of a native African, Father Simeon, of Cumberland Circuit, Kentucky, who, beginning in 1790, served the slave Christian community for fifty years. In 1823 Father Simeon was recruited as a prospect to accompany future Southern Methodist bishop Robert Paine on African missions, but his congregation protested losing him as their preacher and the idea was abandoned.[42]

Only Atkinson featured the story of little known black Methodist, John Charleston from Virginia. Converted in the mid-1780s in a Sunday school run by Thomas Crenshaw in Hanover County, Charleston was freed from slavery in 1809 after Stith Mead and others raised funds for his purchase. Bishop William McKendree ordained him deacon soon afterwards, and he travelled some with Mead. As an imposing figure, six feet six inches tall and weighing 230 pounds, Charleston, Mead reported, "would walk thirty miles a day, and preach three times." His ministry was still vital in 1828, when his story was popularized in *Zion's Herald* and the *Christian Advocate* in New York.[43]

In addition to a few references to the early classes and societies, watchnights and camp meetings, Sunday schools for black children and nine named African Methodist men who became leaders outside the regular system of ordination and conference membership, the historians passed on some institutional history of local African churches. In the supplement to his biography of John Wesley, George Bourne set the stage for later historians to include statistical data about local congregations and circuits with large African constituencies. Finding "the increase of the coloured Methodists" as having been "so unexampled," Bourne reported the "duplicate return" separating white and black members "to shew the relative progress of the Gospel."[44] Beyond Bangs' misleading effort to correlate the secessions from the 1813–22 period with the losses in black membership at the local level, none of the historians did careful statistical work to uncover where the most growth was occurring and why, or to explain any decline in totals of colored members.[45]

Jesse Lee first called attention to the African Church of Wilmington, North Carolina.[46] There were six different historical accounts of the more elusive beginnings of the African Methodism in Baltimore.[47] Until Emory Stevens Bucke's collectively written *History* three decades ago featured the story of the African Church of Charleston and its connection with Denmark Vesey and the early AME denomination, only John Fletcher Hurst had presented that history.[48] Bangs may have had those events in mind when recounting the AME secession of 1816, but he avoided directly mentioning Charleston or the Vesey revolt.[49] Norwood was also the single historian to mention the Zoar (Philadelphia) and Asbury African (New York) congregations.[50]

III. *African Methodist Secessions and Continuities*

It seems both poignant and striking how avoided and unanalyzed is the
effect of racist inflection on the subject. What I propose here is to examine
the impact of notions of racial hierarchy, racial exclusion, and racial
vulnerability and availability on nonblacks who held, resisted, explored, or
altered those notions.

Toni Morrison

George Bourne and Jesse Lee had already published their histories
before the first African Methodist denominational secession occurred.
Like all other subsequent historians except Buckley until 1964, Bangs
was oblivious to the African Union movement out of Wilmington,
Delaware.[51] His report on AME independence in 1816 focused on Allen,
with no mention of Daniel Coker or of the importance of the Baltimore
AME tradition. He knew of the succession of AME bishops from Morris
Brown to Edward Waters but not much of their presence outside
Philadelphia and nothing about the African Church of Charleston. He
shared more details of the Zion church movement, and he had access to
the 1839 minutes of the connection to update its status. Of its origins,
Bangs cited conflicts over supporting white elders, over having to be
dependent on white support and especially because "colored preachers
were not recognized by our conferences as travelling preachers." In
both instances, he denied that colored congregations were oppressed
and he hoped that the ME Church would not be blamed for the
schisms.[52] Later, in discussing the Methodist Protestant movement,
Bangs stated that colored members were not much affected by the
Reformers.[53] He did not know, therefore, of the Charleston, South
Carolina, CMP congregation that emerged in the mid-1830s (see Maser
and Singleton 1964).[54] Nathaniel Peck's secession from the AMEs in
Baltimore to form a CMP denomination occurred after Bangs' volumes
were issued, but it did not become a subject of any later historians'
treatment of black Methodism.

In his multi-volume *History*, Stevens recounted accurately the
Philadelphia and New York African Methodist denominational
movements, reporting their statistical success.[55] His one-volume work
told a more complete story, referring to the charter between Bethel in
Philadelphia and the ME denomination in 1796, to John Emory's letter
expelling the Bethel community as dissident in 1814, and to the career
of Richard Allen as a bishop. He mentioned, as well, the British
Methodist Episcopal (BME) separation in Canada from the AMEs in the
U.S.[56]

As would William Warren Sweet in 1933 and 1954, Scudder saw the
origins of the Bethel and Zion denominations through the lenses of

Civil War and Reconstruction, recording the number of traveling preachers and members in the two churches at the centennial of American Methodism in 1866.[57] Simpson's 1876 history continued the trend. He gave some details of the legal conflicts between Bethel and the M.E. denomination, but the emphasis was on post-Civil-War southern work, including the creation of new colored conferences in the MEC and the Freedmen's Aid Society as the agency for missions and education in the region. Growth of the two northern African Methodist denominations impressed Simpson, and he was the first of our sample to recount the founding of the CME Church in 1870.[58]

McTyeire's history was the initial work to list in a statistical table the Union African Methodist Episcopal (UAME) and the BME denominations alongside the AME, AMEZ, and CME. Not surprisingly, he paid more attention to the success of Southern Methodist missions among the slaves. It was natural, therefore, for McTyeire to celebrate the organization of the CME Church. But he had been diligent in his research on how the AME and AMEZ traditions had originated. Quoting freely from the first *AME Discipline* of 1817, McTyeire delighted in ridiculing abolitionism and its successor, Reconstruction, by highlighting the failures of Northern Methodism in terms of missions to blacks.[59]

Though his work concluded with a survey of world Methodism, Daniels completely ignored the origin stories for AME, AMEZ, and CME churches. They occurred in his volume only in a statistical summary of other Methodist bodies.[60] Only Amherst Kellogg in 1892 rendered black Methodists more invisible: Harry Hosier alone breaks the all-white perspective of Kellogg's volume.[61] In 1861, Porter had been only slightly more interested in the Bethel and Zion denominations, devoting only two pages to them.[62] Halford Luccock and Paul Hutchinson's popular history in 1926 was similar, telling about the beginnings of the AME Church in 1816 but without once mentioning the name of Richard Allen.[63]

Daniels' omission was the clue for Hyde in 1889 to give the first visual representation of African Methodism among all the histories. All the bishops of the AME Church up to that time, along with their school—Wilberforce in Ohio—were pictured. There were also sketches of Gammon Theological Seminary in Atlanta and Claflin University in South Carolina—black M.E. schools. Aware of the success of the M.E. mission into the South after the Civil War, Hyde pointed to the fourteen colored conferences which had been formed, justifying their racial separation by the supposed black preference "to be by themselves" and alerting his readership to the movement to have a black Methodist elected bishop in the U.S. The triumphalist logic of Hyde's perspective on this success suggested to him, when discussing the Zion denomination, that reunion "with mother church" should occur. And he could not resist adding white racial humor in black dialect, calling the AMEs "mudder chu'ch," the AME Zion connection "halleluyee Chu'ch," and the CMEs "de Chu'ch set up by de white foke."[64]

James W. Lee and his two colleagues opened the new century with an even more representative pictorial sampling of African Methodist leadership than Hyde had attempted. They featured the bishops of all three major African Methodist denominations. The accounts of the Bethel and Zion separations were refracted from the post-Civil-War story of these now-national denominations. They did retell the Gallery Incident at Old St. George's Church, dating it 1787, and they traced out the life of Allen until his death in 1831. They credited the Stillwellite movement more prominently than other historians had done in the secession of Zion Church in New York. The three historians conventionally made the CME Church into the logical extension of the pre-war colored membership in the MECS.[65]

Among the historians, Buckley best knew the full range of African Methodism and included the post-Civil-War African Union CMP, UAME and Congregational Methodist (Colored) denominations in his survey. He recounted the early Zion and Bethel congregational histories and reported honestly Richard Allen's point of view about ME harassment leading to the denominational separation in 1816.[66]

Bishop Hurst's two-volume history was also thorough in its coverage of the Bethel Church movement, even attributing its origin to controversies at Old St. George's in Philadelphia over seating to 1786, rather than the traditional date of 1787. He also tracked Daniel Coker's New York and Baltimore years, and he recognized the significance of the African Church of Charleston and its leader Morris Brown, who was pictured in the text—as were three other AME bishops. The AMEZ story fared less successfully in Hurst's account. There were no photographs of their bishops, and as with Lee, Luccock, and Dixon, William Stillwell was more prominent than the early Zion black leaders in the secession story. Hurst did acknowledge the crucial role of the *Southwestern Christian Advocate* for the black M.E. clergy and membership from the late nineteenth century on, evidenced by the picture of editor, I. B. Scott.[67]

Of the three most recent histories, Maser and Singleton in 1964 set the pattern for more accurate and fuller accounts of the origin of the three African Methodist denominations 1813–22. The *History of American Methodism* project also permitted the subsequent histories of the AME and AME Zion churches to be told more fully.[68] Ferguson, while omitting the African Union movement, gave a full rendition of the beginnings of the Bethel, Zion and CME denominations but his account could not do justice to their richer histories or that of the ME, later Central Jurisdictional congregations and clergy.[69]

At the outset in 1974, Norwood addressed the challenge of inclusiveness and the problem of invisibility within Methodism. His work, he wrote, attempted "to recognize the diversity of Methodist witness in various minority forms which continue to insist, and properly so, on the integrity of their own identity."[70] With more sophistication than any historian in the sample, Norwood made clear the distinctions of the early African Methodist congregations and of the denominational divisions that came out of them. These movements occurred in their own appropriate chronological slots, not as some afterthought as the story of Religious Reconstruction began. That was another story for Norwood, and in it CMEs naturally emerged.[71]

Unlike any previous historian, Norwood appreciated the black Methodist abolitionist witness, which he emphasized in the careers of Jermain Loguen, Harriet Tubman, Hosea Easton, Allen, and Coker. Consistent with his intention, Norwood had a larger multicultural view of Methodism—intersecting the black Methodist story with that of Native Americans, Hispanic Americans, German Americans, Scandinavian Americans, and "Oriental" [Asian] Americans with the generic "white" American constituency.[72]

Conclusion

Race has become metaphorical—a way of referring to and disguising forces, events, classes and expressions of social decay and economic division far more threatening to the body politic than biological "race" ever was. . . . racism is as healthy today as it was during the Enlightenment. It seems that it has a utility far beyond economy, beyond the sequestering of classes from one another, and has assumed a metaphorical life so completely embedded in daily discourse that it is perhaps more necessary and more on display than ever before.

Toni Morrison

Given the fact that African Methodism in all its varieties emerged within and alongside a British Protestant Christian system which had come out of Anglicanism in the late colonial and early national periods, these histories, collectively considered, were more inclusive of the black presence than I had assumed they would be. Their narrators may have known unconsciously without saying it, until Norwood emphasized it, that the African presence, to paraphrase Toni Morrison, "is inextricable from the definition of [American Methodism]—from its origins on through its integrated or disintegrating twentieth-century [identity]."[73]

At the same time there was a certain standardization in the accounts of the first generation, and some histories made little of the black presence. The stories most consistently to be remembered were of the careers of the most prominent of black male leaders, Hosier and Allen, and of the denominational separations in New York and Philadelphia. Because many of the histories were written after the Civil War, they often downplayed the actions of 1813–1822 in favor of telling how the independent African Methodist denominations had served the religious needs of the freedpeople. The histories rarely treated the African Union movement or the pre-Civil-War CMP story.

The historians knew only a little local African Methodist congregational history. They did not report in any comprehensive way the powerful spiritual witness of the early African converts in America. They sometimes cited statistical data, but never gave serious analysis to the numbers. They described, without protest, the color line separations—from the early classes, through the denominational schisms (1813–1870) and colored conferences in the MEC (sanctioned by the General Conference of 1876), to the formation of the Central Jurisdiction in the Methodist Church of 1939.

Ironically, for histories skewed to the M.E.-Methodist-United Methodist trajectory, they were the most silent about slave missions in the MEC and MECS traditions and about the separate M.E. congregations in Maryland, Delaware, Pennsylvania, and New York between 1813 and 1864. The failure of the M.E. General Conference to regularize conference membership for black clergy and their churches until 1864 was rooted in its inability between 1820 and 1828 to create an African Conference in order to retain the Zion or reattract the Bethel connections. None of the twentieth-century historians from Sweet, Luccock and Hutchinson, Ferguson and Norwood to Bucke knew Lewis Cox's 1917 work about many of the local black M.E. churches and their pastors.[74]

While the representation of black Methodists exceeded my assumptions prior to making this analysis, their story was consistently a secondary, minor motif in the larger drama of American Methodism. Its success correlated with the "white" westward movement, while Methodist strength in the segregated South into the 1960s remained constant. The European-American dominated Methodist saga occurred in tandem with how race was being constructed socially, economically, and politically in the United States. The key to that interaction was not the racial signifier "black" but "white"—the primary "melting pot" identifier for Europeans who were transcending their origins to become Americans.

From the time of the first Naturalization Act of 1790 until the Walter-McCarren Act of 1952 removed it, the category "white" was the norm for immigration law, and thus for access to citizenship for Europeans coming to the U.S.—35 million between 1820 and 1950. In those 162 years—notwithstanding the fourteenth and fifteenth amendments, the tradition of birthright citizenship, the states' rights challenges to nationally defined civil rights and citizenship, and dissent from African Americans, Spanish-speaking immigrants from the South, and Asian "strangers from a different shore" looking East—American citizenship was normatively a "white" phenomenon.

Understanding these developments may offer some clue why, this far removed from the Walter-McCarren Act and the Brown v. Board of Education Supreme Court decision two years later, and why, beyond the success of the Civil Rights/Black Freedom movement of the 1950s and 1960s, we—Americans and Methodists—agonize over race. Less than a generation past the Second Reconstruction, to use an American historical comparison—less than a generation past American Apartheid, to use the South African metaphor—we struggle with the ghosts of old identities when America was a white man's country.[75]

Given this context about who belonged and who counted racially in the American political community, given the close relationship between Methodism and the American social mainstream from the beginning, given how the construction of race is as self-referential as it is a description of "others," our historians pulled no surprises. The fact of the early black Methodist presence was difficult to ignore, though some did. The fact that most black Methodists separated either in 1813–22 or during Reconstruction into the independent denominations away from biracial fellowship, however limited, in the MEC—Methodist—United Methodist tradition allowed most of the historians to concentrate their focus on racial separation. Only the historians of the last three decades have had the experience, attempted nationally and not just sectionally during a First Reconstruction, of writing in a context of a national consensus that the U.S. is multiracial in its polity, definition of national community, and norms for citizenship.

Such a consensus in the nation or in the denomination is never without controversy. Like the quest for the inclusive church, it remains contested as Methodism enters the new century. Contemporary Methodists can celebrate the small victories of inclusion and expansion where they have occurred in the last two centuries. In doing so they can even link up with the white European-American male preachers of 1796, trying to imagine what it would take to envision "the pure church of God" today to be filled with all the "others" of our time. In that future the challenge will be to articulate a Methodist gospel where "in Christ" there are both male and female in gender diversity; descendants of slaves and of masters, of European dominators and of natives dispossessed of their land in terms of racial history; white and black and brown and red and yellow in color diversity; young and old in life-stage diversity; single, married, divorced, and widowed in relational diversity; gay and straight in sexual orientational diversity. Such a gospel will require an expansive enough Christ to embrace us all, giving good news that we have been made whole, restored to the image of God within us. Meanwhile, having come thus far "Playing in the Dark"—Methodist style, we remember the ancestors from 1796, and beseech heaven for all the wisdom we can obtain about how to have diversity which forges a new definition of unity, and how to have unity which nourishes diversity.

James M. Shopshire Sr.

Part of the task in addressing Gravely's concern is to recover some of the lost, obscured, or neglected aspects of American Methodist history. With regard to African Americans, this does not simply mean paying more attention to the predominantly black Methodist bodies such as the African Methodist Episcopal, the African Methodist Episcopal Zion, and the Colored Methodist Episcopal churches. It also means examining the histories of the African American presence in the predominantly white Methodist bodies.

Historian James Shopshire has opened the inquiry into one such community. The Methodist Protestant Church had its own institutional history for more than a century, and a significant part of its life was its African American constituency. Telling their story demands rigorous candor about the ways that this denomination's democratized polity managed, nevertheless, to adopt mostly segregationist policies. It also must recognize the willingness of the Methodist Protestants to find common ground with Methodist Episcopals (north and south) on attitudes toward race. This is a history that needs to be rediscovered, and it is an example of other ethnic minority stories that are woven into the fabric of American Methodism if not into its written histories.

In recalling this part of Methodist life, Shopshire gives singular attention to the Maryland Annual Conference, whose records suggest that congregations as well as the conference may have been integrated. The statistics he provides do more than recover neglected facts about our collective past. They also raise a contemporary question. Can a small, identified minority of persons in an integrated community become a real presence in the life of that community? Or are they inevitably going to be marginalized by the dominant culture?

Black People in the Methodist Protestant Church (1830–1939)

James M. Shopshire Sr.

Introduction

At a time when the hue and cry in the church is to forget the past and "don't worry, be happy" with our recent steps toward evangelical renewal and racial inclusiveness, this unapologetic effort is made to reconstruct the story of the presence and participation of black people in the Methodist Protestant Church. It is well nigh time for such a project which includes all of the positive and negative implications of those particular black experiences.

The stories of the independent African Methodist bodies and the black mission conferences of the Methodist Episcopal Church having been told and retold, precious little has been systematically reported about the individuals, the congregations, and the mission conferences of black people within the Methodist Protestant Church (1830–1939).

This endeavor focuses particularly, but not exclusively, on the perspectives and experiences of the black people who stayed despite all, and who wanted to be a part of the Methodist Protestant Church in the same ways as other Methodist Protestants. It has been suggested that black people in the Methodist Protestant Church were more interested in autonomy through Methodist Protestant structures than protest against the episcopal powers and lack of lay representation in the Methodist Episcopal Church. Be that as it may, the history of black presence in the larger structures and in their own congregations and conferences, designated "colored conferences," is part of the legacy of race and Methodism from 1830 to 1939 and extending all the way to the present time. The following segments give broad introduction to the matter of race in Methodism and in American culture and otherwise explore the Methodist Protestant Church in black and white.[1]

A Socio-Historical Perspective on Method

Religion functions to do many things for people in social groups. It helps people discover who they are and develop a sense of belongingness. The deepest sorrows and the greatest joys are borne by religion.

The patterned responses of religious belief and ritual as well as the organizations and processes that result compose the very stuff of survival, value formation, and meaning. Religion provides the energy for resistance to suffering, injustice, and oppressive forces of nature and humanity. Religion functions to help people cope with existence, to come to some understanding of what life is all about, and to find their way in a world that is composed of a strange mixture of law and mystery. Religion helps people to withstand the worst horrors and resist the worst tyrannies, to explain and adjust to whatever comes unavoidably or seems unchangeable. Religion functions as a forceful reality that defies explanation in purely rational terms—it supplies the spiritual and mystical dimensions of life—and at the same time religion is a social thing that interacts and, in some peculiar sense, validates the rational foundations of reality in the universe.

By the same token religion can dysfunction and become a destructive force that militates against what is best for humankind, against knowledge, truth, justice, and peace. When, instead of illumination, religion blinds people to the realities of life and directly subverts their well-being, it is a dysfunctional scourge upon the people. When instead of instilling hope and liberating people to aspire to the high calling of their faith, religion suppresses the will to survive, to create and responsibly develop the many resources of the world, it is destructive of the basic fabric of life and all that is inherent in the lively quest for freedom, justice, community, and general well-being.

In studying black Methodist Protestants during the years 1830 to 1939, the case can be made that the religion of African Americans who lived and participated in the Methodist Protestant movement, evidenced aspects of all of the above. As their story amply demonstrates, religious energy fueled the quest for survival with freedom, justice, and dignity in the larger social context of American society. Black people wanted to be free and wanted to be part of all that was good and just in the American experiment. It is a tribute to black people that so soon after the holocaust of American slavery, and with relatively little in terms of economic resources, political power, and social status, the work of organizing and building community was vigorously under way.

Among the already varied Methodist movements, African Americans found themselves joining with white Methodists in protest action that sought a different set of relationships and practices around the principal issues of lay representation, the election of presiding elders, and matters of governance. It is ironic, but not surprising, that black people became a movement within a movement in the Methodist Protestant Church in America.

It was a movement within a movement because the racially segregated structures of American society blindly extended to all social institutions and organizations. As has been amply documented, the churches were no exception. There was no resolve, either during slavery or in its wake, freely to accept African Americans with equity and dignity in the structures of churches principally organized by white people. Black people who might have been part of the Methodist Episcopal Church and who wanted to remain within the parent movement found themselves after 1844 in a split-off movement, the Methodist Episcopal Church, South, in which they were largely required to develop their own church organizations while participating, marginally at least, in the Methodist Protestant Church movement.

Black participation in the religious beliefs and practices that were part of the Methodist Protestant denomination appears to have had the overall effect of redirecting the energies of recently freed slaves away from the critical issues of survival and social and economic development in hostile and difficult times. But although they were indeed Methodist Protestants, they were forced, with one notable exception among the annual conferences, to be black or "Colored" Methodist Protestants.[?] African Americans who were in the Methodist Protestant movement represent another interesting and nearly neglected aspect of the experiences of black Methodists in America.

Therefore, the experiences of black Methodist Protestants will be reconstructed through the use of socio-historical method. The story will be told as it relates to the separate and segregated social contexts of African American people, but also in terms of the social contact and interaction with white Methodist Protestants in the mid-Atlantic, southeastern, and south central portions of the United States of America. This paper is neither comprehensive nor complete. It is an exploratory look at another interesting and nearly neglected aspect of the experiences of African Americans among the predecessor groups of the contemporary United Methodist Church. It focuses initially on the black Methodist Protestants in the predominantly white structures in the mid-Atlantic, northern, and western conferences of the Methodist Protestant Church. It continues by searching the questions why, when, and where did African American missionary structures come into being? It poses the question, what were black people protesting? It looks at the complex web of relationships among black and white Methodist Protestants in different parts of the nation. And finally, it seeks to consolidate and report what appear to be the important outcomes for black people in the Methodist Protestant Church up to the time the Methodist Church was organized in 1939, and to the present day.

Race and Methodism in American Society

Methodism developed parallel with the other American social, cultural, political, and economic structures. It was part and parcel of the democratically oriented spirit of the nation in which autonomism and pragmatism combined to forge new structure and order in the key institutions of the society. It is hardly coincidental that the Colonial period was the time of formation for Methodism as well as for national government. The Declaration of Independence came in 1776, and the founding conference of the Methodist Episcopal Church occurred eight years later in 1784. Ratification of the Constitution in 1787 is further indication that the nation and Methodism were part of the same socio-cultural movement.

One of the regrettable aspects of the movement is located in the already formed attitude of the nation toward the different racial groupings of humankind, especially toward black people. Although biological and other rationalizations were pressed into use, the idea of "race" was as much a social construct then as now. The Bible notwithstanding, the myth of racial superiority came with the European explorers and gained an early foothold on the North American continent. This happened despite the fact that among the self-evident truths of humankind, there was nothing to realistically justify the assumption by one segment of humanity that it was superior to all others.

Indeed, the Bible, the sacred writ of Christian religion, which overall points to the sanctity, dignity, and equality of all human beings under God, became the tool for staking the claim of white supremacy. The religion of white churches became the principal means of establishing the dehumanizingly contrived racism that infected what was and is convincingly one of the best experiments of humankind for ordering and governing social community. The taken-for-grantedness of white supremacy became attached to Christian and civil religious belief so firmly that it took on sacred meaning in the larger culture..

The idea of race, turned into the ideology of white supremacy, was operationalized and institutionalized as white racism. The combination of the two was lethal for black people and became the overwhelming flaw in the honesty and integrity of the founding documents of the American nation. The founding fathers, laden with racialist ideology and economic self-interest, could not agree that slaves (most of whom were black people by the late-eighteenth century) were full human beings (not 3/5 human), endowed by the creator with unalienable rights and entitled to humane treatment and the same rights as white people in the fledgling colonial entity that was trying to become the United States of America. As a result, the Constitution was compromised to exclude black people from full status as human beings in order to reach a defective agreement in the foundational document of the nation.

Unfortunately, the Methodist Episcopal Church became nearly a mirror image of the nation. The founding fathers of the church, in the very presence of black persons, reached essential agreement that dehumanizing slavery was wrong. They were resolute in their insistence that pastors could not be part of the Methodist Episcopal Church and be slave holders too. But their resolve was short lived.[3] The Methodist Episcopal Church and most of the offshoots from it capitulated to the white supremacy and racism bound up in slavery for the sake of unity of the church.

Slavery, segregation, and subversion of African Americans were not the only heated issues challenging Methodism in America. Questions of representation between clergy and laity along with dissatisfaction with an "all powerful" episcopacy were afoot during the same period of time.[4] The winds of discontent with episcopal government began almost immediately after the Christmas Conference of 1784. By the time of the annual conference of 1792 dissatisfaction with oppressive episcopal powers led to an attempt to curtail the power of bishops. The resolution calling for the right of preachers to appeal a bishop's appointment to the conference failed, and subsequently some of the elders and "several thousand members withdrew from the Methodist Episcopal Church.[5]

The year 1795 was another difficult year in dealing with issues pertaining to the powers of the bishops and the presiding elders. "Divisions" and "an uneasy and restless spirit" were present among the preachers and the lay members.[6] The preachers' concerns with the "lordly" powers of the bishops, and the lay members' growing concern that the episcopal and clergy hierarchy would leave them powerless with regard to the Methodist Episcopal Church became increasingly divisive elements of the fledgling denomination.

It was clear that bishops, presiding elders, and a legislative and executive Methodist Episcopal Church in which lay members were left outside with no voice would not be tolerated by the lay people. The surge of various "non-episcopal" groups of the protestant movement gave clear testimony that Methodist clergy and laity wanted to be freed from an unchecked oppressive episcopacy.

The Articles of Association adopted at the General Convention of 1828 make a telling point concerning the stance of the emergent Methodist Protestant Church on the issue of episcopal powers and representation. Most notably, Article VI provided for the organization of one or more annual conference in each state with the requirement of an equal number of ministers and lay delegates. Article VII provided for each annual conference to elect its own *president* and secretary. Article IX provided that each annual conference establish its own pattern of stationing preachers. Articles X through XIV further define the powers and responsibilities of annual conferences and the regulations and duties of preachers in charge. It is apparent that there was no place for bishops and presiding elders in the growing establishment of the Protestant Methodist reformers.

Perhaps the most telling action of the General Convention of 1828 relative to race-based chattel slavery was centered in Article XV, which asserted that "nothing stated in these Articles is to be so construed as to interfere with the right of property belonging to any member, as recognized by the laws of the State within the limits of which the member may reside."[7] This action was the rough equivalent of previous action taken by the Methodist Episcopal Church, in 1784, and in the compromises that were deemed necessary to preserve the unity of that body. Although it is reported that portions of the delegation from the North objected, those from the slave-holding states composed three-fourths of the members of the Convention[8] when this morally objectionable Article was adopted. Compromise of the humanity and the rights of African American slaves had become a matter of record.

Noted historian Edward J. Drinkhouse maintains regarding Article XV: "There was no concealment of its purpose: the protection of slave property in the Southern states. The motives of the author need not be impugned. By him it was intended as a peace measure so far as the infant Church was concerned."[9]

Similar to the slavery issue, over which black people—preachers and lay members—departed to start their own related but autonomous organizations and white "gentlemen" felt compelled to compromise in order to maintain unity in the church, governance issues also began to fractionalize the Methodist Episcopal church within the first decade of its existence. It appears that maintaining church unity in the presence of polity issues was more important than having unity in facing the issue of slavery. An indication of this is the fact that 60 years passed before the major split occurred over slavery (1784 to 1844). The minor fractures in matters of governance, notwithstanding, a major fracture regarding the issues of powers of the episcopacy and lay representation came after only 44 years (1784–1828).

Documentation exists but is spotty with reference to the *participation* of black ministers or lay persons in the early Methodist Protestant movement. This does not dissuade one from the view that black people were there, even if on the margins, from the beginning of the Protestant discontent over governance. What becomes necessary is to locate specific actions and passing references by historians of the movement and in some cases to read between the lines to gain perspective on how African American people participated in the movement.

Hence, the presence and participation of black people in the Protestant wing of the Methodist movement can be summarized as follows: It appears to be the case that African Americans were present and active in the developmental conventions of the non-episcopal Protestant Methodists during the decade of the 1820s. They were present, as occasionally documented, as representatives to the General Conferences and in some of the annual conferences. They were present among the first foreign missionaries of the denomination. They certainly were present in the "colored" missionary conferences of the southern region of the nation. The following section concerns their patterns of participation in the Methodist Protestant Church.

The Methodist Protestant Church's Relationship to Black Members

There were three general categories in which the presence and participation of black Methodist Protestants could be located. First was the individual participation of black people in congregations that were predominantly white. Second was the specific reference to individuals who served as ministers or lay representatives to general or annual conferences or who were missionaries in the "foreign" missions of the church. Third was the general statistical reference to the number of people in congregations of the "colored" mission conferences. A closer look at each of the three categories is necessary. But prior to that, an excursus is necessary to identify what General Conferences of Methodist Protestants deemed appropriate in relating to black people.

Decisions on how to relate to African Americans came early in the proceedings of this offshoot Methodist Protestant denomination. The first *Discipline,* published in 1831, had this to say about how the newly formed church would deal with black people.

> iv. 3. Each annual conference shall have exclusive power to make its own rules and regulations for the admission and government of coloured members within its district; and to make for them such terms of suffrage as the conferences respectively deem proper.

> But neither the general conference nor any annual conference shall assume power to interfere with the constitutional powers of the civil governments, or with the operations of the civil laws; yet, nothing herein contained shall be so construed as to authorize or sanction any thing inconsistent with the morality of the holy scriptures. . . .[10]

Given the agitation against slavery that existed in segments of the newly organized Methodist Protestant Church, especially among the northern and western conferences, such a resolution represented a pragmatic arrangement. It also constituted a compromise with the conferences located in the slave-holding states of the South.

The first paragraph quoted above allowed that black people could be received into the church. Their membership was second class, to the extent that separate and more restrictive rules and regulations were imposed for black people than for white. The second paragraph was virtually a pledge of allegiance to the civil governments to make certain that Methodist Protestants would not interfere with or challenge the institution of slavery in those places where it clearly had government sanction.

A Case in Point: Black Methodist Protestants in the Maryland District

The historical journals of the Methodist Protestant conferences are sprinkled with casual references that acknowledge the presence of African Americans. However, the most explicit early references to black presence and participation in the Methodist Protestant movement among the annual conferences, are found in the proceedings of the Maryland Annual Conferences dating from 1832 and extending to the end of the Methodist Protestant Church in 1939.

Returning to the three categories of interracial contact, the Maryland Conference is again the focal point. Beginning in 1832, the Maryland Conference journal included a column for "whites"and "coloreds" and a total membership column. Thus far, no other conference has been located that made such a concerted effort to show that African Americans were in the church. As the appended table on "African Americans affiliated with the Maryland Annual Conference" illustrates, there were mixed but predominantly black congregations as well as mixed but predominantly white congregations. From 1832 to

1889 the "colored" membership was nearly always reported in the conference journals of the Maryland Annual Conference.

The table in Appendix I shows that after the Civil War there is a precipitous drop in black members reported. A plausible hypothesis is that the changes in the society brought on by the war led black people either to go to the African Methodist Churches or to seek to organize autonomous conferences and congregations. This very likely was the case in the southern region of the nation and in the Maryland conference. There is scant indication that a "Colored Association" continued as a viable organization in the Maryland Conference The infrequent reports from the Colored Association of Maryland were discontinued altogether after the beginning of the special relationship of Maryland Methodist Protestants to black Methodist Protestants in South Carolina.

A second category is that of black leadership or participation in the general church. Occasional reports are contained in the historical record of special endeavors pertaining to black people. Take for example the report on the beginning of foreign mission work at the Centennial Session of the General Conference of the Methodist Protestant Church in Baltimore, 16 May 1928.

> Since it is generally conceded that the place of Missions in church life is central, it is very fitting that a paper, dealing with the history of our missionary work, should have a place in this centennial program. . . .
>
> . . . Much is said of other departments of our church work, but all three of our historians, Williams, Bassett and Drinkhouse, are strangely silent on the beginnings of "Our Obedience to the Great Command."
>
> At that Conference [1834] a Board of Foreign Missions was elected, consisting of twelve members with Rev. S. K. Jennings as chairman. Baltimore was chosen as the headquarters of the Board. Very naturally the first task of this Board was the choice of a missionary field and the securing of missionaries. Somehow the mind of the Board was turned to Africa. A possible reason for this may have been the presence in Cecil County, Md., of a society of about twenty colored folks, ministered to by a colored brother named James.
>
> At least in 1837 we find the Board sending this colored minister, with a number of his people to Liberia, on the west coast of Africa, to found there a Methodist Protestant Mission.[11]

Curiously, in a conference so strongly opposed to slavery, this report seems to reflect affinity to the colonization society as a solution to the problem of white people. Returning black people to Africa was to be desired over fulfilling the national and Christian ideals of living together with freedom and equality for all people."[12] Additional study is needed to get beneath the surface issue of returning African Americans to Africa in the early foreign mission work of the Methodist Protestant Church.

In the same section of the Centennial volume reference is made to a young black woman whose expenses were paid by a successful white businessman to go to Oberlin College. After graduation she "married a young man of her own race," and went in 1846 with her husband to the Mendi Mission on the coast of Liberia.[13]

Other such categorical experiences can be seen in the mention of the Reverend Thomas Wells of Baltimore, the first "colored" person to be seated as a representative to the General Conference.[14]

A third category is the organization of connectional structures for black people. Early in the history of the Methodist Protestant Church, enabling legislation was passed to make it possible for African Americans to form their own societies, after a certain number of persons were gathered to form a group. This was accompanied with the privilege to call a "colored" or a white minister to lead that congregation.[15] The most clear-cut area of development of connectional structures was in the formation of mission annual conference for black people.

Considerable research must be done to reconstruct the whole of the black Methodist Protestant movement. Five "colored" mission conferences have been identified—Alabama, Arkansas, Colorado-Texas, Georgia, and South Carolina. There were others for which no archival materials are yet available. The statistics on mission conferences reported in the *Journal of the Eighteenth Quadrennial Session General Conference of the Methodist Protestant Church*, which met at Atlantic City, New Jersey, 18–26 May 1900, contained eight "colored" mission conferences (p. 128):

Alabama (colored)	Colorado-Texas (colored)
Arkansas (colored)	Dallas (colored)
Baltimore (colored)	North Georgia (colored)
Charleston (colored)	Spring Creek (colored)

On page 129, under Sunday school statistics, a "Southern Georgia (col'd)" conference is reported. One annual conference journal for this conference has be located. As far as the writer can determine, the southern Georgia conference was a related part of the north Georgia group called the Georgia Conference (Colored) of the Methodist Protestant Church. Much detail remains to be uncovered concerning the group of churches in south Georgia around Savannah, Brunswick, Valdosta and as far west as Thomasville, Georgia in Brooks County.

In Volume 2 of Edward J. Drinkhouse's *History of Reform and the Methodist Protestant Church, 1820–1898*, several other references are made to (Colored) annual conferences. Page 499 refers to a "North Carolina (Colored)" conference. Drinkhouse observes on page 581: "Colored Conferences were also organized under the reconstructed Discipline in Maryland, Alabama, Georgia, Texas, and South Carolina."

A footnote on page 587 of Drinkhouse's second volume notes that at the Thirteenth General Conference of the Methodist Protestant Church, which met in Pittsburgh in May of 1880, the "Baltimore Mission Conference (colored) was represented by Thomas Wells." Georgia's G. M. Bargt (a misspelling of Barge), and James Smith were noted as absent. Drinkhouse observes on the next page that "Rev. Thomas Wells (colored), representative messenger from Baltimore, was the first of his race to sit in such a body of the Church; and he was recognized by all sections alike."

In the fourteenth and fifteenth General Conferences of the Methodist Protestant Church (1884 and 1888) "Colored," ministers and laymen representatives were recognized from the Baltimore and Georgia (Colored) Conferences (Drinkhouse 2:613, 634). At the sixteenth General Conference, representatives of the Alabama, Baltimore, Charleston, S.C., and Georgia (colored) Conferences were certified (Drinkhouse 2:653, 656).

At the seventeenth General Conference, held in Kansas City in 1896, representatives were certified from the Colorado (Texas Colored) and South Georgia (Colored) Conferences (Drinkhouse 2:671, 673). The considerable gaps in information for the last decade of the nineteenth century make it difficult to determine if the pattern of certifying and including black ("colored") people at the General Conferences of the Methodist Protestant Church had a significant carryover at the level of the Southern Methodist Protestant annual conferences.

At the present time there are limited holdings at the General Commission on Archives and History at Drew and at Wesley Theological Seminary in Washington, D.C. (the only seminary of the Methodist Protestant Church and probably the place with the most extensive archival holdings on the Methodist Protestant Church). Between those two locations the following assorted years of "minutes" of the five "colored" mission conferences represent the complete holdings on black Methodist Protestant conferences:

Georgia.. 12
Colorado-Texas......................... 8
Alabama 1
Arkansas.................................... 1
South Carolina 6

Black Presence Within the Structures of the Methodist Protestant Church

It should come as no surprise that black people were sympathetic to and involved in the Methodist Protestant movement as well as the movement that gave rise to the Methodist Episcopal Church. The strong appeal of Methodism to black people was present in the various sectarian fractures. In addition to the assessment of black people that the emerging structures of churches in the Wesleyan tradition misappropriated the biblical principle that all people (men) were equal under God, black people were singing, praying, and thinking about theology and polity.

Because of their status as non-people in the sight of American white Christian churches and society, and due to the fact that the life of a black person was not valued, radical statements and precipitous actions concerning the church were not readily made by African Americans. Except for those who decided to form independent African Methodist churches in order to be Methodist without the weight of "black peoples' burden,"[16] those who remained in the Methodist Episcopal Church lived out of the hope that God would change the wrongs and make them right. Looking in retrospect at the experiences of black people, that hope bordered on the absurd.

The presence of "colored" members of predominantly white Methodist Protestant Churches is illustrated most notably by the reports of the Maryland Annual Conference of the Methodist Protestant Church over many years. For example, the statistical section of the Minutes of 1864 contains a column for the "Col'd Members," as do the Minutes for each year from 1832 until 1864. In the year before the end of the Civil War 102 black members are indicated.[17] When the separate column for "colored" and "white" was discontinued, the two special South Carolina circuits that were associated with the Maryland Annual Conference continued to be listed at the end of the report. The seven circuits, stations, and missions reporting black people in their membership were as follows:

	Black	White	Churches
Alexandria	1	120	1
West Baltimore	2	261	6
Cambridge	1	35	3
Harmony	69	179	4
New Town	1	310	7
Pipe Creek	18	376	4
Snow Hill	10	104	4
	102	1,385	30

In the same year the "*Charleston, S.C. Station" was listed, with no membership statistics and with the secretary's note that "Those marked thus * were not heard from."[18]

Enabling Legislation for the Organization of "Colored" Annual Conferences

The Montgomery, Alabama, Convention of 1867 is notable for its effort to provide for "colored conferences" in the Methodist Protestant Church. It appears that the action of this convention set the stage for the formal organization of the "colored" mission conferences as separate bodies related to the General Conference. The Civil War had ended, and the first of the Reconstruction acts passed by Congress took place less than two months before the Montgomery Convention. Typically, no thought was given to the idea of churches and annual conference open to all regardless of race. Instead, this convention got very serious about enabling "colored" conferences.

> A movement was inaugurated for the appointment of a Conference Missionary in each of the Conferences where needed, to "organize the colored people into societies for instruction and evangelization, as shall comport with the genius of the Methodist Protestant Church, and for the formation of Annual Conferences of their own under the style of. . . ." It was further amended: it is highly desirable that we retain our colored membership in our own connection" etc. Under this encouragement various conference of the colored brethren were organized, and a number now exist in the south.[19]

The reconstructed *Discipline* of 1867 set the stage for the General Conference of 1880 to enable the independent organization of mission conferences among African Americans, primarily in the South. A brief sketch of the historic development of "colored" mission conferences in each of five states follows.

A. Alabama

There is virtually no information for Alabama at the present time. Only one conference journal has been located (1932). The identification of church locations across the Black Belt of Alabama, following along highway 14 from Selma north of Montgomery to Wetumpka is the extent of the work thus far. The identification of surviving congregations and exploration of the North Alabama Conference are seen as next steps in fleshing out the socio-historic development of the "Colored" Methodist Conference in Alabama.

B. Arkansas

Although the *General Conference Journal* indicates that a "colored" conference was formed in Arkansas, data is not available to construct an information base for this state. Much work remains to be done concerning black Methodist Protestants in this state to determine the places and congregations that existed, their relative strength, and the level of participation that they maintain in the larger structures of the Methodist Protestantism.

C. Texas (Colorado-Texas)

Only limited data is available on the Colorado Texas Conference. Eight of the colored conference journals have been located, and there are many leads that give indication that future work will allow considerable reconstruction of the development and history of this conference.

D. Georgia

More material is available and more exploratory work has been done on Georgia than any of the other African American missionary conferences. The "Colored" Annual Conference of Georgia was organized by the authority of the forty-seventh Georgia annual conference of the Methodist Protestant Church [White] in its 2–6 November 1877 session in Poplar Springs (Clayton County, Georgia).[20]

Only a year earlier the forty-sixth annual conference of the Methodist Protestant Church of Georgia had formed the Sandy Creek Mission for Blacks which included "Bethlehem, Sandy Creek and surrounding country."[21] There are indications that the black congregations were already organized before they were designated "colored missions" of the white Methodist Protestant Church of Georgia. The following statement lends additional support to the claim:

> Rev. James Robinson, who was received as a delegate from the Colored mission at this conference, was appointed to the Sandy Creek Mission as

Superintendent, and Rev. Silas Montgomery was appointed as his assistant. (Rev. George Barge was appointed to the Campbellton Circuit, which included Zion, Rocky Head, and Poplar Spring)[22]

Hence, the black churches or charges apparently were already formed and functioning. The White Methodist Protestant Annual Conference of Georgia simply helped to constitute the missions and circuits into an organization that became the Georgia Annual Conference of the Methodist Protestant Church (Colored).

The congregations in the Georgia movement had their beginning in the decade of 1870s (or earlier) after the end of what has been termed "Radical Reconstruction" by some historians. The evidence indicates that, from the beginning, the black congregations of Methodist Protestantism were organized by black people for black people, but the "Colored" Methodist Protestant Annual Conference was organized with the assistance of white people in the Georgia Conference of the Methodist Protestant denomination. Placed in perspective, this was not a unique development, as the other white Methodist bodies and other denominations were "solving their race problem" by forming similar segregated structures.

From 1877, when the independent Black Methodist Protestant Conference was organized with the Henry Mission, the Campbellton Circuit, and the Sandy Creek Mission, the matter of autonomy was addressed for black people in Georgia who wanted to be Methodist Protestants. At the same time, the matter of maintaining racial segregation was addressed for Whites.

Although relatively small throughout its history over six decades, the African American branch of the Methodist Protestant Church in Georgia was a viable annual conference organization. Available records show that over the history of its existence the number of congregations and mission of the annual conference did not exceed 20 in North Georgia. If one incudes the South Georgia contingent, that number nearly doubles.

The *Minutes of the Tenth Session of the Georgia Annual Conference of the Methodist Protestant Church (Colored)*, convened in Smith's Chapel, at Ivey's Station, Wilkinson County, 19 October 1887, list the location and dates of the first ten annual conference sessions on p. 4:

ANNUAL SESSIONS

	Place	Time	President	Secretary
1	Rockhead*	Oct. 31, '78	G. N. Barge	J. T. Robison*
2.	Bethlehem	Dec. 13, '79	G. N. Barge	J. T. Robison
3.	Rockhead*	Dec. 9, '80	G. N. Barge	S. D. Wilson
4.	Friendly Hill	Nov. 10, '81	G. N. Barge	J. W. Whittaker
5.	Poplar Springs	Nov. 9, '82	G. N. Barge	I. C. Robison*
6.	Atlanta	Nov. 7, '83	J. T. Robison*	W. E. Spain
7.	Macedonia	Nov. 4, '84	J. T. Robison*	W. E. Spain
8.	Atlanta	Nov. 4, '85	J. T. Robison*	W. E. Spain
9.	Campbellton	Nov. 17, '86	J. T. Robison*	W. E. Spain
10.	Smith's Chapel	Oct. 19, '87	E. Henry	W. E. Spain

*= Spelling differs in several places, and appears to be in error here. J. T. Robinson is the correct name above. Rocky Head instead of Rockhead appears in several of the Minutes.

The printed minutes and records of the Methodist Protestant Georgia Annual Conference (Colored) offer virtually no written reports with reference to the social, cultural, political, and economic condition of African Americans located in a segregated Southern state dominated by Whites. In "post-Reconstruction" Georgia, it was probably the better part of wisdom not to publish statements representing the real attitudes toward racial segregation and subordination in the church and society.

Even after the turn of the century and into the 1930's, the pattern persisted of simply reporting on devotions, scripture titles and hymns, or resolutions pertaining to operations and finance. For example, consider this typical report from p. 12 of the *Minutes of the Fifty-first Session of the Annual Conference of the Methodist Protestant Church (Colored) of Georgia* convened at Rocky Head, M.P. Church, Ben Hill, Ga., 20–24 November 1929.

Friday Night

7:20 o'clock, Bro. E. L. Green led devotions. Lined Hymns 307 and 312. Bros. J. W. Wheat and J. C. Mangram led in prayer. Revs. C. Mangram and E. L. Hickson ascended the rostrum. Rev. C. Mangram lined Hymn 307. Rev. E. L. Hickson arose and selected the text—Daniel 1st chapter and 8th verse. With much power he demonstrated the work intrusted to him. Rev. C. Mangram closed, lining hymn 312. The President led in prayer. The stewards came and collected $2.05.

We stood adjourned.

A few general observations are in order concerning the Methodist Protestant Church (Colored) in Georgia. First, the number of ordained elders who were eligible for conference membership tended to outnumber the missions and circuits that were available for them to serve. It is readily acknowledged that additional study needs to be made of the way ministers were assigned to serve. However, a review of the *Minutes* reveals no distinct pattern. In some years, a number of circuits and missions were not assigned a minister who was a member of the conference and, therefore, had to depend on the services of local preachers or other substitutes. In other years it appears that the stronger churches or circuits received not only what appeared to be the strongest ordained pastoral leadership, but also the benefit of assistant ministers. It is not clear whether those assistant pastors were ordained members of the Annual Conference or lay preachers. The category of "unstationed ministers" was defined by the practices of the annual conference.

Second, the status and role of black women were de-emphasized in the Colored Methodist Protestant Conference of Georgia. In this regard, it appears no different to most Methodist and Baptist churches of the period in the exclusion of women as ministers, relegating them to fund raising, missionary work, and Sunday school work. Although documentation is lacking, it is very likely that women were recognized as evangelists and exhorters but not as pastors, ministers, and preachers.

Third, there were typically Methodist concerns and practices that were carefully attended in the Georgia Conference (Colored) of the Methodist Protestant Church. For example, temperance was emphasized in virtually every annual conference session. In the *Minutes of the Thirty-eighth Session of the Georgia Annual Conference of the Methodist Protestant Church Colored, of Georgia* held in Bethlehem Church, Adamsville, Ga., 16–19 Nov. 1916, a short report was made that gives insight into the social consciousness of black Methodist Protestants in Georgia. The following was given under the heading "temperance."

> We, your Committee, beg to report: Seeing how intemperance is dragging our people down, ruining homes and reducing churches, we beg our people to look high and help save our race. Respectfully submitted, Rev. R. B. Butler, Rev. W. H. D. Gilbert, Rev. S. Mayo, James T. Thurmon, W. F. Davis.[23]
>
> Adopted.

In the year 1925, the *Minutes of the Forty-Seventh Session* indicate that the Conference received the following report from the Committee on Temperance:

> Mr. President and Conference: We, your Committee on Temperance, beg to make this our report:

We recommend that all ministers, preachers, and members refrain from strong drinks, alcoholic or any habits that point downward. Let them act as becomes the saints of God. Be sober, kind, loving and virtuous, true at home and abroad, that their Christian influence may win souls and bring them to Christ, and the church will be an edifice and God will bless our labor.

Respectfully submitted, Rev. W. H. White, Rev. J. W. Robinson, T. M. Varner, G. N. Barge, C. W. Williams.[24]

The Temperance Committee was a standing committee of the Annual Conference as set forth in the Rules of Order. The "Rules" for the Ninth Session of the Georgia Methodist Protestant Conference (Colored) were stated as follows:

COMMITTEES

4.   All Committees shall be appointed by the President, except when otherwise directed in the Book of Discipline or by special vote of the Conference.

5.   Unfinished business—one minister and two laymen.

6.   Finance—three ministers and two laymen.

7.   Itineracy and Orders—three ministers.

8.   Boundaries—seven laymen.

9.   Publication of Minutes—the Secretary.

10. Temperance—three ministers and two laymen.

11. Official Character—three ministers and two laymen.

12. Statistics—one minister and one layman[25]

The committee structure shown above was largely maintained throughout the history of the Black Methodist Protestant Conference in Georgia. Slight variations were made over the years, mainly in terminology, but not function.

Statistics were important enough to merit a Standing Committee in the Annual Conference. The penchant for record keeping was not lost in the "Colored" Protestant Conference of Georgia. A note on page 11 of the *Minutes of the Sixth Annual Conference* encouraged the following: "Brethren, please bring in your papers and statistical reports next term more plainly written than they were before; I may be able to make a more correct minute than this is, Yours sincerely, William E. Spain secretary of conference." Despite what appear to be typographical errors and inconsistencies in the Minutes, the location of statistical records and data may afford a near complete set of information for the 62 years of the Black Methodist Protestant Conference in Georgia.

Education was another continuing concern of the Black Methodist Protestant Conference in Georgia. An education committee was not maintained among the standing committees over the years. Financial concerns with education came often, to which direct responses were made. Support to a theological school is mentioned in several of the conference *Minutes*. The school is not named. A "Literature Committee" is included among the standing committees in the mature years of the Black Methodist Protestant (Colored) Conference. The primary function seems to have been to promote the use of Sunday school and other literature from the Methodist Protestant Publishing Board.

It seems fitting to characterize the cultural agenda as a "split agenda" in the Black Methodist Protestant Conference in Georgia. Such a statement takes into consideration the variety of observable practices and emphases that constituted the way of life for the conference. Temperance was emphasized, as was the case with most Methodist bodies. The same was true for the importance given to maintaining records and statistics, as well as supporting Christian educational endeavors. All the three emphases just mentioned had their roots in Methodism and, therefore, represented the deep attachment of African American people in Georgia to values of the Methodist cultural agenda.

There was another agenda in the practices and procedures of black Methodist Protestants, more subtle, and yet, no less real. That agenda was concerned with survival and accomplishment in times that can only be characterized as hostile for African American people. There were several allusions to things that do detriment to a people, alcholic beverages and other "habits that point downward." Other matters come to light only when the fuller situation in life is considered. The weight of white supremacy and racism on black people was not reflected in the *Minutes* and written records of the conference. The silence of the conference on what was a critical life and death matter reflected the risks and realities of the struggle for survival and social development.

How, then, was the cultural agenda of black people expressed? I maintain that it was expressed in the patterns of worship and praise, and in association and development that echoed the work of the antebellum "Invisible Institution" and the "Underground Railroad." Although deradicalized in the Wilmorian sense,[26] the black Methodist Protestants of Georgia took the opportunity for autonomy and moved on to develop their own organization around some of their vital interests.

Although the content of the worship services and sermons are not available on the written record, the importance of the Bible, the preaching, the worship services, the conference gatherings and the official responsibilities, and to a degree, the caring for the life of the people, is evident in the *Minutes* of each of the conference sessions.

Thus, the split cultural agenda was carried in the full range of experiences of the people, in the blackness and the Methodist-ness of the African American people in the Methodist Protestant movement of Georgia.[27]

E.   South Carolina (and the Maryland connection)

The South Carolina Conference of the Methodist Protestant Church presents an interesting case different from the others. The historical records indicate that the majority of members of the first Methodist Protestant Conference in South Carolina were black or so-called "colored." The president of the Conference in 1881, R. M. Pickens, submitted the following early historical account:

> The first conference was organized with nine hundred and fifty-one members, most of them colored, and seven hundred and fifty-seven belonged to Charleston Station. The second conference reported: Whites, three hundred and ninety-three; colored, seven hundred and sixty-five; in all, one thousand one hundred and fifty-eight, of which eight hundred and sixty-two pertained to Charleston. In 1850, Charles Church was transferred to the Maryland Conference, leaving the South Carolina Conference with six hundred and twenty-eight white members and sixty-two colored. The reports, after this, show small increase until [the] time of the war. And though there was no suspension, yet the conference was so disorganized that when proper reports were made, only about seven hundred and fifty white persons were reported. For a while there was one colored church, which has since been lost sight of. Alexander McCaine was twice, or more, president of this conference, and he was its first ministerial representative to the General Conference (1842).[28]

This sketch is informative, but also leaves unanswered several interesting questions about the Charleston Church, the predominantly black majority around which Methodist Protestantism apparently got its start in South Carolina. Why did the Charleston Church have a longstanding connection to the Maryland Conference? What happened to cause the fraternal relationship and statistical reporting of the black South Carolina churches to end in 1889? Who was Alexander McCaine, and why do references to him disappear from the record after ten years of service, during which time he was "twice or more, president of this conference, and . . . its first ministerial representative to the General Conference (1842)"?[29] Was Alexander McCaine a white minister or black? Is the reference to an Alexander McCaine on p. 8 of the *Minutes of the Maryland Annual Conference of the Associated Methodist Churches* of 1830 the same person referred to above as the first ministerial representative to the General Conference of 1842?

No doubt the answers to these questions rest somewhere in the record and perhaps will be found through more focused research. For the time being, only a sketchy glimpse of Blacks in the South Carolina Conference is available.[30]

From this point, a leap is made to look at the South Carolina Colored Conference of the Methodist Protestant Church. Although conference journals probably were published from 1890 to 1939 for this "Colored" Methodist Protestant Conference, consecutive annual journals have not been discovered so far.

Some type of relationship of the South Carolina Colored Conference to the Maryland Conference was apparently maintained up to the time of the 1939 merger/absorption. As the minutes of the 50th session show, J. H. Straughn, General Conference President of the Methodist Protestant Church, was present at the session. At one point he took the chair during the election of the annual conference president for the ensuing year. Straughn also was given the opportunity to deliver a message concerning the impending merger of the three Methodist bodies.[31]

By way of summary it can be observed that historical records concerning African Americans in the South Carolina Conference of the Methodist Protestant Church are few and difficult to locate. The various archival centers at Claflin College, Spartanburg, S.C., Lake Junaluska, and other places in the Southeastern Jurisdiction have had little to offer.

Concluding Summary

The story now begins to emerge. Black people not only were present but were marginal participants in the life of the Methodist Protestant Church in America. Freedom to participate varied in direct relationship to the proportion of black people in the congregations and conferences of the denomination. Although much more remains to be uncovered, it is apparent that common ground was accompanied by wide gaps in the beliefs and practices of black and white Methodist Protestants. And while a strong and vocal group of Whites believed that the institution of slavery was fundamentally wrong, they could not carry the day against the southern brethren who sought to justify and profit from the "peculiar institution."

White resistance notwithstanding, it is increasingly clear that the similarities of response to slavery and race among the three major, predominantly white Methodist organizations were greater than the differences. Unity was always more important than equity between African Americans and European Americans.

With continued research, a much more revealing story can be told. And although the predecessor Methodist Protestant phase of our history lies far behind us in time, it is informative to know the story in both its honorable and dishonorable dimensions. It is important to celebrate the former black Methodist Protestant congregations that survive as part of the United Methodist Church. And finally, it is redemptive to use the story to help engage in the continuing struggle for unity in a denominational church and global society that are pressed to move toward community which transcends racial-ethnic differences.

APPENDIX 1

African Americans Affiliated with the Maryland Annual Conference
The Methodist Protestant Church (1831–1889)

Year	# "Colored" Members	"Colored" Assoc.	# in SC	# in MD	# White Members	Total Members	% "Col'rd" Members
1832	9		0	9	2,126	2,135	0.4%
1833	90		0	90	3,198	3,288	2.7%
1834	81		0	81	4,146	4,227	1.9%
1835	95		0	95	3,898	3,993	2.4%
1836							
1837	124		0	124	3,494	3,618	3.4%
1838	144		0	144	3,753	3,897	3.7%
1839	145		0	145	4,244	4,389	3.3%
1840	150		0	150	4,915	5,065	3.0%
1841	148		0	148	5,692	5,840	2.5%
1842	334	132	0	466	6,907	7,241	4.6%
1843	497		0	497	8,959	9,456	5.3%
1844	388		0	388	8,672	9,060	4.3%
1845	509	134	0	509	8,352	8,861	5.7%
1846	642	183	0	642	8,502	9,144	7.0%
1847	186		0	186	6,780	6,966	2.7%
1848	171		0	171	6,761	6,932	2.5%
1849	39		0	39	5,477	5,516	0.7%
1850	324	183	0	324	6,023	6,347	5.1%
1851	753		600	153	6,821	7,574	9.9%
1852	775		653	122	6,509	7,284	10.6%
1853	917		750	167	6,686	7,603	12.1%
1854	950		750	200	6,796	7,746	12.3%
1855	835		702	133	6,758	7,593	11.0%
1856	701		549	152	6,634	7,335	9.6%
1857	688		575	113	6,468	7,156	9.6%
1858	752		600	152	6,375	7,127	10.6%
1859	723		539	184	7,149	7,872	9.2%
1860	736		550	186	7,814	8,550	8.6%
1861	735		600	135	7,870	8,605	8.5%
1862	668		550	118	8,056	8,724	7.7%
1863	656		550	106	6,930	7,586	8.6%

Year	# "Colored" Members	"Colored" Assoc.	# in SC	# in MD	# White Members	Total Members	% "Col'rd" Members
1864	102		0	102	7,302	7,404	1.4%
1865	37		0	37	7,604	7,641	0.5%
1866	4		0	4	7,864	7,868	0.1%
1867	4		0	4	8,874	8,878	0.0%
1868	6		0	6	9,669	9,675	0.1%
1869	19		0	19	9,958	9,977	0.2%
1870	332		327	5	10,827	11,159	3.0%
1871	349		327	22	11,435	11,784	3.0%
1872	192		190	2	12,186	12,378	1.6%
1873	282		280	2	10,613	10,895	2.6%
1874	273		270	3	11,824	12,097	2.3%
1875	282		280	2	11,938	12,220	2.3%
1876	282		280	2	11,806	12,088	2.3%
1877	311		305	6	11,806	12,117	2.6%
1878	292		291	1	12,290	12,582	2.3%
1879	660		660	0	12,958	13,618	4.8%
1880	985		985	0	13,995	14,980	6.6%
1881	974		974	0	14,473	15,447	6.3%
1882	977		977	0	14,000	14,977	6.5%
1883	884		884	0	13,490	14,374	6.1%
1884	924		924	0	14,548	15,472	6.0%
1885	940		940	0	15,149	16,089	5.8%
1886	926		926	0	15,042	15,968	5.8%
1887	953		953	0	15,332	16,285	5.9%
1888	1083		1083	0	17,162	18,245	5.9%
1889	1041		1041	0	17,870	18,911	5.5%

Note 1: Zeros ("0") indicate no Black members reported and not necessarily that there were no Black Methodist Protestant members in Maryland or South Carolina.

Note 2: No report could be located for the year 1836.

Note 3: The table above was compiled by James M. Shopshire Sr, using the Minutes of the Maryland Annual Conference of the Methodist Protestant Church.

Stephen S. Kim

The foregoing analyses (and those in Connectionalism, *the first volume in this series*) have demonstrated repeated similarities between the dominant patterns of American culture and the elements that characterize United Methodism in America. What do studies of our missionary outreach indicate about the relationship between church and culture? Stephen Kim, a theologian and professor of world religions, poses that question to a specific missionary endeavor of the church.

In the late-nineteenth and early-twentieth centuries, Methodists were among the many missionaries who introduced Christianity to Korea. Historically, this effort coincided with western cultural and colonial expansion into Asia. Theologically, it connected Methodism and American culture in ways that tended to demean Korean culture, such as by misrepresenting respect for deceased forebears as ancestor worship. Ethically, it confused many Koreans by suggesting that in order to expand their trade and develop their economy they must model their Christianity after their economic partners in the west.

But Kim does more than review a problematic period in Methodist mission history. He also suggests that the episode is indicative of a continuing flaw in our theological perspective. If we limit ourselves to a theology received from within the culture that we occupy, then our doctrine will be unnecessarily narrow, our evangelism will be corrupt, and our outreach will lack integrity.

Yet how can the church be effectively detached from a culture in order to distinguish the holy faith from the human form in which it has taken shape? How can theological work respect diversity without merely casting itself adrift on a sea of differing human experience? How might theological education be changed in order to assist future generations of church leaders to function from a global point of view?

There is no doubt that a defining characteristic of the peoples called Methodist is their commitment to mission outreach. Kim's study of one episode in our missionary history looks back to our past and poses compelling questions about our commitment to be faithful in the future.

Methodist Missions to Korea: A Case Study in Methodist Theology of Mission and Culture

Stephen S. Kim

The Methodist Episcopal Church's missionary enterprises to Korea in the late-nineteenth century can be considered an unparalleled success in terms of both numeric growth and the Church's contribution to the modernization and emancipation of Korea. Some one hundred and ten years since the arrival of the first Protestant missionaries in Korea, the number of Protestant converts has reached nearly one quarter of the entire population of South Korea. The Protestant Church in Korea, however, has shown some of the unsavory characteristics of the dogmatic religion which seemed to have accompanied the early missionaries from North America: parochialism, secularism, and materialism. In addition, the ethnocentric sense of racial and cultural superiority with which the early missionaries came to Korea has been increasingly criticized by young students of history in Korea, which has helped to undermine the splendid achievements of the missionary enterprises. In fact, history shows little critical theological self-evaluation of foreign missions and cultures on the part of most Christian missionary movements, including those of the Methodist Episcopal Church. The conceptualization of the theology of mission and culture of the Methodist Episcopal Church was largely to assume the traditional biblical mandate for conquering the world for Christ with the Gospel (Matthew 28:19), with little consideration of the issues of cross-cultural hermeneutic. In the coming world of diversity and global cooperation, United Methodist missions need to radically reconceptualize the theology of mission and culture in order to be relevant and effective in calling the world to God.

This chapter will examine the Methodist Episcopal Church's missions to Korea in the late-nineteenth century and critically reread the history, reviewing the introduction of Christianity to Korea. My focus is on how and with what consequence Western, particularly American, culture represented by early Protestant missionaries came into conflict with and eventually prevailed over some venerated traditions of Korean culture, particularly ancestor worship. My interest here is to point out that early Protestant missionaries' fundamentalistic iconoclasm of "heathen" culture has kept the Korean Church captive and created a bitter conflict between Korean Protestants and their own culture. Consequently, Korean Protestants in the modern world have found themselves in a spiritual dilemma: on the one hand, missionaries' faith with its attendant parochialism, dogmatism, cultural jingoism, secularism, and materialism, demanding rejection of Korean indigenous values, customs, culture, and faith; or, on the other, a global and humane faith with its promises of appreciation and celebration of the best of Korean spirituality without forced denunciation of biblical faith, and *vice versa*. Ultimately, the dilemma raises questions about the wisdom and appropriateness of missionaries' cultural iconoclasm. As an interim conclusion, drawing from the critique, I will suggest a set of guidelines for doing a new theology of mission and culture from a global and humane perspective.

A Critical Rereading of the History
of Protestant Missions in Korea

Methodist missions to Korea must be understood in the context of at least three major constituent historical developments in the eighteenth and nineteenth centuries to appreciate the fact that early missionaries were, consciously or unconsciously, a part of the political, military, commercial, and cultural aggression against the Asian nations by the Western powers. Those developments are: (1) the Western powers' colonial ambition and imperial expansion in Asia,[1] (2) missionary movements in America, and (3) conflict of cultures and the modernization of Korea.

The West's Colonial Expansion in Asia

The crusading spirit which was the backdrop of what was to become European colonialism was the driving force behind missionary movements in the nineteenth century when European colonialism was at its peak.[2] All of Asia fell victim to European colonialism by the turn of the century. Both Roman Catholics and Protestants sent missionaries to almost every country on earth, and missionaries began to provide medical and educational assistance in conjunction with spiritual help. To the peoples of Asia, however, particularly to Asian rulers who had been humiliated by the so-called "unequal treaties" resulting from the gunboat diplomacy of the powerful Western nations, missionaries did not seem very different from military men and merchants who came to take away Asian peoples' honor and dignity as well as their material goods. As Kenneth S. Latourette observed, the West invaded the East "partly by exploration, partly by conquest, partly by vast migrations, and partly by commerce,"[3] and missionaries were consciously and unconsciously a part of the invasion. The Christian benevolence which missionaries graciously demonstrated was well appreciated, nonetheless.

The Korean intellectual statesmen, who were preoccupied with Confucian ethic and naive political idealism, were desperate for national survival at a time when China and Japan were competing for dominance in Korea, and when Russia, France, Great Britain, and the United States were vying for market and influence. While imperial Japan attempted to cut off China's hold on Korea, which had been an accepted fact for centuries, the Korean market became fair game for the colonialists. When the world around them was crashing in from all sides and the nation's foundation was being crumbled down by internal corruption and factional power politics, the Koreans were still holding on to the Confucian ideals of harmony and resistance to change.[4] For Taewon'gun (father and the Regent of King Kojong, the last King of Yi-Dynasty) and the majority of the officials, absolute isolationism was the only answer. Yet, the revered Chinese emperor had been molested and humiliated by the Western "barbarians" in two Opium Wars, which had broken the Chinese door wide open against her will. The Japanese, who had learned the colonial way from the British and the Americans, were about to use force to take control of Korea.

Protestant missions to Korea coincided with this violent and unwanted opening of Korea to the Western powers. A band of frightened Koreans destroyed a U.S. merchant ship, the *Sherman*, off the coast of Pyungyang in 1866, thereby provoking the assaults by the French in 1866 and the United States in 1871. Korea was forced to sign the Kanghwa Treaty with Japan in 1876, which was the first step toward the Japanese occupation of Korea by force, and also a treaty with the United States in 1877. In 1910, the Japanese took advantage of multinational rivalry and forced a formal annexation of Korea with the Western powers' acquiescence in exchange for trade and missionary opportunities.

It was during this period of national crisis in the final years of Yi Dynasty that the first Protestant missionaries—including Horace N. Allen, Horace G. Underwood, and Henry G. Appenzeller—entered Korea with the help of Dr. Robert Maclay, "the foster father" of Methodist missions to Korea. Maclay, Superintendant in Japan, having secured the royal endorsement to do "educational and medical works only," recommended to the Mission Board of the Methodist Episcopal

Church to "begin educational and medical work using no disguise as to the ultimate object being evangelization."[5] With the donation of five thousand dollars raised by the appeals of the Reverend John F. Goucher, President of Goucher College in Baltimore, and urged on by many articles in *The Christian Advocate*, the leading Methodist Episcopal circular, the Methodist missions to Korea was launched. During the Christmas week of 1884, the Methodist Episcopal Church officially appointed William B. Scranton, M.D., Reverend Henry G. Appenzeller, and Mrs. Mary F. Scranton as its pioneer missionaries to Korea. On 31 March 1885, Dr. Maclay received notification of the formal organization of the Korea Mission from Bishop C. H. Fowler, who appointed Maclay as Superintendent, Appenzeller as Assistant Superintendent, and the newly ordained Scranton as Mission Treasurer. The mission of the Methodist Episcopal Church in Korea began in the summer of 1885. The Southern Methodist Church came in 1895, during the peak time of missionary movements in America.

Missionary Movements in America

The explosion of missionary movements in America during the latter half of the nineteenth century can be ascribed to at least two sources: (1) the Puritan ideal of "a Christian America," which, according to Robert T. Handy, remained a persistent theme throughout the history of Christianity in the United States,[6] and (2) the continuing theme of reform and revival which, according to Frederick A. Norwood, characterized the American Christian evangelical zeal and their sense of moral responsibility for the world as well as for the nation, as demonstrated in two Great Awakenings.[7] While America was becoming a world power at the turn of the century through colonial expansion, evangelicals grew confident with a sense of moral and cultural superiority and felt an urgency to Christianize the world. Thus, the American missionary enterprises exhibited two conflicting characteristics: an evangelical enthusiasm accompanied by humanitarian compassion and commitment to human liberation from "pagan" ignorance and superstitious beliefs, and the colonial habit of mind with its triumphalistic sense of moral and cultural superiority.

Professor Handy has shown how the Puritan ideal of "a complete Christian commonwealth" had dictated the course of both civil and religious history of America by means of religious establishment, moral arguments, and voluntarism. The ideal of "a Christian America" was viewed as a defense for America when "some uncomfortable realities stood in the way of evangelical hopes for the early triumph of Christian civilization in America," or when "serious inner divisions and tensions plagued the Protestant forces," or when "the facts of industrialization, urbanization, and intellectual revolution posed serious challenges to the evangelical expectancies," following the outbreak of the Civil War.[8] In spite of the difficulties, the evangelicals confidently carried forward "the Protestant crusade," firmly based on their Bible-centered, revivalist, and missionary-minded faith.

For these evangelicals with "a characteristically oversimplified, moralistic interpretation of Christian faith,"[9] as Professor Handy claimed, Protestant Christian culture and Anglo-American civilization were closely identified. Thus, "civilizing" the Indians and the foreign pagans became the primary motif for missionary works. This missionary motif was stressed against the papism and pagan religions the nineteenth-century immigrants brought to America with them. Consequently, the idea of Christianity as "the religion of civilization" that would realize the Kingdom of God on earth was more closely associated with the English-speaking, Anglo-Saxon world. Such a theme of the identification of Anglo-Saxonism with Christian civilization had been repeated by many leaders of the major denominations in America, first with regard to the black race and then all the other races. For example, Jeremiah B. Jeter, an influential Southern Baptist leader, wrote in 1869, "to admit blacks into churches on equal basis would lead to 'the mongrelization of our noble Anglo Saxon race.'"[10] Samuel Harris, Episcopal Bishop of Michigan, stressed the identification of American Protestantism with Anglo-Saxonism at the meeting of the Evangelical Alliance in Washington in 1887:

> . . . the consistency of the divine purpose in establishing our evangelical civilization here [in the United States] is signally illustrated in the fact that it was primarily confided to the keeping of the Anglo-Saxon race. By reason of its peculiar characteristics and its training in history, that race was singularly fitted for its task: endowed with a certain race conservatism and a certain persistency of race type, it has sturdily maintained itself, even to the present time.[11]

Continuing this theme, Josiah Strong, a Bishop of the Methodist Episcopal Church, declared that the highest expression of Anglo-Saxon civilization would be in the United States.[12] Furthermore, Anglo-Saxon Christians were God's chosen people to "conquer the world for Christ," as expressed by James H. King, Methodist minister from New York:

> Christianized Anglo-Saxon blood, with its love of liberty, its thrift, its intense and persistent energy and personal independence, is the regnant force in this country; and that is a more pregnant fact, because the

concededly most important lesson in the history of modern civilization is, that God is using the Anglo-Saxon to conquer the world for Christ by dispossessing feeble races, and assimilating and molding others.[13]

Such a sense of racial superiority was coupled with an American expansionism that caused America to purchase Alaska and to go to war with the Spanish in 1898.[14]

Unfortunately, a strong sense of unity based on racial and parochial identification of Christianity with American civilization became the real bond of Protestant unity and eventually the moral and spiritual force behind the missionary activities for the Christian conquest of the world. A number of American Protestant leaders at the close of the nineteenth century (including Sidney L. Gulick, missionary of the American Board of Commissioners for Foreign Missions; W. H. P. Faunce, influential Baptist minister who later became president of Brown University; and Lyman Abbott, the editor of the influential journal *Outlook*), expressed racist, jingoistic, and imperialistic views represented by Matthew S. Kauffman's proclamation in *The Christian Advocate* in 1898:

> American imperialism, in its essence, is American valor, American manhood, American sense of justice and right, American conscience, American character at its best, listening to the voice of God, and His command nobly assuming this republic's rightful place in the grand forward movement for the civilizing and Christianizing of all continents and all races.[15]

Such a confidence gave a new intensity to the missionary concerns of the evangelicals, and foreign missions provided the means for the world conquest and thus a unifying partnership among denominations despite various theological tensions.

The Protestant zeal for foreign mission gave birth to many missionary societies, especially among college students: the Young People's Society of Christian Endeavor, the summer Bible conferences, and the new and extensive activity of the Young Men's Christian Associations. Many of the pioneer missionaries to Korea were trained during this period. However, it was not until the early 1900s before both the Methodist Episcopal Church and the Methodist Episcopal Church, South formally established Boards of Foreign Mission separate from Boards of Home Mission. The number of foreign missions and Missional Annual Conferences was steadily growing. More than half of the Protestant missionaries were women.[16] The Woman's Foreign Missionary Society of the Methodist Episcopal Church (W. F. M. S.), the Woman's Board of Foreign Mission of the Methodist Episcopal Church, South (W.B.F.M.) in the south, and the Woman's Union Missionary

Society (W.U.M.S.) of the Methodist Protestant Church were organized in the late-nineteenth century.

Methodism's Asia mission began in this period of general Protestant missionary zeal coincident with European colonial expansion in Asia: first India with the establishment of Britain's East India Company (1814), then China in the aftermath of the first Opium War (1844), and Japan with the coming of Commodore Matthew G. Perry (1853). American Protestants' Korea missions began when Robert S. Maclay of the Methodist Mission of the Northern Church in Japan, along with Henry Loomis of the American Bible Society and George W. Knox of the Presbyterian Mission, became acquainted with liberal-minded Korean students in Japan who were intent on the modernization of Korea as the only way to Korean independence and dignity. Some progressive Koreans saw an opportunity for a new Korea by means of modern learning, which was called "Suh-Hak" (Western Learning), referring to the modern science of medicine and the education introduced by the missionaries,[17] including the missionaries' contribution to the revitalization of native language *Hangul* and human rights movements.[18] These missionaries, for a time, seemed to be the only hope for Korea. Indeed, they played a significant role in preparing the Koreans to come to the modern world, unfortunately at a questionable cost.

Theological education at most seminaries where early missionaries were trained was saturated with Enlightenment-era pietism and the evangelical spirit of the conquest of the world for Christ. A conversion experience as well as a conviction of personal salvation was a requirement for early Methodist missionaries. Compulsory attendance at daily chapel and deeply pious religious life were main features at many seminaries, of which Drew was exemplary. When Appenzeller was a student at Drew, Bishop Edmund S. James summed up aims of Drew education, as well as those of many Methodist seminaries, with these words on one opening day of classes:

> We do not expect these who go from this institution simply to stand in the rank and file of Immanuel's army; nor to be mere gunners simply to load afire, especially if they use a paper cannon. We expect every man to be competent to be a leader, and lead God's sacramental hosts onward and upward until all the cohorts of error are driven from the world, and the standard of Christ is triumphant over all the lands.[19]

Referring to Drew as the West Point of Methodism, the Bishop continued to urge:

If a young man comes here with the lion in him, do not begin to pare his nails, or trim his mane, or tone his voice or tame his spirit, but let his claws grow, let his mane thicken, let his spirit wax until by his roaring he send terror to all the haunts of wickedness and dismay to all the dens of iniquity.[20]

The missionary call was viewed as the highest of all the full-time professions for the seminary graduates, for it required personal sacrifice to go to a "heathen" country to serve Christ, although there also was considerable ambivalence regarding the volunteers.[21]

Most of the young missionaries were theologically orthodox, or even conservative, with high hope of the urgent and imminent victory of Christian civilization, which was characteristic of the theology of that period. They showed uncritical confidence in their theology and no sense of appreciation and respect for values and cultures other than their own. They made no effort to understand why the Korean people were in such a dire condition of poverty, and even mistook poverty as laziness.[22] Thus, the modernization of Korea was to be characterized by the influence of young, immature, self-confident and uncritical self-appointed apostles of theological conservatism and American superiority. With a prematurely formed low opinion of the Korean people on the one hand, and a sense of compassion for them on the other, they treated the poor in the hospitals and taught their values and faith in the schools.

Modernization of Korea

Missionaries at the turn of the century played a significant role in the modernization of Korea. However, they had to operate within the confines of international politics; the imperial Japanese ambition of hegemony in Asia began to move against China, Russia, and the United States; the Korean peninsula, which offered a strategically convenient and advantageous springboard to achieving that ambition, was their first target. Many young nationalist Koreans were desperately seeking ways to save their motherland by looking to Russia, others to China, still others to the United States. There were also a number of young Korean men who went to Japan to learn the secrets for their nation's survival.

Of those young Koreans in Japan who tried to convince Queen Min and the Korean government officials of the need for modernization, Min Young-Ik, a nephew of the queen and a prominent official, with whom the Reverend Goucher got acquainted, and Kim Ok-Kyun, an official at the Department of Foreign Affairs befriended by the Maclays, eventually proved to be consequential in opening the Korean door to mission work, although their efforts were not fruitful initially. Ultra-progressivists such as Kim Ok-Kyun, Park Hyo-Young, Yoon Chi-Ho, Suh Kwang-Bum, and Suh Jae-Pil stressed not only the need to learn modern science and technology but also Christian faith to help the nation become independent, strong, self-reliant, and peaceful.

The first missionaries began their work in medical and educational areas which contributed a great deal to the modernization of Korea. The first modern hospitals were established by Dr. Horace Allen (*Jejoongwon* in 1885) and Dr. Scranton (*Shibyungwon* in 1886). The first schools opened by missionaries—both endorsed by King Kojong—were *Pai-Jai Hakdang* (Hall for Rearing Useful Men) established by Appenzeller and *Ehwa Hakdang* (The Pear Blossom School) established by Mrs. Scranton, Dr. Scranton's mother and the first missionary of the Women's Missionary Society of the Methodist Episcopal Church. From these schools, many of the future leaders of Korea were to come, and, indeed, the schools ultimately turned out to be the most effective means of the evangelization of Korea.

The translation and publication of the New Testament in 1900 and the ensuing revivals in early-twentieth century opened the way to slow growth under the Japanese occupation from 1910 through 1945. The fact that Underwood and Appenzeller, with the help of Korean translators, published both New and Old Testaments in *Hangul* had evangelical as well as literary significance since Hangul was the language of the poor and low class. It was said to be the most significant event in the history of the Korean language.[23] Hymnbooks published by the missionaries were another way to contribute to Korean literary culture, as were newspapers and magazines, which were established to bring "light to the darkness and help the modernization of Korea move forward"[24] and to inculcate Christian faith. Many pages were used to introduce Western culture and modern technology, including farming, child care, and other practical knowledge to improve the standard of life. Magazines published in English by the missionaries led the movement toward modernization as well as evangelization. In fact, the modernization of Korea was monopolized by the missionaries so much that Christian faith and Western culture to which the Koreans were exposed were almost exclusively those interpreted and introduced by the missionaries. Theological and cultural assumptions included the world views and values associated with the Puritan ideal of "a Christian common-wealth," "Anglo-Saxonism," and the sense of divine commission for the world conquest on the part of the evangelicals. This was to have a long-lasting influence on the thought and practice of many Korean Christians.[25]

As the various missionary enterprises became settled and institutionalized during the years of Japanese control, the missionaries took a neutral stance in political matters. Through this darkest period of the Korean history, however, the Christian leaders who grew up under the tutelage of missionaries were the backbone of the unceasing struggle to gain freedom, independence, and dignity from Japan's most cruel exploitation and domination. The Korean Methodist Church, among other denominations, grew steadily throughout the war years. In the 1960s and 1970s, its growth exploded, along with the success of three Five-Year Economic Plans of President Park Jung-Hee's military regime, in relative peace in spite of the constant threat of North Korean invasion.

Christian Theology of Mission: A Problematic Theology for a Humane Global Future
The Korean Church Historians' Critique of Missionary Iconoclasm

An examination of the Korean church historians shows three major historiographical tendencies: (1) missionary history, represented by L. George Paik,[26] (2) nationalist history, represented by Kyung-Bae Min,[27] and (3) Minjung (oppressed people's) history, represented by the historians under the leadership of Man-Yul Lee at the Institute of Korean Church History Studies.[28] Whereas the first is decidedly affirmative of the "missionary" character of the Korean Church, having been written in the late 1920s when the nation was under Japanese control, the last two groups are critical of missionary Christianity for having impaired the Koreans' self-understanding and ability to make Christian witness and confession for and by themselves. Theology, culture, and rituals imposed on Korea by the missionaries, according to these younger scholars, had remained "foreign" in contradistinction to the Korean religious and spiritual identity.[29]

In concluding his pioneer work on the history of Christian missions in Korea, George Paik characterized "the inherent conservatism of the Church, the want of the social application of Christianity, and the low intellectual standard of the Korean Christians"[30] as outstanding "defects" of the Korean Church. He stopped short of listing these "defects." Some historians and theologians claim that the Korean Church suffers from a serious confusion about its identity both personally and culturally, from *Gibok Sasang* (contradictory faith in "other-worldism" or escapism, simultaneously demanding immediate blessing in terms of secular and worldly gains) and to superstitious practices, parochial intolerance, supermarketism, smorgasbordism, and mammonism. Dr. Paik also stopped short of saying that these defects were related at least partially to early missionaries' parochial and narrowly defined pietistic evangelicalism, burdened as it was with a sense of triumphalism and ethnocentrism motivated by a racial and cultural superiority complex.[31] The immature and inexperienced young missionaries, who were filled with spirit and zeal but short on understanding and respect for "foreign" values and cultures, failed to make a fair and reasonable attempt to understand what values and faiths were considered important in Korea and why they were significant before they labeled the "old religions" of Korea "ridiculous" and "superstitious." They lacked the basic wisdom to perceive their own assumptions. Iconoclasm, a conflict between cultures, was the result, and that iconoclasm has created an ongoing tension between the traditions of Korean culture and the process of modernization. In this struggle, the practice of ancestor worship that make up the fabric of Korean autonomy and unity has become one of the most poignant cases of iconoclasm.

The Controversy over Ancestor Worship

Ancestor worship is actually a misnomer because the Confucian Asians do not consider their ancestors as deities, although the extent to which they express their respect and gratitude and the manner in which they perform the rites do go beyond what is involved in a simple memorial service. The term "Je-sa," the Confucian ritual to honor and memorailize ancestors, does not connote any sense of expressing adoration and praise that Christians and other deity-worshipping believers would normally do. The term properly means "paying respect and expressing gratitude to the dead ancestors." It was only within the context of a controversy initiated by Christians with the Western cultural baggage that the term was translated as "worship."[32] And such elaborate rites, resembling worship and close enough to be considered idolatrous, are due to the depth and breadth of people's love and respect for their ancestors but have nothing to do with the holy. The large family system is the basic unit of the Confucian social order, and the rites to remember and express respect and gratitude for giving birth to posterity are essentially a component in Confucian moral and social philosophy for maintaining order and harmony in a nation. The entire oriental moral, social, political order is based on such family values and has little or nothing to do with idolatry. The concept of idolatry does not exist in Asian culture. If idolatry is giving ultimate loyalty to something other than supreme reality, then for the Asians who were brought up in a Confucian system of values, refusal to pay respect to ancestors would be it. Such a refusal would also be an act against the supreme temporal authority of the King, who was believed to have been endowed with parental authority. Therefore, refusal to observe ancestor worship is an act against the King and Heaven, by which the King was appointed to maintain moral, social, and political order and peace for the people.

Missionaries approached Korean culture with total disregard for this age-old Korean custom that has been an essential part of the Korean culture for centuries. Such an iconoclastic attitude to ancestor worship, one of the most important family and social customs sustaining the spiritual force of Korean culture, was in fact the source of the Korean people's distrust of and ensuing conflict with the early Roman Catholic missionaries in the eighteenth century. This instance resulted in a series of the bloodiest persecutions of missionaries and converts in the history of Christianity for a period of more than one hundred years from the time the first martyr, Kim Bum-Woo, was exiled and died in 1784. In five large persecutions between 1784 and 1886, hundreds of missionaries and thousands of Korean converts were put to death for the cultural ideology they were amalgamating with their faith. Of these five persecutions, the first was the Jinsan persecution in 1791, in which Yoon Ji-Choong and several of his colleagues were arrested and hanged for refusing to perform Je-sa and burying ancestral tablets. Their refusal was motivated by a desire to obey Bishop Gouvea's injunction prohibiting ancestor worship,[33] in violation of the government's decree outlawing Christianity, and the act was serious enough to be considered an act against the government. Hundreds, indeed thousands more were to be sacrificed over this issue in the next hundred years. The Roman Catholic Church was to finally accept the Korean custom as legitimate and not idolatrous in 1984, when Pope Paul VI canonized more than one hundred Korean and foreign martyrs. Protestant Koreans are still adamantly against the rites of sacrifices to ancestors, condemning the rites as idolatry, primarily due to their tutelage under iconoclastic missionaries.

Missionaries did not realize the rites were as much a means of finding comfort and hope for a secure and prosperous future for the lowly Minjung class, as it was a means to perpetuate the rights, authority, and privileges of the upper Yangban class. The missionaries' iconoclastic attitude reflects an ignorance and disregard of how deeply and comprehensively the rites are a part of Korean culture and how they hold one meaning for the upper class and another for the lowly Minjung. Perhaps this was one of the most attractive features of the Christian teaching for the commoners and thoughtful, progressivist intellectuals. From this perspective, the missionaries' Christianity was a religion of the personal savior for many Korean converts. What missionaries and their loyal converts did not realize was that the prohibition of the rites also meant denial of opportunities for comfort-seeking, hope-giving, and community-building for the oppressed Minjung. When the two-class system as an official institution was outlawed in modern Korea, the cultural and spiritual significance of the rites should have been re-evaluated by Protestant churches as has been done by the Catholics. These rites are still the most significant spiritual strut of family, community, and nation even after the explosive growth of Protestantism in the late-twentieth century. The Koreans would abandon them only at the risk of a total loss of the sense of family which is the sacred foundation of life and meaning in Korean society. Many find it difficult to go against the entire family, and end up in secret participation in the rites, or in non-committal kneeling, rather than bowing, at the ceremonies. The Protestants, still bound by nineteenth-century missionary theology, are holding on to the papal decree of 1704 (*Acta Causae Rituum seu Ceremoniarum Sinensium Complectentia*) even today. In the meantime, the Catholics who sowed the seeds for evangelization by sacrificing so many of the faithful over the rites issue are now making remarkable progress in working with Korean culture, and the Catholic Church's numeric growth has exceeded that of the Protestant Church in the last three decades of the twentieth century. Protestants have also recorded an unprecedented numeric growth in the same period, but there are ominous signs of inner struggle and general disregard for the church's official position regarding ancestor worship and other traditional rites among the new converts.

Many Christian intellectuals in Korea today agree that the rites are the most efficient means of community building and consider them an important spiritual force. The concept of family as the basis and context of individual identity and social cohesion, which is the core significance of the rites, can contribute to the world community coming together in the next century. The point of argument is that any missionary effort in the future can be iconoclastic only at the expense of disrupting all potential for peace and harmony among nations and cultures; ignorance may have a chance for improvement, but disrespect and disregard for the values of others would mean no dialogue, no cooperation, no community, no harmony, no peace.

Iconoclasm reflects a superiority complex that manifests itself in the dogmatism, parochialism, and factionalism that plague the Korean Church today. Early missionaries' attempts to sustain their authority and power as the Christian enterprises they helped establish became large and institutionalized revealed immaturity and inexperience in handling cultural, denominational, and theological differences. Sadly, many Korean pastors and theologians learned the lesson of theological conservatism too well to appreciate the diverse ways of biblical witness and the necessity of demythologizing and remythologizing the Gospel message for proper translation of faith from one culture to another. All attempts to "tamper" with the purity of the Gospel are condemned as heresy, and the conservative evangelicals do not even realize that they are throwing out the baby with the bath water. For example, the Reverend Yong-gi Cho, pastor of the well-known Yoido Full Gospel Church, had given a rather tolerant counsel to new converts who were troubled with the issue of ancestor worship in his public sermon delivered on 30 November 1979, saying "ancestor worship is nothing but honoring one's parents."[34] He was severely criticized in public press by a number of theologians and pastors and eventually changed his view regarding ancestor worship. Professor Sun-hwan Byun of Seoul Methodist Theological Seminary, a prominent advocate of religious pluralism, experienced the same difficulty when he wrote "ancestor worship is a social product of a large-family system."[35] Professor Myung-Hyuk Kim writes against the two "liberals":

> It is time that we Evangelicals should be alerted to a full understanding of the relation between the Christian Gospel and secular culture and should provide clear-cut solutions in concrete situations. It would be well for us to realize the criticizing, transforming, and recreating function and power of the Gospel in various cultures as others have done throughout the history of Christianity.[36]

Such a view is the result of uncritical reading of history and ignorance of one's own culture. The hold of "missionary theology" is indeed long-lasting. Contradictions and distortions mainly due to the lack or denial of cross-cultural valuation add to the serious problems of dogmatism, parochialism, and anti-critical spirit. Due to the adoration of missionaries and gratitude for their sacrifices, as well as respect for their honorable accomplishments, missionaries' "faults" and failures are unpopular subjects. These "faults" of missionaries were essentially the products of time and culture, to be sure, but they were faults nevertheless.

Their sacrificial contributions to the evangelization and modernization of Korea and emancipation of the Korean people notwithstanding,
missionaries were a part of the Western powers' mercantile and cultural
invasion, and many Korean converts do not even realize that their
religio-cultural identity and dignity are being trivialized. But the new
generation of Koreans are different; they feel a need for affirming their
identity and dignity as legitimate and contributing partners in the new
world of global and humane cooperation. And this need is becoming an
important factor in re-evaluating and learning from the work of early
missionaries.

Preliminary Questions and Some Guidelines for Doing Theology of Mission and Culture

In view of the above discussion, a few questions about the
relationship between Christian mission and culture can be identified,
and answers to these questions will serve as guidelines to a Christian
theology of mission and culture for the humane global future in the
coming century. To what degree and in what sense has Christian faith
sublimated Korean culture and its sacred traditions and "liberated"
Korean Christians from superstition, parochialism, and dogmatism, or
do Christian faith and Korean culture stand against each other? Can
Christian faith be transferred from one culture to another without
theological reinterpretation? In short, how could our experience in
Korea contribute to the articulation of a United Methodist theology of
mission and culture? And how could such a theology of mission and
culture inform United Methodist self-understanding and mission in
terms of reinvigorating the Methodist impulse to be once again a
significant partner in reinventing an American culture that is
compatible with, and partaking in, a humane global culture that is
emerging at the dawn of the twenty-first century?

The following are the essentials of doing a holistic cross-cultural
theology of mission and culture:

— It becomes evident that absolute claims, dogmatic or cultural, are not
only futile but hazardous to any mission activities. "The humane" is an
attitude that will help minimize conflicts.

— Theology of mission and culture should articulate a vision for a
humane global community. In addition to the so-called "clash of
cultures," the issues of race and class have been most disturbing for
wholesome, dignified life in today's world as was revealed in the Los
Angeles uprising in 1992.

— The task of a humane theology of mission and culture is to humanize (or "humane-ize") dogmatic theology, for dogmatic theology traditionally speaking, is by definition idealistic and absolutist, and therefore imperialistic. Thus, a humane theology, begins with a conviction that all persons are unique and sacred—and are therefore beings of incalculable worth, decency, and dignity—regardless of their ethnic and racial origin, cultural sophistication, and religious persuasion.

— In a pluralistic context, a humane theology needs to deal with the encounter of peoples who may have different sets of assumptions, views, and convictions. An authentic encounter presupposes the authenticity of the persons encountered, each meaningful and valid not only in each person's own value system but in that of the whole. Implicit in such an encounter is pluralism, and particularly, religious pluralism, which presupposes cultural pluralism.

— The major assertions of a humane theology can be summarized as follows:

(a) "Humane" refers to that quality of person which commands the integrity and respectability of all persons regardless of external conditioning influences. Persons of different intellectual, social, and religious orientation are not only to be equally treated but deserve, to equal degree, respect for the sacredness of being persons participating in the life of, in a Christian term, God.

(b) Salvation/liberation, or a meaningful, authentic life, of all persons is the vocation of the supreme reality. Religion, understood in terms of the dynamics relating faith and religious traditions whether theistic or non-theistic, concerns itself with persons universally.[37] However variegated the expressions of this ultimate reality may be, all symbols of faith are religiously valid (or true) insofar as the transformation of relationship which is "humanely" significant occurs, although the forms of expression of faith that charges the encounter experience may be culture- and time-specific.

(c) Therefore, the theology of mission and culture that is relevant to the contemporary world, which is pluralistic and global, must be such that its horizon is truly open and diligently self-critical lest it become another absolutism.

— Underlying these assertions are the assumptions here simply noted: the integrity of every person as "humane" being consists in the consideration of others as being equally persons of integrity; and this "humaneness," while participating in the Transcendent, falls short of It (or Him or Her). It is an intelligent admission that human intelligence cannot penetrate the mystery of the divine.

— Doing such a humane theology, therefore, requires a hermeneutic that is capable of providing a common means for us to grasp and articulate the meaning of relationship between person and the Transcendent in the pluralistic and global world as a common context: a "hermeneutic of integrity" as complementary to the methodology of "the hermeneutic of suspicion" put forward as a challenge to traditional Euro-American rational theology by liberation theologies of Third World countries. Such a critical hermeneutic is a sound and liberating practical application of metahermeneutical principles of which at least three critical points are implied: the critique of absolutism, dualism, and dehumanization.

— Theology of mission and culture in the coming century should be a Theology of Human Dignity for a Global Community. It has first of all to undo the myth of racial and cultural superiority and thereby to prevent gross dehumanization by humanizing the oppressor's theology. It is a search for a way to articulate a God, free of the distorted historiography of the Church, who pervades and continues to sustain the human Church and validates the claim of worth, decency, respectability of every disenfranchised individual and community, the reluctance and resistance of the "established" Church notwithstanding.

— Pluralistic, cross-cultural mission theology guides us to reflect on the meaning of God in behalf of the whole of creation in search of the more holistic, more just, more humane community in which we all must coexist. This theology is a commitment to transcend particularity without losing integrity and to participate in seeking common contexts in which each community can articulate its own identity and dignity without being coerced to an ideology and without losing the sense of family kinship of all human beings.

— God is just and compassionate. As such, God is a critique of the imbalance in hearts and systems that creates anarchy and tyranny, "the twin evils" which dehumanize. God's vocation is to promote "humaneness" (humanity) in an inhumane world. Persons, or love and respect for life of all persons, not the truth of dogmas, are God's ultimate concern. Doing mission theology in the global world is in fact a cooperative exercise to articulate a common norm for all theological reflection, which I claim is human dignity.

Three major principles for a holistic theology of mission and culture can be summarized as follows:

— (a) Doing a theology of mission and culture in a pluralistic world should begin with a genuine respect for, and (as much as humanly possible) an unbiased objective study of, religio-cultural values and traditions different from our own, a collaborative interfaith and intercultural dialogue, and a serious study of religious pluralism in addition to doing traditional theology; in short, a theology of religions without dogmatic absolutism.[38]

— (b) Church growth and strength must be measured by social, political, and cultural transformation that is creative, humanely significant, and reflective of compassion and justice ("passion for holiness and compassion for humanity")[39] as well as by increase in numbers and funds.

— (c) The ultimate purpose of Christian mission, therefore, is to broaden the Kingdom of God by enhancing the dignity of human beings and nature as God's creation, based on the sense of global responsibility and ethic.[40]

Concluding Remarks

Such a global and humane theology of mission and culture that is reflective of United Methodist commitment to biblical faith and human dignity signfies the crucial role of United Methodism in American culture to once again take leadership, with compassion and humility, in globalizing the biblical faith and humanizing the globe, only this time without ethnocentrism, parochialism, and exclusivism. To be able to do that, all concerned, both lay and ordained, women and men, natives and immigrants, sophisticated and simple, must come together to do theology together through dialogue or colloquy. This can be initiated by the next phase of the project, much the same way the Duke Conference was organized. The project leaders might consider writing another proposal to funding agencies to continue to sponsor dialogues through conferences and other means. The General Board of Global Ministries and related boards and agencies of the Church could set "Global Theology," or "Cross-cultural Theology," as their missional priority, which then could be relegated to Annual Conferences and local churches for study and implementation. Denominational seminaries and researchers/scholars could be summoned to contribute to the articulation of theology, and new graduate programs in the area of ecumenics and cultural study can be established. Global Theology or Cross-cultural Theology could be required for ordination. Bishops' study would enhance the endeavor. God willing, perhaps it will lead to a new awakening.

Bibliography

Board of Missions, *Korea Annual Conference, Methodist Episcopal Church, South*, 1926.

Chun, Taek-Boo. "Gidok-gyo wa Hangul" [Christianity and Hangul], *Nara Sarang* 36 (1980): 142.

Clark, Allen D. *History of the Korean Church*. Seoul, 1961.

Cobb, John B., Jr. *Beyond Dialogue: Toward a Mutual Transformation of Christianity and Buddhism*. Philadelphia: Fortress, 1982.

Cunningham, John T. *University in the Forest*. Madison, N.J.: Afton, 1972.

Griffis, William E. *A Modern Pioneer in Korea: The History of Henry G. Appenzeller*. New York: Fleming H. Revell, 1912.

Han, Woo-Keun. *The History of Korea*. Ed. Grafton K. Mintz. Transl. Lee Kyung-Shik. Honolulu: East-West Center, 1970.

Handy, Robert T. *A Christian America: Protestant Hopes and Historical Realities*. 2d ed. New York and Oxford: Oxford University Press, 1984.

Hogg, W. Richey. "The Missions of American Methodism." Vol. 3, pp. 59–128 in *The History of American Methodism*, ed. Emory Stevens Bucke. New York and Nashville: Abingdon, 1964.

Hunt, Everett Nichols, Jr. *Protestant Pioneers in Korea*. Maryknoll, N.Y.: Orbis, 1980.

Kim, Chan-Hie. "Christianity and the Modernization of Korea." In *Traditional Thoughts and Practices in Korea*, ed. Eui-Young Yu and Philips. Los Angeles: Center for Korean Studies, California State University, 1978.

Kim, Myung Hyuk. "Ancestor Worship: From the Perspective of Korean Church History." Pp. 29–30 in *Ancestor Worship and Christianity in Korea*, ed. Jung Young Lee. Lewiston, N.Y.: Mellen, 1988, 29–30.

Kim, Stephen S. "The Burning Heart: Passion for Holiness and Compassion for Humanity." Pp. 3–17 in *The Burning Heart*. N.Y.: General Global Ministries National Mission Resources, 1990.

Küng, Hans. *Global Responsibility: In Search of a New World Ethic*. New York: Crossroad, 1991.

Latourette, Kenneth S. *A History of Christianity*. Vol. I, New York: Harper & Row, 1975.

Lee, Man-Yul, et al. *Hanguk Gidokgo eui Yoksa* [A History of the Korean Church]. 2 vols. The Institute of Korean Church History Studies. Seoul: Christian Literature Press, 1989.

Lee, Jung Young, ed. *Ancestor Worship and Christianity in Korea*. Lewiston, N.Y.: Mellen, 1988.

Maclay, Robert S. "A Fortnight in Seoul, Korea, 1884" *The Gospel in All Lands* 22 (August 1885): 11.

Methodist Episcopal Church Report, 1884.

Min, Kyung-Bae. *Hanguk Gidok Gyohoesa* [A History of the Korean Christian Church]. Seoul: Korea Christian Press, 1982.

Moltmann Jürgen. *On Human Dignity: Political Theology and Ethics*. Transl. M. Douglas Meeks. Philadelphia: Fortress, 1984.

Norwood, Frederick A. *The Story of American Methodism: A History of the United Methodists and Their Relations*. Nashville: Abingdon, 1974.

Paik, L. George. *The History of Protestant Missions in Korea, 1832–1910*. Seoul, Korea: Yonsei University Press, 1970 (Ph.D. dissertation, Yale University, 1929).

Ro, Young-Chan. "Ancestor Worship: From the Perspective of Korean Tradition," in *Ancestor Worship and Christianity in Korea*. Ed. Jung Y. Lee. Lewiston, N.Y.: Mellen, 1988.

Smith, Wilfred Cantwell. *Meaning and End of Religion*. San Francisco: Harper & Row, 1962; repr. 1978.

———. *Towards a World Theology: Faith and Contemporary History of Religion*. Philadelphia: Westminster, 1981.

Woman's Foreign Missionary Society of the Methodist Episcopal Church. *Fifty Years of Light in Commemoration of the Completion of Fifty Years of Work in Korea*. Seoul: Woman's Foreign Missionary Society, 1938.

Justo L. González

For Stephen Kim, Methodism's missionary outreach into Korea was compromised by its bondage to American culture, and that history compels our denomination to find for itself more diverse, expansive, and global theological perspectives. For Justo González, American Methodism can experience some liberation from its limitations if the church will seriously embrace the contributions such as those that Hispanic United Methodists have to offer to the denomination.

González, whose work has ranged widely in the fields of historical theology, liberation theology, and preaching, proposes that the tiny fraction of United Methodists who are Latino and Latina can alter our theological self-understanding in positive and constructive ways. He draws our attention particularly to the theology and practice of community. It is not unusual, for example, to have a local United Methodist congregation highlight its commitment to the family. But familia as a Hispanic term has a connotation that differs from the sense in which the vast majority use the term family, and that difference could offer an important viewpoint for the larger culture to embrace.

Further, wonders González, could United Methodist worship be markedly improved if it were understood in the Hispanic way, as fiesta? Could United Methodists improve their sense of identity if we thought of ourselves as members of the familia of God rather than as occupants of a professional or social class? Could our evangelism improve if we planted new churches where people need ministry and not where economically self-sufficient congregations can be grown? Could our Christian nurture foster more intimate communities of faith if we carried the gospel to people's homes rather than expecting people to leave their homes and come to great church buildings?

And if the answers to any of these questions is affirmative, then how might a minority influence and reshape the whole of United Methodism in America?

Hispanic United Methodists
and American Culture

Justo L. González

I have been asked to address the subject of this study "United Methodism and American Culture," from a Hispanic perspective. Allow me, before even broaching the subject, to clarify the way I understand my task on two points. First, as I understand my task, it has to do with Hispanics or Latinos and Latinas in the United States, and not necessarily or directly with the presence or impact of United Methodism in Latin American. Second, even though the title of this study speaks of "American" culture, I understand that I am to deal with the mainstream of culture in the United States, and not with other cultures that could equally be called "American": Cherokee, Nahuatl, Patagonian, Mexican, and Panamanian. Since "United-Statesian" is a rather awkward word, I shall speak of "North American" culture.

It is also clear that the subject "United Methodism and American Culture from a Hispanic Perspective" could mean several things, or could be approached in several different ways.

One approach, and probably the simplest would be to ask, how have Hispanic United Methodists influenced North American culture? It would be the simplest because the question itself is ridiculous. Even thinking about it, I am reminded of the story of an elephant that jumped into a swimming pool, and a flea on its back shouted, "boy, am I making waves!" In the large pool of North American culture, Hispanic United Methodists have made very few and very small waves.

A second approach would be to inquire to what degree North American culture has influenced Hispanic-American United Methodists. That would be a more relevant question and one deeply affecting the lives of Hispanic United Methodists. It is the question of acculturation, and to what degree the very fact of becoming United Methodists is part of the process of acculturation of Latinos and Latinas into this country. For us Hispanics, this is an important question for two reasons. First of all, it is a question that has significant bearing on the subject of what we are accomplishing in our evangelistic efforts. We are aware that people join the United Methodist Church for a number of reasons, and usually for more than one of them at the same time. Yet, to the degree that people are coming into the United Methodist Church as a way of joining the cultural and social mainstream of this country, and not in order to become disciples of Jesus Christ, to the degree that we have been promoting membership in our denomination as the religious equivalent of physical immigration, and not as joining a community longing for and working for the Rule of God, to that degree we have failed in our evangelism.

But that question is also important to us for a different reason. It is important because repeatedly throughout our history, our non-Hispanic brothers and sisters in positions of power have tried to answer it for us, and the consequences have been tragic both for us and for the United Methodist Church.

Back in 1920, the Methodist Episcopal Church, South, had a Florida Latin District with nine churches. That district continued growing and even sending missionaries to Cuba. Then, in 1939, with the merger of three branches of Methodism, the authorities of the church decided that there was no reason for such a district, since we were all one church. After all, they reasoned, the Latinos in South Florida should be encouraged to join the mainstream of North American culture. On that supposedly wise counsel, the Latin District was abolished. The event marked the beginning of decline for the Hispanic church in South Florida, to the point that by 1948 only one church remained, and no new churches were organized until the time of the Cuban Revolution in 1959 and the resulting exodus from Cuba. Thus, if we now have Hispanic churches in South Florida, it is not thanks to those wise church planners who decided that we ought to become acculturated, but thanks to Fidel Castro, and thanks to other upheavals that have shaken the Caribbean in recent years. In Southern California, Hispanic work was organized in 1940 as a Provisional Annual Conference which built on a long history of survival, success and increasing self-determination. There again, wise church planners with crystal balls whose crystal was not so clear decided that Hispanics who became United Methodists might as well go all the way in the process of acculturation, and the Provisional Annual Conference was dissolved in 1956. Decline had begun two years earlier, as word got around that the Provisional Conference was to disappear. Almost forty years after merger, Hispanic Methodism in Southern California still has not reached the size or the impact that it had in the days of the Provisional Conference. The consequence is that, now that some areas are 50% Hispanic, the United Methodist Church is hardly a player in the religious scene of those areas.

In Texas and New Mexico, we still have a Hispanic Annual Conference. Again, non-Hispanic United Methodist leaders, people who love the church and its Lord dearly, but who apparently do not understand how a people can love their culture even when it is suppressed and oppressed, are suggesting that the Rio Grande Conference be absorbed into the other geographic conferences of the region. If they succeed, I fear that United Methodism will be closing itself out of what will soon be half the population of those two states.

In short, the question of the degree to which North American culture has influenced or should influence Hispanic-American United Methodists, and how far we should assimilate and acculturate, is a question of life and death for our institutions and judiciaries.

And yet, even that is not the most important question that I feel compelled to raise. Many Hispanic United Methodists are convinced that there is an even more important question, one which has to do not only with the future of Hispanic United Methodism, but also with the future and even the present of United Methodism itself. The question that to us is so important and that I would like to explore is: what do we as Hispanic United Methodists have to contribute to the United Methodist Church at large?

When I pose the matter in such terms, my first thoughts run to the concept of the church as the family of God. I know that I need to explain that term, because there are many reasons—actually many good reasons—why some in the majority culture do not like to hear talk of the church as family. The problem is that when we speak of "familia," we mean something very different than the U.S. Bureau of the Census means when it speaks of "family," or when some politicians today speak of "family values." If someone asks me in English, "How many were there in your family when you were growing up?" I would answer "four." If someone were to ask me in Spanish, first of all I would be surprised, for it is not a question that makes any sense. In my "familia," there were my two parents, my brother, my two living grandparents, some great-uncles and great-aunts, my Godfather and my Godmother, half a dozen aunts and uncles and their spouses, more than a dozen first cousins, two or three dozen second cousins, and on, and on, and on. As a matter of fact, a familia has no clear limits. By its very nature its borders are indefinite and permeable, and new people are always joining, not only by birth or by marriage, but even by baptism. Thus, while a family in the current English language is easily defined with clear lines of demarcation, a familia is by nature fluid and even elusive in its definition. And while a family is by nature exclusive, guarding its own privacy is an important value, a familia is by nature inclusive and open. As a matter of fact, in Spanish there is not even a term for "privacy" as a value; and our term for "private"—privado—also means "deprived." For us, to be too private is also a privation.

You have to understand this meaning of familia in order to understand how it is that most Hispanics look at their church. For a number of reasons the familia can no longer give us the support it was supposed to provide. For those who are immigrants, the reason for this is quite clear. Most of the familia has remained in the old country. We keep in contact with them. They are still our familia, but we can no longer meet with them regularly and draw strength from those meetings and from their support. For those who have lived here for generations, the old longing for the familia still remains—and in many cases there is still the actual experience of such a familia. But the modern industrial society, with its enormous mobility, means that no matter whether born here or there, very few of us can enjoy the support of a familia. And to make matters worse, there are even some of us for whom the very act of becoming Protestants has meant a breach with the more traditional in the familia, who now consider the convert as the straying sheep of the familia and a threat to its unity.

What this means is that for many Latino Protestants, the church becomes the new familia. It is in that community that we find the support and the understanding we used to find in the familia in the older country—or the support that our cultural tradition tells us we ought to have, but that we have never enjoyed in this society of privacy and mobility.

It also means that when we speak of the new birth, we mean not only the change in personal allegiances and lifestyle that is commonly implied in that notion, but also a new birth into a new familia. For many of us, the words of 1 Peter 1:23 are very true: we "have been born anew, not of perishable seed but of imperishable, through the living and enduring word of God." And as a result of this new birth, we who were not people, not a family, are now God's own people, God's own family; once we had not received mercy, but now we have received mercy (2:10).

I suspect that it is something like this that John Wesley had in mind when he spoke of "the people called Methodist." He did not mean that conglomeration of people or of nuclear families called Methodists. He meant that new family, that new social reality that gave the lie to much of traditional social reality, that new people who were not a people and who are now called Methodist.

All of this would help those United Methodists who do not belong to the same culture and traditions understand some of the strange features of the Latino church. In many of our churches, particularly in small towns and rural areas where going out at night is still relatively safe, Hispanic churches often have services practically every night of the week. That is because such services are the gathering place for the familia, and it is inconceivable to have to wait until Sunday to get together with family when we have need of it—or when we simply want to express our love and celebrate who we are. In larger cities where travel at night has become dangerous, the relatively large central churches that have reduced their services to Sunday morning and perhaps Wednesday evening are struggling, while people are congregating for worship and fellowship in smaller living-room or store-front churches in their own communities where they can actually attend more frequently. It is not a matter of size, as if we felt better in smaller churches. It is rather a matter of availability. For us what is important is that the familia of the church, no matter whether large or small, be readily available and not just on Sundays. We need the familia near at hand. We need to gather often. We cannot conceive of a familia that only gathers on Sunday mornings and then for a carefully measured hour of exactly fifty minutes.

For the same reason, our services are genuine love feasts. We embrace when we arrive. If the pastor insists that we ought to be quiet in the sanctuary, we stay outside chatting until the formal service is about to begin or has already begun. Then when the passing of the peace comes around, we get up and mill around for a good five or even ten minutes, embracing each other once again, until the pastor or the piano calls us back to order. When the service ends, we stay talking to each other, sometimes for a longer time than the service lasted. And then, just before we part, we embrace still once again.

In this family gathering, the sharing of concerns and the announcements are also of crucial importance. The announcements may be printed on the bulletin. There may be a list of those who are sick. Still, the announcements must be read verbally, and sometimes even discussed; and there must be an up-to-date report on the condition of the sick, the bereaved, the unemployed, those who have a motive for celebration, etc. Not to do this would make as much sense as arriving at a family gathering and being handed a list of the relatives who are sick, or a notice that an aunt has died and will be buried Thursday.

Since we are a single familia, and not a conglomeration of families trying to guard their own privacy, it is not unusual when concerns are being shared to have a sister stand up and ask for prayers because she is unemployed and may not be able to pay next month's rent or a brother say that he and his wife are having problems and they need prayers and support. We are a familia. We can air all of these problems in church. And, lest it be thought that I am romanticizing reality, let me hasten to add that we can also have huge and long-lasting family quarrels. These become even more painful because they are not disagreements with people we can ignore when we return to the bosom of our families; they are quarrels in that very bosom.

That the church is a familia also means that our primary identification is not, as in the dominant culture, as lawyers, teachers, carpenters, janitors, or even pastors. Our primary identification is as Christians, and as Christians who gather together as this particular branch of the great *familia de Dios*. I am always surprised when I visit a white church and the first question that people ask, after I given them my name is, "What do you do?" In fact, I am so surprised that most times I can only respond with a rather facetious, "as little as possible." In the churches to which I am most accustomed, the first thing people ask is, "What is your home church?" Or sometimes, "Where do you congregate?"—*¿Dónde te congregas?*—meaning, where do you gather with others as the familia of God? To those who are not used to this question, this may seem as an opening gambit in a proselytizing move, as if the purpose were to invite the visitor to change churches or denominations. But that is not at all what is taking place. What is actually happening is simply that cousins in the same familia are trying to establish the nature of their kinship—as when in a family reunion someone asks, "Are you related on Uncle Joe's side or on Aunt Mary's?"

The establishment of those bonds, and of the identity that goes with them, is one of the main purposes of worship in the Latino church. We live in a society that constantly denies our true identity. In daily life, in the outside world, society gives us identities and labels with which we must live. We are "welfare recipient," "undocumented alien," "janitor," "successful professional," and "unwed mother." We need to gather, not just once a week, but as often as possible, to be told again and again and to tell ourselves that any such description is at best a secondary identification, and at worst a lie, that our true identity is "Christian," "child of God," "member of the *familia de Dios*." The list is so strong, its power of persuasion so strong, that we need to hear the story again and again. We never tire of hearing it, not just because it is a good story, but because we need it; because without it Mariá may come to believe the lie that her true self is "unwed mother"; Pedro may come to believe the lie that what really defines him is "undocumented alien"; and I may come to believe the lie that what I really am is a "successful professional."

This is the first thing that as a Hispanic-American United Methodist I covet for the United Methodist Church at large in this North American culture that tells all of us such lies as to who we are. How I wish the United Methodist Church at large were able to see itself, not as a conglomeration of families, each guarding its privacy and each trapped in the four walls of its own suburban home, but as the household of God, as the great *familia de Dios*! How I long for a church where my friend Arthur does not have to keep to the pretense that he is successful businessman, but can share his pain and his anxieties and be embraced as he hurts, and be embraced as he arrives, and be embraced as he leaves, and be told again and again that he is not really a businessman, successful or not—that he is really our brother, and a child of God. How I long for a church where Mary can speak out loud of her fear that Joey may be on drugs, and be embraced and lifted up in arms of prayer. How I long for a church that is willing to give the lie to the culture around it and say to people: "You are not defined by what you do. That is a lie. You are not defined by how much you make. That is a greater lie. You are not defined by how much credit you can muster and how much you owe. That is an even greater lie. You are defined by the face of God. And grace defines you as a member of the household of God, as a child of God. In fact, as Paul would have said, "you have died and your life is hidden with Christ in God."

Then, because we are familia, our worship is a family reunion, a fiesta. This does not mean that all is light and happy. In the familia, people gather for all sorts of occasions. They gather for births, they gather for baptisms, they gather for weddings, they gather for funerals, and they gather just for the sake of gathering. Some of these occasions are happy and others are painful. But all have at least an undertone of fiesta, for we are gathered *en familia*. If you do not believe this, go to a Latino wake! The same is true in our worship services. We rejoice in the grace of God, and we bemoan our sinfulness. We hear God's loving promises, and we also hear God's loving and harsh judgment. And because all of this takes place in familia, there is a sense of celebration about the whole thing.

That is something else that as a Latino I covet for the United Methodist Church at large: a real sense and experience of worship as fiesta, as celebration. Here is another of those points in which, as a person belonging to a different culture, sometimes I fear that the United Methodist Church has come to reflect its culture too closely. For all kinds of reasons, North American culture—especially middle-class North American culture—tells us that people should not get too excited over religion. It is OK to jump and shout at the stadium. It is OK to applaud and shout "bravo" at the concert hall. But in church you are supposed to hear the Story of the Ages and at best respond with a demure and rather mumbled "Thanks be to God." That too is part of the lie of culture. There is nothing wrong with being excited about what God has done, is doing, and has promised to do. There is nothing wrong with showing that excitement. That too is something Wesley learned, even against the expectations of his own culture and his proper British upbringing. And it is something that the United Methodist Church must learn once again, even against its own dominant culture, if it is to reclaim the joy of the Gospel and the wonder of God's amazing grace.

The 1992 General Conference approved a National Plan for Hispanic Ministries. The Plan is in its third year and seems to be well on the way to a resounding success. There is one point, however, at which it has failed, or at which at least it has not yet made the impact we had hoped for. When a national committee wrote this Plan, we were hoping it would be a plan for the entire United Methodist Church and not just for Hispanic leaders and others directly involved in Hispanic ministries. That does not mean that we expected everybody in the Connection to make Latino ministries a matter of first priority. We are well aware that there are many other equally important ministries, and that there is a variety of callings. What we had hoped was that the vision of the church and its mission that is embodied in the National Hispanic Plan would at least be known and discussed by the church at large, not just as a vision of this small segment of the denomination that happens to be Hispanic, but also as a vision that might enrich the entire denomination. Frankly, that has not happened. Others who for years have studied the theme of "United Methodism and American Culture" can perhaps would tell me whether this is due to the pragmatism of North American culture or to the pragmatism of United Methodism (and whether there is any difference between the two sorts of pragmatism). But the fact is that many people, deeply committed to the United Methodist Church and its ministry, see the words "Hispanic Ministry" on the title of a document and set it aside as having nothing to do with their particular calling or their setting for ministry.

I invite you to look again at that document, not just for what it says about Hispanic ministries, but also for what it says about the vision of the church and its ministry that we as Latinos and Latinas would like to share with the church at large. Along those lines, I would like to highlight some of the features of that plan.

First of all, it is a plan that calls the church to take risks in evangelism and mission. There are many drawbacks in being a so-called mainline denomination. One of these is that once we begin taking pride in being "mainline" and respectable, we can no longer afford to fail. Thus, we have set up carefully thought-out guidelines for new church planting, requiring demographic surveys, feasibility studies, committee decisions, financial commitments, and so on. The purpose of all this is to make certain that wherever we plant the United Methodist flag, we shall not have to call retreat. (As a result, we are retreating almost everywhere.) It is also to make certain that we invest our resources in those places and settings that are most likely to produce results, with viable, self-sustaining churches developing in the shortest possible amount of time. The problem is that nine out of ten questions we ask in making these decisions are the same questions that I suppose Kentucky Fried Chicken asks before opening a new franchise. I imagine that in making these decisions, Kentucky Fried Chicken executives do not ask "who needs chicken?" but rather, "who can afford chicken?" I submit to you that in many subtle ways, often quite uncon-sciously, the question we ask when planning new church development is not so much "who needs the gospel?" as "who can afford our United Methodist brand of the gospel?" And the fact is that very few Hispanics—in fact, very few poor people of whatever race or culture—can actually afford to be United Methodists. Oh, yes, we do plant a few churches in poor barrios and ghettoes; otherwise, we could hardly be called Methodists or heirs of John Wesley. But the expectations that we lay on a congregation in order to be considered "viable" are such that most of those new churches will never fulfill the requirements. Meanwhile, churches recently planted in newly affluent communities flourish. "Good stewardship," therefore, directs us to invest more resources on those churches that will soon become "viable," and fewer in the churches among the poor, that most likely will eventually be declared "non-viable." Significantly, the result is that our United Methodist denomination, which has taken such an admirable position of leadership in combating redlining by banks and lending institutions, ends up practicing what amounts to ecclesiastical redlining. What I find surprising is that this point, which is so obvious for those of us who look at United Methodism from the perspective of other cultural experiences, does not seem to be noticed by the vast majority of United

Methodists. I suspect that this is one of those points at which United Methodism has become too identified with North American cultural values, and may profit from a dose of criticism from those of us who look at matters through a different cultural prism.

Along the same lines, there is something else that, as someone who looks at it from the perspective of a different culture, I find surprising and even distressing in North American United Methodism. I am a church historian by training, and most of my ministry both in this country and elsewhere, has centered around the teaching of church history. I remember how scandalized I was when over forty years ago, I heard for the first time that during the Middle Ages church positions were bought and sold. As you know, we call that practice "simony," after Simon Magus, who apparently tried to buy the power of the Holy Spirit from the apostles. I also remember how scandalized I was when I leaned that, contrary to what was practiced in the Methodist Church in which I grew up, in the Methodist Church in the United States pastors earned different salaries according to the churches they served, that the appointive system had to take such matters into account, that large and rich congregations had considerable say in what pastors were appointed to them, and that some poorer churches had to take whatever pastors nobody wanted. I remember precisely the occasion when I first became aware of those matters. I was still a seminarian, sitting at dinner with a bishop from the United States, who was explaining how the appointive system was being adapted to take into account such economic realities. With the recklessness of youth, I asked the bishop, "How does that differ from medieval simony?" The bishop was not happy, and I must confess that his answer did not satisfy me either. In fact, I am still looking for a fully satisfactory answer. In the meantime, I live with the nagging suspicion that this may be another of those points in which the cultural captivity of the North American church is such that those of us who are part of it have a hard time seeing it.

The National Plan for Hispanic Ministries is well aware of these dynamics, and therefore sets up a different procedure for the planting of new churches. It does not call for sophisticated feasibility studies to determine where new Latino congregations might succeed. It does not call for subsidies for vast numbers of Hispanic ordained ministers to be supported while they develop new churches. It calls instead for hundreds of "lay missioners"—both Hispanic and not—with the commission and the freedom to establish and nurture as many "faith communities" as possible. These lay missioners are to work in teams, normally with the participation and supervision of ordained ministers, but in such a way that it may be possible for a single ordained ministry to supervise the work of several faith communities. We avoid calling these faith communities "new church developments," and we do that on purpose for fear that, if they are seen as new church development projects, immediately all the categories of "viability" will be applied to them, and they will feel the pressure of trying to meet all the disciplinary requirements for becoming an organized church. The Plan clearly stipulates that from the very beginning these faith communities will be involved in Bible study, prayer, worship, evangelism, and community ministries, and that when they gather, offerings will be collected both for their work and for the work of the entire Connection. When participants in these faith communities are ready for it, they will become members of the United Methodist Church though one of its established congregations, but they will normally continue participating in the life of their faith community. Faith communities function as the presence of the church in the neighborhoods where people live. And yet, their primary purpose is not to become organized churches. That may happen or may not happen. Their primary purpose is to witness of Jesus Christ in their communities, to sustain and develop the faith of their members, to serve the community in the name of Jesus Christ.

Part of what stands behind this vision is a way to assess the success of our work that is different from that of the mainstream of North American culture. We do not value the success of our work by the permanence of the institutions founded, and even less by their economic viability. This is one of the reasons why our culture has often been criticized as being too personalistic. It is said that, in contrast to North American culture, which makes decisions on the basis of institutions and procedures, we make decisions on the basis of personal relationships. That may well be the case. But that may not be all bad. If, as a part of the work of the church, we are able to found faith communities that for a while sustain the lives of one or two dozen people, and that is all we achieve, we should be quite content. If, beyond that, some of those faith communities, either by themselves or by joining others, are eventually organized as United Methodist churches, we shall be even more content. Still, the fundamental goal by which our work is to be measured is not the upbuilding of the United Methodist Church as an institution, but the service of those needing the ministries of the church—a point on which, if I had more space, I would relate what we are proposing to Jesus' insistence that people ought to be healed even if it goes against the institution of the Sabbath.

It is our expectation that most of these faith communities will meet, at least initially, in people's homes. There is ample precedent for that, both in the early church and in the early Methodism classes. For us, it has much to do with our sense that the church is a family. It is quite normal for families to gather in homes. In our extended families, one does not build up the familia by requiring all family members to gather once a week in a park, a theater, or some other form of neutral territory. A familia does not even need a special meeting place. On the contrary, the familia is built up by numerous gatherings in the living rooms or in the backyards of various family members. These are gatherings in which we celebrate life's momentous events—births, death, marriage— but in which most often we gather simply in order to celebrate and to experience the fact that we are a familia.

Thus, what the National Hispanic Plan contemplates is taking the church back to where the family of God leads most of its life—to their very homes. Furthermore, like our various familias in our own culture, these faith communities will be encouraged to relate to each other, to meet with each other, so that they may celebrate the fact that by virtue of the Gospel they are all the same family. If, after sufficient time for growth both spiritually and numerically, a faith community or several communities together find that they need a larger place for regular meetings, that will be the time to look for a more traditional church building. Again, rather than determining beforehand what these communities must become, or what they must be, or how they must be organized, the main goal is to serve the people, to nurture them in the faith, and to allow them to find their own institutional way.

There is something here that I also covet for the United Methodist Church at large. It is the vision of taking the church back to where the people live, back to the gatherings at which they celebrate their most important and their most intimate joys and sorrows. That is where the Methodist tradition has seen some of its finest hours, and some of us wonder whether, in becoming as many of our churches have become, commuter churches, United Methodism has not allowed itself to be unduly influenced by North American culture. We live in a society in which there is a gap between life and work. Life takes place where we live. Work takes place in offices and factories to which we commute. For an ever-increasing number of people, no matter what we might say to the contrary, work is not the place from which we derive meaning in life. Such people commute from life to work, and back to life. The place to which they commute is a parenthesis of their lives—a necessary parenthesis, because without it they could not afford rent or food or leisure, but a parenthesis nevertheless. And then, there are denominations that call ourselves mainline. Quite often our churches are on Main Street and people commute to them just as they commute to work. Is there not the risk that for such people the church may become one more element in that parenthesis to which they commute? Is it possible that this may be one of the reasons why our so-called mainline denominations are losing their influence, not only on the life of the nation and its culture, but also in the lives of their own members? I do not know the answer, but it is worth pondering.

In summary, the National Hispanic Plan takes very seriously the fact that the vast majority of Hispanics in this country are poor. If it is true that most Hispanics cannot afford to be United Methodist, this leaves us with only two options: either the United Methodist Church gives up on Hispanics and other poor constituencies, or we find a different way of being United Methodist. (I was inclined to say a "new" way until I realized that much of what we are proposing goes back to the original ways of Methodism in the days of the Wesleys.) That is part of what we are attempting by proposing the recruitment and training of lay missioners, by recommending the establishment of faith communities, and by seeking ways in which it is possible for poor people to be part of United Methodism. But I would hope that the National Hispanic Plan will do much more than that. I hope it will challenge the United Methodist Church to think about its connection, both positive and negative, with the mainstream of American culture, and to evaluate the price it is paying for the right to consider itself a "mainline" denomination—perhaps the most "mainline" of all denominations in the United States. It is true that the United Methodist church has gained much from its connection with the mainstream of North American culture; but it is also true that is has paid a high price— the price of connection with the poor and the marginalized in North American society. In short, I would hope that the National Hispanic Plan and the presence of Hispanics and other minorities in the United Methodist Church will force us to consider seriously the harsh but unavoidable question: in a society in which ever-growing numbers are increasingly marginalized, is it legitimate for a church to call itself at the same time both "mainline" and "Christian"? This may be a harsh question, but it certainly is a question worth pondering.

Barbara Troxell and Patricia E. Farris

If the relative importance of events can be measured by the amount of controversy they create, then one of the most important episodes for American Methodists in the twentieth century would have to be the Re-Imagining Conference in November 1993. Years afterward, the mere mention of it produces polarizing conversations among antagonists in United Methodist and ecumenical circles. Was it a gathering so radically out of touch with the center of the denomination's theology and discipline that its participants and their perspectives should be deplored by the church? Or was it an event so remarkably consistent with the way women have had to bring about change in the church that it stands at the center of our denominational story?

Barbara Troxell, a practical theologian, and Patricia Farris, a pastor and district superintendent, look back into some of the history of American Methodist women and find that earlier efforts were also as controversial as they were creative. They also look into the future of the denomination, toward what they believe the church is becoming, and they urge the church not to be threatened by the beckoning transformation.

Using the tools of historical research in print resources, oral history, and a variety of interviews with contemporary participants in the life of the United Methodist Church, Troxell and Farris pose a number of questions. Will those who are eager to re-engineer the structures of the church find common ground with those who wish to re-imagine new ways for United Methodists to be the church? Is the great tradition being creatively reclaimed or destructively re-defined by affirming the principles of trinitarian worship as Troxell and Farris propose to do? Is the practice of a holistic spirituality a temporary fancy, or is it essential to recovering the power of the past if our church is to have any promise for the future?

One Eye on the Past, One Eye on the Future: Women's Contributions to the Renewal of the United Methodist Church

Barbara Troxell and Patricia E. Farris

Introduction and Intent

We intend to explore women's contributions to renewal of the United Methodist Church based on:
— historical data,
— interviews with contemporary churchwomen, and
— our own projections of future options.

Issues of authority and ministry are critical to this exploration, as are elements within Christian spiritual traditions that nurture faith journeys and aid church revitalization. We assert that attending to the marginalized voices and acting on the witness of women and racial ethnic persons within the United Methodist Church are essential elements towards renewal and revitalization. We further assert that renewal of the self and renewal of the church go hand in hand for women in United Methodism. In this paper, we move back and forth between personal renewal and ecclesial renewal, finding, at base, that personal and social holiness and transformation are always interconnected, else they are neither holy nor transformative.

I. History Informs Us

At a time when the United Methodist Church is hungering for renewal and new vision, a time when the denomination is groaning in labor pains as it awaits the birth of a new purpose and structure, at such a time as this, the denomination finds itself once again at a point of embracing or rejecting the contributions of women to its renewal and revitalization.

The Re-Imagining Conference of November 1993, considered by many of its critics as a radical aberration from Christian work and faith, can be seen in another light as a continuation of the work of women in the churches based in the formation of the women's missionary societies of the last century. For the last century and a half, women in

Protestant churches have been organizing for dialogue, theologizing, ministry, and mission, in ways often perceived by male leadership as threatening to the larger church body, but which, in fact, have furthered not only the participation and emancipation of women in church and society but also the mission and ministry of the church.

The Women's Missionary Societies of the last century were created in the years following the Civil War in the United States. For Methodists and America, this was an era of denominational growth, increasing prosperity, industrialization, urbanization in the nation, and belief that improvements in the lives of women at home and abroad would serve to improve the whole human race. Increasing economic prosperity afforded many women opportunities to volunteer energy and involvement outside the home. Missionary work came to be seen as an extension of the "women's sphere" and thus acceptable work for Christian women. The missionary societies were created to fund, by "second-mile giving," the women's mission projects at home and abroad and to preserve for women the funding and control of their organizations.[1]

From the beginning, several factors distinguished the women's societies from the boards and agencies of their male counterparts. Minutes of meetings reveal passionate discussion of controversial issues, with consensus as the goal. Truly democratic leadership was their style. Plans for continual self-study and re-evaluation were built into their organizations. A strong "sisterly" feeling of support within the groups and with the missionaries was nurtured by extensive letter-writing and prayer.[2]

Monies were raised through the sale of crafts and baked goods and through whatever means the women could create using the limited resources available to them. The women's groups eagerly worked with their ecumenical partners. Not having the funds for extensive publication of books, they shared information, prayers, and Bible study materials in thousands of leaflets and tracts. Funding for all the work came from monies gathered by the women themselves and given on top of their regular church contributions.

Underlying all their work was a strong spiritual base with both strength and flexibility to face changing conditions. The slogan of the women's missionary society of the Methodist Episcopal Church South was "Grow we must, even if we outgrow all that we love."[3]

Several of their organizations, such as the Women's Home Missionary Society, took very active progressive social stands on issues such as temperance, child labor, law enforcement, causes of war, neglected children, polygamy, violations of the Bill of Rights, share croppers, race relations, and immigration. Participation in the work of the women's missionary societies often led members to work for broader recognition and authority both within the life of the church (for example, towards becoming deaconesses and achieving laity rights for women) and in the broader society, as seen in the creation of social work as a profession and the development of women as speakers and leaders in such movements as the Woman's Christian Temperance Union.

Through it all, the women and the work of the church grew and prospered. Case in point: the annual income of the Woman's Foreign Missionary Society of the Methodist Episcopal Church South grew from $4,014 in 1874 to $259,178 in 1909. Their number of auxiliaries grew from 150 to 4,201. By 1909, they had sent 92 missionaries, were supporting 107 schools, and had responsibility for $200,000 worth of property.[4]

The success of the women proved too threatening to the official agencies of the church. In action similar to those in the other Methodist bodies of the time, the 1910 General Conference of the Methodist Episcopal Church South—at which women had neither laity nor clergy rights—voted to combine the Woman's Home and Foreign Missionary Societies under the denomination's Board of Missions.

In language strangely prescient of present-day deliberations, an active Methodist woman wrote to her friend in 1910: "I fear women will lose their independence of thought when they lose responsibility for, and management of, their own affairs. . . . I fear the future will see the most intelligent women seeking a field of usefulness elsewhere and leave the church lacking the leadership that leads to enthusiasm and further development. . . . We are a helpless minority in a body where the membership is made up largely of men opposed to the independence of thought in women."[5]

As a bridge between the nineteenth-century women's missionary societies and the contributions of women today, we wish to name three highly intelligent women, within American Methodism of the last 130 years, whose "independence of thought" thankfully did *not* lead them to seek "a field of usefulness elsewhere." These three were not alone, yet they stand out as foremothers and sisters whose witness after their deaths continues to inspire and renew women and men of faith within and beyond our denomination.

Ida B. Wells-Barnett (1862–1931) was a remarkable journalist and advocate for social justice whose primary contribution was within the anti-lynching movement. When a yellow fever epidemic killed her parents and a younger sister, Ida Wells, at age sixteen, supported five brothers and sisters as a school teacher in Memphis. She soon became a newspaper columnist and then editor. "Through these columns, Wells created a standard for herself, her people, and United States society. She forged a deep and abiding spirituality rooted in the black church of the South."[6]

Wells was an ecumenical person, involved in Congregational, African Methodist Episcopal, and Presbyterian churches at various times in her very full life. Her "strong sense of Christian duty"[7] led her into unwavering social advocacy for the rights of blacks who were being lynched and otherwise oppressed by all classes of whites in U.S. society. She wrote, spoke, and acted forcefully against oppression. Townes writes, "She yoked Christian duty and womanhood with justice, moral agency, and vocation. . . . Wells-Barnett *lived* out her faith and sense of vocation. . . . Her high social, moral, and religious standards demanded a just society. . . . [She] blazed the trail for others to follow."[8]

Georgia Elma Harkness (1891–1974), "the first woman theologian to teach in a Protestant seminary in the United States," combined in her creative life a deep spiritual commitment to God in Christ, an unwavering passion for justice and peace, and an ability to teach theology plainly and clearly. These were not divided for her but woven into the tapestry of a faithful life. Rosemary Keller, who wrote the definitive biography of Harkness, observes in a separate book, "Georgia Harkness's prophetic witness for social justice throughout her adult life was closely tied to her faith commitment as an evangelical liberal."[9]

Nurtured in the faith in Harkness Methodist Church, in upstate New York, she continued as an ecumenical Methodist and United Methodist her entire life. A pacifist throughout her adult life, Harkness also worked intensively against racism, for women in ministry, and against militarism in very specific ways (including, for example, speaking out against the internment of the Japanese people on the Pacific Coast of this country during World War II). She grew into such unwavering justice commitments out of a deep faith in the incarnation of God in Jesus Christ. Georgia Harkness certainly "stands as both forerunner and role model," as Rosemary Ruether writes in her "Introduction" to Keller's biography of Harkness.

Thelma Stevens (1902–1990) was a Southern white woman who at age sixteen witnessed part of a lynching of an African American teenager. "The experience profoundly changed Stevens' life, for she vowed that 'if the Lord would ever let me live long enough I would spend the rest of my life working for basic fairness and justice and safety for black people.'"[10] As director of a Methodist women-sponsored Bethlehem Center in Augusta, Georgia, from the late 1920s to late 1930s, Stevens organized interracial camping programs and other social justice and outreach programs.

Later she would become head of the Bureau of Christian Social Relations of the Methodist Episcopal Church, South, and, in 1940, the full-time executive of the Department of Christian Social Relations of the Woman's Division of Christian Service of the Board of Missions of the Methodist Church. She was the primary writer of the 1952 Charter of Racial Justice; built strong ties between Methodist women and the United Nations, including sparking construction of the U.N. Center. After retirement in 1968, Stevens worked strongly against sexism in the church, volunteered with Church Women United, and helped in the formation of the UM General Commission on the Status and Role of Women. She worked for justice for gay men and lesbians, and was a wonderful mentor for younger women.

We lift these three women as examples of the many faithful women, known and unknown, named and unnamed in our written histories, whose life stories are part of our sources for renewal of the United Methodist Church. These three women are "bridge mothers" between the women of the missionary societies of the nineteenth century and the women within the UMC today.

II. Tensions of Authoritative Leadership Experienced by Women

As we consider renewal, we highlight tensions of authoritative leadership experienced by women. We understand authoritative leadership to be the creative exercising of authority in community, the legitimation of power to name, to influence, to change people and situations. Since it is *legitimated* power, authority requires relationship and is most full expressed when shared in mutual ministry. We explore three tensions women church leaders have experienced as they seek to express and live out authoritative leadership. These are particularly apposite to our theme of "Women's Contributions to Renewal of the United Methodist Church," for these tensions delineate a context in which many church women find themselves today.

A. Backlash and Silencing Eroding Women's Authority

As part of the backlash against women in leadership in church and society, movements have arisen which seek to silence the voices of women theologians, pastors, and church executives. Witness, for example, the huge brouhaha over the "Re-Imagining" Conference in November 1993, including the actual loss of jobs of certain women who gave planning leadership to this excellent theological event. In response to the backlash, women in the United Methodist Church are variously expending enormous amounts of time and energy defending their positions and their work, becoming angry and reactive, acquiescing in the face of such silencing, or going underground. In all cases the inner wisdom and valuable leadership of women, seeking to follow the call of God in their lives, is muted or denied.

In a series of interviews on authority and mutual ministry among UM women in leadership in the church, facilitated by Barbara between 1990 and 1995, the following statements were made:[11]

—A retired staff person of a general agency: "I see so much violence against women and oppression of women within the church escalating in the United States and in various parts of the world. I am very sad and angry about this violence born of patriarchy. This violence must be named and talked about openly in the church so it can be confronted and addressed."

—A former district superintendent of a south central annual conference: "Though I have been affirmed as a key leader in terms of the general church, as a good representative of our conference, I find immediate colleagues stomping on me. It is as if they are threatened by me. Would that be the case if I were a man? There seems to be an issue here of inability to share power."

—A bishop noted that early in her episcopacy she felt categorized by being seen and received primarily as a "role" or an "office" rather than as a real person. This was not so much "backlash" as it was a feeling of being "reduced to a role." She learned that she needed to let go of her own need to insist that others see the "real me." She began to accept the new office in a "reconstructive" way, affirming the inner knowledge that she was a whole person called to a particular office of bishop in the church.

—Another bishop expressed hope that clergywomen in the UMC "will not ricochet at defensive postures" in the coming years. "The backlash is on, and my plea is that they take their authority in good stride and remember how they came to be where they are out of the kind of mutual exercise of power for each other and on behalf of each other."[12]

With the backlash against feminist, womanist, mujerista, Asian women, and Native women theologians, pastors, and diaconal ministers, how do women continue to offer constructive leadership?

What sources of renewal allow women to minister within an often abusive institution in ways that are authentic, faithful, inclusive, and prophetic? How do we continue to call the church to its God-given task of exposing the idolatries of sexism, racism, and disempowerment? What are sources of renewal in this context?

B. Accountability systems in conflict

There is a deep struggle when authority systems are in conflict with one another, when, for example, scripture, tradition, reason, and experience war against each other. The struggle is most painful when personal authority clashes with institutional authority, when new patterns of partner-oriented leadership are denigrated by hierarchical systems. Many women, through the interviews and in informal conversations we have had, spoke passionately about these conflicts. For the most part, those named related to the struggle between what the church ("tradition") expected and what the "inner witness" of the Spirit directed.

—Barbara's own experience: "When struggling in 1980 and 1984 with the pressure from colleagues and friends in the church to consider being nominated for the office of bishop, I discovered that tradition, reason, and the perceptions of others were in conflict with the 'inner witness.' The outer voices, as well as the voice of reason ('Of course you would be a good bishop; you can do it') were saying one thing. The inner voice kept quietly insisting, 'This is not your calling at this time. You can do it, but you may lose your soul.' Thus, I withdrew from consideration."

—A bishop spoke of her approach to authority as one of being honest, truthful, direct in confronting, and even apologizing to her cabinet for mistakes. Cabinet colleagues were shocked at such expression of vulnerability, for they felt it subverted or undercut her authority as bishop. She responded that apologizing when she is mistaken is part of her taking authority appropriately.

—General agency staff colleagues said: "Authority is what we are authored to do, which is connected with who we are as persons." They spoke of the occasional "cacophony of voices" which then must be heard and sorted out until there is some clarity about where God's voice is in all of this. They also used the image of the "human body" which "includes a very complex system that exists to keep us alive and well. The image is one of dynamic interaction with all of creation, in the sorting out of our ministries."

How do we remain accountable to God, to other persons, and to our own best selves in healthy ways, rather than becoming numbed or co-opted by institutional systems of dominance/subordination? How do we take courageous leadership on strongly conflicted issues while being open to hearing and acknowledging diverse viewpoints and those who hold them? How do women create styles of leadership different from the rewarded models of competition and "one-upsmanship," or the new mega-church super-pastor as "lone-ranger-knows-best"? When inner authority contravenes authority of office or authoritative statements of the denomination (as in *The Book of Discipline*), how do we cope with that basic contradiction? What are sources of renewal, when accountability systems are in conflict?

C. Challenges of Chaos and of Law-and-order

For many in today's world, all that seems real is chaos; disorder; situations, people, and events that are out of control. Alternatively, in a society sick or fearful of chaos, the clarion call is for "Law and order!" and "Rules and regulations!" We have become caught in this nation and in parts of our denomination in what Walter Wink calls "the myth of redemptive violence."[13] That is, we are convinced that God has called us to bring order out of chaos through whatever means are necessary, including combat and violence. In the process, we forget that chaos has been the milieu for creation and for the birthing of the new.

Boundaries in our church and world are either too loose or too rigid. Many women and some men, both clergy and lay, are leaving the church or our particular denomination—because their creative leadership is not honored and they do not feel heard or supported. They feel stifled, bound too tightly by denominational restrictions. Others leave because they feel the denomination has become too loose, too "liberal," not standing for orthodox convictions of Christian faith.

— A bishop and others named in interviews the pain they felt about clergywomen who leave the active ministry because these women feel they cannot be heard or received in the church as they are. Their stories are not honored. Yet, the interviewees stated, "these are some of the most courageous, visionary, and gifted women." The boundaries have become too tight for them, around images of God, styles of worship and music, sexual orientation, lifestyle.[14]

— Agency executive: "God created life out of chaos! We don't really believe that. We have such a linear idea of what life is. Yet life is a cyclical spiral of evolution. We often will revisit what we have been through before in similar yet different ways."

— Agency executive: "Part of mutuality in ministry is to allow whatever gut-level reaction comes, rather than having to be so linear, statistical, numerical." But this way, she pointed out, feels like chaos and persons being out of control, and "that is scary and not orderly enough for many people in the church."

How do we lead with strength and conviction when all that seems real in the world is chaos, disorder, situations and people out of control? Alternatively, how are we to be creative when, in a society sick of violence and fearing chaos, the clarion call is for "Law and order!" "Rules and regulations!" and "Tighten up!"? What are sources for renewal when chaos frightens us and boundaries constrict us?

III. Present Elements and Future Options for Renewal

It is clear that the United Methodist Church is currently experiencing an existential crisis of direction and definition. Buffeted by societal forces of economic change, increasing racial/ethnic diversity, urbanization, a new populism suspicious of all large-scale organizations and their leadership, growing polarization between rich and poor, the decline of U.S. hegemony as a world power, etc., a range of prognoses, paradigmatic models, and new structures are being discussed and explored at all levels of church life.

It is troubling to note that within church circles and publications, as well as in conservative groups within the denomination, "Re-engineering" is being embraced but women's work of "Re-Imagining" is attacked as heresy. Stereotypically male forms of language and thinking are accepted as new paradigms for church development, whereas concepts and styles that come from church women themselves are received with suspicion and even disdain. Perhaps not surprisingly, Re-Imagining as been formatted into a convenient target for derision and fear-mongering by the Good News organization, the Presbyterian Lay Committee, and their larger umbrella organization, the Institute for Religion and Democracy.

In point of fact, the Re-Imagining Conference was for many the most public and visible manifestation of women's theologizing, organizing, and visioning. As such, it has become a powerful beacon of hope for many in the church. One very significant perspective is revealed in the recent study out of the Hartford Theological Seminary, *Defecting in Place: Women Claiming Responsibility for Their Own Spiritual Lives*.[15] This Lilly-funded study, based on research surveys of some 3,746 Roman Catholic and Protestant women, documents the fact that the Re-Imagining Conference, in both form and content, was not an aberration.

The research clearly documents a widespread development within the churches of circles of women who are not content with the limited theology they often receive in their local churches, who are frustrated by the obstacles placed by the church to their full participation and recognition of their authority, and who are nevertheless working within the church for transformation and renewal of their own lives and of the institution itself.

We can note many examples of contemporary women's contributions to the renewal of the UMC, contributions that embody creativity, courage, and deeply transformative faith commitments that are renewing the women themselves even as they renew the institution:

— Bishop Sharon Brown Christopher and Conference Lay Leader Aileen Williams from the Minnesota Conference are risking bold new initiatives based on the Quest paradigm.

— Phyllis Tyler Wayman, recently of the Board of Discipleship, has offered prophetic leadership in grounding the Covenant Discipleship Group experience in ministries of justice and peace-making.

— Retired Bishop Leontine Kelly continues to witness to a denomination by being engaged in public social involvement around issues of universal health care and nuclear testing, as well as the elimination of racism.

— Nobuko Miyake Stoner, See Hee Han and others are providing powerful, redemptive leadership and modelling around issues of international and ethnic truth-telling, confession and reconciliation through their work on Japanese-Korean relations.

— Jeanne Audrey Powers has offered public witness as a lesbian woman with decades of experience as a denominational leader and ecumenist.

— Tweedy Sombrero and Anne Marshall speak passionately about the theft of Native American spirituality by church and commercial opportunists.

— District Superintendent Tembo Kalenga from Zaire, and others from Liberia and other places of horrendous violence and suffering, are challenging traditional roles for women while living out ancient/new models of church as source of forgiveness and reconciliation, as well as hope and joy in the power of the Holy Spirit.

These women, and many others like them, are seeking to renew the denomination from within as they themselves are transformed through the practice of ministry at the intersection of faith and the world.

Theological renewal and transformation of church and society go hand in hand, as they have since the first ministries of women in the church.

Out of our historical and present experience as women of the church, we are pointed towards sources of renewal in the United Methodist Church, some of which are being overlooked, deliberately misreported and/or trivialized. We here lift up eight for discussion and serious consideration.

IV. Contributions of a Transformative Ecclesiology to Renewal of the United Methodist Church

1. Living within communities of faithful people who support, challenge, pray with us, study Scripture with us, and hold us accountable to our visions and covenantal commitments

Support communities are essential to renewal of the church. Every one of the twenty-five women whom Barbara interviewed named support communities as essential to the nurturing of her relationship with God and her continuing in ministry within the United Methodist Church. Support communities for these women leaders include women and men, young and old, families and friends, colleagues and spiritual guides, laity and clergy, persons within and outside of the United Methodist denomination.

We must stay within embodied, living communities of faithful ones who both support and challenge us, and hold us accountable to our visions, voices, and promised commitments. They help us speak out and act when we feel called by the Spirit of God.

These contemporary forms of "Christian conference" are one of the essential means of grace. Jesus knew this. The Wesleys knew this. Members of class meetings in the Wesleys' day, and members of covenant discipleship groups in our day knew and know this. The nineteenth-century women in missionary societies knew this. Ida B. Wells-Barnett, Georgia Harkness, and Thelma Stevens knew this. Can we do less? The renewal of the United Methodist Church depends on such communities of support and accountability.

2. Practicing discernment within a holistic spirituality

Holistic spirituality involves interconnectedness with God, with others, with our world, with the earth and all creatures, and with ourselves. For Christians, it is the quality of relating all of life to the presence and guidance of God as God is known in Jesus Christ. The ways this quality of interconnectedness is developed are many. We name some which we heard again and again in our conversations and interviews with women in United Methodism:

— Take sabbath time intentionally (daily, weekly, monthly, yearly) as a way of attentiveness to God and God's call in one's life. This is a way of caring for our soul's and body's well-being. Make time and space for prayer and whatever else nurtures your relationship with God.

— Know the importance of our "inner life" connected with our "outer life." Several women interviewed were clear that it was only in mid-life that they became aware that they had an inner life that required tending; they now find that tending a great joy and grace.

— Develop a holistic spirituality which honors body, as well as spirit and mind, embracing the whole of creation.

— Begin and end each day with special rituals for re-connecting, gathering, centering.

— Engage regularly with a spiritual director or spiritual companion who keeps us honest and aids our discernment (our "listening" and "sifting").

— Trust the "means of grace." Keep a balance of "works of piety" and "works of mercy"—together with "no-works," but simple resting in God.

"We must learn to ground our spirituality in what European theological traditions most fear—physical embodiment, cultural particularity, and the unavoidable reality of multifaceted interdependence and cosmic interconnection."[16]

3. Claiming authority from God in the self and in the community of faith, trusting that God in Christ speaks through inner wisdom within diverse persons and communities of discernment

We are called in our baptism to claim the power of God, for "through baptism (we) are incorporated by the Holy Spirit into God's new creation and made to share in Christ's royal priesthood."[17]

Let our styles of leadership and organization reflect this affirmation, through greater participation and mutuality among *all* persons, honoring the gifts of persons of diverse genders, races, classes, educational levels, sexual orientations, and cultures. Let us affirm that God *does* speak through diverse theological perspectives, new ways of preaching Jesus Christ, and diverse expressions of faith; for at the center is Jesus Christ, not creed, tradition, or even scripture.[18] In women's experience, such centering on Jesus Christ eschews triumphalism and arrogance, as well as forms of patriarchal control often associated with Christ-centered faith.

As Jean Miller Schmidt writes: "the power to transform the world must be rooted in profound spirituality, biblical faith, and theological reflection (and not simply human effort), while insisting equally that this must *not* mean conforming to a particular type of piety."[19]

Will we (to use Nelle Morton's apt phrase) "hear one another to our own speech, to our own stories?" Part of claiming God's authority within us is surely to aid one another in finding our voices, in speaking our stories and struggles of faith.

4. Naming alienating sins

Dare to name all forms of exclusion, repression, and violence against marginalized persons, as antithetical to the liberating gospel of Christ.

This confessional contribution to renewal is grounded in our baptismal covenant. Our vows (or in the case of an infant, the vows of parents or sponsors) include accepting "the freedom and power God gives to resist evil, injustice, and oppression in whatever forms they present themselves."

Dare to name the violence against women and continuing oppression of women and children as serious obstacles to true renewal in the church. Name all forms of exclusion and repression (racism, sexism, homophobia, handicappism, ageism) as antithetical to the liberating gospel of Christ. Name also the contradictions.

Letty Russell writes of four contradictions that we must name and reject if we would be a church faithful to Jesus Christ:

> (First) Coalitions and safety are a contradiction. . . . There are no coalitions without risk. . . . A second contradiction . . . is that of trying to solve conflict without sharing power. . . . Persons of privilege cannot solve conflict without giving up or sharing power. . . . A third contradiction is that we think we can create community without diversity. . . . (C)ommunity is not built on sameness. Community is built out of difference. . . . Finally, we need to develop a spirituality in which we recognize the contradiction of celebrating liberation without struggling for justice.[20]

We are called not only to name, but to resist; and such resistance includes praying, acting, speaking with authority and intentionality, and "interceding for the *souls* of institutions."[21]

5. Dialoguing with integrity

In the current context of fabricated polarization, backlash, and fearfulness, it cannot be assumed that true dialogue is always possible nor that it will lead readily to reconciliation. Authentic dialogue is predicated upon self-affirmation on the part of those involved, moves to mutual examination and criticism and on towards mutual affirmation.

The tensions and conflicts that currently mark the United Methodist Church with respect to both theological and social issues cannot be minimized. Symptomatic of the larger "culture wars" of the broader American context, these tensions call for discernment and intentional attention.

Given that women still move into dialogue on these highly conflicted issues from positions of marginalization and vulnerability in the institution, new forms of conversation and relationship-building—which draw on the experience of the early women's missionary societies as well as the spirit of Wesley's class meetings—are called for.

Such dialogue was experienced by participants in the Re-Imagining Conference. Unanimity of thought was neither assumed nor sought. On the contrary, diversity of perspectives on such difficult issues as abortion, homosexuality, inclusive language, and christology was apparent. Difference was embraced, as women spoke from their own life experiences and stories. Mutual respect, trust in a God larger than human diversity, and affirmation of a common orientation towards justice-making and faithful discipleship allowed and even encouraged great latitude in thought.

Based on the experience of women with whom we have worked and worshipped, women we have interviewed and read, women's experiences of dialoguing offer sources of renewal to the larger church: creating safe places for honest sharing which assume confidentiality and mutual respect; giving careful and consistent attention to the presence and the leading of God's Spirit and wisdom; assuming that diversity in the body is expected and healthy; grounding the experience in the worship of the triune God.

6. Affirming the ministry of the laity as we recall the Wesleyan model of small groups led by laity, based in the ministry given in our baptism

Remember the historic Wesleyan model of class meetings, bands, select societies often led by lay leaders. Laity in these small, faithful, regular groups followed the means of grace, and questioned one another about their faithfulness to these disciplines. They did not emphasize dogma, doctrine, or busywork on church committees.

Together, before any laying on of hands for ordination or consecration, we have been baptized. Thus we are called to honor the daily ministries of the laity in their places of service and prayer. There will be no renewal of the United Methodist Church without laity.

It is striking to us that the Re-Imagining Conference in November 1993 included a large percentage of laywomen. The majority of participants were intelligent active laywomen of diverse Christian communions. While inclusive of clergywomen and of men, many of the participants came from traditional women's groups and offices in the denominations, similar to those of their foremothers in the women's missionary societies.

We are ever invited to be involved in covenant groups of laity and clergy, together seeking the will of God. It is imperative that we affirm and encourage coalitions of lay women and clergywomen, together with men, who want to share power out of abundance, rather than compete in an atmosphere of scarcity and competition. Trust the laity as thinkers, doers, reflective practitioners from whom clergy can learn a lot!

7. Encouraging deep ecumenism and internationalism

As we are interconnected in this world, we must develop commitment to an ecumenical and international way that celebrates diverse gifts and contributions of all members, basing life together in relationships of mutual respect and engagement.

Encourage an international scope which keeps the material and social needs of the poor at the center of the church's agenda for mission and ministry. Honor diverse practices or disciplines of Christians from various nations, cultures, denominational traditions (and also those of other living faiths).

Engage in cross-cultural dialogues, action, projects. Listen, listen, listen. And be willing to be vulnerable and open about one's own faith as well. Remember that we are interconnected; when we lose sight of our connections, we sin against one another and against God.

As colleagues in Shalom Ministries have written: "Great religious themes are controversial and debated for centuries. These discussions affect the ways people deal with their cultural setting as well as how the church understands itself and its mission."[22] They note that a key religious question confronting us now is: "How will we relate to other people? What does it mean to follow Jesus' teaching to love our neighbor?"[23]

8. Worshipping the Triune God undergirds and enlivens all other contributions to renewal.

At the center of our lives as United Methodist Christians is worship in all its facets of praise and thanksgiving, confession and forgiveness, word and table, hymn singing and silent waiting, intercession and engagement in God's mission for holiness/wholeness in the world. Even as the persons of the Triune God are ever in relationship with one another, so do we lift up our hearts and reach out our hands to be in relationship with one another through the power of the One who first loved us.

Women have sought the transformation of vital worship through emphases on: "worship in the round"; involvement in worship of "the whole person"—body-mind-spirit—in every age and stage, in all beginnings and endings within one's life; and awareness of all of creation within Christian worship. Renewed emphasis on the sacraments, together with regular weekly celebration of the eucharist in many (though not yet the majority of) United Methodist churches, has deepened our life in God.

A transformative ecclesiology, renewing the United Methodist Church, requires honest, open, celebrative, authentic worship of the Triune God.

Conclusion

The title for this paper is taken from Madagascar, where a proverb speaks of the chameleon, an amazing creature whose two eyes can turn independently, thus allowing a large field of vision embracing many directions at once. The Malagasy people say that the chameleon has one eye on the past and one eye on the future.

Thus, with one eye on the past and one eye on the future, it is our conviction that attending to the marginalized voices and acting on the historical and present witness of women within the United Methodist Church are essential elements as we live into the future.

It remains to be seen whether or how women's perspectives and contributions will be sought and incorporated into new models of church and denomination. Will women's theological and ecclesiological contributions be embraced at the heart of denominational restructuring, or will they—metaphorically speaking—remain in the basement with the statues of Susan B. Anthony, Elizabeth Cady Stanton, and Lucretia Mott, still awaiting their place in the rotunda of the U.S. Capitol, in this year of the seventy-fifth anniversary of women's suffrage?

In this time of renewal of our denomination, we assert that our Wesleyan, United Methodist tradition has never been about drawing sharp lines, but about depth inquiry, asking questions, embracing diversity—in commitment to the Gospel which liberates persons, society, and even the church itself.

Every movement arising from the wind of the Spirit re-imagines. In a recent address, Dr. Marjorie Suchocki, Dean of the School of Theology at Claremont, asserted that "what was in the beginning, is now, and ever shall be *is* the process of transformation—that is, God making all things new."[24]

Ellen Kirby, active United Methodist, writes: "I dream about the church as a place where people from all walks of life find interesting and challenging ways to serve their community, where women's and men's talents are equally shared and recognized, where faith and action are integrated into tangible expressions of social healing. I dream about the church as a living witness to society of the most important messages of love and justice that the Christ presence in and among us can offer. . . ."[25]

It is our hope that women's voices and styles of leadership, women's insights in theology and spirituality, women's gifts, graces, and wisdom will be seen by the denomination not as threats, but as profound and faithful sources of renewal and revitalization.

CONCLUSION

Donald G. Mathews

One could read the disparate accounts of the peoples called Methodist at the risk of descending into despair over the fragmentation in the present and the forgetfulness about the past that seem to characterize the denomination. But Donald G. Mathews, a historian of church and of culture, reads the panorama comprehensively and finds some remarkably unifying forces at work.

For Mathews, American Methodism arose as a theological option that offered an alternative self-consciousness to people. It provided not only the rhetorical possibility of becoming a "new creation," but also the spiritual power of grace and discipline to accomplish it. And it did so as a creative force both for individuals and for communities (or, more properly for Mathews, "publics"). As a result, in American culture, (United) Methodism has served a personal and a public mission.

What Mathews describes, in subtle and sensitive ways, is the multiple levels of meaning involved in describing American Methodism as a "popular" movement. It is not the same thing as "celebrity." That is, a movement of the people, a "popular movement," is one which fosters a similarity of discipline among persons and groups, one which forms and fosters a collective will, one which founds institutions for exercising that discipline and will, one which has the capacity to embrace internal tensions yet to offer a transforming testimony of faith.

This is a daring vision of United Methodism in American culture. It pleads with us to recover our forgotten history, to enter into dialogue with our adversaries, and to forge a discipline for faithful living in the public as well as private arena. One comes away from reading Mathews convinced that this is the way it has been and must be for Methodist peoples. But are we ready to take it seriously?

United Methodism and American Culture: Testimony, Voice, and the Public Sphere

Donald G. Mathews

The polarity of "United Methodism and American culture" masks a complex reality. The two are scarcely equal: one is swallowed up in the other. Such a relationship—although more symbiotic than that of Jonah and the great fish (Jonah got transportation but the fish gained nothing)—is not easily explained. Boundaries between the two are indistinct and permeable, the exchanges too many and too subtle, and the fragmentation of each mirrors that of the other. Indeed, this fragmentation suggests to some commentators that American society is not one culture but a mosaic of many and that United Methodism is not one of the many but is itself a mosaic of cultural pluralism. That the denomination is such a small replica of the larger society suggests that American culture has overwhelmed Methodist identity. And that is how students usually conceive interaction between the two: it has been more common to talk about how American culture affected Methodism[1] than how Methodism affected American culture.[2] This is in part because United Methodism has been so thoroughly integrated into the larger society, that identities other than Methodist have engaged members along gendered, ethnic, and ideological lines. Moreover, Methodists' stories have been part of other stories rather than primarily their own; American religious historians have long labored under the rigidity of the Puritan paradigm that made American culture the historical exposition of the Puritan psyche.[3] Accordingly, the story of Methodism was told as part of a Calvinist story. As the paradigm weakened, Methodism became part of a widespread, popular, democratic transformation of American Protestantism that repudiated traditional Calvinism and helped contour American culture between the Declaration of Independence and the Civil War.[4] Methodism became part of an Evangelical story;[5] it was one of many phenomena in a long and complex historical process.

It still is. If this accounts for the difficulty in discussing United Methodism and American culture, it means also that there will be varied and conflicting ways of doing so; but all attempts should somehow concede that there once was a time when, in the early

279

Republic, boundaries between the surrounding culture and Methodists were clearer and more substantial: when their contributions were more obvious; when they were not quintessentially "American" but a peculiar people—indeed, far too peculiar to suit their critics. In those peculiarities one may infer the original Methodist appeal, which in turn can provide an understanding of a Wesleyan public consciousness and encourage discussion as to what the Methodist past might suggest for a Methodist future. Historical knowledge is not, however, a prescription for returning to the past—impossible on its face; nor is it a search for heroes, heroines, or practices to emulate. Such a view freezes history, denying its vitality and humanity as well as the historicity and malleability of the present. Such a use of history is as naive and insipid as the view that innovation for its own sake is worthwhile. The idea that we must cut all ties with the past leaves us bereft of the most valuable of cultural tools—historical memory.

A People's Movement

Memory tells us that it was not difficult to see Methodists in the early Republic. They were a movement of the people that separated individuals from status, class, rank, gender, family, or race as a source of personal worth—in their own minds, at least. In a hierarchical society in which social position was established by wealth, family, dress, and education, Methodists insisted that such things did not dictate a person's worth. That worth, they said, lay in a new consciousness of self at odds with meanings traditionally associated with invidious social distinctions and the ascriptive characteristics of gender, race, and beauty. Methodists did not denounce these distinctions as the way in which powerful people sustained their authority over common folk, nor attack the social and political systems as oppressive; but what they did say was as revolutionary as if they had done these more confrontational things. They simply told each person that she or he could live a new life at once; the decision was up to them. The message was formidably simple even if it did rely on assumptions about divine grace and presence, and it could seem incredible even if devoutly to be wished, but thousands did in fact come to believe it. The radical nature of the message was probably at its most dramatic when white preachers visited slaves' quarters, for such an event was at odds with the ordinary rules of the world even if consistent with the circuit riders' belief that they had been called to "proclaim liberty to the captives." [Isaiah 61:1–2]. White people did not usually enter the homes of slaves to tell them they could become children of God. Blacks usually were not conceded a voice among whites. If such demeanor meant an assault neither on slavery nor racism, it did suggest the value of each individual heedless of rank. The simple act of entering a slave shack to kneel with the people there could speak more eloquently than a treatise on human equality. If such action were not so radical in a white family, it could nonetheless convey the same message and elicit a similar voice.

That message was not a simple formula such as repent-believe-on-Christ-and-be-saved although it could at times appear partially in this fashion. Nor was the message new doctrine—truth to be learned—although it could be defended doctrinally; it was not the Apostles' Creed nor the Twenty-Five Articles nor (yet) a catechism. The message was more personal and complex than any of these things; it could not be separated from the various ways in which it was conveyed or the way in which it affected those who received it. It was *embodied* in holy men who entered domestic space heedless of social and gendered order; it was *dramatized* by the various ways in which women and men, blacks and whites, youth and elders shared with each other the sense of *being released* from the great burden that alienated them from self, others, and God. The expressiveness of worship from those responding to such *liberty* was essential to the message received; so was the collective act of organizing classes and societies in which people could share themselves and their salvation freely with each other. The message thus was *enacted* in such ways that people from different backgrounds who could not receive what they needed from strict doctrine, careful ritual, and normative polity now received personal assurance of salvation. That the enacted message of salvation should have been conveyed in the spoken and sung word—preaching, testifying, shouting, singing, and groaning—was significant because the psychodynamics of orality brought the "interior life of each person out into a communal sharing of the drama of salvation and commitment."[6] This focus on word, act, and response, and the insistence that response was essential to the message rested on the fact that every early Methodist preacher knew he was delivering his message when his audience told him so through audible and physical responses. Salvation was delivered in encounter and response; and response was public testimony.

People heard repentance to be sure, but the words would not have meant the same to enslaved Africans, anxiously pregnant wives, boisterous young white men, or sorrowful old women who had lost husbands in battle and daughters in childbirth. "Sin"—for which repentance was demanded with the promise that it could be effected—may have been symbolic of any habit, failure, loss, or guilt in the heart and memory of each individual. The *desire* to be free from agony like unto that upon a cross meant (the preachers promised) that God would accept and heal and renew. And in this renewal with its accompanying self-discipline, each could discover oneself as "a new creature." The true evaluation of self lay not in personal pasts or current situations but in the value to be inferred from the news that Christ had died for all to make each new; each person could receive grace to live a new life as a victory of the self over the self sustained by great effort but enabled by divine grace. Thus, each person was empowered to receive by what one believed was an experience of the supernatural so vivid and so associated with feelings of relief that bodies of the newly faithful could involuntarily express the state of their souls in groans, cries, shouts, and tears.[7] The appeal of the Methodist message was that those who received it seemed to be the very ones who contoured it to their own personal needs. *Emotional catharsis*—identified with divine presence and love, sensed in Methodist worship, and given credible substance by human need, relief, and hope—conveyed the message of being born again. The message was only partially cognitive; it was not simply emotional; it was deeply personal; it was holistic. The anarchy of celebrating could be transformed into the enthusiastic singing of salvation in hymns and songs that expressed earnest and intense relief, faith, hope, and piety. Later the songs and hymns would provide emotional power when the shouting had all but died. Such effusiveness was thought by many contemporaries to be unseemly at best and blasphemous at worst, but early Methodism appealed to people who fused the memory of their innermost sorrows, losses, and failures with the healing power of renewal coming from beyond themselves. To them it was the power of God.

In this process were two important innovations in the way people thought about themselves and their destinies. There was (1) a psychological change within religious tradition and (2) an erosion of traditional habits of deference. The psychological change lay in breaking the Calvinist paradigm of salvation on one hand and sloughing off a latitudinarian, tepid, and bland faith on the other. The Calvinist tradition—as Wesleyans understood it—left humans helpless before the uncertainty of salvation. Emphasis on the sovereignty of God and the idea that, because of this sovereignty and the irresistibility of divine grace, Christ could die only for the elect chosen before Adam's fall left one with no way of knowing if she or he were saved. Methodists insisted that humans could know that they were saved through the witness of God's Holy Spirit quickening their religious affections. Calvinists were deeply suspicious of such affections lest one be led mistakenly to believe salvation sure when it was not; but Wesleyans told people to trust their innermost sentiment and celebrate their salvation. The two moods were distinctly different even if they both attempted to prevent a false sense of spiritual security. Wesleyans did this by following their founders' insistence on living a life of aggressive love, which they called holiness, Christian perfection, or entire sanctification. This emphasis on living a holy life complemented the convert's knowledge of personal salvation and religious affections; it emphasized that the Christian life was earnest enough to challenge what was perceived as careless attention to such things among the conventionally religious; and it made life a rewarding struggle for achievement. In emphasizing a dynamic confidence in religious affections and holy living, Wesleyans helped not only to make salvation sensible, but also to sacralize earnestness and personal discipline. This holy living became the hallmark of Wesleyan preaching. Deference to others' evaluation of the self was impossible for someone embued with a continuing struggle for perfection.

This message—which made even the lowliest of the enslaved a child of God—was preached by those recruited from among the people themselves. Methodist preachers lacked the long and relatively careful formal education expected of ministers in Episcopal, Congregational, Reformed, and Presbyterian churches. Indeed, Methodist preachers seemed rough, untutored, naive, young, and brashly disrespectful of authority not based on an experience of divine grace or of religion not expressed in earnest personal testimony or celebrated in song. Thus, the nature of the Methodist clergy—like the democracy of affections to which they appealed, also suggested the popular character of the movement. At first, preachers were laymen within the Church, and when some were ordained after 1784, a complex interweaving of laity and clergy remained as classes and societies selected the men who would eventually be ordained. Essential to selection was the power to move people to the affectionate sensibility so valued by the movement. Traveling in circuits that grew out of the homes of faithful people, these young men were under the tutelage not only of brother ministers, but also of women in the households in which they lived and of older laymen who led the classes. If preachers encouraged converts to live lives of self-consciousness, self-denial, and self-discipline, they could do so only by a democratic confirmation by Methodist women and men that what they preached was true. Thus, if in a world where dress expressed self, circuit riders could preach plain and modest clothing; if, in a world where people drank spirits with abandon, circuit riders could preach abstinence; if, in a world where youth frolicked in erotic celebration, they could condemn dance; and if, in a world of fashionable gaiety and wit, they could caution sobriety, they did all these things by permission of the people they served. Such attention to costume, demeanor, and mood reflected a collective belief that a clear line divided the children of God from the "world" and carried a warning against crossing it as well as the willingness to heed the warning. In early Methodism boundaries were clear at least in theory, which is to say in sermons, exhortations, and the idealized practice of perhaps two generations.

Methodists crafted broad networks of societies, churches, publishing ventures, and other institutions through a flexible polity that seemed designed especially for an expansive, changing society. The flexibility lay in combining a democratic sensibility in recruitment, worship, and expressiveness with the ability to dispatch ministers where they were needed. Just how important bishops were to the process is difficult to say; senior elders in annual conference could have been as efficient as general superintendents in deciding where to send circuit riders—and might have known their men better, too. This democratic insight led some Methodists now and then to break off from the central body of Wesleyanism which retained bishops, but without a convincing and successful theological defense of their apostolic office. Virginians had originally been able to conceive a connectional system without episcopacy, but the way in which Francis Asbury came to dominate the American Wesleyan imagination through his iron will, fierce piety, clever maneuvering, fabled ubiquity, self-discipline, and monumental life—which he carefully constructed—fixed the episcopacy upon most of the Methodist communion. And Asbury's episcopacy was a people's episcopacy for all his dictatorial ways. He lived on popular largess, for one thing, relying upon Methodists directly for food and shelter as if to say in his dependence that the man who assigned the circuits, chaired the annual conferences, and kept the connection together in his person was nothing without them. By thus submitting himself actually and symbolically to the people—by visiting and praying with them in their homes, he brought the connectional system into their everyday lives and personally mediated the universal church to Methodists in all sections. He and the bishops who came immediately after him seemed to personify the people by reflecting their backgrounds, achievements, style, aspirations, and values in ways that made bishops credible representatives of a broad constituency. Later, when bishops and annual conferences—ministers all—began to work with prominent laity to build schools, institutes, and colleges to serve the educational needs of the laity of both sexes these seemed to be grounded in the needs of the people generally rather than in the designs of an elite. There were complaints, to be sure, that Methodists were losing their popular identity; but these were not convincing, for "the people" were finding that they needed such institutions in an increasingly complex, fast-developing, capitalist culture that demanded education and rewarded disciplined behavior.

Essential to Methodism as a people's movement was, as we have seen, its ability to reach across class, racial, gender, and cultural lines. That Methodists' preaching had the capacity for eliciting profound emotional responses across these lines suggested the catholicity of its offering salvation to all and its malleability in allowing people to express themselves in familiar and homely ways. This did not mean that Methodists were casual when it came to repentance or behavior; both were important for the sanctified life. But this catholicity did mean that the Methodist style was *vernacular*; it allowed people to express their faiths in the various vernaculars of their understanding. Methodists allowed greater leeway than other faith communities in converts' expressing their salvation in language that was natural and with concepts that were familiar to them. In dealing with the Cherokee people, for example, Wesleyans were catholic enough to ease the transition to Christianity through the catharsis of emotion rather than the rigors of theology. They allowed converts to grow in grace and knowledge after acceptance as Christians rather than to impose rigid requirements before admission to the household of faith: theology would come later. They saw in Cherokee practices such as mass meetings, communal singing, and water rituals forms that could be used for Christian camp meetings, hymn sings, and baptisms.[8] Wesleyans conceded authenticity to religious practices of peoples from other cultures, African as well as native American; language, the sense of awe, obedience to the divine and celebration in the spirit could be expressed in actions, sounds, words, and images familiar yet converted to Christian usage. This implied not a rejection of Christian exclusiveness so much as appreciation for universal human seeking.[9] In English-speaking culture, too, honoring the vernacular meant understanding that folk belief about spirits, visions, and dreams betokened an openness to the supernatural that could receive its highest expression in a "witness of the Spirit." Methodists were also notorious among their critics for using secular ditties and drinking songs for sacred purposes.[10]

A vernacular tone and mood that encouraged people to express themselves vividly encouraged them, too, to step out of their accustomed places. As a movement, Methodists acquired a reputation for being disorderly in such a way as to challenge relationships in which power and authority were implied. These included class, gender, and racial relationships in which persons traditionally deferential and dependent sloughed off habits of self-abnegation to celebrate themselves made new in Christ and in so doing seemed to challenge social and political order. The most obvious and revolutionary step was to raise questions about slaveholding which became an abortive and forthright attack on the practice when the movement began to become a church in the waning days of 1784. Antislavery preachers could express their anguish and anger in a chanting denunciation of oppression and blood; they could write pamphlets against slaveholding and encourage the laity to manumit their slaves. And there was enough agitation and soul searching to enable a few Wesleyans to develop an antislavery reputation for the church that would last until the 1830s even in the far reaches of Mississippi. Slaveholders responded with lashes, laws, vigilantism, and outraged piety eventually to silence antislavery testimony. The frail antislavery impulse fell victim to the catholic inclusiveness of Methodist evangelical preaching, to slave-holders who did not experience an impulse for emancipation in the "witness of the spirit," and to the fact that whites, not blacks, made policy. What remained was a commitment on the part of a few whites to converting slaves and widespread communities of African Methodists who fought the implications of their enslavement with the implications of their Christian liberty even after Emancipation failed to deliver the promised freedom.[11]

Methodists invited opposition, too, for emphasizing a life of self-denial-and-discipline. Their reproof of amusement and play evoked contempt, ridicule, vandalism, denunciation, and various forms of violence because their attempts to set themselves apart from "worldly" behavior suggested false pride to some and envy to others.[12] Such a posture on the part of Methodists was at one level merely the attempt to change values of people within the movement. But their ability to recruit ever-greater numbers suggested a subversion of social distance; it implied that common folk—including African Americans—were thinking more highly of themselves than they "should have"; worse, it seemed to be threatening gendered order as well. Methodists opposed such traditional male rituals as fighting, drinking, horse-racing, and gambling; they sometimes objected to husbands' treatment of their wives; and they relied on women to nourish the movement. Early

Methodist memories are dominated by "mothers in Israel" who made the church possible by posting appointments for the circuit riders, giving them room and board, and living lives of extraordinary devotion that provided the rich biographical confirmation of the authenticity of Methodist preaching. They led classes, donated money, provided counsel, and encouraged itinerants; they became unordained leaders within a movement that could not have existed without them. With circuit riders, women formed a coalition that could draw scandalous accusation from their enemies[13] and create a popular suspicion, among certain husbands at least, that Methodism had been designed to steal their wives away. Fabled stories of Methodist women who eventually won their husbands to the new faith suggested their own aggressiveness and the meaning of Methodism for women whose demeanor belied historians' canard that evangelicals imposed a domestic tyranny upon women. Indeed, Methodism early in its development created considerable social and psychological space in which women could develop their own sensibility as to gendered spirituality and therefore their power.[14]

That the Methodists' movement had an impact on American culture can be inferred from the fact that they grew from 5,000 members and 14 preachers in 1773 to over 200,000 members and 2,000 preachers in 1816.[15] Numbers reflected the "popularity" of the movement. Growth continued to be dramatic until the Civil War; and if afterwards the drama was less, the results by the end of the century were nonetheless impressive indeed. Methodism had been able to flourish in a society that was changing radically with each decade of the nineteenth century. Americans were moving west and southwest; building canals, turnpikes and railroads; improving communications; expanding inter-regional and international trade; developing a new economic system by doing things they had never done before and—at least some of them—becoming people they had never been before. Such changes transformed ideals, values, goals, and behavior, that is, the culture. Methodists were part of this change, and their chief contribution was that they made Protestantism different from the way it had been preached and practised before their advent. This is not to say that Methodism was the only force affecting the Reformed tradition; but it was the most widespread and aggressive and the best organized. Most recent interpretations of nineteenth-century American culture agree on the great impact of evangelical religion then. Of course any informed historian would be quick to insist that it is as impossible to extricate the spread of the evangelical mood from capitalism as it is to extricate Methodism from the broader evangelical mood, but there was a major, significant innovation which may be assigned to the Methodist movement. That was the way in which Methodists' insistence on a person's "gracious *ability*" to respond to Christ's offer of salvation and the subsequent emphasis on the struggle for *perfection* freed people psychologically to make themselves anew.

There were many assaults on traditional Calvinism[16] but the one that spread throughout the United States in the most organized and effective fashion was Methodist. When a Presbyterian cleric, Charles Grandison Finney, adopted Methodist rituals, style, mood, and aggressiveness in his own work; and when he embraced "perfectionism"—the most characteristically Wesleyan of doctrines—he fused part of the Reformed tradition to the most popular and fastest-growing religious movement in the United States. The activism inherent in compelling and confident recruitment became one counterpart to the entrepreneurial genius of nascent capitalists; it also crafted a reform movement, merging elements of the vestigial Puritan regard for civic life together with perfectionist assumptions, and thus effected change. The nature of evangelical reform—its itinerant lecturers, its national conferences, its conspicuously large number of women—reflected the original Methodist priority of the Christian life over doctrine, its model of continual and tenacious agitation, and its reverence for women as "mothers in Israel," those birthing the new Israel. The political activism of antebellum American evangelicals, however, came not from the Methodist drive for perfection but from the way in which those within the Reformed tradition combined the surge for perfection with their own habits of civic consciousness. It took the Civil War with its fusion of civil religion, post-millennial optimism, and self-dramatizing righteousness finally to bring Methodists into whole-hearted commitment to using political means to achieve perfectionist goals.[17] Before the war, Methodists had joined with other evangelicals in helping to forge the Republican party and secure its opposition to slavery, to be sure;[18] but they had harbored abolitionists uneasily within their midst and with few exceptions had not been among the most radical leaders of reform. If the Methodists' movement had helped make activism possible by appealing to the power of an "experimental divinity"[19] to cut the Gordian knot of Calvinist inability, empower women, and demonstrate the utility of aggressive organizing, they had yet to make modern the Wesleyan desire "to reform the nation."

Methodist Publics

When Methodists burst into the offended consciousness of the Revolutionary generation, they were not monolithic. As a people's movement they represented the many divisions of society and culture. They spoke different languages—German, Gullah, Geechee, English; remembered different pasts—Irish, Scottish, Welsh, English, German, African, Native American; prayed in different postures—standing, kneeling, sitting; carried different burdens as slaves, masters, men, women, and children; and worked in different ways as farmers, planters, artisans, servants, merchants, laborers, and in various relations to the household and public forum. That Methodists encouraged religious testimony from persons heedless of status and gender and thus allowed exchanges amongst themselves not sanctioned elsewhere did not necessarily dictate a democratic uniformity even under the ecstatic conditions of worship. Even the intimacies of class meetings and family prayer which seemed to provide the conditions sufficient for an accord lacking in the broader movement, could harbor interior demurrers based on sex, age, and race. The quarterly meeting of the circuit and other meetings of society could include a multiplicity of experiences among participants, and the chasm between the practices of quarterly conferences themselves and the expectations of the general conference could be great indeed. The demolition of antislavery rules after the founding conference of 1784 is a case in point. This diversity— perhaps latent divisiveness—within Methodist catholicity did not foil Methodist solidarity, even if it made it difficult. Within Wesleyan inclusiveness, preachers used conferences, camp meetings, public address, and private guidance from the General Rules and *Discipline* to maintain regularity. Doctrinal *standards* were illuminated by writings from John Fletcher and John Wesley that provided comment, insight, and encouragement in preachers' sermons as they encouraged believers along the path to Christian perfection. And the preachers themselves were (theoretically) kept in line with every annual passage of their "character." The tension between multiplicity and unity was tamed through what Russell Richey has reminded us was "conference" as a means of grace,[20] and also by preaching, and practice. These helped to create a Methodist public sphere.

"Private" Methodists also became a "public" through engaging issues of collective concern. The idea of a public sphere has been addressed by Jürgen Habermas and by friendly critics who have responded to his discussion of the rise and fall of the "bourgeois public sphere."[21] Habermas found the basis for this field of action in the transformation of family life from a mere economic unit into an intimate association so bonded by "human closeness" that it underscored the essential worth of each individual, a quality not to be denied by either status or wealth. The sentimentality of popular literature, Habermas suggested, helped to reinforce this sense of human worth through cultivating self-knowledge and empathy; and literary criticism helped observers within the public sphere transform this self-knowledge into rational assessments of state authority.[22] Through communication, discussion, and the conflict arising from them, there developed a public opinion that could address issues of concern to itself and encourage collective resistance to authority. Critics of Habermas have suggested refining his analysis to take into account a plurality of "publics"; others have suggested greater attention to the role of religion in developing the public sphere. The criticism is a tribute to his contribution to our understanding of the dynamics of collective and public life in the modern world.[23] Habermas' insight into the familial basis of a developing emphasis on the worth of the individual helps see the broad implications of a movement such as that of Wesleyans on both sides of the Atlantic. Bracketing for the moment his thesis that an expanding market provided an essential driving force in creating the bourgeois public sphere, we see in the Wesleyan movement that included slaves, workers, and women—which the bourgeois public sphere did not—an event of great importance for strengthening the emotional basis of individual worth and a network for sustaining that value beyond the family and into a public domain.

The process of creating a Methodist public[24] ran through three stages, the first of which did not appear to fulfill Habermas' theory that the public sphere would sustain a rational criticism of the state (only in the third stage would such expectations be implied—and then only problematically). The first stage in creating a Methodist public begat and birthed a similarity of practice and thought over a relatively broad geographical area and created ways to guarantee its regularity. This was followed by a discussion of issues that was to lead to a collective will. This stage in turn and in various ways led to founding institutions and sustaining them through continuing discussion and tacit commitment. The maturing of these institutions led to an erratic process in which Methodists could develop the rational criticism of public policy one would expect of a body *claiming* loyalty to a value system not dictated by class, race, gender, and secular authority.

We have already seen the first stage through which Methodism began to become a "public" as a people's movement. The second phase—that of developing a collective will—was advanced by conflict over just what it meant to be a Methodist. Such encounters of course will never end so long as being a Methodist continues to be important—as current controversy suggests. The nature of identity for any long-lasting collectivity is a continually contested matter; certainly the millennia of discussing what it means to be a Christian have not resolved that particular issue. The controversies that afflicted Methodism in establishing its collective will and sanctioning a public presence revolved around slaveholding, authority, and doctrine (entire sanctification). The earliest public controversies within Methodism were those involving slaveholding and slavery, and they continued even after Emancipation (1863–65). The Christmas Conference of 1784 created not only an institution but also a public outcry from within as well as from outside the Methodist Episcopal Church and resulted in an uneasy truce between opponents and apologists of slaveholding. The conflict was never fully resolved, even when the General Conference agreed to divide the Church approximately along lines coinciding with slaveholding and non-slaveholding conferences (1844–48). The division allowed Methodists to assume public responsibilities according to sectional loyalties: a few became abolitionists in the North and fewer still became missionaries to slaves in the South. Neither party to the division ever fully engaged in the rational criticism of the state and authority imagined by those who expect it from the public sphere; rather each became a constituency in the creation of a broad public opinion that supported the social system of each section.[25] There were exceptions of course; most, but not all, were black. That issues associated with slavery were not merely among white Methodists over whether or not slaveholders should receive communion is clear from controversies in Philadelphia, New York, Wilmington [Del.], and Charleston, South Carolina between 1794 and 1834. These were between black and white Methodists over equality in seating arrangements and at the communion table; blacks as sisters and brothers in Christ expected respect and recognition of their human dignity in a place where the ordinary rules of the world should not have applied; whites with different expectations denied them. The institutional results of these conflicts were the African Methodist Episcopal, the African Union, and the African Methodist Episcopal Zion churches; the Colored Methodist Episcopal Church developed after 1870 in the South. African Americans and a very few white sympathizers would be the only early Methodists to fulfill the expectation for a public discourse critical of the "state."

Creating a collective identity also resulted from debates over authority and doctrine. In one sense the issue of authority is continuous, often smoldering for years until bursting into periodic flame, frequently in conjunction with other issues associated with doctrine, race, gender, or sex. Contention over the power or need for an episcopacy resulted in the O'Kellyite schism in the 1790s and the formation of the Methodist Protestant Church in the late 1820s and early 30s. When Methodists identifying themselves as Wesleyan (1843–44) and Free (1860) created new denominations, they also repudiated episcopacy, both to be consistent with their antislavery and perfectionist emphases and to secure a more democratic participation and primitive simplicity in dress, worship, and public councils.[26] In these conflicts, Methodists contested with each other over who was to decide—and how closely and strictly—the nature of piety and discipline. There was a persistent, recurring cycle of controversy over Christian perfection in which definition and redefinition seemed not only to affect the doctrine itself but also to shatter the institutional solidarity of Methodism and suffuse the surrounding religious culture with a penumbra of holiness and charismatic effects. In conflicts, too, with their Calvinist opponents, Methodists contended for a collective identity. The result, writes Randy Maddox concerning formal theology, was to deviate from Wesley's affectional model of moral psychology and expropriate a more rationalistic model. Faith was becoming less a grace-inspired response of religious affections to God's offer of salvation and more a rational assent to Christian revelation.[27] It is no wonder that some Methodists turned to the affectional assurance of a second blessing and even more charismatic gifts!

Conflict over a "collective will" demanded discussion of "public policy"—matters of vital concern not only to private prayer and devotion but also to the face that Methodists presented to other religious groups and to the world at large. But before there was conflict, there was the characteristically Methodist privilege—or was it an obligation?—of testifying to one's religious experience before others. In one sense a responsible Methodist could not keep quiet; and once the private experience was expressed, conflict was sometimes possible when the insight, experience, or vision reflected uncomfortable political realities. When a black woman testified that she foresaw all slaveholders writhing in Hell,[28] testimony had become political discourse as well as moral commentary. When such testimony as this became broadcast through the publishing revolution, a public forum was created. Publication of private testimony was usually less confrontational than that of the slave woman, although the long-term effects could be subversive indeed. Consider the role that publication could play in creating a Methodist female public voice. The *Ladies Repository*, which was printed first in 1839, was merely developing new timbre in a Methodist public voice already expressed in a range of periodicals. By the time the *Repository* began publication as an evangelical antidote to the secular *Godey's Ladies Book*,[29] Methodist periodicals had for twenty years been speaking publicly in ways that complemented the books and tracts of the publishing house, which had been helping define Methodist identity since the eighteenth century. When by the 1830s a renewed antislavery testimony erupted into print and began to unsettle Methodists throughout the connection, conservatives could probably find relief in the *Repository's* devotion to religion instead of "politics."

The slow transformation of the *Repository*, however, demonstrates in one specific case the nature of the cultural process deemed so significant by Habermas and represented in Methodist sensibility: establishing the worth of each person heedless of invidious and ascriptive characteristics. This worth was expressed and reinforced in public testimony to one's inner thoughts. On its face, such testimony did not appear to be the beginning of a revolution, but it was, as Joanna Bowen Gillespie explains in an insightful and compelling study.[30] Unlike *Godey's*, the *Repository's* editors did not engage women in the kitchen, sewing room, or closet, but in the mind. Women were expected to wrestle with psychology and religion, i.e. abstract thinking, self-development, and spiritual autonomy. The male editors began to print the response to their encouragement, and the male voice diminished as the female voice became more audible. Farm girls, young mothers, college students, and older women talked about their religious experience and their innermost thoughts, and thus shared themselves in a public forum where women—according to historians and many people at the time—were not supposed to be. Printing often contradictory essays, letters, and poems of varying quality and insight, the editors allowed self-expression to such a degree that women felt comfortable in telling stories about their children as well as their interior selves. Many women wrote who were rejected for publication—but in merely taking up the pen, they assumed that there was a public out there of which they were a part and which they could help to create through their own sentiments and words. As women gained confidence in exercising the strength and daring which they had suppressed for so long, they expressed themselves in surprisingly dramatic and assertive ways:

And I vowed I would not flinch or falter,
Tho' through *fire* led on my path of life—
Dare the strife,
Dash ahead and *force* a way through life.

A young woman could even find a critical voice, charging certain aspects of "old fashioned Methodism" with having neither refinement, nor feeling, nor the "love of God" in them.[31] Such expressions were part of a broader transformation, Gillespie notes; like much long-range but significant change, they suggested a trajectory that led to a more assertive voice and even more independent behavior. They were learning, as the young poet above wrote, to "Dash ahead and *force* a way through life." Women were becoming more public as Methodists, as women, and eventually as citizens.

In seeking a collective will, Methodists were expressing themselves in more than one voice, as befitted a catholic and malleable movement. The vast Methodist testimony meeting of public discourse evoked Cherokee, Gullah, German, Algonquian, Yankee, and Southern accents in both a masculine and feminine timbre. When testimony became discussion, and discussion became debate, and debate became conflict, and conflict became rancor, it was obvious that achieving a Methodist public voice through trying to establish a Methodist collective will in fact never attained that will. There were too many voices for unity, they were spoken in too many accents for clarity. Thus they were not always heard; if heard they were not always heeded; and if heeded they were not always considered guides for action. Yet the many voices themselves bespoke a public forum. The *attempts* to create a collective will themselves were the creative dynamic. Public debate about slaveholding, episcopacy, presiding elders, laity rights, laity rights for women, entire sanctification, congregational singing, and stained glass windows was carried out in print, various conferences, and special meetings in such ways as to elicit and confirm public identity. With each controversy, those disagreeing with decisions had to decide if they would remain a loyal opposition within the public domain, withdraw to private devotion and reluctant adaptation, or leave. Those remaining sustained the institutional continuity of a United Methodism into the third phase of creating a public presence; they were forging from a coalition of different Methodist publics such lasting institutions as colleges, seminaries, universities, and the bureaucracies that characterize modern life and seem to vitiate local variation and ingenuity.

The process began in the early nineteenth century with the founding of Augusta [Ky.], Randolph-Macon [Va.] , Wesleyan [Conn.]

and Emory [Ga.] Colleges and the acquisition of Allegheny [Pa.], Dickinson [Pa.], and Wesleyan Female [Ga.] Colleges. After the Civil War came universities and seminaries and the proliferation of boards and offices which together with churches throughout the country made the public presence of Methodism appear almost as ubiquitous and solid as the U.S. postal service. Critical thinking associated with higher education was possibly of no greater value than a diploma's certification that its holder was verifiably middle class; both were necessary to a modernizing society. If camp meetings were giving way to middle-class assemblies of genteel self-improvement such as Chatauqua, and if self-education was yielding to the formal schooling of divinity schools, the Methodist consistency remained nonetheless sufficiently broad to include the ministry of both an Oklahoma Sac and Fox justice by the name of Cloud and a Boston theologian with a German Ph.D. by the name of Bowne. It could include African American craftsmen and farmers as well as white supremacist lawyers; mill workers and owners as well as social workers and deaconesses. Such catholicity meant differences in public testimony. And differences in testimony meant continuing conflict, especially if they reflected variations in the inner lives of people who had to act on the basis of such testimony. Once the differences were uttered in public there was no denying them—nor was there any inclination to do so. Thus the continuing testimony of Methodist women led them to participate in public life in ways vindicated by the vision and activism of Frances Willard; in cooperating with women of other denominations to drive a woman's agenda in the WCTU, they were moving toward suffrage in both church and state. They had crafted their own organizations, edited their own periodicals, and taken independent action to serve the needs of city women in all sections of the country. They were continuing the trajectory suggested earlier by the increasingly outspoken consistency associated with the *Ladies' Repository*.[32] In continual pressure, controversy, and criticism, women sustained the public sphere every bit as much as the bishops and ministers who resisted them.

The kinds of issues about which Methodists fought are familiar to the present generation: gender, race, class, unity, purity, and authority. In each of these categories we seem to be no closer to a collective will than we were one hundred years ago. True—the differences are more nuanced now, but for that reason are more difficult to address. When the issue was whether or not men should concede women full laity rights, shades of vestigial "sexism" and "male oppression" were irrelevant in part because the words and concepts had not been invented yet to deal with them, and also in part because the issue was "yes" or "no." The emotional "let down" felt by women after such rights were granted betokened the need for language that could in fact define what was to be called "sexism" and "male oppression," but that was in the future. When the future arrived and the issue became whether or not to ordain women and receive them as full members of annual conferences, the issue was still easier because it could be decided by a clear "yes" or "no." So was the issue relating to women bishops. In both cases, however, even with language supplied by feminist analysis, and even with the attempt on the part of men to learn from that analysis, fair minded persons would have to agree that there is still an "edge" between articulate men and women within Methodism. This is so even among those who have tried to understand the nuanced and shaded differences that distinguish the intersubjective feelings of one from the other. This is not so much true of personal relationships as it is of public personae when ascriptive characteristics immediately create invidious distinctions condemning a speaker as illegitimate because of his or her sex, race, age, and place of birth. This is true, no matter where in the spectra of politics, gender, ethnicity, or theology one stands.

   Issues relating to race were most dramatic during the long negotiations between the Methodist Episcopal Church and the Methodist Episcopal Church, South that ended with the uniting conference of 1939 that merged these two churches with the Methodist Protestant Church. Although it is probably not true that union was postponed for forty years because General Sherman's troops marched through Warren Akin Candler's hometown of Villa Rica, Georgia in 1864, the Bishop never forgot the trauma of that event and his allies fantasized for years about what authority a black bishop might have in a general conference attended by white Southerners.[33] In the end the latter's fears dictated policy with the creation of a jurisdictional Methodism that postponed indefinitely confronting issues relating to race that still confound a United Methodist church.[34] True, Southern Methodists were prominent in the so-called "inter-racial" movement of the 1920s, and Southern Methodist women sustained work by the Association of Southern Women for the Prevention of Lynching,[35] and many of those who fought in the civil rights revolution were Methodists. But public testimony is still scrutinized for accents and cadences that betoken failure to understand the meaning of ethnic identity; and it is still heard with an ear sensitive to any betrayal of the prejudice that the only racial and ethnic divisions among Americans and Methodists are black and white—which they are not.

Beyond gender and ethnic issues, Methodists contended for purity, unity, and authority. Although most authoritative discussions of modernist controversies at the turn of the twentieth century ignore the extensive debates within Methodism because they did not adhere to a Calvinist paradigm,[36] Wesleyans were every bit as contentious as their Reformed brethren. An intense debate about the spectrum of thought ranging from Christian perfection, to the second blessing, to the "baptism of the Holy Spirit" occurred at the same time Calvinists were contending with each other over a dated if intellectually rigorous Princeton theology and an ingenious dispensational premillennialism. Wesleyans, too, fought over the authoritativeness of higher criticism and the relevance of natural selection; they disputed about immanence and transcendence; they argued over what they feared other people might be thinking, and they usually feared the worst. Some were so enthusiastic about harboring a major new theologian such as Borden Parker Bowne in the Wesleyan house of faith that they failed to appreciate just how much he deviated from traditional belief. But his enemies tried to redress that fault with a heresy trial. Others were so impressed by the piety and earnestness of Wilbur Fisk Tillett that they ignored the "liberal" implications of his theory to the great frustration of conservatives.[37] Methodists from all sections engaged in debate: some left the church to participate in more recognizably holiness and charismatic publics; some postponed union as long as possible to sustain the doctrinal purity of Southern Methodism; some embraced union as a way of making Methodism more relevant to an industrial society. Conflict over the social gospel afflicted Methodism in all sections as women began to engage the problems of cities and racial division. The purity of the faith, a few believed, lay not only in the refining fire of the Holy Spirit but in service through home missions and the sisterhood of deaconesses, home missionaries, and supporting networks.[38] Some, like Belle Harris Bennett combined both the fire and the sisterhood with the service. Converted under the preaching of a famous Presbyterian holiness evangelist, Bennett became—in function and dignity, if not in title and office—the first "general superintendent" of Southern women's work. She shared Lucy Rider Meyer's vision of activist women in service to the Master and was probably one of the two most widely revered woman in the South when she died in 1922.[39] If Bennett is remembered as a fighter for women's rights within the church, she should also be remembered as a partisan for broad-based authority and faithfulness to the traditional Wesleyan suspicion of narcissistic antinomianism that elevates experiential authenticity above service to the kingdom.

The Methodist public sphere which developed through recurring conflict and institution-building remains a conflicted forum. It has been conflicted for a very long time; and it is to be hoped that creative tension will remain. And this creativity requires continuing public testimony from the rich variety of peoples identified with the United Methodist Church. Private testimony made public was the genius of Wesleyanism from its inception. For a historian of Methodism, the movement remains an evocative story of origins with suggestions for the future—but not for its Edenic qualities. Eden would not include African slavery, gender inequality, draconian punishment, and primitive anti-intellectualism. Remembering an Edenic moment would not suggest a strategy for recapturing lost influence: history and politics would combine to prevent it. Recapturing the language of origins would not re-create the vitality of movement for a bureaucratized institution, because certain meanings have changed and conceptual nuances have been lost; but the language of origins does suggest the nature of the original "movement." *The movement provided a process through which ordinary people found their own voices.* They spoke. Others listened; and then they, too, spoke. Others joined them. They sang and wept and felt renewed—in the love of Christ. *The language of origins was dynamic and evocative; its testimony in the vernaculars of the people was the dynamic creativity of the movement.* What people said in that testimony was certainly important and is to be part of understanding the voices of the past. What the movement claimed to be speaking, however, was not merely a new Wesleyan language but the Christian language of salvation. *Testimony* was not merely a technique for finding oneself— although it was surely that; but it *was also the means of discovering personal responsibility*. Early American Methodism was realized not only in conference as a means of grace,[40] but also in *testimony* as to the power of that grace. A Methodist public sphere was fabricated in conference after conference where heirs to the movement contended with each other over the meaning of the many, disparate, and often contradictory *testimonies*.

Testimony, Voice, Multiculturalism and United Methodists

Despite persistent contention within the public sphere, Methodists no better than any other body of believers fully appreciated the meaning of *multiplicity* in American life. The word which everyone coming to majority in the 1950s thought was "correct" for referring to the varied experiences of American life, *pluralism*, never captured the realities represented by the concept of many cultures in a society. This was so because pluralism implied a consensual politics negotiated in public exchanges rather than "recognition" that there were many cultures in the United States and that each deserved respect. In the last generation, a politics of recognition has affected not only the governing of the Republic, but also the teaching of children, the training of teachers, and a general understanding of the public sphere. Government, schools, colleges, and universities have been severely criticized for failing to respect the many cultural identities of American citizens— hence a plea for "multiculturalism." The richly textured debates about African American, Native American, Asian-American, and Latin or Hispanic cultures during the 1970s and 80s resulted in widespread insistence on recognition and respect. The multiplicity of collective identities has been complicated by more than thirty years of feminist criticism and a corresponding movement by women away from their traditional roles that forced broad re-negotiations of gender identity and power. In the process, gendered behavior came under even more radical scrutiny; people whose erotic (or at least amative) orientation was centered on persons of the same sex demanded respect and acceptance on a par with heterosexuals. This separating of sexuality from procreation—already popularized by a [hetero]sexual revolution facilitated by "the pill"—in one sense had nothing to do with cultural identity. But it did reflect a *collective* identity that explains why sexual and gender identity have become part of the generic reference to "multiculturalism."

The ideal makes sense in a country such as the United States; and it certainly makes sense in a church which so uncannily reflects the demographic, cultural, ideological, and gendered spectra of American society. It makes sense, too, for an institution—such as United Methodism—which was built on its ability to elicit many voices from a broad range of peoples. The multicultural ideal of mutual respect should have been essential to Christian discourse that engages people not only through their individual lives but also through their collective identities. Those whose only self-conscious collective identity is Christian and "American" have often been unaware of the ways in which unexamined assumptions about the "normality" and unexceptionable character of their own identity have affected treatment of others. The multicultural character of a liberal democratic state within which persons live who are not Christian demands that "Christian" citizens concede civic legitimacy to all engaged in non-violent public debate. The same multiplicity of culture suggests that being "American" is a broad, inclusive category not restricted by sectarian assumptions about normality; confirming citizenship and the rights of citizenship is not grounded on the same rubrics of taste we use to define our friends. The same is true of confirming the Christianity of those proclaiming their commitment in a faithful voice. The genius of the early Wesleyan movement was its including people who had been left out of favorable categories of inclusiveness by elites and their mimetic constituencies. This was also true of the primitive church, and no determined searching for proof texts to the contrary can justify a vengeful repudiation of the command that we love—that is, respect one another before the humbling agony of the cross.

The absence of an "s" in the project's title, "United Methodism in American Culture," thus was not a repudiation of multiculturalism although wary project participants feared that it was. Some suspected that the adjective "American" was too restrictive, too, and that it carried too condensed a meaning with normative connotations; but it was actually meant to focus on Methodism in the United States for purposes of manageable analysis. The assumption was that talking about world Methodism would be even more difficult and analytically diffuse than talking about Methodism derived from social experience in the United States. *Culture*, if condensed, could have the connotation of normativeness, too, but "culture" in this case was meant to be ambiguous, and implied all the ways in which people identify themselves beyond their association with United Methodism. The rubric was thus broad enough to invite participants to address in some fashion the various cultural contexts within which Methodists live. Far from assuming a condensed connotation, restricted to an orthodox view of what constitutes "culture," those who selected the word hoped to elicit from all who participated in the project their own understanding of culture so that in the end we would begin to have a broader view of the tensions within the rubrics "Methodism" and "Culture"—whether in Los Angeles, California; Lima, Peru; or Kuna, Idaho. From various specifics we hoped to bring scholarship, pastoral experience and reflection to bear on conversations about ways to renovate the denomination. From different testimonies on a range of issues it was hoped that we would initiate—if not a great love feast (which would have historical precedence if not realism in its favor)—then at least meaningful dialogue in which we could engage each other honestly in the Methodist public sphere.

Achieving such a dialogue is probably the most impossible task one can conceive in the United States at the present time. The fragmentation of American society and the poisoning of political discourse by partisan warfare that demonizes opponents and exaggerates difference to achieve notoriety if not power has afflicted United Methodism as well as the society within which it exists. Attempts to restrict theological range, impose sectarian purity and renounce the best insights of feminism—similar to the fundamentalists' purge of the Southern Baptist convention—represent to some United Methodists a turn away from the openness of communion and the inclusiveness of theological discourse which generations fought to achieve. Attempts to extend theological range, relax disciplinary expectations, and embrace New Age "spirituality" represent to some United Methodists a turn away from the essential core of Christian preaching and the meaning of a Christian life. The traditional Wesleyan tension between seeking authentic reassurance in the Spirit (the subjective confirmation of faith) and seeking aggressively to serve and reform in advancing the Kingdom persists. The conflict between these "parties" (each with indistinct boundaries) is, of course, confusing to many United Methodists who would rather not side with either on the sure premise that living a faithful life is difficult enough without the added pressures of partisanship. Yet our memory tells us that the Methodist public sphere is sustained by rich and continuing debate.

Much of that debate as suggested above has been carried on with reference to issues associated with multiculturalism and has not so much been "rich" as impoverished by a chronic deafness. Anyone who has been even remotely a part of multicultural discussions knows that they tend to be a series of exchanges that sound like litanies with mandated responses. Listening to what "opponents" say and engaging their concerns instead of merely waiting one's turn to attack them is almost impossible. This results in part from the logic of special pleading; but it also results from postmodern theorists' insistence that there are no such things as real engagement and dialogue in attempting to arrive at certain truths; there are only political arguments made in the contest for power. The failure to listen and engage may also result from rejecting historical understanding because history is presumed to be the story of oppression on one hand and because, on the other, history has been used to justify an unexamined continuity. Historical investigation and understanding—even in controversy in order to be of use to anyone does, however, suggest a way to approach conflict. First of all, historical inquiry requires a patient listening to others in order to ensure that they have been heard correctly; it insists on getting the stories straight. Second, it concedes a history to all parties in conflict, thus demanding attention to continuity not as a normative prescription for the future but as a condition of understanding how we arrived at our present condition. Moreover it accepts the importance of memory in sustaining what the church calls the communion of saints and what others call collective identity; but it acts, too, to correct flaws in memory. Historical understanding is the enemy of cherished myth and legend—which possibly accounts for the suspicion with which it is regarded. Historical understanding cannot prevent conflict and faulty memory, but it can call to mind conflicts in which lack of respect for the ethnic [racial] and cultural identities of others rent the Wesleyan [Christian] community in such ways as to belie protestations of Christian love and mutual respect. Historical understanding can lay bare the starkness of past violations with a florescent glare that shames the communion of saints. It can insist on the role of public testimony in attracting converts to the Church, but it cannot provide the *will* to make us listen to the testimony of all peoples in the present. That *will* must come from other sources if each group in the Church in its continuing testimony hears only its own voice and not the voices of others. Christians ought not to require being told where those sources are.

Participants in the final session of the project, "Methodism and American Culture," (St. Simon's Island, Georgia, August 1995) heard a thoughtful minister speak eloquently and directly to the issue of multiplicity and conflict within the United Methodist Church. He observed that he and another minister who were almost theological opposites had conversed several times and had come to understand each other in positive ways: they had not only heard each other but had also listened. He confessed that the experience suggested what could happen in the church at large, for here was an example of conference as a means of grace. These and other comments which elicited positive responses from laity present implied a desire for the understanding, comity, and collective solidarity that one could hear in the singing of familiar hymns. If other experiences were more discordant, dissonance is natural in a fugue of public discourse even when it suggests John Cage rather than J. S. Bach. Testimony may sometimes bristle at the familiar in Wesleyan history as "patriarchal"; it may embrace innovation as a matter of principle; it may repudiate it for the same reason; it may be modulated in familiar moods and accented in unfamiliar ways. It may be voiced in annoying and discordant ways, but it is authentic for the people who speak. As Methodism first spoke in such a way as to enable testimony from all heedless of condition, accent, modulation, timbre, grammar, or syntax, so it waxed in significance and influence as it fabricated a public sphere. That sphere was impoverished and the church fettered whenever voices were silenced, or if not silenced, ignored, or if not ignored, not heeded. One wonders about the condition of the Methodist public sphere now—the voices that speak and the state of public hearing.

Testimony has been almost sacramental when uttered in conference. Originally testimony was to the power of God among the people of God who received public expressions from others as evidence of the love that bonded all in Christ. It also demonstrated the power of the Spirit-liberated self which could, as the anonymous young woman wrote in *The Ladies' Repository*, then "dash ahead and *force* a way through life." It was originally not accusatory but celebratory; for accusation breaks the sacramental character of testimony unless it is leveled against the self, in which case it then celebrates being freed from the logic of condemnation. Essential to testimony was that it be heard by others humbled before the power of God but elated, too, at the liberation of those who spoke. At least, that was the theory at its best, even if the best was effaced, diminished, and eroded by historical reality. Thinking of the dialectic between elated testimony and the selective and chronic deafness of the past, one wonders how hearing occurs now. What is the response to voices raised in authentic testimony? When the voice is male or when it is female, is the timbre instead of the *voice* heard? Does testimony now focus on oppression rather than liberty; does it smart from evil done and cast on "others" as sin inflicted wrongly upon those who testified in the same voice before? Does this testimony then silence that of others thus condemned? Can a tradition in which public testimony is so important dare lose the dynamic of its public life by enforcing silences when voices sound too little like one's own?

This train of thought is not about historical reality—always the enemy of sacramental occasions; and this is not about ignoring issues to which believers are passionately committed. It is about conceding to fellow believers the authenticity of their voice and the traditional Wesleyan commitment to its being audible, that is, public. It is also about the problems derived from the speaking *that must be done* and freely given without self-censorship for fear of pervasive contempt remembered or anticipated for those who do not see with "true vision" or speak with a "pure voice." In such ways are testimonies hidden and voices denied. There are things we do not want to hear, whether we oppose or support multiculturalism, whether we are "liberal," evangelical, orthodox, charismatic, or liturgical. There are things to which we will not testify for fear not of opponents, but of friends. There are things we will not hear from women, blacks, Asians, or homophiles, things we will not hear because we ourselves are not on a list in the intentionally restricted first clause of this sentence—but should be. If we hear voices unlike our own we do not listen; and we still our own voice when we know it may condemn us.

This condition is not unique to the United Methodist Church. A society in which segmented coalitions readily expose the "sins" of **others** is one that supports no public confession of one's **own** sins. A narcissistic culture cannot even conceive the meaning of "sin" when Christian understanding itself is so disabused of the notion despite images of Holocaust[s] and "Bosnia," and the American intoxication with violence and self. Knowing no sin, the society knows neither responsibility nor forgiveness; knowing no forgiveness, it asks for none, grants none and therein lacks the capacity for understanding the ideals of multiculturalism which rest on recognition and respect as well as *confession*. But the Church does know forgiveness, for it has heard the Word; so how does it excuse its inability to listen when it was called into existence through the Word that evoked voices of many peoples and invested testimony with a sacramental quality? If the church cannot provide the sacramental ethos in which the Word made flesh is celebrated in the solemnity and full meaning of the word "communion," who will take it seriously as the Body of Christ? If the church is intent on excommunication instead of communication; if it silences voices, mutes testimony, and thus restricts the Spirit, who will take it seriously as a house of faith? Those who listen to other voices only to determine if they bespeak the right thoughts in an approved ideological grammar risk restricting creativity in the testimony of others and thus impoverishing the public forum. Testimony must be met with testimony—not silence—if it is to be meaningful; in this we are not surrendering cherished convictions, but conceding that others unlike ourselves cherish convictions, too. The goal is not consensus but testimony in love and the capacity for approaching the Table in confession and repentance to receive forgiveness for our own sins, find "delight" in the Divine will, and discover the capacity for walking in God's ways. The Holy Communion does not silence but rather establishes the ground on which voices become audible and testimony is made public.

Early Methodists were not afraid of taunts that heard their cacophony of voices as noise; they knew that silenced voices meant a muted Word. They somehow knew, if they did not totally comprehend the implications of their knowledge, that silence was worse that "noise." If *they* did not listen as well as they should have, perhaps *their* failure to do so can shame *us* out of our own.

Contributors

Jackson W. Carroll is Ruth W. and A. Morris Williams, Jr., Professor of Religion and Society as well as director of the J. M. Ormond Center at Duke Divinity School in Durham, North Carolina. He is the author of *As One with Authority: Reflective Leadership in Ministry* (Louisville: Westminster/John Knox, 1991) and a co-editor of *Beyond Establishment: Protestant Identity in a Post-Protestant Age* (Louisville: Westminster/John Knox, 1993). A sociologist and an ordained United Methodist minister, he has done major work in the field of congregational studies. Before assuming his present position at Duke, he spent eighteen years at Hartford Seminary.

Patricia M. Y. Chang is an assistant professor in the Department of Sociology at the University of Notre Dame. Educated at Stanford and at the University of California at Berkeley, she served at Hartford Seminary and Yale University prior to accepting her present position. She is the author, with Barbara Brown Zikmund and Adair T. Lummis, of *An Uphill Calling: Ordained Women in Contemporary Protestantism* (Louisville: Westminster/John Knox, 1997).

Patricia E. Farris is Superintendent of the San Diego district in the California-Pacific Annual Conference of the United Methodist Church. Formerly the pastor of United University Church, adjacent to the University of Southern California in Los Angeles, she was educated at the School of Theology at Claremont, the University of Delaware, and at Harvard. She attended the Seventh Assembly of the World Council of Churches in Canberra, and she has chaired the theological education committee of United Methodism's General Commission on Christian Unity and Interreligious Concerns.

Justo Luis González is Executive Director of the Hispanic Theological Initiative at Candler School of Theology at Emory University in Atlanta. The author of many volumes on church history and the history of Christian thought, he also has co-authored volumes on preaching. He is an ordained United Methodist minister.

Will Gravely is a professor in the Department of Religious Studies at the University of Denver. A historian with special interests in southern religion and in tracing the history of African American church life, he was educated at Drew University and earned his doctorate at Duke.

John C. Green is Director of the Ray C. Bliss Institute of Applied Politics at the University of Akron in Akron, Ohio. He is a political scientist and frequently serves as a commentator on the American electoral process. His recent publications include *Religion and the Culture Wars: Dispatches from the Front* (Lanham, Md.: Rowman and Littlefield, 1996) and *The Politics of Ideas: Intellectual Challenges to the Party After 1992* (Rowman and Littlefield, 1995).

James L. Guth is Professor of Political Science at Furman University, Greenville, South Carolina. A graduate of Harvard and of the University of Wisconsin, he has published a number of works on American political life. They include *The Bible and the Ballot Box: Religion and Politics in the 1988 Election* (Boulder: Westview, 1991), which he co-authored with John C. Green, and *The New Christian Right: Mobilization and Legitimation* (New York: Aldine, 1983), to which he contributed along with Robert Wuthnow and others.

Stephen S. Kim is Assistant Professor of Historical Theology and the History of World Religions at Claremont School of Theology. His education includes a doctorate from Drew and an undergraduate degree from Yonsei University in Seoul. In addition to his teaching and research, he directs the local pastors course of study program at Claremont.

Donald G. Mathews is Professor of History at the University of North Carolina, Chapel Hill. His book, *Religion in the Old South* (Chicago: University of Chicago Press, 1977) is a definitive study in its field. He has also published works on Methodism and slavery. A doctoral graduate of Duke University, he has served as a member of the Advisory Board for United Methodism and American Culture.

William McKinney is President of Pacific School of Religion in Berkeley, California. The co-author of several volumes, including *American Mainline Religion: Its Changing Shape and Future* (New Brunswick, N.J.: Rutgers University Press, 1987), he formerly served as professor and dean at Hartford Seminary.

Rolf Memming is a United Methodist clergyman who has served as a pastor in Morrisville, Vermont, and Islip, New York. Prior to entering the pastoral ministry, he earned a doctorate at the University of Nebraska, later doing his theological education at Drew. He has been conducting major studies of pastoral ministry records, including commissioned work for the United Methodist General Board of Higher Education and Ministry.

Daniel V. A. Olson is Professor of Sociology at Indiana University South Bend. Educated at the University of Chicago, he has published numerous articles concerning the sociology of church and congregational life. With William McKinney, he has written *Of Two Minds: Leadership Directions among Protestant Church Leaders*.

Wade Clark Roof is J. F. Rowny Professor of Religion and Society in the Department of Religious Studies at the University of California, Santa Barbara. Educated at the University of North Carolina and Yale, he is the author and editor of numerous works concerning the sociology of religion. One of his most recent volumes is *A Generation of Seekers: the Spiritual Journeys of the Baby Boom Generation* (San Francisco: HarperSanFrancisco, 1993).

James M. Shopshire is Professor of the Sociology of Religion at Wesley Theological Seminary in Washington, D.C. He has studied the Pentecostal movement among African Americans and the neglected history of African Americans in the Methodist tradition. His education includes a doctorate from Northwestern University and a divinity degree from Gammon Theological Seminary in the Interdenominational Theological Seminary in Atlanta. An ordained United Methodist minister, he is a clergy member of the Iowa Conference.

Barbara Troxell is Assistant Professor of Practical Theology, and director of field education and spiritual formation, at Garrett-Evangelical Theological Seminary in Evanston, Illinois. Formerly a district superintendent in the California-Nevada Conference of The United Methodist Church, she was educated at Union Theological Seminary in New York and at Swarthmore College. Her published work includes material on clergywomen and the exercise of ministry.

Charles E. Zech is Professor of Economics at Villanova University. He was educated at the University of Notre Dame and has a special interest in the economics of religious organizations. Among his recent books are *The Mainline Church's Funding Crisis: Issues and Possibilities* (Grand Rapids: Eerdmans, 1995), co-authored with Ronald E. Vallet, and *Money Matters: Personal Giving in American Churches* (Louisville: Westminster/John Knox, 1996) with Dean Hoge and others.

Editors

William B. Lawrence is Professor of the Practice of Christian Ministry and Associate Director of the J. M. Ormond Center for Research, Planning, and Development at The Divinity School, Duke University. He has served as the project associate for this study of United Methodism and American Culture. His recent publications include *Sundays in New York: Pulpit Theology at the Crest of the Protestant Mainstream, 1930–1955.* A graduate of Duke, Union Theological Seminary in New York, and Drew, he served as a United Methodist pastor and district superintendent prior to assuming his present position.

Dennis M. Campbell was Dean of The Divinity School and is Professor of Theology, Duke University. Dr. Campbell has served as President of the Association of United Methodist Theological Schools since 1992. He is the author of *Who Will Go For Us? An Invitation to Ordained Ministry* and *The Yoke of Obedience.* Dr. Campbell is codirector of United Methodism and American Culture.

Russell E. Richey is Professor of Church History at The Divinity School, Duke University, in Durham, North Carolina. Dr. Richey is a member of the Historical Society of the United Methodist Church and the American Society of Church History. He is the author of *The Methodist Conference in America* and coauthor with James Kirby and Kenneth Rowe of *The Methodists.* Dr. Richey is codirector of United Methodism and American Culture.

Endnotes

Notes to "INTRODUCTION"

1. Penny Long Marler and C. Kirk Hadaway, "Methodists on the Margins: 'Self-Authoring' Religious Identity," in *Connectionalism: Ecclesiology, Mission, and Identity*, ed. Russell E. Richey, Dennis M. Campbell, William B. Lawrence (Nashville: Abingdon, 1997), 295.

2. See the chapter by John C. Green and James L. Guth, "United Methodists and American Culture: A Statistical Portrait," 27.

3. This does not count the assets of the denomination, such as the properties or endowments held by its general boards and agencies. It does not include similar assets owned by the annual or jurisdictional conferences. Nor does it include the assets of corporations affiliated with or controlled by the annual, jurisdictional, or general conferences of the denomination.

4. See *General Minutes of the Annual Conferences of the United Methodist Church, 1995* (Evanston: The General Council on Finance and Administration), 29, 72–73, for statistical data on the annual conferences and local churches of the denomination. Other supporting data can be found in the various chapters of this volume.

5. *The Book of Discipline of The United Methodist Church—1996* (Nashville: The United Methodist Publishing House) ¶ 65J, pp. 90–91.

6. Ibid., ¶ 65G, esp. p. 89 ("Homosexual persons no less than heterosexual persons are individuals of sacred worth. All persons need the ministry and guidance of the church in their struggles for human fulfillment, as well as the spiritual and emotional care of a fellowship that enables reconciling relationships with God, with others, and with self. Although we do not condone the practice of homosexuality and consider this practice incompatible with Christian teaching, we affirm that God's grace is available to all. We commit ourselves to be in ministry for and with all persons"), and ¶ 304.3 ("While persons set apart by the Church for ordained ministry are subject to all the frailties of the human condition and the pressures of society, they are required to maintain the highest standards of holy living in the world. Since the practice of homosexuality is incompatible with Christian teaching, self-avowed practicing homosexuals are not to be accepted as candidates, ordained as ministers, or appointed to serve in The United Methodist Church").

7. *The Journal of the General Conference of The Methodist Episcopal Church, 1912*, 629–30.

8. Ibid., 631.

9. See, for instance, William Easum, *Dancing with Dinosaurs* (Nashville: Abingdon, 1993), and Andy Langford and William H. Willimon, *A New Connection* (Nashville: Abingdon, 1995).

10. See, for instance, William J. Abraham, *Waking from Doctrinal Amnesia: The Healing of Doctrine in the United Methodist Church* (Nashville: Abingdon, 1995).

11. *The Book of Discipline 1996* ¶ 17, p. 26.

12. *Ibid.,* ¶ 33, p. 31; ¶ 604.6, p. 314.

13. *Ibid.,* ¶ 204, p. 116.

14. Thomas Edward Frank, *Polity, Practice, and the Mission of the United Methodist Church* (Nashville: Abingdon, 1997), 156–57.

15. *Discipline 1996,* ¶ 216, p. 123.

16. See, for instance, the discussion in Richard P. Heitzenrater, *Wesley and the People Called Methodists* (Nashville: Abingdon, 1995), 214ff.

17. Martin Luther King Jr., *Why We Can't Wait* (New York: Harper and Row, 1963), 77f.

18. Russell E. Richey, *Early American Methodism* (Bloomington, In.: Indiana University Press, 1991), 5ff., passim.

19. *Discipline 1996,* ¶ 605.6, p. 316.

20. Kenneth E. Rowe, "Redesigning Methodist Churches: Auditorium Style Sanctuaries and Akron-Plan Sunday Schools," *Connectionalism: Ecclesiology, Mission, and Identity,* ed. Russell E. Richey, Dennis M. Campbell, William B. Lawrence (Nashville: Abingdon, 1997), 131.

21. *General Minutes, 1968,* 29, 66.

22. Data from the *General Minutes, 1995,* indicate that the United Methodist Church in the United States had 36,559 local churches with 8,611,021 members at the close of 1994.

23. *The World Almanac and Book of Facts, 1997* (Mahwah, N.J.: Funk & Wagnalls), 477.

24. *A Profile of United Methodists* (Dayton: General Council on Ministries, 1995), 4–5.

25. *Discipline 1996,* ¶ 65C, p. 87; ¶ 65G, p. 89; ¶ 806.12, p. 426; ¶ 304.3, p. 172; 306.4f., p. 176.

26. William R. Hutchison, "Protestantism as Establishment," in *Between the Times: The Travail of the Protestant Establishment in America, 1900–1960,* ed. William R. Hutchison (New York: Cambridge University Press, 1989), 4.

27. *Newsweek* (27 January 1997), 52.

28. Noted in a sermon delivered by Bishop Woodie White to the General Commission on Religion and Race in August 1992.

29. "The Financial Commitment of the United Methodist Church, 1997–2000" (Evanston: General Council on Finance and Administration, September 1996), 5.

30. See the chapter by Charles Zech, who indicates that a perceived financial crisis at the denominational level may not generate additional church revenues.

31. See the chapter by Justo González, who says that fast food franchises like Kentucky Fried Chicken do not open new restaurants where people like chicken or need chicken, but where they can afford chicken.

32. George D. McClain, "Pioneering Social Gospel Radicalism: An Overview of the History of the Methodist Federation for Social Action," in *Perspectives on American Methodism: Interpretive Essays*, ed. Russell E. Richey, Kenneth E. Rowe, Jean Miller Schmidt (Nashville: Kingswood, 1993), 383.

33. "The Financial Commitment of the United Methodist Church 1997–2000 (Evanston: The General Council on Finance and Administration, 1996), 5.

34. *General Minutes 1968*, 29, 67, 69, and *General Minutes 1995*, 29.

35. Zech notes the implications of this for deliberations about church size. Small-membership congregations place a high value on belonging to, caring for, and knowing one another. They understand how much they need one another, and how much they need one another to be good stewards. Large congregations must build those same values through small-group life if they are to be effective in matters of stewardship.

36. Richard P. Heitzenrater, "A Critical Analysis of the Ministry Studies Since 1948," in *Perspectives on American Methodism: Interpretive Essays*, ed. Russell E. Richey, Kenneth E. Rowe, and Jean Miller Schmidt (Nashville: Kingswood Books, 1993), 431–47.

37. William B. Lawrence, "The Theology of the Ordained Ministry in the United Methodist Church," in *Leadership Questions for the Twenty-first Century* (Nashville: Abingdon, forthcoming).

38. The United Brethren and, thereafter, the Evangelical United Brethren had a single ordination to the office of elder.

39. Jackson W. Carroll, "Small Membership Churches in North Carolina United Methodism: A Social Profile and Analysis" (Durham, N.C.: The J. M. Ormond Center, 1997), 37.

Notes to "United Methodists and American Culture: A Statistical Portrait"

1. The General Social Surveys (GSS) were conducted by the National Opinion Research Center, University of Chicago (Davis and Smith 1972–93), and distributed by the Roper Center for Public Opinion Research, University of Connecticut. The 1992 National Election Study (NES) was conducted by the Center for Political Studies (Miller et al. 1993), and distributed by the Inter-university Consortium for Social and Political Research, both at the University of Michigan. The collectors and distributors of these data are not responsible for the interpretations made here. The 1992 National Survey of Religion and Politics

(NSRP) was conducted at the University of Akron by the present authors and colleagues (Kellstedt et al. 1994). More details are available from the authors. Similar patterns are found in the Gallup surveys and a host of media polls.

2. For the denominations coded as mainline and evangelical Protestants see Kellstedt and Green (1993).

3. Religious commitment was calculated on the basis of four variables: religious salience, frequency of prayer, church attendance, and views of the Bible. Respondents with low scores on any three of these measures were placed in the "Nominal" category. The remaining respondents were divided on the basis of views of the Bible, with biblical literalists assigned to the Traditionalist category and non-literalists to the Moderate category. These variables were employed because they occurred in all three surveys in approximately the same form. See Kellstedt (1993) for more on this procedure.

4. Surveys generally have few measures of theological liberalism, but those that do exist suggest that the Moderate category contains a number of different theological perspectives. We combine these groups on the basis of their relative heterodoxy compared to the Traditionalists.

5. The 100% inerrancy score of the Traditionalists reflects the way the category was constructed.

6. Traditionalist Methodists frequently refer to themselves as "evangelicals." More than one-fifth of this category actually applied this term to themselves, and nearly as many used the related terms "fundamentalist" and "charismatic," so that three-fifths of the category saw themselves in the evangelical camp broadly defined. In contrast, four-fifths of the Nominals and two-thirds of the Moderates described themselves as "moderate to liberal." Interestingly, only about one-fourth of each category described themselves as "mainline." These data come from the 1992 NES and NSRP.

7. These data come from the GSS.

8. These data are consistent with Roof and McKinney (1987, chap. 4) who used an earlier version of the GSS, and with denominational data for church members (Griffith 1995).

9. For ease of presentation, clerical and farm occupations are included with blue-collar workers; the patterns are the same.

10. The data in Tables 4 through 7 were corrected for demography by means of multiple classification analysis.

11. The only dramatic difference between the original data and the statistical control occurred on party identification. Absent the correction, Traditionalists and Nominals have the same low level of Republican identification. But once the effects of demography—principally race, region, and education—are taken into account, Traditionalists are more Republican and Nominals less so.

12. The survey of Methodist clergy was conducted in 1989; see Guth et al. (1991) for details.

13. The survey of Republican activists was conducted in 1987, and a counterpart Democratic survey was conducted in 1989; see Green et al. (1991) for details.

Notes to "UNITED METHODIST CONGREGATIONS"

1. This statistic is reported in Robert L. Wilson and William H. Willimon, *The Seven Churches of Methodism* (Durham, N.C.: The J. M. Ormond Center, 1985).

2. We selected congregations in both regions representing several types of institutions: downtown ("Old First Church"), middle-class suburban, and a relatively young congregation. We acknowledge our deep appreciation to the pastors and laity of these six churches, who allowed us full access to their congregational life and gave generously of their time and insights in interviews and conversation about their churches. We have tried to report what we saw and experienced as faithfully as possible; although we are aware that brief descriptions of the kind to which space has limited us will seem to many members to have barely scratched the surface of their life together and to have missed (we hope not misrepresented) some significant dimensions.

3. Warner writes: "The congregational form of local organization is the sanctioned, official norm among only a few of America's religious communities. . . . Nonetheless the congregational mentality has great practical force as an unofficial norm in American religious life" (73). See his article, "The Place of the Congregation in the American Religious Configuration," pp. 54–99 in *American Congregations*, vol. 2, ed. James P. Wind and James W. Lewis (Chicago: University of Chicago Press, 1994).

4. Andy Langford and William H. Willimon, *A New Connection: Reforming the United Methodist Church* (Nashville: Abingdon, 1995).

5. See Milton J. Coalter, John M. Mulder and Louis B. Weeks, *Vital Signs, The Promise of Mainstream Protestantism* (Grand Rapids: Eerdmans, 1996), 59ff. See also Jackson W. Carroll and Wade Clark Roof, eds., *Beyond Establishment, Protestant Identity in a Post-Protestant Age* (Louisville: Westminster/John Knox, 1993).

6. See Samuel S. Hill, *Southern Churches in Crisis* (New York: Holt, Rinehart, and Winston, 1966), and Samuel S. Hill et al., *Religion and the Solid South* (Nashville: Abingdon, 1972).

7. John Shelton Reed summarizes the general religious data in his *One South: An Ethnic Approach to Regional Culture* (Baton Rouge: Louisiana State University Press, 1982), 134–38. The Methodist data come from a four-state survey conducted in 1989 by Wade Clark Roof and Phillip E. Hammond.

8. See Rodney Stark and William S. Bainbridge, *The Future of Religion* (Berkeley: University of California Press, 1985), 68–95.

9. Eldon Ernst, "Religion in California," *Pacific Theological Review* 19 (Winter, 1986), 43–51.

10. See Wade Clark Roof, *A Generation of Seekers* (San Francisco: Harper-SanFrancisco, 1992).

11. Assisting with the field work were Sally Bates, Jennifer Berentsen, Lyn Gesch, Charles Reynolds, and Julie Steele. We are grateful for their careful and helpful work.

12. Her perception of the denomination's openness to gays and lesbians is only partially correct. While the denomination affirms homosexual persons as "individuals of sacred worth" and welcomes them into the church's fellowship, it does not condone homosexuality and views it as "incompatible with Christian teaching." The denomination also does not permit the ordination of "self-avowed, practicing homosexuals" or their appointment to serve as United Methodist ministers. See *The Book of Discipline of the United Methodist Church, 1992* (Nashville: United Methodist Publishing House, 1992), pp. 92, 202.

13. Religious census data (Martin B. Bradley et al., *Churches and Church Membership in the United States, 1990* [Atlanta: Glenmary Research Center]) show significant differences in the religious makeup of the two states: North Carolina is dominated numerically by Southern Baptists, with Methodists a somewhat distant second; California is dominated by Roman Catholics. United Methodist statistical data for the two annual conferences also show that the California-Pacific Conference is much more ethnically diverse than the North Carolina Conference. Survey data from the two states that Roof gathered in connection with his study of baby boomers (see note 6 above) also show differences in how Methodists in the two states view the church and their involvement in it.

14. Paul J. DiMaggio and Walter W. Powell, "The Iron Cage Revisited: Institutional Isomorphism and Collective Rationality in Organizational Fields," *American Sociological Review* 48 (April 1983):147–60. While most congregations conform in important ways to the basic patterns of their organizational field, they also respond to other influences, both internal and external, that lead them to develop different, often innovative patterns that may have little to do with being part of a particular denomination.

15. See Arlen Rothauge, *Sizing Up a Congregation* (New York: Episcopal Church Center, n.d.).

16. Alisdair MacIntyre, *After Virtue: A Study in Moral Theory* (Notre Dame: University of Notre Dame Press, 1981).

17. Dorothy C. Bass, "Congregations and the Bearing of Traditions," in *American Congregations*, vol. 2, ed. James P. Wind and James W. Lewis (Chicago: University of Chicago Press, 1994), 199.

18. T. S. Eliot, "Tradition and the Individual Talent," sect. 1, *Egoist* (London, Sept. and Dec. 1919), reproduced in *Selected Prose of T. S. Eliot*, ed. Frank Kermode (San Diego: Harcourt Brace, 1975), 37–40.

19. "Living in a Post-Traditional Society," quoted in *Reflexive Modernization,* by Ulrich Beck, Anthony Giddens, and Scott Lash (Stanford: Stanford University Press, 1994), 64.

20. See Anthony Giddens, *The Consequences of Modernity* (Stanford: Stanford University Press, 1990), 21ff.

21. "Methodists on the Margins: The 'Self-Authority' of Religious Identity," in *Connectionalism: Ecclesiology, Mission and Identity*, ed. Russell Richey, Dennis Campbell and William B. Lawrence (Nashville: Abingdon, 1997).

22. The quotation is from Dean R. Hoge, "Who Are the Lay Liberals?" *Congregations* (September/October 1995): 3. The larger study of Presbyterian baby boomers is *Vanishing Boundaries*, by Dean R. Hoge, Benton Johnson, and Donald Luidens (Louisville: Westminster/John Knox, 1994).

23. Nancy T. Ammerman, "Golden Rule Christianity: Lived Religion in the American Mainstream" (Unpublished paper).

Notes to "PATTERNS OF GIVING AMONG UNITED METHODISTS"

1. The author acknowledges his gratitude to Dean Hoge, Patrick McNamara, Michael Donahue, Peter Zaleski, the members of the United Methodism and American Culture study, and the Lilly Endowment for their financial support.

2. See Charles E. Zech, "Determinants of the Denominational Mission Funding Crisis" in *Connectionalism: Ecclesiology, Mission, and Identity*, ed. Russell E. Richey, Dennis M. Campbell, and William B. Lawrence (Nashville: Abingdon, 1997).

3. Graphic by Stephen Hart, "Religious Giving: Patterns and Variations," Annual Meeting of the Religious Research Association, November 1990. All figures appear at the end of the chapter.

4. Jackson W. Carroll and David A. Roozen, "Congregational Identities in the Presbyterian Church," *Review of Religious Research* 31, no. 4 (June 1990), 351–69.

5. Most previous studies have shown the relationship between religious contributions and their determinants to be curvilinear. This means that changes in the determinant variables affect giving at either an increasing or decreasing rate. To put this relationship into equation form, the square root of per member contributions was taken. Taking the square root is one of the techniques that one can use to estimate a curvilinear relationship.

Prior testing of the equation showed it to be affected by heterscedasticity, a statistical problem in which the error terms are not independent. To resolve this problem, the White correction was used to adjust the equation. See G. S. Maddala, *Econometrics* (New York: McGraw-Hill, 1977) 265–67.

6. Matthew 28:17-20.

7. The figure of 80% of the Administrative Board members who spend their free time reading the bible is exceptionally high. It may be accounted for by the fact that Administrative Board members are extraordinarily committed, or it might be an artifact of Board members responding with what they wish were the case, rather than what it actually is.

8. See Dean R. Hoge, Benton Johnson, and Donald A. Luidens, *Vanishing Boundaries* (Louisville: Westminster/John Knox, 1994), and Wade Clark Roof, *A Generation of Seekers* (San Francisco: HarperSanFrancisco, 1994).

Notes to "UNITED METHODIST LEADERS: DIVERSITY AND MORAL AUTHORITY"

1. Robert Wuthnow, *The Restructuring of American Religion: Society and Faith Since World War II* (Princeton, N.J.: Princeton University Press, 1988).

2. James Davision Hunter, *Culture Wars: The Struggle to Define America* (New York: Basic Books, 1991).

3. The results presented here are based on a book in progress tentatively titled *Protestant Church Leaders: Divergent Visions and Cultural Tensions*, by Daniel V. A. Olson and William McKinney.

4. Dean R. Hoge, *Division in the Protestant House: The Basic Reasons Behind Intra-Church Conflicts* (Philadelphia: Westminster, 1976); Martin E. Marty, *Righteous Empire: The Protestant Experience in America* (New York: Dial, 1970); David A. Roozen, William McKinney, and Jackson W. Carroll, *Varieties of Religious Presence: Mission in Public Life* (New York: Pilgrim, 1984); Richard J. Mouw, "New Alignments: Hartford and the Future of Evangelicalism," in *Against the World For the World: The Hartford Appeal and the Future of American Religion*, ed. Peter L. Berger and Richard John Neuhaus (New York: Seabury, 1976); Jeffrey K. Hadden, *The Gathering Storm in the Churches* (Garden City, N.Y.: Doubleday, 1969); Harvey G. Cox, *The Secular City: Secularization and Urbanization in Theological Perspective* (New York: Macmillan, 1966); Henry J. Pratt, *The Liberalization of Americanism: A Case Study in Complex Organizations* (Detroit: Wayne State University Press, 1972); Harold E. Quinley, "The Dilemma of an Activist Church: Protestant Religion in the Sixties and Seventies," *Journal for the Scientific Study of Religion* 13 (March 1984): 1–21; Richard J. Coleman, *Issues of Theological Conflict: Evangelicals and Liberals* (Grand Rapids: Eerdmans, 1972); James Davison Hunter, *American Evangelicalism: Conservative Religion and the Quandary of Modernity* (New Brunswick, N.J.: Rutgers University Press, 1983); Richard Quebedeaux, *The Worldly Evangelicals* (San Francisco: Harper & Row, 1974); R. Stephen Warner, *New Wine in Old Wineskins: Evangelicals and Liberals in a Small-Town Church* (Berkeley: University of California Press, 1988); Robert Wuthnow, *The Restructuring of American Religion: Society and Faith Since World War II* (Princeton, N.J.: Princeton University Press, 1988); Hunter, *Culture Wars* [see above, n. 2]. For an excellent summary of the "two party thesis" see Jean Miller Schmidt, *Souls or the Social Order: The Two-Party System in American Protestantism* (Brooklyn, N.Y.: Carlson, 1991), xxvi-xxxii.

5. The scales used here are actually factor scores created using the the SPSSPC VARIMAX routine. While this routine artificially "forces" the two scales to be orthogonal, other results using OBLIMAX, a routine that does not force the scales to be orthogonal, have only an R-squared of .0576. In technical terms, less than 6% of the variation in social activism scores are related to variation in evangelism scores. However, other analyses not shown here reveal that this negative

correlation is entirely due to denominational differences. Within denominations, the actual correlation between leaders' evangelism and social activism scale scores is actually slightly positive.

6. Recall that since there are many more oldline leaders, the averages for the entire sample are tilted towards the oldline denominations.

7. Fred Kniss, "Culture Wars(?): Conceptualizing the Battleground," paper prepared for presentation at the Annual Meeting of the American Sociological Association, Miami Beach, Florida, 1993.

8. Andy Langford, "Affirmations of a New Connection," paper presented at the meeting of the Duke Divinity School Project on United Methodism and American Culture held 24–28 August 1995 at Epworth by the Sea, St. Simons Island, Georgia. For more extensive treatment of these issues see Andy Langford and William Willimon, *A New Connection: Reforming the United Methodist Church* (Nashville: Abingdon, 1995).

9. Judith Smith, "Leadership," Paper presented at the meeting of the Duke Divinity School Project on United Methodism and American Culture held 22–25 September 1994 at Duke Divinity School, Durham, North Carolina.

Notes to "United Methodist Ordained Ministry in Transition"

1. Richard B. Wilke, *And Are We Yet Alive? The Future of the United Methodist Church* (Nashville: Abingdon, 1986), 96ff.

2. For a comprehensive review of seminarians, see Ellis L. Larsen and James M. Shopshire, "A Profile of Contemporary Seminarians," *Theological Education* 24, no. 2 (Spring 1988).

3. Larsen and Shopshire note that "no current figures are readily available regarding those who leave ministry" (ibid., 38). The relational database of this Duke-Lilly research project can track the careers of elders year by year from ordination through any appointment category listed in the Disciplinary Questions, Part Two, of any annual conference. These categories include various appointments beyond the local church (ABLC), school, sabbatical leave, family leave, leave of absence, honorable location, and various categories of termination as well as disability leave, death, and retirement.

4. Richard E. Koenig, "Research and Reformation: The Presbyterians' self-scrutiny" (Christian Century, Sept. 22–29, 1993), 900–903, emphasis added. The full Presbyterian study to which Koenig refers is published under the title *The Presbyterian Presence: The Twentieth-Century Experience*, ed. Milton J. Coalter, John M. Mulder, and Louis B. Weeks, 7 vols. (Louisville: Westminster/John Knox, 1992).

5. The results of this research project are copyrighted as "DOM/Memming Longitudinal Clergy Study." At present it consists of the computerized records of 15,178 UM elders ordained in 69 UM conferences between 1974–93. The relational database is a complete census of everyone ordained elder during this period.

6. Lovett Weems, "Leaders and Servants," in *Truth & Tradition: A Conversation About the Future of United Methodist Theological Education,* ed. Neal F. Fisher (Nashville: Abingdon, 1995), 61.

7. Schubert Ogden, "Ogden's Scholarly Interests Brought Him to Perkins" (an interview), *Perspective: A Newsletter for the Alumni/ae and Friends of Perkins School of Theology* (Winter 1993), 11–12, cited in Fisher, *Truth & Tradition,* 62.

8. Weems, "Leaders and Servants," 73.

9. "Taking the Measure of UMC Clergy," *Christian Century* (8 August– 4 September 1996): 807–8.

10. It remains to be seen whether the fluctuation in UM female ordinations reflects a "leveling off" in female seminary enrollment as per Larsen and Shopshire, "Profile," 94.

11. National Center for Health Statistics, *Vital Statistics of the United States, 1978,* Vol. 1, DHHS Pub. No. (PHS) 82–1100, Public Health Service (Washington, D.C.: U.S. Government Printing Office, 1982). Table 1–20, "Live Births By Sex. . . ."

12. Wade Clark Roof and William McKinney, *American Mainline Religion, Its Changing Shape and Future* (New Brunswick, N.J.: Rutgers University Press, 1987), 17.

13. "Poll Finds Major Drop in Church Attendance," *The United Methodist Review* (20 September 1996), 8.

14. How does this square with Lyle Schaller's view that "the greatest openness to women becoming ministers appears to be in the North" ("When Will Women Become A Majority Among UM Clergy?" *Circuit Rider* [October 1993], 17)?

15. This declining trend contrasts with the observation made in Larsen and Shopshire, "Profile," 94, that the numbers of "young, male seminarians has remained rather constant throughout this period." This may be true in other denominations, but to judge from ordination numbers, it is not true in the United Methodist Church. Some 445 men were ordained elders at age 30 and younger (≤ 30) in 1974, and 83 in 1993. If the number of ≤ 30 men really has remained constant, where have they gone by the time of orders?

16. Joseph P. O'Neill and Richard T. Murphy, "Changing Age and Gender Profiles Among Entering Seminary Students," *Ministry Research Notes* (Princeton, N.J.: Educational Testing Service, Spring 1991), 13.

17. For discussions of pastors who leave parish ministry from Congregational (UCC) and United Methodist perspectives, see Gerald J. Jud, Edgar W. Mills Jr., and Genevieve W. Burch, Ex-Pastors—Why Men Leave the Parish Ministry (New York, Pilgrim, 1970); and Bary R. Fleet, Leaving the Parish: A Study of the Southern New England Annual Conference, 1977–1984, unpublished D.Min. project report, Boston University School of Theology, 1986.

19. The percentages do not total 100%. By their tenth anniversary, clergy may be attending school; on leave of absence, sabbatical leave, maternity leave, or disability leave; in honorable location; or deceased.

20. The term "retention rate" (RetRate) refers strictly to elders in parish ministry as of their tenth anniversary unless another time period is specifically indicated.

21. The retention rate twenty years out for the classes of 1974–75 is 42.1%.

22. The conferences tagged with (*), that is, Southern New England, Maine, and New Hampshire were merged into a new entity in 1994, the New England Annual Conference. In the same year, the conferences tagged with (#), namely North and South Dakota, were merged into the Dakotas Annual Conference. The appearance of these five conferences in such close proximity to each other on the low end of this list is a striking coincidence.

23. Ellis L. Larsen, "A Profile of Contemporary Seminarians Revisited" (Theological Education, The Association of Theological Schools), 68. (A galley proof of this monograph, dated Spring 1994, was graciously provided by Nancy Merrill.) Larsen's statement refers to men age 45 and older (≥ 45). The ten-year-out retention rate of this subset is 57.3%, which is almost the same as, but certainly not higher than the 30 and younger subset's rate of 60.3%.

24. Dewey W. Grantham, *The South in Modern America: A Region at Odds* (New York: HarperCollins, 1994), 318.

25. The interpretation of recruitment and retention rates was suggested in correspondence with William B. Lawrence, Duke Divinity School, 6 June 1996.

26. For definition of four categories of appointments beyond the local church (ABLC), see *The Book of Discipline of the United Methodist Church—1996* (Nashville: United Methodist Publishing House, 1996), ¶ 335.1.a-d. The records of ABLC clergy in this project are categorized accordingly.

27. Larsen, "Profile . . . Revisited," 79. Larsen notes that more than a third of all seminarians in his survey of students in 1986 came from a denomination other than the one in which they eventually sought ordination.

28. For definition of different categories of termination, see *The Book of Discipline of the United Methodist Church*, ¶¶ 356–357. The records of terminated clergy in this project are categorized accordingly.

29. Career sequence analysis indicates that when clergy in honorable location (hon. loc.) make a change in their appointment status, they select termination over reappointment in parish ministry by a ratio of 10 to 1. Therefore, it seems appropriate to note that, of the elders ordained from 1974–83, an average 4.4% were in hon. loc. ten years out. As a trend, 6.4% in the 1974 class were in hon. loc., a figure that fell to 3.1% for the 1978 class and subsequently fluctuated around 3.2% for the 1979–83 classes.

30. In one conference, virtually all women clergy serving in parish ministry turned to non-parish ministry or terminated during the episcopacy of a certain

bishop. The memory of this exodus continues to hamper recruitment of women ordinands there.

31. The ten conferences that were the most popular destinations of clergy who transferred included (in descending order of preference) Virginia, Texas, California-Nevada, Western North Carolina, Central Pennsylvania, New Mexico, Oklahoma, West Michigan, and New York.

32. Conversation with DOM Director Robert Kohler, 12 October 1995.

33. Their retention rate in parish ministry is markedly lower than that of the Whites who do not transfer conferences; their ABLC and termination rates, on the other hand, are considerably higher.

34. The retention rate of African Americans who transfer, as well as the rate of persons in ABLC jobs ten year out, are both conspicuously higher than those of Blacks who do not transfer.

35. The seminary affiliation of nearly every elder ordained from 1974 to 1993 who held an M.Div. degree from a UM seminary is captured in this database. The seminary data of elders who graduated from non-UM theological schools is not as complete. Nonetheless, about 91.1% of the elders in the 1974–83 classes have their seminary connection identified.

36. About 94.8% of the people ordained elder from 1984 to 1993 have their UM and non-UM seminary status determined.

37. Larsen and Shopshire state that "young, male seminarians" in their 1988 survey, presumably younger than 30 years old, account for "48% of the total M.Div. enrollment" ("Profile," 94). Only 17.2% of the men ordained elder during 1990–93 fit that age category.

38. Fisher, *Truth & Tradition*, 113.

39. A representative of the theological school with the lowest retention rate expressed some surprise when the author shared this data with her. She went on to explain, however, that the data was consistent with the school's emphasis on training people for work in UM boards and agencies. In fact, only a middling percentage of clergy who left parish ministry actually worked in UM nonparish jobs of any description. A significantly above-average percentage had terminated.

40. Conversation with author, 9 November 1995.

41. Ronald L. Flaugher, "A Survey of American Clergy," unpublished report prepared by the Princeton-based Educational Testing Service, funded by the Lilly Endowment.

42. Is there a "morale problem" among UM clergy that needs to be addressed?

43. Thomas C. Oden, *Requiem: A Lament in Three Movements* (Nashville: Abingdon, 1995).

44. Ibid., 40.

45. Jackson Carroll, Barbara Hargrove, and Adair T. Lummis, *Women of the Cloth: A New Opportunity for the Churches* (San Francisco: Harper & Row, 1981), 128.

46. See G. Lloyd Rediger, "Clergy Killers," *The Clergy Journal* (August 1993), 7–10.

47. See Christina Maslach, *Burnout, The Cost of Caring* (Englewood Cliffs, N.J.: Prentice Hall, 1982), 60ff., for a discussion of factors relevant to pastoral ministry that help account for why the first five years are the "crucial period" for retention.

48. Loren B. Mead, *The Once and Future Church: Reinventing the Congregation for a New Mission Frontier* (Washington, D.C.: The Alban Institute, 1991), 39. For discussions about how tenuous denominations are at the turn of the century, see Robert Bruce Mullin and Russell E. Richey (eds.), *Reimagining Denominationalism: Interpretive Essays* (New York: Oxford University Press, 1994).

49. See Donald E. Messer (ed.), *Send Me? The Itineracy In Crisis* (Nashville: Abingdon, 1991), especially the introductory and concluding chapters written by Messer.

Notes to "Paying the Preacher Her Due: Wages and Compensation Among United Methodist Clergy"

1. The number of men and women who reported salary information was 3,034. Of these, not all indicated how many hours they worked, and only 2,718 reported that they worked full-time.

2. Dummy variables for denomination are included to adjust for denominational differences in average wage levels.

3. The pairwise correlation between age and total labor force experience is .472.

4. Classifications are taken from the ATS Bulletin of Theological Schools 1994.

5. We asked respondents to classify their current position from one of the following: senior pastor, sole pastor, associate/assistant pastor, co-pastor, interim pastor, regional staff, national staff, secular work, "other." We also asked them to identify their job title and coded these positions into a more detailed occupational classification. For purposes of cross-denominational comparison, the first schema is considered more valid and is used in these analyses.

6. Because of the smaller sample size and the relatively large number of variables in the equation, significance levels of coefficients are not reported.

7. It should be noted that there is a general trend among UM conferences to move toward longer pastorates. Also, the frequency of moves will vary according to the types of appointments served and the stage of a pastor's career.

8. Underemployment occurs when one takes a job for which one is overqualified.

9. Of those clergy who were paid for less than 30 hours a week, 71 were men and 353 were women.

Notes to "'PLAYING IN THE DARK'—METHODIST STYLE: THE FATE OF THE EARLY AFRICAN AMERICAN PRESENCE IN DENOMINATIONAL MEMORY, 1807–1974"

1. Toni Morrison, *Playing in the Dark: Whiteness and the Literary Imagination* (Cambridge: Harvard University Press, 1992), 65. (Subsequent epigraphs from Morrison's book are taken from pp. 90, 46–47, 11, and 63. All are used by permission of Harvard University Press.) Morrison is using "Africanism" to refer, not to specific cultural continuities of African peoples in the diaspora from their homelands, but to a general Africanist presence in the North American context. The term "African" was the common self-designation by African Americans and by others in the period until 1830, after which it was replaced by "colored American." In this essay I use the terms African American and Black interchangeably; for the early period of Methodist history, I use the terms "Africans" and "the African presence."

2. Nathan Bangs, *History of the Methodist Episcopal Church*, 3rd ed., vol. 2 (New York: G. Lane and C. B. Tippett, 1845), 21–24; Abel Stevens, *History of the Methodist Episcopal Church in the United States of America*, vol. 3 (New York: Phillips & Hunt, 1867), 347–48. There is no mention of either the Fast Day or Thanksgiving by Methodists in 1796 in Elmer T. Clark, et al., eds., *Journal and Letters of Francis Asbury* (London: Epworth, 1958).

3. The unpublished essay, "'. . . many of the poor Affricans [*sic*] are obedient to the faith': Reassessing the African-American Presence in Early Methodism in the United States, 1769–1809,'" was first presented at the Oxford Institute in England in 1992, and then in a revised version at the Conference on Methodism and the Shaping of American Culture at Asbury College in October 1994.

4. There was no racial differentiation in the first statistics of the American conferences down to 1786. Two decades later the African Church of Charleston claimed 1000 members, Bethel in Philadelphia totalled 711, and Baltimore counted 755. Two circuits in the Baltimore Conference (Prince George's with 1,038 and Calvert with 1,664) and another in the Philadelphia Conference (Dorchester at 1,198) numbered more than a thousand members. *Minutes of the Annual Conferences of the Methodist Episcopal Church, for the Years 1773–1828* (New York: T. Mason and G. Lane, 1840), 137–39.

5. My own interest in these issues was first sparked by "Francis Asbury and the Development of African Churches in America," a paper presented by David H. Bradley Sr. at the World Methodist Historical Society meeting in Denver in 1971 and published in *Methodist History* 10 (October 1971): 3–29. See also L. M. Hagood, *The Colored Man in the Methodist Episcopal Church* (Cincinnati: Cranston & Stowe, 1890); I. L. Thomas, ed., *Methodism and the Negro* (New York: Eaton & Mains, 1910); Harry V. Richardson, *Dark Salvation: The Story of Methodism As It Developed Among Blacks in America* (Garden City: Doubleday, 1976); William B. McClain, *Black People in the Methodist Church: Whither Thou Goest?* (Cambridge: Schenkman, 1984); Grant S. Shockley, ed., *Heritage and Hope: The African-American Presence in United Methodism* (Nashville: Abingdon, 1991).

6. In chronological order, the sample is: (1) George Bourne, *The Life of John Wesley . . . and a Comprehensive History of American Methodism* (Baltimore: George Dobbin & Murphy, 1807); (2) Jesse Lee, *A Short History of the Methodists in the United States of America* (Baltimore: n.p., 1810); (3) Nathan Bangs, *History of the Methodist Episcopal Church*, vol. 1 (New York: Carlton & Porter, n.d. [1839]; 3rd ed., vol. 2 (New York: G. Lane & C. B. Tippett, 1845; vol. 3 (New York: T. Mason & G. Lane, 1840); 9th ed., vol. 4 (New York: Carlton & Porter, n.d.); (4) James Porter, *A Compendium of Methodism*, 20th ed. (New York: Carlton & Porter, 1861); (5) Abel Stevens, *History of the Methodist Episcopal Church in the United States of America*, vol. 1 (New York: Eaton & Mains, n.d. [1864]); vol. 2 (New York: Eaton & Mains, n.d.); vol. 3 (New York: Phillips & Hunt, 1867); vol. 4 (New York: Eaton & Mains, n.d.); (6) Abel Stevens, *A Compendious History of American Methodism* (New York: Carlton & Porter, 1868); (7) M. L. Scudder, *American Methodism* (Hartford: S. S. Scranton, 1870); (8) Matthew Simpson, *A Hundred Years of Methodism* (New York: Phillips & Hunt, [1876]); (9) John Atkinson, *Centennial History of American Methodism* (New York: Phillips & Hunt, 1884); (10) William H. Daniels, *The Illustrated History of Methodism* (New York: Phillips & Hunt, 1884); (11) Holland N. McTyeire, *A History of Methodism* (Nashville: Southern Methodist Publishing House, 1884); (12) Ammi Bradford Hyde, *The Story of Methodism Throughout the World* (Springfield, Mass.: Willey, 1889); (13) Amherst W. Kellogg, *A Concise History of Methodism in England and America* (Milwaukee: H. O. Bruce, 1893); (14) J. M. Buckley, *A History of Methodists in the United States* (New York: Charles Scribner's Sons, 1900); (15) James W. Lee, Naphtali Luccock, and James Main Dixon, *The Illustrated History of Methodism* (St. Louis: Methodist Magazine Publishing Co., [1900]); (16) John Fletcher Hurst, *The History of Methodism*, vols. 4–5, *American Methodism* (New York: Eaton & Mains, 1903); (17) Halford E. Luccock and Paul Hutchinson, *The Story of Methodism* (New York: Methodist Book Concern, [1926]); rev. ed., with Paul Garber, New York: Methodist Book Concern, 1949); (18) William Warren Sweet, *Methodism in American History* (New York: Methodist Book Concern, 1933; rev. ed., 1954); (19) Emory Stevens Bucke, ed., *The History of American Methodism*, 3 vols. (New York: Abingdon, 1964), hereafter referred to with specific contributors and chapters in *HAM*; (20) Charles Ferguson, *Organizing To Beat the Devil: Methodists and the Making of America* (Garden City: Doubleday, 1971); (21) Frederick A. Norwood, *The Story of American Methodism: United Methodism and Its Relations* (Nashville: Abingdon, 1974).

7. Niebuhr, *The Social Sources of Denominationalism* (1929; reprint, New York: Meridian Books, 1972). An important essay that defends a historiographical focus on race and religion in the U.S. is David Wills, "The Central Themes of American Religious History: Pluralism, Puritanism and the Encounter of Black and White," *Religion and Intellectual Life* 5 (Fall, 1987), 30–41.

8. Morrison, 6, 12–13.

9. Sydney E. Ahlstrom, *A Religious History of the American People* (New Haven: Yale University Press, 1972), 12. For my review of the book, see *Journal of Religious Thought* 33 (1976), 106–8.

10. Bangs, 1:63; Stevens, *History*, 1:103; Stevens, *Compendious History*, 123.

11. Bangs, 1:90–108. The same flaw occurs in Clark, et al., *Journal and Letters of Francis Asbury*, 207–24, where no effort was made to correlate the printed account by Rankin and Jarratt with Rankin's rich manuscript journal.

12. Bangs, 1:114; Porter, 133–34; Daniels, 451–53.

13. Coen G. Pierson, "Methodism and the Revolution," *HAM*, 1:171 [See n. 6, item 19].

14. Lee, *A Short History*, 131, 134; Bangs, 1:265.

15. Atkinson, 228.

16. Lee, *A Short History*, 301, 308.

17. Atkinson, 233.

18. Lee, *A Short History*, 72; Bangs, 1:261; Stevens, *History*, 2:496; Buckley, 308; Norwood, 168; McTyeire, 381. Bishop McTyeire made his inclusion of these instructions into a partisan point in order to attack retrospectively abolitionism in early and later Methodism.

19. Atkinson, 180–83. This event has more often been linked to the anti-abolition sentiments of some people in Charleston who took offense at the Address of the General Conference of 1800 to state legislatures urging the end of slavery. See also Lee, *Short History*, 134; Buckley, 271; and Richard M. Cameron, "The New Church Takes Root," *HAM*, 1:274–76.

20. Daniels, 453; Arthur Bruce Moss, "Methodism in Colonial America," *HAM*, 1:116.

21. Potts, "Methodism in Colonial America," *HAM*, 1:85; King, "United Methodism, 1940–60," *HAM*, 3:486.

22. Norwood, 167, 201; Atkinson, 232–33.

23. Ferguson, 119, 229.

24. Hurst, 5:572.

25. Hyde, 351–52.

26. Buckley, 108.

27. Moss, *HAM*, 1:104–5; Norwood, 67–68.

28. Ferguson, 202.

29. Hurst, 4:44; McTyeire, 671. In his ongoing sectional polemics, Bishop McTyeire gloated in telling the story that the first Methodist society in New York owned Williams as a slave.

30. Stevens, *Compendious History*, 245–46; Hurst, 4:290–91, 437; Daniels, 493; McTyeire, 346–47, 386; Hyde, 408–9, 428; Buckley, 239–40, 269–70; Norwood, 168; Ferguson, 106–7; Norman W. Spellman,"The Formation of the Methodist Episcopal Church," *HAM*, 1:210; Lee, Luccock, and Dixon, 256.

31. Stevens, *History*, 2:174–77; Daniels, 494. The failed petition by Colbert and 18 other signatories "to the Methodist Episcopal Bishops and Philadelphia Conference at Chestertown, May 1, 1805 in behalf of Henry Hoshure [*sic*]" is in the Philadelphia Conference archives at Old St. George's Church, Philadelphia.

32. Norwood, 168. Daniels, 494 and Stevens, *History*, 2:174–77 had perpetuated the 1810 date.

33. Lee, *A Short History*, 270–71 mentioned other ordinations in New York, Philadelphia and Lynchburg, VA. See also Bangs, 2:97–98 and 3:30; Stevens, *History*, 4:173–77; Stevens, *Compendious History*, 417; Hyde, 469; Hurst, 5:849; Buckley, 310; Frederick E. Maser and George A. Singleton, "Further Branches of Methodism Are Founded," *HAM*, 1:604; Ferguson, 216; Porter, 163–64; Scudder, 506ff. Norwood reported the legislation but without mentioning Allen, 168.

34. Simpson, 84.

35. Bangs, 3:30 and 2:97–98; Porter, 163–64; Scudder, 506ff. If Allen was a "local elder," none of the historians of the rise of the AME Church in Philadelphia or of his biographers has followed up on the point.

36. Maser and Singleton, *HAM*, 1:602–3.

37. Stevens, *Compendious History*, 447; McTyeire, 565. Hyde confused some of the details of Allen's life, in terms of his role as AME bishop, with his successor, Morris Brown, 766.

38. Bangs, 3:166–67, 232, 246–51 (spelled Steward); Stevens, *History*, 4:435–37, 477; Hyde, 507–8; Hurst, 5:696–98; Lee, Luccock and Dixon, 486–87; Norwood, 177, 330; Ferguson, 148; W. Richey Hogg, "The Missions of American Methodism," *HAM*, 3:65; Luccock, Hutchinson, and Garber, 307–9; Sweet, 190–91.

39. Stevens, *Compendious History*, 435–38; Stevens, *History*, 4:221ff.; Hyde, 475–76, 545; Hurst, 5:735.

40. Stevens, *History*, 4:214–16, 225; Stevens, *Compendious History*, 432.

41. Stevens, *History*, 3:358–62.

42. McTyeire, 446–47.

43. Atkinson, 174–76.

44. Bourne, 350. The statistical information was Bourne's only mention of the presence of African Methodists. Given his later career as a Presbyterian abolitionist, this omission and total neglect of the antislavery controversy in early Methodism are surprising.

45. Bangs, 3:79–80.

46. Lee, *A Short History*, 208–9; Buckley, 285; Hurst, 4:457; Lee, Luccock, and Dixon, 289.

47. Lee, *A Short History*, 49; Stevens, *Compendious History*, 68; Hyde, 368; Norwood, 170–71; Maser and Singleton, *HAM*, 1:605–6; Shockley and Haynes, *HAM*, 2:527.

48. Hurst, 5:851; Maser and Singleton, *HAM*, 1:608–9; Grant S. Shockley and Leonard L. Haynes, "The A.M.E. and the A.M.E. Zion Churches," *HAM*, 2:536.

49. Bangs, 3:30. Buckley knew of the early strength of African Methodists in Charleston, but he did not tell the story of Vesey, 299–300.

50. Norwood, 168–69, 173.

51. Buckley, 347; Maser and Singleton, *HAM*, 1:616; Shockley and Haynes, *HAM*, 2:528.

52. Bangs, 3:30, 79–80, 95–98.

53. Ibid. 3:433.

54. Maser and Singleton describe this in "Further Branches," *HAM*, 1:677–78.

55. Stevens, *History*, 4:246, 260–63.

56. Stevens, *Compendious History*, 447–49.

57. Scudder, 506–8; Sweet, 313–14.

58. Simpson, 309–14, 322–23.

59. McTyeire, 687, 386–87, 523, 669–70, 671, 564–66.

60. Daniels, 702–3.

61. Kellogg, 178.

62. Porter, 163–64.

63. Luccock and Hutchinson, 484–85.

64. Hyde, 483–84, 571, 680–81, 744–45, 766–75, 485–86, 548.

65. Lee, Luccock, and Dixon, 460, 462, 464, 474–75, 651–52, 659–61, 478.

66. Buckley, 311, 346–48, 582–99.

67. Hurst, 5:848–55, 819–22, 871.

68. Maser and Singleton, *HAM*, 1:601ff.; Shockley and Haynes, *HAM*, 2:527ff.

69. Ferguson, 211–17, 298, 417.

70. Norwood, 10.

71. Ibid. 169–74, 271–81.

72. Ibid. 188–91, 282–84, 443–44, 284–86, 289–91, 333, 435–36, 370–75.

73. Ibid., 65.

74. Lewis Y. Cox, *Pioneer Footsteps* (Cape May, N.J.: Star and Wave, 1917).

75. The work of Ronald Takaki convinces me that a multicultural approach to race, taking it beyond the binary categories with which this chapter has been concerned, re-contextualizes the issues. Much of the previous three paragraphs has been shaped by my learning from his *Strangers from a Different Shore: A History of Asian-Americans* (New York: Penguin, 1989) and *A Different Mirror: A History of Multicultural America* (Boston: Little, Brown, 1993), especially chaps. 1, 14.

Notes to "Black People in the Methodist Protestant Church (1830–1939)"

1. The Methodist Protestant Church in black and white represents the primary focus of this chapter. It takes into consideration the fact that mission conferences were constituted for a number of reasons, and race represented one of them. In the attempt to extend the mission of the church to the world, mission conferences were organized in Asia, including China, Japan, and India. It does not appear that the restrictive rules concerning black or "colored" people pertained equally to those of Asian nationalities. Perhaps distance was enough to preclude the essential concerns of inclusiveness with Asian and other mission conferences. In some aspects it is clear that Asians had different status to that of black people. At Westminster Seminary (now Wesley in Washington, D.C.) Asians from the mission conferences studied and graduated in the late-nineteenth century. This was a period when Black people could not study at Westminster. As a matter of fact, there is no record of a Black graduate from Westminister until 1952, thirteen years after the 1939 merger that created the Methodist Church.

2. Researches of the records of the conferences of the Methodist Protestant Church show that the Maryland Annual Conference recorded the number of black members in the various congregations, many of which had predominantly white memberships. This was true from the very beginning as recorded in the *Journal* of 1832 and continued through the Reconstruction period.

3. Recall that the Methodist Episcopal Church, for the sake of unity, refused to hold to the position against slave-holding established in the Christmas Conference of 1784. A number of historians point out that the veritable reversal of the original position was done in order to placate the southern brethren.

4. Historians of the Methodist Protestant Church point out that the assumption of power by the clergy and bishops and resistance to representation for the laity go to the very origins of the Methodist Episcopal Church. The Christmas Conference of 1784 was hastily called and excluded many of the elders, not to mention the laity. Ancel H. Bassett makes the following observation:

> The notice was so short, the season so adverse, and the preachers so far dispersed, there was not a full attendance, some not having received notice of the call. Even Jesse Lee, the early historian, was five hundred miles away, and in feeble health, and found it impossible to attend. About sixty were present, and most of these were young men. Such was the account afterwards given by Dr. Coke. Yet, such an assembly laid the foundation of an ecclesiastical interest, involving the welfare of thousands and even millions! (Ancel H. Bassett, *History of the Methodist Protestant Church* [Pittsburgh: James Robison; Baltimore: W. J. C. Dulaney, 1882], 27)

Bassett continues with the following critique of what happened:

> The official account of this conference is thus given by Mr. Asbury himself [see Lee's *History of the Methodists*, 127]: "It was unanimously agreed at this conference, that circumstance made it expedient for us to become a separate body, under the denomination of the Methodist Episcopal Church." And again: "Therefore, at this conference, we formed ourselves into an independent church."

Let the reader note particularly the personal pronouns here used by this body of preachers. "We," "ourselves," "us" as being the persons who organized *themselves* into an independent church, assuming the name of the Methodist Episcopal Church! It is notorious that the laity were not at all consulted in this matter. Many of them, there is ample reason to presume, hundreds of miles distant, had no knowledge of the transaction till the whole was consummated. Yet, here was set on foot an exclusively clerical government, which was saddled upon the whole Methodist lay people. Not a local preacher nor a layman had a seat in the body which consummated this important legislation, and the conference, we presume, as was usual for many years, held its sessions with closed doors. (Bassett, 27–28)

5. See the account offered by Ancel Bassett in which James O'Kelly and William McKendree left the church.

6. Bassett, *The History of the Methodist Protestant Church*, 33.

7. Quoted from the Articles of Association for the government of the Associated Methodist Churches, as reproduced on pp. 84–85 of Bassett's *History of the Methodist Protestant Church.*

8. Another source confirms that the "vast preponderance of its membership" (mother church)"was in the South," and "of the entire Reform Convention all but eighteen hailed from slave territory." "Methodist was, so to speak, a Southern religion" (Edward J. Drinkhouse, *History of Methodist Reform, synoptical of General Methodism, 1703 to 1898, with special and comprehensive reference to its most salient exhibition in the History of the Methodist Protestant Church*, vol. 2 [Baltimore: William J. C. Dulany, 1899], 212).

9. Ibid.

10. *Constitution and Discipline of the Methodist Protestant Church* (Baltimore: John J. Harrod/Methodist Protestant Church, 1831), 21–22.

11. Thomas Lewis, ed., *Centennial Anniversary of the Methodist Protestant Church, 1828–1928* (May 1928), 91.

12. In fact, there is documentation of interest and support of the Colonization Society in the Maryland Conference. In the *Minutes of the Maryland Annual Conference of the Associated Methodist Churches held in Baltimore from March 31 to April 6, 1830*, the following resolution was recorded: "Whereas, The objects contemplated by the Colonization Society, are such as merit the approbation of Christians of all denominations throughout the United States,—therefore, Resolved, 1.—That the members of this conference do highly approve of the institution, and will use their best endeavors to promote its interests. 2.—That the ministers of every circuit and station, within the bounds of this Conference, take up a collection, on or about the 4th of July next, to aid the funds of said society; which collections, when made, shall be forwarded to the Conference steward, Brother James R. Williams, Baltimore, who shall hold the same, subject to the draught of the treasurer of the Colonization Society."

13. *Ibid.*, 92.

14. Drinkhouse, 2:588.

15. The *Minutes of the Baltimore Conference, The Methodist Protestant Church, 1831*, p. 4 include a six-part resolution on dealing with colored persons. The second part is explicit that "In organizing their classes, they shall have the privilege of electing their leader from among the white or colored members of the church: Provided, that if he be a coloured man, he shall be over the age of 21 years, and be free, and shall have no vote in any case excepting it refers exclusively to his own colour."

16. The term used here, "black peoples' burden" is a reappropriation of the common colonialist attitude and practice called the "white man's burden." A deep understanding of the traditional African and Christian worldviews led African Americans, most of whom were slaves, to the morally appropriate view that there was no superior race, and all are equal under God. It becomes clear that the real burden was borne by African American people. One of the planks of the white supremacy ideological platform has always been that they are burdened with the responsibility to care for and correct the childlike peoples of other cultures that they systematically exploit, and to convert the pagans to a form of Christianity makes them docile and servile, but neither free nor equal in society or under God.

17. *Minutes of the Maryland Annual Conference*, 1864, Statistical Section. There is no way to determine whether the total number of 102 "colored" members is a reasonably close count or simply a reflection of the fact that only seven of 50 churches bothered to report the black persons in their membership. It is not unlikely that there were other African Americans who were not counted or included in the official record. It is noteworthy that the fifty-first church on the 1864 listing was the Charleston, South Carolina Station, the predominantly black congregation that was affiliated with the Maryland Annual Conference of the Methodist Protestant Church.

18. *Ibid.*

19. Edward J. Drinkhouse, *History of Methodist Reform and the Methodist Protestant Church*, The Board of Publication of the Methodist Protestant Church (Baltimore: Wm. J. C. Dulaney; Pittsburgh: F. W. Pierpont, 1899), 488. Drinkhouse inserts an interesting footnote pointing to African or "colored" Methodist Protestant groups. The interest arises from presenting highlights of a group that seceded from the African Methodist Episcopal Church in 1848 and the documented fact that the African Union Methodist Protestant Church was one of two "African" churches formed after a dispute arose over the appointment of a white pastor to the Ezion Methodist Episcopal Church in Wilmington, Delaware, and after Peter Spencer, William Anderson, and forty other Black members withdrew from Asbury Church in that city in 1805. Their withdrawal came as a result of being denied the sacraments because of their race. (See also Wardell Payne, ed., *Directory of African American Religious Bodies*, Washington, D.C.: Howard University Press, 1991, 75–76, 80–81).

20. See the sketch "The History of the Bethlehem United Methodist Church" in the 111th Anniversary program booklet (unpublished; Bethlehem United Methodist Church, 1987).

21. See p. 2 of "The History of Bethlehem United Methodist Church" in the 111th Anniversary Booklet for information compiled about the Forty-Sixth Annual Conference of the Methodist Protestant Church, Centerville (Walton County, Georgia), 2–4 November 1876.

22. Ibid.

23. See *Minutes of the Thirty-eighth Session of the Georgia Annual Conference of the Methodist Protestant Church Colored, of Georgia,* 1916, 10. Similar statements were made in subsequent years.

24. See p. 11 of the *Minutes of the Forty-seventh Session of the Methodist Protestant Annual Conference (Colored) of Georgia,* which convened at Rocky Head Methodist Protestant Church, 18–24 November 1925.

25. For the complete text see pp. 13–14 of the *Minutes of the Ninth Session of the Georgia Annual Conference, Methodist Protestant Church, (Colored)* convened at Zion Church, Campbellton,Ga., 17 November 1886.

    The term "stationing committee" was used more or less interchangeably with "itineracy and orders committee" down through the years. Appointments of ministers were recommended by this committee to the president of the conference in session. Presidents were restrained from changing or otherwise manipulating appointments between the annual conference sessions.

26. This reference rests on an interpretation of Gayraud Wilmore's idea of the deradicalization of the Black Church in his book *Black Religion and Black Radicalism* (Maryknoll: Orbis Books, 1983). Despite the deep immersion of black people into Methodist belief and practice, the white Methodist churches never fully received and appreciated the presence, participation, and gifts of African American people. Slavery occasioned the first compromise in the eighteenth century. The second compromise came with segregation in the nineteenth century, in order to maintain some sort of unity in a supposedly universal church and union of states that summarily marginalized and dehumanized black people in particular. The decision of many black people to stay and morally persuade white people to change—in relative silence—epitomized a deradicalized Black Methodist Protestant Church.

27. It seems most likely that there was contact between the historically Black congregations of the Methodist Protestant (Colored) Conference and the Black Mission/Annual Conference of the Methodist Episcopal Church in Georgia. The latter was formed in the year 1867 and the former in 1877. Existing Methodist Protestant records located to date do not report much about the fact or the nature of the contact that almost certainly took place. Both were absorbed and pressed into the Central Jurisdiction ofthe Methodist Church in 1939.

28. Ancel H. Bassett, *A Concise History of the Methodist Protestant Church,* 2d ed. (Pittsburgh: James Robison; Baltimore: W. J. C. Dulaney, 1882), 146–47.

29. *Ibid.*, 146.

30. On p. 393 of his *Concise History,* Bassett includes under the general heading "Addition Articles" the following statement which sheds more light on the matter of black people in the Methodist Protestant Church in South Carolina.

A COLORED CHURCH IN CHARLESTON, SOUTH CAROLINA

At page one hundred and thirty-one, was mentioned the organization of a Methodist Protestant Church in Charleston, South Carolina. For many years it was recognized and supplied by the Maryland Conference. During the late civil war, the church came to suffer embarrassment, their edifice being seriously shattered by shot and shell. In consequence, they were induced to merge with a Lutheran Church, and were lost to our denomination. But a little band of colored members stood firm. They were led by Francis Brown, a preacher of their color, whose labors have been remarkably blessed, and his success wonderful. In a letter to the author, some months ago, he gave us the following statement:

"Before the war, the white and the black worshiped together, in a church on Wentworth Street. After the war, the white went Lutheran, and the colored was broken up. The greater part went African Methodist, excepting myself, with three brethren and nine female members. With these twelve, we hired a room for worship. Here we so increased that the place was soon too straight for us. We applied to the government for the use of a large hall on the citadel green. It was granted. This we fitted up for worship, and there held our meetings and Sunday school. We soon increased from twelve to one hundred in membership. After about one year, the government notified us that the hall was wanted. We were now at a loss—but, providentially, we were soon enabled to secure the use of an unoccupied church belonging to the Independents. After worshiping here for six months under rent, we arranged with the trustees to buy the property, for twenty-five hundred dollars. We began almost without money, but, thank God, through His blessing, our obligation has been fully met, and we owe not one cent to-day. We have, in the city, a membership of three hundred and fifty, and a Sunday-school of one hundred children and seven teachers. Also, a small organization out of the city of sixty members. At Berkeley, about forty miles from the city, we have six hundred members and six churches, all Methodist Protestant—property worth two thousand dollars. All this growing out of our small beginning of twelve members since the war closed."

This church is reconized by the Maryland Conference. Both Francis Brown and E. R. Washington, who is now in charge of the Berkeley Churches, have received ordination; and in each of the charges are several licentiates, in prospect for the ministry. Nearly one thousand members are reported from these two charges. Brother Valiant, of Baltimore, reports a very pleasant presidential visit to those churches in the winter of 1881–'82.

31. *Minutes of the Fiftieth Session of the S. C. Colored Conference of the Methodist Protestant Church*, held in Greeh Hill M. P. Church, Pineville, S.C., 17–20 November 1938, 2–3.

Notes to "METHODIST MISSIONS TO KOREA"

1. W. Richey Hogg, "The Missions of American Methodism," *The History of American Methodism*, ed. Emory Stevens Bucke (New York and Nashville: Abingdon, 1964), 3:59–128.

2. Kenneth S. Latourette, *A History of Christianity* (New York: Harper & Row, 1975), 1:413.

3. *Ibid.*, 2:924.

4. Han Woo-Keun, *The History of Korea*, ed. Grafton K. Mintz, transl. Lee Kyung-Shik (Honolulu: East-West Center, 1970), 336–83.

5. *Methodist Episcopal Church Report*, 1884, 204–5.

6. Robert T. Handy, *A Christian America: Protestant Hopes and Historical Realities*, 2d ed. (New York and Oxford: Oxford University Press, 1984).

7. Frederick A. Norwood, *The Story of American Methodism: A History of the United Methodists and Their Relations* (Nashville: Abingdon, 1974).

8. Handy, 57.

9. *Ibid.*, 70.

10. *Ibid.*, 92.

11. Samuel Harris, "Necessity of Cooperation in Christian Work," *National Perils and Opportunities: The Discussions of the General Christian Conference Held in Washington DC December 7th, 8th, and 9th, 1887*, Evengelical Alliance for the United States (New York: Baker and Taylor, 1887), 305, cited by Handy, *Ibid.*

12. Handy, 91.

13. *Ibid.*

14. Lee Man-Yul et al., *Hanguk Gidokgo eui Yoksa* [A History of the Korean Church], 2 vols. The Institute of Korean Church History Studies. (Seoul: Christian Literature Press, 1989). 1:174–75.

15. *Ibid.*, 108–9.

16. Hogg, 69.

17. William E. Griffis, *A Modern Pioneer in Korea: The History of Henry G. Appenzeller* (New York: Fleming H. Revell, 1912), 53ff.

18. Chan-Hie Kim, "Christianity and the Modernization of Korea," in *Traditional Thoughts and Practices in Korea*, ed. Eui-Young Yu and Earl H. Phillips (Los Angeles: Center for Korean Studies, California State University, 1978), 116–27.

19. John T. Cunningham, *University in the Forest* (Madison, N.J.: Afton, 1972), 64.

20. *Ibid.*, 65.

21. Everett Nichols Hunt Jr., *Protestant Pioneers in Korea* (Maryknoll, N.Y.: Orbis, 1980), 86.

22. After his first visit to Korea to survey for the possibility of mission work at the urge of Dr. Goucher, Maclay wrote, "Indolence is written on every feature of their faces. Indeed it surprised me that people who were so lazy could be troubled to make so much noise, or could be roused to fight so easily" (Robert S. Maclay, "A Fortnight in Seoul, Korea, 1884" *The Gospel in All Lands* 22 [August 1895]: 11).

23. Chun Taek-Boo, "Gidok-gyo wa Hangul" [Christianity and Hangul], *Nara Sarang* 36 (1980): 142.

24. *The Christian Advocate* 1, no. 1 (8 April 1897): 9. Missionary publications included *The Christian Advocate* (Appenzeller in February 1897), *The Christian News* (Underwood in April 1897), *The Korean Repository* (Ohlinger in 1892), *The Korean Review* (Hulbert in 1901), *The Korea Field* (Vinton in 1901), *The Korea Methodist* (1904), *The Korea Mission Field* (1905), *Shinhak Wolbo* ("Theology Monthly" by Jones in 1900), *Eunhye Jinri* ([Grace and Truth], Norimatz in 1904), *Jesugyosuh Hoebo* ([Christian Circular], Vinton in 1904), and *Epworth Hoebo* ([Epworth Circular], Jungdong Methodist Church in 1904).

25. Lee Man-Yul, 1:206.

26. L. George Paik, *The History of Protestant Missions in Korea, 1832–1910* (Seoul: Yonsei University Press, 1970; Ph.D. dissertation, Yale University, 1929).

27. Kyung-Bae Min, *Hanguk Gidok Gyohoesa* [A History of the Korean Christian Church] (Seoul: Korea Christian Press, 1982).

28. *Ibid.*

29. *Ibid.*, 193.

30. Paik, 427.

31. Lee Man-Yul, 174–75.

32. As Young-Chan Ro has noted, ancestor worship is a form of worship, and one needs to consider the world view, life style, and value system, i.e., *Weltanschauung*, in which the specific form of worship was created before generalization. However, I disagree with Professor Ro in his assertion that the term "worship" is appropriate even when it causes confusion. When one considers the *Weltanschauung* of the Korean people in "worship" of their ancestors, one can appreciate Professor Ro's concern, but "worship" is an imported term with Western Christian cultural baggage, and it does not accurately describe the values and *Weltanschauung* associated with the Korean way of memorializing ancestors. See Young-Chan Ro, "Ancestor Worship: From the Perspective of Korean Tradition," in *Ancestor Worship and Christianity in Korea*, ed. Jung Young Lee (Lewiston, N.Y.: Mellen, 1988).

33. *Ibid.*, 76–77. Bishop A. Gouvea of Peking, China, was a Franciscan who had a strong opinion against ancestor worship in accordance with the Papal decree in 1704 forbidding the use of *T'ien* (Heaven) and *Shang T'i* (Supreme Lord) in the translation for God, and commanded the use of *T'ien Chu* (Lord of Heaven), a term which Mateo Ricci used. Christians were commanded not to participate in sacrifices to Confucius or to ancestors. This put an end to the so-called Rites Controversy over which the Pope disbanded the Jesuits who had honored the age-old Chinese traditional customs (Latourette, 349–56).

34. Myung Hyuk Kim, "Ancestor Worship: From the Perspective of Korean Church History," in *Ancestor Worship and Christianity in Korea,* ed. Jung Young Lee, 29–30.

35. *Ibid.*, 31. Two years before his retirement, Professor Byun was fired from the seminary for his "liberal" teaching.

36. *Ibid.*

37. See Wilfred Cantwell Smith. *Meaning and End of Religion.* San Francisco: Harper & Row, 1978.

38. Wilfred Cantwell Smith, *Towards a World Theology: Faith and Contemporary History of Religion* (Philadelphia: Westminster, 1981). John B. Cobb Jr., *Beyond Dialogue: Toward a Mutual Transformation of Christianity and Buddhism* (Philadelphia: Fortress, 1982).

39. Stephen S. Kim, "The Burning Heart: Passion for Holiness and Compassion for Humanity," *The Burning Heart* (New York: GBGM National Mission Resources, 1990), 3–17.

40. Jürgen Moltmann, *On Human Dignity: Political Theology and Ethics*, transl. M. Douglas Meeks (Philadelphia: Fortress, 1984); Hans Küng, *Global Responsibility: In Search of a New World Ethic* (New York: Crossroad, 1991).

Notes to "One Eye on the Past, One Eye on the Future"

1. See Halford E. Luccock and Paul Hutchinson, with 2 final chaps. by Robert W. Goodloe, *The Story of Methodism* (Nashville: Abingdon-Cokesbury, 1949), 140.

2. See Mary Isham, *Valorous Ventures: A Record of Sixty and Six Years of the Women's Foreign Missionary Society of the Methodist Episcopal Church* (Boston: Women's Foreign Missionary Society, Methodist Episcopal Church, 1936), 37, and Elaine Magalis, *Conduct Becoming to a Woman: Bolted Doors and Burgeoning Missions* (New York: Women's Division, Board of Global Ministries, The United Methodist Church, 1973), 16.

3. Noreen Tatum, *A Crown of Service: A Story of Woman's Work in the Methodist Episcopal Church, South, from 1878–1949* (Nashville: Parthenon, 1960), 386.

4. See Helen Barrett Montgomery, *Western Women in Eastern Lands* (New York: Macmillian, 1910) and Anne Firor Scott, *The Southern Lady: From Pedestal to Politics 1830–1930* (Chicago: University of Chicago Press, 1970).

5. Anne Firor Scott, *The Southern Lady: From Pedestal to Politics 1830–1930* (Chicago: University of Chicago Press, 1970), 142.

6. Emilie M. Townes, "Because God gave Her Vision: The Religious Impulse of Ida B. Wells-Barnett," in Rosemary Keller, ed., *Spirituality and Social Responsibility: Vocational Vision of Women in The United Methodist Tradition* (Nashville: Abingdon, 1993), 140.

7. Emilie M. Townes, "Because God Gave Her Vision: The Religious Impulse of Ida B. Wells-Barnett," in Rosemary Keller, ed., *Spirituality and Social Responsibility: Vocational Vision of Women in The United Methodist Tradition* (Nashville: Abingdon, 1993), 152.

8. Emilie M. Townes, "Because God Gave Her Vision: The Religious Impulse of Ida B. Wells-Barnett," in Rosemary Keller, ed., *Spirituality and Social Responsibility: Vocational Vision of Women in The United Methodist Tradition* (Nashville: Abingdon, 1993), 155.

9. From the chapter on Harkness in *Spirituality and Social Responsibility: Vocational Vision of Women in the United Methodist Tradition,* ed. Rosemary Keller (Nashville: Abingdon, 1993), 206. The biography is *Georgia Harkness: For Such a Time as This,* by Rosemary Keller (Nashville: Abingdon, 1992).

10. From Thelma Stevens' own "oral (auto)biography and interview" quoted in Alice Knotts, "Thelma Stevens, Crusader for Racial Justice," in *Spirituality and Social Responsibility: Vocational Vision of Women in The United Methodist Tradition,* ed. Rosemary Keller (Nashville: Abingdon, 1993), 232.

11. Quotations are not attributed to persons by name, unless previously published, esp. in Barbara B. Troxell, "Honoring One Another With Our Stories," *Spirituality and Social Responsibility: Vocational Vision of Women in The United Methodist Tradition,* ed. Rosemary Keller (Nashville: Abingdon, 1993).

12. Judith Craig, interview, July, 1990, in Barbara B. Troxell, "Honoring One Another With Our Stories," 308.

13. Walter Wink, *Engaging the Powers* (Minneapolis: Augsburg Fortress, 1992), 13–31.

14. Susan Morrison and others, in "Honoring One Another With Our Stories," 297–98, 307.

15. Miriam Therese Winter, Adair Lummis, and Allison Stokes, eds., *Defecting in Place: Women Claiming Responsibility for Their Own Spiritual Lives* (New York: Crossroad, 1994).

16. Beverly W. Harrison, in *Defecting in Place,* 230.

17. Baptismal Covenant I, in *The United Methodist Hymnal* (Nashville: The United Methodist Publishing House, 1989), 37.

18. Paraphrased from the Trinity UMC, Atlanta, statement, as reprinted in *Social Questions Bulletin* (New York: Methodist Federation for Social Action, May-June, 1995).

19. Jean Miller Schmidt, "Reexamining the Public/Private Split: Reforming the Continent and Spreading Scriptural Holiness," in *Perspectives on American Methodism,* ed. Russell Richey, Kenneth Rowe, Jean Miller Schmidt, (Nashville: Abingdon, 1993), 244.

20. Letty Russell, *Church in the Round* (Philadelphia: Westminster/John Knox, 1993), 194–96.

21. George D. McClain, *Claiming All Things for God: A Guide to Prayer, Discernment, and Ritual for Social Change* (unpublished D.Min. thesis, New York Theological Seminary, 1995), 124.

22. *Shalom to You* Newsletter (Portland, Oregon: Shalom Ministries, May, 1995), 4.

23. Ibid.

24. Author Patricia Farris's personal notes, United Methodist Clergywomen's Consultation, Atlanta, August 1995.

25. June Steffensen Hagen, ed., *Rattling Those Dry Bones: Women Changing the Church* (San Diego: Luramedia, 1995), 124.

Notes to "UNITED METHODISM AND AMERICAN CULTURE: TESTIMONY, VOICE, AND THE PUBLIC SPHERE"

1. For example, my dated monograph on *Slavery and Methodism: A Chapter in American Morality 1785 to 1845* (Princeton: Princeton University Press, 1965) focused on how Methodists embraced slaveholding rather than opposed it; Hunter Dickenson Farish, *The Circuit Rider Dismounts* (Richmond, Va.: Deitz, 1938) showed how the Methodist Episcopal Church, South accommodated to the modernization of the South. Further examples abound.

2. Nathan Hatch, *The Democratization of American Christianity* (New Haven: Yale University Press, 1989) does discuss how Methodism in conjunction with other popular movements affected American society; see also Hatch, "The Puzzle of American Methodism," *Church History* 63 (June 1994): 175–89.

3. See Sidney Ahlstrom's classic, *A Religious History of the American* (New Haven: Yale University Press, 1972. As another brilliant example of the genre, see Sacvan Berkovitch, *The Puritan Origins of the American Self* (New Haven: Yale University Press, 1975).

4. Hatch, *Democratization of American Culture.*

5. Daniel Walker Howe, "The Evangelical Movement and Political Culture in the North during the Second Party System," *Journal of American History,* 77 (March 1991): 1216–39; Richard A. Carwardine, *Evangelicals and Politics in Antebellum America* (New Haven: Yale University, 1991).

6. Donald G. Mathews, "Evangelical America—The Methodist Ideology," in *Perspectives on American Methodism: Interpretive Essays,* ed. Russell E. Richey, Kenneth E. Rowe, Jean Miller Schmidt (Nashville: Kingswood Books, 1993): 20;

also Walter J. Ong, *The Presence of the Word: Some Prolegomena for Cultural and Religious History* (New Haven: Yale University Press, 1967), esp. chap. 3.

7. The unsympathetic could be offended at such "noise" from white people. See Mathews, "Evangelical America—The Methodist Ideology" in Richey et al., *Perspectives on American Methodism*, 19.

8. See William McLoughlin, *Champions of the Cherokee: Evan and John B. Jones* (Princeton: Princeton University Press, 1990), 20, 33–35, 85; also William McLoughlin, with Walter H. Conser Jr., and Virginia Duffy McLoughlin, *The Cherokee Ghost Dance: Essays on the Southeastern Indians 1789–1861* (Macon, Ga.: Mercer University Press, 1984), 13–37, 47–48, 402–3.

9. See, for example, Mechal Sobel's nuanced and insightful, *The World They Made Together: Black and White Values in Eighteenth-Century Virginia* (Princeton: Princeton University Press, 1987), 204–13.

10. See not only Hatch, *Democratization of American Culture*, but also Jon Butler, *Awash in a Sea of Faith: Christianizing the American People* (Cambridge Mass.: Harvard University Press, 1990), 222–23, 238–39, 241.

11. Reginald Hildebrand, *The Times Were Strange and Stirring: Methodist Preachers and the Crisis of Emancipation* (Durham, N.C.: Duke University Press, 1995; Mathews, *Slavery and Methodism*; William Montgomery, *Under Their Own Vine and Fig Tree: The African-American Church in the South 1865–1900* (Baton Rouge: Louisiana State University Press, 1993; Clarence Walker, *A Rock in a Weary Land: The African Methodist Episcopal Church During the Civil War and Reconstruction* (Baton Rouge: Louisiana State University Press, 1982).

12. See, e.g., *The Journal and Letters of Francis Asbury*, ed. Elmer T. Clark, J. Manning Potts, and Jacob S. Payton (Nashville: Abingdon, 1958), 1:399, John Lednum, *A History of the Rise of Methodism in America* (Philadelphia: by the author, 1859), 56, 126, 148–49; Robert Paine, *The Life and Times of William M'Kendree, Bishop of the Methodist Episcopal Church* (Nashville: Publishing House of the MECS, 1869), 88.

13. See, for example, William Colbert, "A Journal of the Travels of William Colbert, Methodist Preacher, through Parts of Maryland, Pennsylvania, New York, Delaware and Virginia in 1790 to 1828" typescript copy at Methodist Center, Drew University, 24 January 1794. See also Sarah Jones, *Devout Letters, or, Letters, Spiritual and Friendly*, corr. and publ. by Jeremiah Minter, (Alexandria: Samuel Snowden, 1804 [American Imprints, second series 6572]), 42, 143, 158.

14. See Rosemary Skinner Keller, ed., *Spirituality & Social Responsibility: Vocational Vision of Women in the United Methodist Tradition* (Nashville: Abingdon, 1993.

15. *Minutes of the Methodist Conferences Annually Held in America from 1773 to 1813, Inclusive* (New York, 1813), xx and 612.

16. Hatch, *Democratization of American Christianity*, 227–43.

17. See the brilliant discussion of "The Evangelical Movement and Political Culture in the North during the Second Party System," by Daniel Walker Howe [n. 5 above]; see also George M. Thomas, *Revivalism and Cultural Change: Christianity, Nation Building, and the Market in the Nineteenth Century United States* (Chicago: University of Chicago Press, 1989).

18. Carwardine, *Evangelicals and Politics in Antebellum America*.

19. Robert E. Cushman, *John Wesley's Experimental Divinity* (Nashville: Kingswood Books, 1989): 23–25.

20. Russell E. Richey, *Early American Methodism* (Bloomington: Indiana University Press, 1991), 65–81. See also *The Methodist Conference in America* (Nashville: Abingdon, 1996).

21. Jürgen Habermas, *The Transformation of the Public Sphere: An Inquiry into a Category of Bourgeois Society*, transl. Thomas Burger, with the assistance of Frederick Lawrence (Cambridge, Mass.: MIT Press, 1989), 27: "The bourgeois public sphere may be conceived above all as the sphere of private people come together as a public; they soon claimed the public sphere regulated from above against the public authorities themselves, to engage them in a debate over the general rules governing relations in the basically privatized but publicly relevant sphere of commodity exchange and social labor. The medium of this political confrontation was peculiar and without historical precedent: people's public use of their reason."

22. Craig Calhoun, "Introduction" to *Habermas and the Public Sphere*, ed. Craig Calhoun (Cambridge, Mass.: MIT Press, 1989), 9, 11–12.

23. See David Zaret, "Religion, Science, and Printing in the Public Spheres in Seventeenth Century England" in Calhoun, ed., *Habermas and the Public Sphere*, 212–35; also the essays by Mary P. Ryan, Geoff Eley, and Nancy Fraser in the same volume.

24. The word "public" could be plural.

25. In the process that allowed this outcome, a Methodist public seemed merely to reflect the class differences of its members. After the Civil War, northern Methodists tried to use federal power and white southern weakness to gain control of Methodist property in the South and enlarge their constituency by appealing to anti-secessionist whites and former slaves. See Ralph Morrow, *Northern Methodists and Reconstruction* (East Lansing: Michigan State University Press, 1956).

26. John Leland Peters, *Christian Perfection and American Methodism* (Nashville: Abingdon, 1956), esp. 124–32.

27. Randy Maddox, "An Untapped Inheritance: American Methodism and Wesley's Practical Theology," unpublished paper.

28. Mathews, "Evangelical America—The Methodist Ideology" in *Perspectives on American Methodism*, ed. Richey, Rowe, and Schmidt, 27.

29. Sarah Josepha Hale was editor of the magazine; she was a Presbyterian, a supporter of missions, and an opponent of slavery. None of these things was obvious in the magazine.

30. Joanna Bowen Gillespie, "The Emerging Voice of the Methodist Woman: The Ladies' Repository, 1841–61" in *Perspectives on American Methodism*, ed. Richey, Rowe, and Schmidt, 248–64.

31. Ibid., 261.

32. John Patrick McDowell, *The Social Gospel in the South: The Woman's Home Mission Movement in the Methodist Episcopal Church South, 1886–1939* (Baton Rouge: Louisiana State University Press, 1982); Lucy Rider Meyer, *Deaconesses, Biblical, Early Church, European, American* (Cincinnati: Cranston & Stowe, 1892); C. Goldner, *History of the Deaconess Movement in the Christian Church* (Cincinnati: Jennings & Pye, 1903); Ruth Bordin, *Women and Temperance: The Quest for Power and Liberty 1873–1900* (Philadelphia: Temple University Press, 1981).

33. Robert Sledge, *Hands on the Ark: The Struggle for Change in the Methodist Episcopal Church, South, 1914–1939* (Lake Junaluska. N.C.: United Methodist Church Commission on Archives and History, 1975).

34. Dwight W. Culver, *Negro Segregation in the Methodist Church* (New Haven: Yale University Press, 1953).

35. Jacquelyn Dowd Hall, *Revolt against Chivalry: Jesse Daniel Ames and the Women's Campaign Against Lynching* (New York: Columbia University Press, 1979).

36. See, e.g., Norman F. Furniss, *The Fundamentalist Controversy 1918–1931* (New Haven: Yale University Press, 1954); George M. Marsden, *Fundamentalism and American Culture: The Shaping of Twentieth Century Evangelicalism 1870–1925* (New York: Oxford University Press, 1980).

37. George W. Wilson, *Methodist Theology vs Methodist Theologians: A Review of Several Methodist Writers* (Cincinnati: Jennings and Pye, 1904), 15–124, 225–321.

38. See McDowell, *Social Gospel in the South*.

39. The other one was Charlotte Diggs [Lottie] Moon, the legendary Baptist missionary to China. See Catherine B. Allen, *The New Lottie Moon Story* (Nashville: Broadman, 1980); Mrs. R. W. [Tochie] MacDonell, *Belle Harris Bennett: Her Life and Work* (Nashville, Tenn.: Board of Missions of the Methodist Episcopal Church, South, 1928).

40. Richey, *Early American Methodism*, 65–81.